Also by Christiane Bird

NEITHER EAST NOR WEST: ONE WOMAN'S JOURNEY
THROUGH THE ISLAMIC REPUBLIC OF IRAN

THE JAZZ AND BLUES LOVER'S GUIDE TO THE U.S.

BELOW THE LINE: LIVING POOR IN AMERICA
(COAUTHOR)

NEW YORK HANDBOOK

A Thousand Sighs,

a Thousand Revolts

BALLANTINE BOOKS

NEW YORK

A Thousand Sighs,
a Thousand Revolts

,,,,,

JOURNEYS IN
KURDISTAN

Christiane Bird

A Ballantine Book
PUBLISHED BY THE RANDOM HOUSE PUBLISHING GROUP

COPYRIGHT © 2004 BY CHRISTIANE BIRD

Five lines from *Shanidar, the First Flower People*,
translation copyright © 1971 by Ralph S. Solecki.

www.ballantinebooks.com

LIBRARY OF CONGRESS CATALOGING-IN-PUBLICATION DATA
Bird, Christiane.
A thousand sighs, a thousand revolts : journeys in Kurdistan / Christiane Bird.
p.   cm.
ISBN 0-345-46892-9 — ISBN 0-345-46939-9 (pbk.)
1. Kurdistån (Iraq)—Description and travel.   2. Kurdistån (Iraq)—Politics and government.
3. Kurds—Iraq—Social life and customs.   4. Bird, Christiane—Travel—Iraq—Kurdistan.
I. Title.
DS70.65.B57 2004
956.7'2—DC22

Manufactured in the United States of America

FIRST EDITION: MAY 2004

10 9 8 7 6 5 4 3 2

Map by © Jeffrey L. Ward

Text design by Barbara M. Bachman

The mountains, always the mountains,
held the old man's gaze.
There is a fascination about them that it is not necessary
to be a Kurd or a Persian to be able to acquire.

TO MESOPOTAMIA AND KURDISTAN IN DISGUISE,
Ely Bannister Soane

Contents

ऽ ऽ ऽ ऽ

Acknowledgments

THIS BOOK COULD NOT HAVE BEEN WRITTEN WITHOUT THE HELP of many Kurds and scholars. Many magnanimously opened their homes and lives to me; others gave generously of their time and expertise.

For the Iraq section, I am especially indebted to Nesreen Mustafa Siddeek Berwari, who filled me in on many aspects of life in Kurdistan, hosted me in Erbil, and provided me with numerous introductions, and to Diane E. King, who gave me much invaluable advice and insight, and read the Iraq chapters in manuscript. A special thanks, too, to my kind hosts in Dohuk, Majed Sayyed Saleh and family, who helped me in innumerable ways, and to Carole A. O'Leary, who first introduced me to Iraqi Kurdish affairs and also read the Iraq chapters in manuscript. Shayee Khanaka was an astute and helpful reader as well.

I am indebted to many other Iraqi Kurdish families who hosted me during my stay. My thanks to the Shamdeen family in Zakho, Muhsen Saleh Abdul Aziz and family in Amadiya, Kamerin Khairy Beg and family in Baadri, Yassim Muhammad Wossou and family in Erbil, the Rozhbayani family in Erbil, the students at the University of Salahuddin in Erbil, Guergis Yalda and family in Diana, and the family of Hamin Kak Amin Bilbas in Raniya. In Syria, the Shweish family and others who prefer to go unnamed warmly welcomed me into their homes and provided me with an excellent introduction to their country.

I also owe a great deal to the many Iraqi Kurds who went far out of their way to serve as my guides and translators, usually on an informal and voluntary basis. In Dohuk, Dr. Shawkat Bamarni, Dilovan Muhammad Amin, Dr. Saadi Namaste Bamerni, Bayan Ahmed, Yousif Chamsayidi, Zerrin Ibrahim, Dr. Khairy, Mr. Fadhil, and Dr. Jasim Elias Murad were especially helpful, with Dilovan serving as my ad hoc research assistant after I returned home. In Zahko, Nazira Shamdeen gave me especially perceptive insight into her world and culture. In Erbil, Fawzi Hariri, Rezan Yousif, Hozak Zahir, Himdad Abdul-Qahhar, Othman Rashad Mufti, and Yonadam Kanna helped me explore the city, while in Barzan, Dr. Abdullah Loqman and Saleh Mahmoud Barzani did the same. In Suleimaniyah, Nizar Ghafur Agha Said and Dildar Majeed Kittani were translators par excellence, while Safwat Rashid Sidqi, Dr. Fouad Baban, Rewaz Faiq, and Yousif Hassan Hussein showed me parts of Kurdistan that I would not have seen without them. In Halabja and Suleimaniyah, Dr. Adil Karem Fatah took much time out of a busy schedule to help me conduct numerous interviews. Also most helpful were my translators Khalid Muhammad Hassan Sharafani in Sumel, Hickmat Mustafa Mahmoud in Amadiya, Imad Salman in Chamsaida, Janet Iskail in Diana, and Ayub Nuri in Suleimaniyah.

Before leaving for Iraq and Syria, I was in contact with many experts who both encouraged me to make the trip and helped prepare me for my journey: Michael Rubin, Omar Sheikhmous, KDP and PUK representatives in the United States and Damascus, Mike Amitay, Deirdre Russo, Joost Hilterman, Dr. Ali Sindi, Kathy Fuad, and David Hirst. After I returned home, the Washington Kurdish Institute, and Stafford Clarry and Ann Mirani in Kurdistan did a superb job of sending me news stories about the Iraq war, its aftermath, and other developments in the region.

For the Iran section, I am especially grateful to Soleyman Soltanian in Tehran for his advice, hospitality, and many introductions, and to his son Babak for first introducing me to his father. My thanks as well to the Bahri, Sedighi, and Najafi families, who hosted me in Mahabad, Sanandaj, and Kermanshah respectively, and to Hiwa Soofyeh, who gave me much poetic insight into Kurdish culture. Hasham Salami introduced me to Iranian Kurdish folklore, his son Siamand Salami filled me in on the music of the Ahl-e Haqq, Fatah Amiri and family welcomed me in Bukan, and Mehrdad E. Izady offered me pretrip advice. Shirin Rewaz was my gracious host in Urumieh, Nasreen Jaferi and Parang Shafai served as my able guides and hosts in Mahabad, and the Greenway conference organizers were my enthusiastic escorts in Sanandaj.

For the Turkey section, I am especially indebted to Kani Xulam, who provided me with many contact names and answered many of my questions, and to the Sevinc family in Istanbul, who went far out of their way to help me in my research. In addition, I would like to thank Henri J. Barkey for reading the Turkey chapters in manuscript; A. Celil Kaya, Sedef Esirgenc, and Hivda Ustebay for serving as my translators; Suzan Samanci for her delightful company and hospitality; and Kevin McKiernan, Sennacherib Daniel, Jordan Bell, and Gregory Scarborough for their pre-trip advice. I am also deeply grateful to Kurdologists Martin van Bruinessen and David McDowall, whose exhaustive works inform much in the following pages.

I would like to thank my editors: Wendy Hubbert, without whose enthusiasm this book might never have been written; Nancy Miller, for her unfailing insight and friendship; and Dana Isaacson, for his skillful tightening and line editing. A special thanks also to my agent Neeti Madan for her belief in this project, to my friends Barbara Feinberg and Kim Larsen for reading early drafts of several chapters, and to Jerry Brown and my family for their steadfast support throughout the research, writing, and publishing process.

Author's Note

BECAUSE OF POLITICAL CONSIDERATIONS AND TO PROTECT some individuals' privacy, I have changed some names and identifying details in this book. Because there is no standard transliteration from Kurdish, Persian, or Arabic into English, I have generally chosen to spell words as simply as possible and according to how they are pronounced. I have spelled people's names according to their personal preferences.

Preface

THROUGHOUT 2003, THE WAR IN IRAQ AND ITS AFTERMATH dominated the media. Early in the year, thousands of pundits, journalists, and talking heads—along with everyone else—speculated on when the war would begin, whether weapons of mass destruction would be found, and what the overthrow of Saddam Hussein would mean for Iraq and the rest of the Middle East. That spring, from the first attack on Baghdad on March 20 through President George W. Bush's declaration of the end of major combat on May 1, reporters delivered visceral, blow-by-blow accounts of the conflict, bringing a virtual war into nearly every living room. And after the "shock and awe" was over, and the statues of Saddam Hussein came tumbling down, the media roar continued; it became apparent that the Iraq story had legs that would carry it well into the future.

Yet for me, the barrage of media coverage often obscured more than it revealed. I had spent three months in northern Iraq in the spring of 2002—a year before the war—and two months in the bordering Iranian and Turkish regions the following fall, exploring Kurdistan, or the land of the Kurds—a country that exists on few maps, but in many hearts. I got the most tangible news from the region not from the media but in e-mails from my Kurdish friends in Iraq, Iran, and Turkey. Their messages were often short and simple, and written in broken English, with much of the drama between the lines.

SUBJ: SITUATION CALM
DATE: 1/14/03
FROM: AMIN, DOHUK, IRAQ

Dear Christiane, So happy to hear from you. Here in Kurdistan the situation is calm and no tension yet. All the people are happy to hear the words of war and they all hope it will be the end of the 13 years sad and tragic story. Iraq without Saddam will be better. Sincerely, Amin

SUBJ: HAPPY NEW YEAR
DATE: 1/15/03
FROM: HIWA, SANANDAJ, IRAN

Hello Christiane, Happy New Year to you. I see you are very curious about war but here in Iran it is an ordinary matter and the poverty is the most important thing. *Enshahallah* the war will not occur. Best wishes, Hiwa

SUBJ: ABOUT WAR
DATE: 2/14/03
FROM: CELIL, DIYARBAKIR, TURKEY

Dear friend: Every day we are getting closer to war. And people who are living in this area are getting more anxious. I hope it won't happen. But the Turkey government is insisting on war. And this situation makes us worry. I hope you are trying to do something to prevent this dirty war. Best wishes, Celil

SUBJ: THANK YOU FOR YOUR E-MAIL!
DATE: 2/26/03
FROM: AMIN, DOHUK, IRAQ

Dear Christiane—The people here are preparing themselves to go to the mountains in case of war. The situation is bad, and people are frightened. The real tension began a week ago with hearing news that the Turkish armies might participate in the campaign against Iraq. Most of the Kurds think they will have to fight Saddam and the Turks at the same time.

About me, I'm also preparing with my family to escape; you don't need to be so smart to know that there will be a bloody conflict. And it will be like a hell. I'm going to prepare a bag with every thing we will need after escaping. Medical needs, food, heavy clothes. And I have a further plan. In middle of turmoil I will cross the border out of Iraq. I'm not going to wait till the war to end, there will be no end for it.

Till your reply to this message, take care of your self. The time is exactly 11.15 PM, while I'm writing to you, I already opened the window, snow, snow! Best, Amin

SUBJ: RE: HOW ARE YOU?
DATE: 2/27/03
FROM: ZERRIN, DOHUK, IRAQ

Dear Ms. Christiane, So far I'm fine and still in one piece. Not only me but almost all the people are ready to leave to the mountains if needed. We are afraid from Satin Saddam if he decided to revenge against us for being close friend to the US.

Yes, I still feel danger from Baghdad as my head is still wanted. I still have my bodyguards assigned by the Governor and I go around with them.

I'm VERY WORRIED about the Turkish troops in northern Iraq. For two days, I have been visiting the Refugee Camps and was trying to calm them down. They are TERRIFIED and I can understand their fear. I cannot wait until I see your brothers and sisters when they arrive. MY DREAM IS BECOMING TRUE!

We have a lot of snow here and it is VERY cold. There is a big shortage on Fuel. Lots of love. Always, ZERRIN

SUBJ: SALAAM KHOSHGEL!
DATE: 3/23/03
FROM: HIWA, SANANDAJ, IRAN

Dear Christiane: As you know the war has began and now Iraq is conflicting with several problems. You know, many years we Kurds have been in war, it's really an ordinary matter to us. More people in Iran follow the news for their curiosity. Nearly all the people wish Iraq to resist because they think western forces are cruel. Perhaps refugees will come to Iran in next days, this has occurred when Saddam attacked Halabja by chemical weapons.

Today is 3rd day of 1382, so that we are in New Year vacations, weather is very good, everywhere is calm, I want to wander every day I can! (The great poet hiwa!) Tell me about yourself and write more. Your friend, Hiwa

SUBJ: RE: WHAT A SIGHT!!
DATE: 4/12/03
FROM: ZERRIN, DOHUK, IRAQ

Dear beloved Christiane, Thank you for your congratulations to see the statue of Saddam coming down! But first of all, let me congratulate YOU and all AMERICANS for the great Job and VICTORY. We LOVE your country and are proud of your soldiers because they FREE us from Satin Saddam.

Secondly, for the first time today, I went to the office without my body guards. I can not believe it. Is not that wonderful? I'm planing to make a BIG PARTY in the UN CLUB and you are MOST WELCOME to attend it. I'm SO HAPPY you can not imagine. Remain in touch and lots of love. Sincerely, your sister in FREE IRQ, Zerrin

SUBJ:
DATE: 4/13/03
FROM: NIZAR, SULEYMANIAH, IRAQ

Dear Christiane, You can not imagine the joy of the Kurdish people, I have never seen them so happy. Whatever the future will be it will not be worse than what we had, so everyone is optimistic. The best business today in Sulaimany is the shop who makes American, British, and Kurdish flags (16 hours a day). Photos of President Bush on cars, shops, and in homes. Dancing and music until late evening. People are looking forward to travel to Baghdad without restriction, fear and discrimination. Regards, Nizar

SUBJ: LETTER
DATE: 4/28/03
FROM: SOLEYMAN, TEHRAN, IRAN

Dear Christiane, No, there is not any extra pressure on kurds in Iran because of the war. We are very happy about the overthrowing of Saddam's Regime. Our governmental officials are also very happy because Saddam and his friends were very dangerous enemy of Iran's people. But there is a very important question: What is the next target for USA? Which regime will join Saddam's system? Good Luck, Soleyman

SUBJ: REPLY
DATE: 5/2/03
FROM: AMIN, DOHUK, IRAQ

Dear Christiane, The art institute is open again, and we have a very hard task to get things back to normal, especially the student's mood. In Dohuk things are fine, and you can meet many American's soldiers in the streets. The American's are welcome here, people love them and showing great admire. No soldier can walk alone, people simply follow and stopping him to shake hands, saying (hi), or to print a kiss on his cheeks.

During the war, I tried to cross the border, but no luck. After a few days I was back again in Dohuk. Hugs, Amin

SUBJ: FROM HEART TO HEART
DATE: 6/21/03
FROM: BAYAN, DOHUK, IRAQ

Dear Miss Christiane, I am so sorry because I haven't sent you a message for a long time. As you know, I am so busy at work and at home also. Anyway Miss Christiane if you are asking about Iraq in general, I don't think that the situation is stable. We don't have a president and a government so how we will have stability, but anyway I am very happy because the regime was down so soon. Day by day the Iraqi people are discovering new mass graves. I can not imagine how savages Saadam and his followers were. Concerning Kurdistan the situation is different but also people here are anxious and worried. People didn't get their wages and everything is expensive but it is better than in the other parts of Iraq. I hope this will soon be over. With best wishes. Bayan

During much of 2003, I thought that I would return to Iraqi Kurdistan postwar to gather material for this book's final chapter. For months, my plans were to revisit the former "northern no-fly zone" to see firsthand what changes had occurred since the toppling of the Baath regime. But as the future of Iraq seemed to grow less rather than more settled, I realized that even safety issues, travel expenses, and publishing deadline pressures aside, I didn't want to go back. Like the barrage of media reports surrounding the war, I feared that for me, going back would obscure more than it revealed. Whatever insights I had gained into one of the world's oldest yet leastknown cultures during my 2002 travels would not be honed by a hasty trip to view what was still only a thin layer of political change. Wars in Kurdistan came and went; life went on.

This is not a book about Kurdish politics, or about how the Iraq war will affect the Kurds, or even, strictly speaking, a book about Kurdish history or culture, although all those elements can be found herein. This is a book about the Kurdish people, an examination of an often-overlooked society that has been rocked and at times devastated by some of the most catastrophic events and tragic political policies of the last eighty years. This is also a book about journeys—some my own, but most, the Kurds'.

—New York City, November 2003

A Thousand Sighs,

a Thousand Revolts

KURDISTAN

RUSSIA

BLACK SEA

GEORGIA

CASPIAN SEA

ARMENIA

AZERBAIJAN

MT. ARARAT △

Euphrates *River*

TURKEY

Dogubayazit

Tunceli

Bingol

Mus

Tatvan

Lake *Van*

Van

Lice

Kulp

Bitlis

Diyarbakir

Sirnak

Lake *Urumieh*

Tabriz

Silopi

Hakkari

Urumieh

Cizre

Zakho

Amadiya

Urfa

Qamishli

Dohuk

Aqra

Barzan

Mahabad

Rowanduz

Haj Omran

Mosul

Raniya

Erbil

Baneh

Kirkuk

Chemchemal

Sanandaj

Suleimaniyah

No Sud

IRAN

Tehran ★

Halabja

Paveh

Tikrit

Kalar

Kermanshah

Qasr-e Shirin

SYRIA

Khabur *River*

Euphrates *River*

Tigris *River*

ZAGROS MOUNTAINS

Baghdad ★

IRAQ

JORDAN

Tigris *River*

Euphrates *River*

Basra ·

0   100   200 Miles
0   100   200   300 Kilometers

KUWAIT

PERSIAN GULF

Kurdish Regions

SAUDI ARABIA

© 2004 Jeffrey L. Ward

CHAPTER ONE

Through the Back Door

THE MALTAI FAMILY LIVED IN A BIG AIRY HOUSE ON THE outskirts of Dohuk in northern Iraq. Out front stretched their even bigger garden, its borders etched with fluttering purple blossoms mixed with penny-sized red wildflowers that the patriarch, Aziz Maltai, had transplanted from the mountains. Here and there bloomed flowers grown from seeds sent by friends in Europe. In the middle splashed a hand-carved fountain, water spilling from cup to cup to cup into a violet pool below.

"Flowers are like young sheep," Aziz Maltai said, examining a rosebud on our way into the house. "The more time you spend with them, the more they grow."

At the door, a line of women waited—dressed in floor-length gowns of lilac, black, deep green, and bright red, their long lacy sleeves tied behind their backs while still allowing for freedom of movement. Most of the older women's heads were covered with gauzy black or white scarves, most of the younger women's heads were bare. "B'kher-hati, b'kher-hati," they all cried—welcome, welcome—and kissed me on both cheeks before ushering me into a large room furnished only with Oriental carpets, a kerosene heater, and shiny benchlike couches lining two walls.

Women sat on one side, men on the other, as Aziz was joined by some of his nine sons and other male relatives. In contrast to the patriarch, who was wearing a Western suit and red tie, many of the men were dressed in the Kurdish *shal u shapik*, or trousers and jacket. Resembling billowing aviators' jumpsuits, traditionally made of goat's hair, the *shal u shapik* come in a variety of muted hues—browns, tans, blacks, and whites—and are cinched around the waist with elaborately woven cummerbunds, which can be up to twenty feet long when unwound. The style of the *shal u shapik* varies depending upon region or occasion, but today, all were wearing their finest: it was Newroz, or New Year's.

Tea was served in delicate, tulip-shaped glasses, along with cookies stuffed with walnut paste, made specially for the holiday. Then we were off—Aziz and his wife, most of his sons and their families, cousins visiting from Baghdad, and me. Moving out into the garden, amid excited children's cries, we climbed into a cavalcade of gleaming BMWs and sport-utility vehicles. Proudly mounted on the lead car was the striped green, red, and white flag of Kurdistan, a yellow sunburst in its middle.

Aziz seated me in a BMW next to his son Siyabend, a small, wiry, dapper man wearing fashionable minimalist glasses and a starched military-style *shal u shapik* made of khaki. He and I had both spent time in Iran, and Aziz hoped we would be able to communicate in Persian.

Kurdish music spinning from the tape deck, we headed north toward the Turkish border and then east toward Iran. The snowcapped mountains of Turkey's Kurdistan appeared, along with an expansive plain shining like an enormous silver tray as it soaked in the rays of the sun.

"There's Silopi, and that's Mount Cudi." Siyabend pointed out several sites across the Turkish border. Later, I learned that Silopi had suffered especially badly during the Kurdish-Turkish civil war that ended in 1999, and that Mount Cudi, along with the better-known Mount Ararat, is believed by many Kurds to have been the resting place of Noah's Ark.

Turning off the paved road, we headed up a grassy mountainside. Although only midmorning, the slope was already half filled with parked cars and sturdy white tents shaped like miniature big tops. Children played ball, men built bonfires, and women socialized or cooked, the lush fabrics of their gowns blinking in the sun.

After parking, the men quickly set up a tent, into which the older women immediately retired, and started a fire. Many of the rest of us set off to roam the mountain and to look for wildflowers—white *nergiz* (narcissus), scarlet or purple *sheqayiq* (ranunculus), daisylike *hajile*.

When we returned, much of the family was already seated on padded cushions around a now-roaring fire. One of the younger wives, a handsome chestnut brunette, was boiling water in a battered teapot. Another woman was handing around small cakes, and a third, a bag filled with nuts. Two young men were playing a game, moving pebbles between six small holes dug into the earth.

I gazed out over the plain before us. A river cut a clear meandering path across a land that changed color as it went—from browns to reds to greens

Preparing tea at a Newroz picnic

and back again. The mountain ranges beyond the plain started small, but then rose and rose, each range thrusting higher into the cobalt sky until cresting into Turkey's crystalline blue-white peaks.

On the plain immediately below stood a dozen or so red and orange buses hired by picnickers too poor to own vehicles of their own. And on the mountain slopes to our left and right, tents had popped up almost as far as the eye could see.

Aziz talked about his garden. "I have always loved nature, ever since I was a small boy," he said. "And when I was a *peshmerga*, fighting in the mountains, I would shout 'Oh!' whenever I stepped on a flower. My friends would think I had stepped on a mine." He slapped his knee, laughing.

Lunch was served, on a big plastic tablecloth spread out near the fire: *biryani* rice made with raisins, nuts, and chicken; *tershick*, or wheat patties, filled with vegetables and lamb; grilled kebabs, served with tomatoes and onions; thin crisp bread, baked in an outdoor oven that morning; *du*, the Middle Eastern drink made of yogurt and water; and platefuls of mysterious, pungent greens gathered fresh from the mountains.

On the slope below, a trio of musicians was traveling from tent to tent, the sound of their cylindrical drum, the *dohul*, and conical flute, the *zirnah*, penetrating deep into the mountains. Wherever the musicians stopped, people dropped what they were doing to form a long line and begin a Kurdish dance. Joining hands, swinging arms, moving shoulders in deliberate, hypnotic rhythm; two steps to the right, one to the left, back, forward, kick. The first person in the line often twirled a handkerchief high in the air as people merged in and out, men and women and children dancing together.

When the musicians reached our tent, Siyabend and his wife pulled me to my feet and showed me how to link my little fingers with theirs as we joined the line. The dance had simple footwork that even a child could follow, but just as I was relaxing, a more intricate dance began. Everyone started singing, with one side of the line answering the other in a love song about a girl with dark hair. In and out the line moved. I stumbled, then dropped out.

A short while later, the musicians started a bold wild tune, chasing all but five men from the dance floor. Most dressed in *shal u shapik*, they were stomping, jumping, bending, and twisting in a dance that seemed as old and resilient and self-contained as the mountains. Watching them, the world around me vanished—the men seemed alone on a barren slope, Kalashnikovs piled beside them, winds and snows howling around them, taking a break from the fierce guerrilla war that has raged off and on in Kurdistan for over one hundred years.

The musicians moved on. The dancing stopped as abruptly as it had started, leaving an emptiness behind. Two of the youngest men, dressed in black sweaters, sunglasses, and jeans, took off in the newer, cooler, black SUV, while the rest of us returned to the now-dying bonfire. The sun was setting. A tall, skeletal blind beggar, led by a blond girl, wandered from tent to tent.

"The worst people in the world are the Turks, and then come the Arabs," Siyabend said.

I looked at him, not knowing what to say. Uncomfortable subjects had been bumping back and forth unspoken between us throughout the day. Until now, neither one of us had wanted to articulate them; the day had been too beautiful, there had been too much hope in the air.

"See over there." Siyabend pointed toward a Turkish mountain in the distance, its tip now blue-black, dipped in darkening snow. "That's where we went after the uprising. We stayed in a refugee camp there for two months and then they sent us to a camp near Mardin. We stayed there four years."

"Four years?" I said, surprised. Only my third day in Kurdistan, I still had much to learn. "The whole family?"

He nodded.

"Four hundred people died in the first camp," said one of his brothers.

"They tried to poison us with bread in the second," said one of the wives.

"The Turkish soldiers hit the women."

"They kicked the children like footballs."

"But we couldn't come back. Saddam—"

"He gassed his own people."

"He destroyed four thousand Kurdish villages."

"More than one hundred eighty thousand people disappeared."

"How did we survive?"

"God helped us."

FROM THE MOMENT I arrived in Kurdistan, I felt as if I had fallen through the back door of the world and into a tragic magic kingdom—the kind of place where tyrants' castles reigned over mist-filled valleys, beautiful damsels ran away with doomed princes, and ten-foot-tall heroes battled scaly green dragons as good clashed swords with evil. In reality, there was no kingdom—at least not of the type found in fairy tales—but I did find evil, as well as good, and castles and valleys, damsels and princes, magic and tragedy.

THE KURDS ARE the largest ethnic group in the world without a state of their own. Probably numbering between 25 and 30 million, they live in an arc of land that stretches through Turkey, Syria, Iraq, Iran, and parts of the former Soviet Union, with the vast majority residing in the region where Turkey, Syria, Iraq, and Iran meet. About eight hundred thousand Kurds also live in Europe, with about five hundred thousand of those in Germany, while some twenty-five thousand Kurds live in the United States and at least six thousand in Canada.

Not a country, Kurdistan cannot be found on modern maps. The term was first used as a geographical expression by the Saljuq Turks in the twelfth century and came into common usage in the sixteenth century, when much of the Kurdish region fell under the control of the Ottoman and Safavid Empires. For the Kurds themselves, Kurdistan is both an actual and a mythical place—an isolated, half-hidden, mountainous homeland that has historically offered sanctuary from the treacherous outside world, and from treacherous fellow Kurds.

I became interested in the Kurds during a 1998 journey to Iran. While there, I traveled to Sanandaj, Iran's unofficial Kurdish capital, where I was immediately struck by how different the area seemed from the rest of the Islamic Republic—heartbreaking in its lonesome beauty, and defiant. Despite a large number of Revolutionary Guards on the streets, the men swaggered and women strode. These people are not cowed, I thought—no wonder they make the Islamic government nervous.

In Sanandaj, I stayed with a Kurdish family I had met on the bus, and attended a wedding held in a small pasture filled with about two hundred people in traditional dress. To one side were the city's ugly concrete buildings; to another, empty lots strewn with litter. But the people and their costumes, framed by the far-off Zagros Mountains, transcended the tawdry surroundings. Women in bright reds, pinks, greens, blues, and golds. Men in baggy pants, woven belts, and heavy turbans. Boys playing with hoops. Girls dreaming by a bonfire. Musicians on a mournful flute and enormous drum, followed by circling men dancing single file, one waving a handkerchief over his head.

After I returned home, I began reading more about the Kurds. Who are these people, and why don't we know more about them?

The Kurds are the fourth-largest ethnic group in the Middle East—after the Arabs, Turks, and Persians—accounting for perhaps 15 percent of its population. They occupy some of the region's most strategic and richest lands. Turkey's Kurdistan contains major coal deposits, as well as the headwaters of the Tigris and Euphrates Rivers—important irrigation sources for Syria, Iraq, and Turkey. Iraqi Kurdistan holds significant oil reserves, and Turkey's and Syria's Kurdistan, lesser ones. Much of Iraqi and Syrian Kurdistan also lies in the fertile valley of and adjoining northern Mesopotamia, one of the world's richest breadbaskets and most ancient lands.

The Iraqi Kurds, numbering about 5 million, constitute between one-fourth and one-fifth of Iraq's population. Despite much repression, they have always been recognized by the state as a separate ethnic group. Iraqi Kurds have at times held important government and military positions, and between 1992 and 2003, ran their own semiautonomous, fledgling democracy in Iraq's so-called "northern no-fly zone." Post–Saddam Hussein, the Kurds are assuming a central role in the forging of a new Iraq.

Numbering 13 or 14 million, or one-half of all Kurds, Turkey's Kurds comprise at least 20 percent of their nation and boast a birthrate that is nearly double that of their compatriots—promising an even greater presence in the future. Turkey's Kurds have been brutally repressed both culturally and politically since the founding of the modern Turkish Republic in 1923. Turkey is now striving to join the European Union, however, and its acceptance therein will depend largely on an improvement in its human rights record toward the Kurds.

Numbering about 6.5 million, or 10 percent of Iran's population, Iranian Kurds ran their own semiautonomous state as early as the 1300s. Today, they have about twenty reform-minded representatives in Iran's Parliament, who, along with many others, are pushing for more liberalization in the Islamic Republic. Syrian Kurds, although numbering only about 1.4 million, constitute 9 percent of their country's sparse population, with the Syrian capital of Damascus home to an influential Kurdish community since the Middle Ages.

Exact population figures for the Kurds are unavailable because no reliable census has been conducted for decades. All of the countries in which they reside regard them as a political threat and downplay their existence. And without a nation-state of their own, the Kurds have been slow in letting their presence be known to the outside world.

This is changing. Thanks in part to recent political developments, of which the Iraq war of 2003 is only the latest, and in part to a growing diaspora, satellite communications, and the Internet, today's Kurds are both rapidly developing a national consciousness as a people, and overcoming the geographic and psychic isolation that has plagued them for centuries. And as they do so, questions of nationalism, multiculturalism, and a possible future redrawing of international boundaries arise.

The Kurds possess an ancient and romantic culture, which many Kurds trace back to the Medes, a people mentioned in the Bible and other early texts. Inhabitants of the Kurdish lands may have pioneered agriculture as early as 12,000 B.C., while the first probable written mention of the Kurds appears in *Anabasis*, penned by Xenophon the Greek some twenty-four hundred years ago. In his account of a 401 B.C. battle, which pitted ten thousand Greek mercenaries against the Persian forces, he writes of the "Karduchoi"—probably Kurds: "The Greeks spent a happy night with plenty to eat. Talking about the struggle now past. For they passed through the country of the Karduchoi, fighting all the time and they had suffered worse things at the hands of the Karduchoi than all that the King of Persia and his general, Tissaphernes, could do to them."

The Arab armies arrived in Kurdistan in A.D. 637, bringing with them the new religion of Islam. At first, the Kurdish tribes put up a fierce resistance, but as the enormous might of the Arabs became clear to them, they gradually converted to Islam, nominally submitting to the new central power. However, in a pattern that has continued up into the modern era, the Kurds' first loyalty remained to their tribal leaders, who retained considerable local authority.

In the tenth century A.D., the Kurds entered what some scholars call their "golden age." Kurds served as generals in the Islamic army, scholars and administrators in the Islamic court, and rulers of wealthy semiautonomous fiefdoms, which thrived on trade from the Silk Routes then passing through the area. The most famous Muslim warrior of all time, Salah al-Din, or Saladin, was a Kurd born in A.D. 1137 in Tikrit—also the hometown of Saddam Hussein, the infamous former president of Iraq. Of the Hadhabani tribe, Saladin reconquered Jerusalem from Richard the Lionhearted during the Crusades. He established the Ayyubid dynasty, which ruled in some form until the end of the fifteenth century. It is unlikely, however, that Saladin thought of his central identity as Kurdish; first and foremost, he was Muslim.

The vast majority of today's Kurds are also Muslim, with at least 75 percent belonging to the Sunni branch and 15 percent to the Shiite. Sunnis and Shiites are the two great factions of Islam, a schism based largely on the question of leadership succession. The Sunnis, who comprise about 90 percent of the world's 1.1 billion Muslims, believe that the Prophet Muhammad's successors should be chosen by consensus; the Shiites, who live mostly in Iran, believe that his successors should be his direct descendants. But whether Sunni or Shiite, most Kurds view themselves as moderate Muslims. The political side of Islam has also at times created tension between their Muslim and Kurdish identities. Some nationalist Kurds even say that Islam is detrimental to their people, as it subjugates the Kurdish cause to the larger Islamic goal of a united world community of believers. "Don't have any confidence in a holy man even if his turban should be straight from heaven," goes one Kurdish proverb.

The Kurdish region is religiously diverse, with many other Kurds belonging to one of three small religious groups—the Yezidis, Ahl-e Haqqs or Kakais, and Alevis—whose faiths combine pre-Islamic and Islamic beliefs; some scholars classify the Ahl-e Haqqs and Alevis as Muslim. Non-Kurdish Christian groups such as the Assyrians and Chaldeans (a Catholic branch of the Assyrians) also live in the area, as do evangelical Christians and a few Armenians, though most Armenians left the region following the Turks' massacres of their communities in the 1890s and 1915. A large Jewish Kurdish community once lived in Kurdistan, but departed the area after the founding of Israel.

The 1200s and 1300s brought disaster to the Kurdish lands. First came waves of Mongol invasions headed by Hulagu, grandson of Genghis Khan, destroying many Kurdish villages and major towns. Then came the invasions of the emperor Tamerlane and his son, who, after capturing Baghdad and Damascus, again sacked hundreds of Kurdish settlements.

But by the sixteenth century, the region was again flourishing. Under the reign of the Ottoman and Safavid Empires, which rose to power in

Turkey and Persia respectively in the early 1500s, Kurdish princes ruled over emirates with such romantic-sounding names as Bahdinan, Bitlis, and Jazira bin Umar. Often only loosely controlled by their Turkish and Persian overlords, the princes had powerful militias—composed of nominally allied tribes—at their command, and courts filled with musicians, poets, scientists, and religious scholars. A complex social and political order was maintained, as the Kurdish princes, Kurdish tribes, Ottomans, and Safavids successfully balanced power among them for about three hundred years.

With the passing decades, however, cracks appeared in the system. The importance of the Silk Routes declined, the rule of the empires became more oppressive, and quarrels among Kurdish princes and tribes turned into wars. Plagues devastated the region, and, by the mid-1800s, Kurdish high culture had again all but collapsed. Entire tribes were eviscerated or deported, and the Kurds' sedentary agricultural communities gave way to their more traditional nomadic lifestyle, already in existence for thousands of years. A chaotic tribal order, with an economy based on raiding, emerged. European travelers passing through Kurdistan in the nineteenth century wrote of meeting ruthless bandits and warring tribes, adding more fuel to the Kurds' by-then well-established reputation for ferocity. "It is better to fight than to sit idle"; "One crowded hour of glorious life is worth an age without a name," go two old Kurdish proverbs.

Many Kurds today downplay their tribal heritage, fearing that it portrays them as a primitive people. But to many outsiders, it is part of their distinction. There are dozens of tribes, and hundreds of subtribes, some of which date back centuries. In the past, many tribes had their own distinct dress, folktales, music, and social customs. Some were known for specific characteristics, such as red hair, broad builds, boorishness, or courage. Tribal affiliations united as well as divided people and, though much diminished in importance today, are still central to many Kurds' identity and to Kurdish politics. There are also many nontribal Kurds, living primarily in the cities and on the plains. The nomadic tribal lifestyle has all but disappeared. Only "seminomads" remain, living in villages in winter and in goat-hair tents in summer as they move their flocks between their lowland and mountain pastures.

After World War I and the collapse of the Ottoman Empire, the Kurds came close to achieving national independence. The 1920 Treaty of Sèvres recognized their political rights and left open to possibility the establishment of an autonomous Kurdistan. But the treaty was never ratified, and, three years later, with the rise of Turkey's Mustafa Kemal Atatürk, another treaty was negotiated. The 1923 Treaty of Lausanne recognized a new Turkish republic; paved the way for the new British Mandate of Iraq to acquire the oil-rich Kurdish province of Mosul; and made no mention of the Kurds, then in a state of political disarray, torn apart by tribal loyalties. Shortly thereafter, the Western powers finalized the modern international borders of Turkey, Syria, and Iraq—new countries carved out of the old Ottoman Empire—while reaffirming those of Iran, then known as Persia. In a few short strokes of the pen, Kurdistan—never more than a vaguely delineated land divided among many tribes—was literally erased from the map and the Kurds were parceled out among four nation-states.

Then a foreign concept to the Middle East, the nation-state is still an idea with which the entire region struggles. Many Kurds have never really accepted the West's imposed borders, which in some places severed tribes and even families in half. "A thousand sighs, a thousand tears, a thousand revolts, a thousand hopes," goes an old Kurdish poem about the Kurds' determination to be masters of their own lands. Meanwhile, the erstwhile nation-states, desperate to establish a national identity based on a unified culture, have marginalized and persecuted the Kurds.

Yet the Kurds have also been their own worst enemy. Their history is strewn with gut-wrenching tales of infighting, brutality, and betrayal. One recent definitive instance occurred in 1996, when the Iraqi Kurdish leader Massoud Barzani turned to Saddam Hussein—the Kurd's most lethal modern enemy—to help him defeat his rival Jalal Talabani, who had earlier solicited help from another traditional Kurdish enemy, the Iranian government. Saddam had been instrumental in manipulating the two leaders' actions, which occurred in the wake of a failed CIA-backed coup attempt to oust him from office, and the events enhanced his standing internationally while diminishing that of the Kurds.

Just what is it about the Kurds, I thought as I read about one revolt after another, that gives them their courage, determination, and cussedness? What is it that makes a people a people? And, conversely, why *haven't* the Kurds been able to establish their own state? How does a people evolve into a nation?

Some of the answers to these questions must lie in the mountains, I thought. Mountain people all over the world—Scotland, Appalachia, Afghanistan, Chechnya—are a notoriously independent, stubborn, rebellious, and proud lot. Isolated in their craggy fortresses, they are accustomed to taking care of themselves, and don't cotton well to being told what to do. There's a reason why one of the first great rebels of all time, the Greek god Prometheus, "guilty" of bringing fire to man against Zeus' wishes, was banished to a mountain in the Caucasus.

And some of the answers must lie in the extraordinary repression the Kurds have suffered—and survived; as the hackneyed saying goes, what doesn't kill you, makes you stronger. In the last two decades alone, the Kurds have endured multiple aerial bombings and lethal chemical attacks, the ruthless destruction of thousands of their villages, the assassination of their leaders, killings and kidnappings, torture and inhuman prison conditions, crippling economic conditions, the banning of their language and culture, and the deprivation of that most basic right of all: the right to call themselves "Kurds."

This last violation occurred in Turkey, one of the most democratic of Middle Eastern countries, between 1924 and 1991, during which time Kurds were declared to be "mountain Turks who have forgotten their language." Anyone who said otherwise risked arrest and torture. In contrast, modern Iran and Iraq, despite their repressive regimes, have never denied the Kurds their identity. Up until 1975, Saddam Hussein even made regular visits to Kurdistan, posing for the cameras in Kurdish dress, while Iran's Islamic government has always granted the Kurds some basic cultural—though not political—rights.

How do a people function after such a horrific history? How do they rebuild after attempted genocide? How does trauma shape and filter lives?

The Arabs have an old term for places such as Kurdistan—*bilad es-siba'*, meaning "land of lions"—i.e., land not controlled by central government. Once applied to the most inaccessible areas of the Middle East, including its mountains, deserts, and marshes, the term connotes regions inhabited by isolated peoples who listen more to their hearts and traditions than to "civilization." Some scholars even once posited a kind of division of labor "between the tame and the insolent, the domesticated and the independent" with the rebels keeping "the urban civilization of the Middle East refreshed and in motion." But in our age of telecommunications and cyberspace, urbanization and globalization, it's questionable how much longer such lands will exist—if indeed they still do. Once remote Kurdistan, for one, is now in the throes of rapid modernization, with the Internet, satellite dishes, and supermarkets making their arrival. How are the Kurds coping with jumping one hundred years in the space of a decade, maintaining a sense of self as their traditional world tips, whirls, and shudders around them?

I wanted to travel to Iraq to explore these questions. I wanted to find out more about these mysterious, stubborn, seemingly inextinguishable people called Kurds. And the world needs to know more about them, too, I told my friends and editors—the Kurds are important; they're central to the future of Iraq, Turkey, Iran, and Syria, and hence to the whole Middle East.

But I also had a more personal reason for wishing to travel to Kurdistan: I wanted to return to the Middle East. I had loved Iran—not for its politics, but for its complex people, its paradoxical culture, its rich history, and, most of all, for the way in which it had challenged every last one of my Western assumptions.

MUCH OF THE MODERN Western world first became aware of the Kurds at the end of the Gulf War in 1991, when President George Bush encouraged the Iraqi Kurds to rise up against Saddam Hussein, in the hopes of destabilizing him. They did so in good faith, retaking many of the areas they had lost in the 1980s, when Hussein attacked his own citizens with chemical weapons and destroyed over twelve hundred Kurdish villages in the infamous Anfal campaign. When the Gulf War ended, however, the United States failed to follow through on its promise of military aid. Fearing more attacks, panicked Kurds fled to neighboring Turkey and Iran by the hundreds of thousands. Journalists covering the enormous migration—thought to comprise at least 1 million people—brought the world's attention to the Kurds' suffering for the first time in modern history. With a refugee crisis on hand, a shamed United States, along with other Western powers and the United Nations, set up a "safe haven" in northern Iraq, to which the Kurds could return without fear.

This safe haven was supposed to be a temporary arrangement, pending a final settlement of the whole Iraq question. But by the time of my visit to the region in the spring of 2002, the safe haven, by then also known as the "northern no-fly zone," had evolved into an extraordinary, quasi-permanent experiment in democratic self-government. Guarded by the U.S. and British air forces, and relatively flush with aid from the United Nations "oil-for-food program," northern Iraq—the size of Swit-zerland—was flourishing with three universities, fifty-odd newspapers and magazines, two satellite TV stations, satellite dishes, Internet access, "kurdicized" school curricula, small factories, social programs, and leaders regularly received by foreign states. Prosperity hadn't exactly come to Iraqi Kurdistan, but these northern provinces, which until 1991 had been among the most backward regions of Iraq, were now much better off than those under Saddam's control.

Although fewer Kurds live in Iraq than in either Turkey or Iran, I focused my travels on Iraq both because it represented an extraordinary chapter in Kurdish history—the first time the Kurds had governed themselves since the 1946 Kurdish Republic of Mahabad, Iran—and because Iraq was the easiest country in which to do research. From what I could ascertain while in the United States, neither Iran nor, especially, Turkey welcomed foreigners snooping around into sensitive Kurdish affairs, and although I also intended to visit both those countries, I wasn't sure how deeply I'd be able to penetrate their Kurdish cultures. As it turned out, both Iran's and Turkey's Kurdistan, which I visited on a second trip to the region the following autumn, proved easier to explore than I'd initially thought. Nonetheless, neither country was anywhere near as accommodating as northern Iraq—a land filled with both officials and ordinary people eager to show off their experiment in democracy.

Since Saddam Hussein's Baath regime did not generally grant visas to foreigners wishing to travel to northern Iraq, I had to enter through one of its bordering countries—Turkey, Iran, or Syria—using a crossing permit issued by that country in conjunction with one of the two political parties then ruling Iraqi Kurdistan—the Kurdistan Democratic Party (KDP) or Patriotic Union of Kurdistan (PUK). Syria, I was told, was the easiest of the three countries to work with, while Turkey, once relatively open, had since the mid-1990s become the hardest. I therefore applied through Damascus, to which I flew one cloudy afternoon in mid-March, and took the overnight bus to Qamishli, a Syrian border town. Arriving just as a pink dawn stole down wide muddy streets flanked by rough cement buildings, I slept for a few hours on the floor of the home of an Arab English teacher I'd met, surrounded by his six lightly snoring children. Then came a Jeep ride past fields flush with new wheat and barley, and solitary oil derricks bobbing against the horizon like hungry black crows picking at seed. The ride ended on a dirt road leading to an isolated military outpost, where an official, boredom rimming his eyes, wordlessly checked my papers and pointed me down a hill to the river below.

On the banks waited a handful of burly men in red-and-white turbans, and two creaky wooden skiffs equipped with outboard motors. One of the men tossed my suitcase—suddenly too new looking, though it was at least five years old—into one of the skiffs, another pulled me aboard, a third started the motor. We sputtered away from shore. Dead ahead was Iraq, and to the east was Turkey, followed by Iran. To the immediate west lurked the forces of Saddam Hussein, and to the northeast was the spot at which the Greek mercenaries had defeated the "Karduchoi" in 401 B.C. Below flowed the Tigris River, its mythical waters high now with the rush of early spring, but not high enough to hide huge mounds of pebbles rising from its current like beached whales.

A few moments later, our skiff grated against the Iraqi shore at Fesh Khabur. "Welcome to Kurdistan," said a lean young man in perfect English. WELCOME TO KURDISTAN read a sign in English behind his back. And "Welcome to Kurdistan" nodded an unsmiling guard armed with a Kalashnikov as I retired to a reception room for my first glass of Kurdish tea.

CHAPTER TWO

Arrival

FROM FESH KHABUR, I TOOK A TAXI HEADING SOUTH TO Dohuk, the northernmost of the three largest cities in Iraqi Kurdistan. Beneath a smudged gray sky, the road slipped through a dreamy landscape, jade knolls in the foreground and gaunt peaks in the distance. We passed miles of belching oil trucks headed toward Turkey, and isolated, still-life villages built of clay and cement. Few people were about that morning. The world seemed watchful, waiting.

Dohuk was tucked between two steep, boulder-strewn mountains, rising from the country's high plateau like crumpled hats. On the outskirts of town presided a ten-foot-tall, golden bust of Mulla Mustafa Barzani, father of the Kurdish liberation movement, and a row of mansions that had once belonged to Baath Party officials and now belonged to their Kurdish political counterparts. We passed a modern supermarket of an odd violet-blue color, and various faculty buildings of the University of Dohuk. Signs for nongovernmental relief agencies were everywhere: UNHCR (the United Nations High Commissioner for Refugees), WHO (World Health Organization), WFP (World Food Program), KRO (Kurdistan Reconstruction Organization), PWJ (Peace Winds Japan), Diakonia (Swedish), Help Age International (British).

Turning up a short hill, we arrived at the Jiyan, or "Life," Hotel—my home for the next few nights. Originally meant to become a Sheraton, the Jiyan was the hostelry of choice for foreign aid workers, journalists, politicians, and businessmen passing through town. In the rain that was now streaming from the heavens, however, the hotel had an almost abandoned feel. The "good afternoons" of the two smartly uniformed young men who greeted me in English as I came in were swallowed up by the silence of the dark lobby beyond. The electricity was out.

From my eighth-floor hotel window, I looked directly across the town to a mountain ridge spiked with conical pines. In the valley below, empty streets skirted clumps of cement-poured buildings, most two or three stories tall. The skies churned with dark clouds spitting out sheets of rain, while dense clots of black smoke from burning tires rose here and there. Today was the day before Newroz, or New Year's, and the streets had been emptied and the tires lit in celebration.

All in all, a dismal scene. I wondered, not for the first time, if I really knew what I was doing here. I was more interested in culture than in politics, in society than in the machinations of a possible new war, which thanks to President G. W. Bush's "axis of evil" speech, naming Iraq a worldwide pariah just two months before, suddenly seemed frighteningly imminent. My nebulous project involving—what? Attempting to understand how the Iraqi Kurds had reinvented themselves, seemingly overnight, from a fractured tribal people into a fledgling democracy? But whatever my questions or reasons for being here, they suddenly seemed woefully inadequate now that I had finally arrived in this land that was neither country nor state, both united and divided, bristling with hostilities directed both externally and internally.

CONFLICTS BETWEEN THE central Iraqi government and the Kurds erupted almost immediately after British rule was established in Iraq in 1920, following the demise of the Ottoman Empire. Although the British made some early promises of self-government to the Kurds, these were quietly forgotten as they struggled to control the artificial nation cobbled together out of three distinct and hitherto unrelated groups—the majority Arab Shiites, the minority Arab Sunnis, and the minority Kurds, also Sunnis. The British had selected the Arabian Emir Faisal to be king of Iraq after their mandate ended in 1932. But while Faisal claimed direct descent from the Prophet Muhammad, he was Sunni Muslim, which angered the majority Shiites. He had also never been to Iraq before, which angered others, including most Kurds. Why how familiar, I thought months later of the U.S. struggle to control Iraq postwar, with history repeating itself right down to the Pentagon's initial endorsement of Ahmed Chalabi, a former banker who had spent most of his life outside Iraq (and was wanted for embezzlement in Jordan), as the country's interim leader.

As Britain's intentions for Iraq's future became clearer, the Kurds reacted with armed resistance. First came the revolts of Shaikh Mahmoud in 1919 and 1922 to 1923, then the provocative actions of Shaikh Ahmad in the late 1920s, which led the British to bomb about eighty Kurdish villages—another early foretaste of what was later to come. And when the British duly instated King Faisal and his Hashemite monarchy in 1932, the legendary Mulla Mustafa Barzani rose to the fore.

Born in 1904, Mulla Mustafa is the best-known hero of the Kurdish nationalist movement. A larger-than-life warrior-leader, whose picture can be found in virtually every home in northernmost Iraqi Kurdistan, he succeeded against all odds in uniting nonliterate men from rival tribes with educated urban professionals to fight for a then-seemingly impossible cause. Though his first revolt of 1943–45 was small and eventually defeated, forcing him into exile in Iran and the Soviet Union, when he returned to Iraq thirteen years later, at age fifty-four, he effectively waged a war against the Iraqi government that in its essence continued into the 2000s.

Mulla Mustafa returned to Iraq with the fall of King Faisal's Hashemite monarchy, overthrown in 1958 in a coup d'etat by Brigadier Abd al-Karim Qassem, who at first promised a bright future for the Kurds. With the blessing of Qassem, Mulla Mustafa took up residence in Baghdad, assumed leadership of Iraq's Kurdistan Democratic Party (KDP), which had been formed during his exile, and began drawing up a list of Kurdish demands. But three years later, in 1961, Barzani's relationship with Qassem soured irrevocably, as it became clear that they could never agree on the extent of Kurdistan's autonomy. The KDP was banned, and a full-scale Kurdish-Iraqi war began, to be waged with only short interruptions until 1970.

In 1963, Qassem himself was overthrown, in a coup d'etat by the Baath Party. Another exile hurried home: Saddam Hussein, hiding out in Egypt because of his earlier attempt to assassinate Qassem. Nine months later, the Baath Party fell from power in a third coup d'etat. It resumed control again in 1968, to reign with ever-increasing brutality until the Iraq war of 2003.

Initially, the Baath regime expressed interest in negotiating with the Kurds. Then–Vice President Saddam Hussein traveled to Kurdistan to meet with Mulla Mustafa, and together they drafted the 1970 March Manifesto, which promised the creation of a semiautonomous Kurdish state, to be phased in over a four-year period. But as the four years went by, various articles of the manifesto failed to be adequately implemented. The boundaries of the Kurdish state were never established. Distrust escalated on both sides, and, in March 1974, hostilities broke out again.

The Kurds resumed the war with military aid from the Shah of Iran, who was in turn supported by the United States, giving the Kurds high hopes of victory. But only one year later, on March 6, 1975, the shah and Saddam Hussein suddenly signed the Algiers Accord—a devastating moment in Kurdish history that is still lived and relived every day in Iraqi Kurdistan. The accord abruptly ended the shah's support of the Iraqi Kurds in return for territorial rights. Overnight, the Kurdish resistance movement crumbled. A defeated Mulla Mustafa, forced into exile once again, declared the Kurdish war finished.

It was then that the modern chapter of Iraqi Kurdish politics began—a chapter still unfolding at the time of my visit and defining much of what I observed around me. I was traveling through a Kurdistan that was a divided country within a divided country. Its two northernmost governorates— Dohuk and Erbil—were controlled by a reinvigorated version of Mulla Mustafa's old party, the Kurdistan Democratic Party. The third and southernmost governorate—Suleimaniyah—was controlled by a newer party, the Patriotic Union of Kurdistan (PUK).

The seeds of this division had been sown during the earliest days of the KDP, when the party was split between its more traditional elements, headed by Mulla Mustafa, and its more urban, intellectual branch, led by Ahmad and Jalal Talabani. The latter pair, who had a socialist agenda, endured Mulla Mustafa only because of his strong following and military capabilities. But Barzani's unilateral decision to end the Kurdish war was the last straw for the leftists, and, in 1976, citing the "inability of the feudalist, tribalist, bourgeois rightist and capitulationist Kurdish leadership"—i.e., Barzani—to wage an effective revolution, Jalal Talabani declared the establishment of his new party. The PUK then resumed the Kurdish war against the Iraqi government, to be joined in the fight shortly thereafter by a regrouped KDP. Relationships between the two parties remained extremely hostile, however, all too often erupting into bloodshed.

After the Gulf War and the establishment of the Kurdish safe haven in 1991, there were questions over who would govern the zone. Many outside analysts did not believe the divisive Kurds capable of peacefully governing themselves, but, in May 1992, they more than rose to the occasion by holding democratic elections—the first in Iraq in thirty years—a remarkable achievement anywhere, but especially so in the Middle East. For the most part, international observers deemed the elections to be free and fair, with the KDP and PUK receiving a near equal number of votes. A jointly controlled Kurdish Parliament was set up, with fifty representatives from each party and five representatives from minority parties. The new government moved quickly to establish order, altering existing Iraqi laws to better serve the new quasi-state, outlawing the Baathist methods of repression, and, most impressively, announcing the formation of a Kurdish federal state, with the hopes of eventually being incorporated into a post-Saddam federation. Ordinary Kurds rejoiced in what seemed the beginning of a new era.

However, before long, an old pattern reestablished itself. The KDP and PUK began accusing each other of misappropriating funds and of being more interested in accruing power than in developing the region. Desperate economic conditions, terrorist bombings, and attempted assassinations raised tensions to the breaking point. In the spring of 1994, fighting broke out. Thousands died in a tragic and unnecessary internal war that led to the division of Kurdistan into two separately governed zones—a situation that would endure until six months after my visit, when a joint KDP–PUK session of the Kurdish Parliament met on October 15, 2002, for the first time in six years.

LATER THAT DAY, I met Dr. Shawkat Bamarni in the hotel lobby. Head of Dohuk's Public Relations Office, and thus an influential member of the KDP, it was his job to meet foreigners like myself and help us maneuver through Kurdistan. As a writer, I also needed Dr. Shawkat's help to line up interviews and gather background information.

A broad-shouldered man dressed in a neat dark suit with a pearl gray tie, Dr. Shawkat had a heavy, lugubrious air about him. Throughout that visit, and on numerous others, he seldom smiled, though he was always exceedingly generous and kind, and even told the occasional joke, most of which didn't quite translate into English. Later in my stay, I saw a photograph of him as a young guerrilla fighter, attending a conference with Massoud Barzani, in which Dr. Shawkat looked angry, untamed, and desperately ill at ease, as if longing to bolt out of the strange conference room and back to his familiar mountains. Now, though, hair thinning and eyes tired, he seemed all too accustomed to meeting foreigners in conference rooms and glass-sheathed hotels, both in Kurdistan and "outside."

"Welcome," Dr. Shawkat said in good English, motioning me toward a cluster of armchairs. From the other end of the room came the familiar tinkling sound of AOL's "you've got mail" signal. The Internet had arrived in Kurdistan in the late 1990s, and the Jiyan Hotel was host to a cybercafe.

Dr. Shawkat's eyes lit up when he heard I'd spent some time in Iran— he'd lived there for many years. He asked me a few questions about my background and talked about the other foreign visitors he'd recently hosted. Then, he got down to business.

"Don't ever go outside by yourself—always go with a friend. And when you travel outside Dohuk, you must take a bodyguard," he said.

"Is that really necessary?" I asked. Before leaving the United States, I had talked to several Americans who'd spent much time in Iraqi Kurdistan, as well as to a number of Kurds. The subject of bodyguards had come up, but no one had been able to tell me definitively if they were necessary. Some had said that they were more of a formality than anything else, while others had hedged on the subject by saying that bodyguards were sometimes needed, sometimes not; it all depended . . . on what, they couldn't specifically say. I didn't understand their answers until after I'd spent some time in Kurdistan, and then found myself answering the question in the same ambiguous way. Most of the time, the guards *were* a formality, but at times, I heartily welcomed their presence.

"If they're not really necessary, I'd rather not use them," I said. "They'll just get in the way."

"You know the situation here," Dr. Shawkat said.

"Yes," I said, but I also knew that I really didn't. I knew about Saddam Hussein, of course, and about the high probability—the certainty, really— of his agents' presence in Kurdistan, along with agents from Iran, Turkey, and Syria, all countries with interests in destabilizing northern Iraq. As a semiautonomous, Western-supported state, Kurdistan posed a threat—a

democracy in a region generally hostile to democracy. Kurdish independence here might encourage Kurds elsewhere to rise up against their governments. In the mid-1990s, Saddam had targeted Americans in northern
Iraq for assassination, which led President Bill Clinton to pull all U.S. aid
workers out. Since then, however, that Iraqi government policy had ended.
I had no reason to believe that anything would happen to me, but I was in a
volatile part of the world, where things could change at any time. No one
really *knew* the situation here.

We moved on to more personal topics. Dr. Shawkat had hundreds upon
hundreds of books, he said, and thousands upon thousands of photographs.
He took pictures of everything and everyone, and documented and indexed
all his images carefully, in an intricate cross-referencing system. He also
wrote in his journal every night, as he had for decades, and saved and
indexed every letter. Kurdistan was history in the making, he said proudly,
reminding me of something I'd read: The Kurds like photographs because
the images confirm their existence—otherwise too often denied.

"How do you find the time?" I asked.

He shrugged. "I don't know, but I must."

Dr. Shawkat, I would later decide, was a quintessential KDP man.
Throughout northern Iraq, I met many like him—big, broad, middle-aged
men dressed in dark suits, which often didn't quite fit. There were plenty of
younger, slimmer KDP officials as well, but in general, they didn't take
their jobs quite as seriously, weren't quite as committed to the party or to the
idea of a semiautonomous Kurdistan. Already one generation removed
from the armed Kurdish struggle, many of the younger officials seemed
more focused on their own desires than on communal needs. To them, the
KDP was a job, not a mission, as it was to men like Dr. Shawkat.

Mulla Mustafa had passed away in 1979, but the KDP was still headed
by the Barzani confederation and still had a reputation for old-fashioned
tribal politics. Mulla Mustafa's son—the round-faced, boyish Massoud
Barzani—was now the KDP president, and Nechirvan Barzani, Massoud's
nephew, was the KDP prime minister. Like his father, Massoud tended to
dress in traditional *shal u shapik* and keep his thoughts to himself.

Jalal Talabani, in contrast, who still headed the PUK, was a round, gar-
rulous lawyer who dressed in Western suits. He reputedly held more liberal
and socially progressive positions than his rival. But Talabani was often crit-

icized for his unpredictability and willingness to compromise, whereas Barzani was generally regarded as more steadfast.

The Iraqi Kurds continually pointed out the differences between the two parties to me, and I did notice some contrasts between them, as represented by both their policies and the officials I met, most of whom were men. KDP officials tended to be more formal and reserved; PUK men were more forthcoming and spontaneous, though more disorganized. Overall, however, I found the two parties to be essentially much alike. Both were powerful institutions that revolved around their strong-willed leaders, maintained strict party hierarchies, controlled an astonishing number of activities, paid close heed to tribal politics, and supported their own militias.

EACH OF KURDISTAN'S three governorates, all named after their capital city, had a distinct personality, which loosely corresponded to the personality of its governing party. KDP-controlled Dohuk was the smallest, most conservative, and tribal of the three, so much so that Iraqi Kurds elsewhere sometimes poked fun at it. But Dohuk was also the most quintessentially Kurdish, as it had been least subject to urban influences. PUK-controlled Suleimaniyah was relatively modern and liberal, at least as far as its largest cities were concerned. Suleimaniyah city was the site of the first Kurdish university, established in 1968, and had been the center of Kurdish publishing since 1920. Erbil, the headquarters of the KDP and seat of the Kurdish Parliament, fell somewhere in between Dohuk and Suleimaniyah, both geographically and in terms of character, except when it came to religion. The city of Erbil was said to be the most devout of the three large cities. It was also the largest, with a population of nine hundred thousand, as compared to Suleimaniyah's seven hundred thousand and Dohuk's four hundred thousand.

The boundaries of the governorates loosely corresponded to those of the old Ottoman Empire emirates. Most of Dohuk governorate had once belonged to the Bahdinan emirate, Erbil was at times ruled by the Soran princes, and Suleimaniyah was the former capital of the Babans. Under the Ottomans, the Kurds had inhabited sixteen large emirates and about fifty smaller Kurdish fiefdoms, all located in what is now Iraq and Turkey; the Safavids had ruled over a fewer number of Kurds in what is now Iran. Most

Kurdish princes had sided with the Ottomans after a decisive 1514 battle between the two empires at Çaldiran (Turkey), which established the border between them. The Kurdish princes supported the Ottomans largely because the Turkish Sultan offered them semiautonomous, self-governing powers, in return for paying taxes and providing military support, while the Safavids did not.

In the long run, this semiautonomous arrangement proved to be a double-edged sword. Because whenever a Kurdish prince rebelled against the Ottoman authorities, he inevitably had a brother, son, or nephew who was happy to obey the sultan and literally stab the prince in the back. Threats from disgruntled relatives was a major theme running throughout Ottoman history, and one that resonates in Kurdistan to this day, as individuals jockey for position within families, tribes, and the government.

I WENT TO Dr. Shawkat's office to talk about my itinerary. He sent one of his drivers to pick me up, and we drove to a low-slung building surrounded by a wall and overgrown garden. Sitting on plastic chairs outside the wall, AK-47s between their knees, were several guards in the machine-woven, military-style *shal u shapik*, better known as *khak* (like the English word *khaki*, both derived from Persian), and red-and-white turbans that are the trademark of the Barzanis and their supporters. Wound tightly around the head over the base of a skullcap, the turbans are usually one cloth high; Barzani family members wear two, one piled on top of the other.

One of the guards ushered me into the dank KDP building, chilly with the rains of early spring. Behind a large desk, beneath a photograph of Massoud Barzani, sat Dr. Shawkat, today dressed in a handsome brown suit and golden tie. Rising with a big smile, he kissed me on both cheeks and apologized. He still had other business to attend to, would I mind waiting? He directed me to a couch nearby, beneath a photograph of Mulla Mustafa. An assistant lumbered in with tea, balancing the delicate hourglass and saucer carefully between his large hands.

A man in a Western suit and double-tiered turban big as a birthday cake entered, followed by a slight Armenian priest in black robes and a collar, and an older man in an exquisite *shal u shapik* of a lustrous beige striped with thin brown. Each man sat with Dr. Shawkat for about fifteen minutes, discussing his concerns over a glass of tea while I watched them curiously.

The diversity and occasional magnificence of the male Kurdish costume, coupled with their often striking faces, seemingly carved by the elements, fascinated me throughout my visit, even after their initial novelty wore off.

I studied the walls. On one hung a detailed map of northern Iraq, and on another, a dusty wreath of dried red, yellow, and green—the colors of Kurdistan. On a third was a woven plaque, also of red, yellow, and green, commemorating the KDP's establishment, while in a corner flickered a television, silently tuned to a Kurdish satellite station.

Nowhere in sight was a map of Greater Kurdistan—a red-hot political issue in the Middle East. Depicting all of the lands that are inhabited by Kurds, the Greater Kurdistan map is about four times larger than the Iraqi Kurdistan map, as it includes over a third of Turkey, a fifth of Iran, slivers of Syria and Armenia, and an Iraqi Kurdistan expanded to encompass the oil-rich cities of Mosul and Kirkuk. Many non-Kurds assume that an independent Greater Kurdistan is what most Kurds are pushing for, and that independence is, in fact, what the whole trouble with the Kurds is all about. Yet I found the reality of the situation to be far more complex and nuanced. Although the creation of an independent Greater Kurdistan is certainly the dream of many Kurds, many realize that it is just a dream, and are primarily focused on achieving equal rights in the nations in which they live. Certainly neither the KDP nor the PUK, as I was told repeatedly, was pushing for an independent Greater Kurdistan. They simply wanted a semiautonomous state within a federated Iraq; they were Iraqis as well as Kurds, they often said.

"You see how busy I am," Dr. Shawkat said, finally joining me. "I have so many visitors. I have no time."

I nodded. "Did you talk to the governor?" I asked.

Dr. Shawkat had told me that before doing anything or talking to anyone in Dohuk, I had to meet with the province's governor—it was a matter of protocol and respect.

"No, he is busy right now. A delegation is here from the United Nations."

"Oh," I said, surprised. Dr. Shawkat had told me that I'd be meeting with the governor that morning—the reason why I'd arrived at his office at nine A.M. sharp.

Dr. Shawkat stared at me intently while I glanced surreptitiously at the clock. It was already ten-thirty.

"When will he be free, do you think?"

"At twelve. Do you want another cup of tea?"

I nodded again. An hour and a half wasn't too bad. I'd already settled into the slower rhythms of the Middle East.

Dr. Shawkat kept staring at me, and I shifted uncomfortably.

"Do you mind if I take your picture?" he said. "For my files?"

Almost before I could answer, he called to an assistant, who entered a moment later with a camera, obviously accustomed to this request. We posed on the couch, and then Dr. Shawkat returned to what I was discovering to be his favorite subject.

"I had to destroy some of my files when I left Iran," he said. "I had to leave in a hurry—I only had a few days, and I couldn't take everything. I divided my letters into two groups—one just personal, the others with information. I took pictures of the personal ones, and then, I had no choice, I had to burn them." Tears rose in his eyes. "Some of them said nothing, just 'hello' or 'thank you,' but still I think—that person took the time, bought the stamp, went out to mail—"

His words trailed off, and he drummed his fingers on his armchair.

"What were you doing in Iran?" I said, surprised at his emotion. I thought of all the mundane letters I'd thrown out in my lifetime.

Slowly, that morning and on subsequent visits, Dr. Shawkat's story came out, as stories came out everywhere I traveled in Kurdistan. They usually began with one simple hint, a sort of string that I tugged at, to open up dark, labyrinthine tales.

The son of an army guard, Dr. Shawkat had started working with the Kurdish resistance in 1961, at age fourteen. Two years later, he was arrested—one of his comrades, tortured by the Iraqi police, had given up his name and those of thirteen others. On the morning of his arrest, he'd been home, eating breakfast with his mother, who was epileptic. His last sight of home was of his mother running after the police car and collapsing on the road in a seizure.

The police first took him to Dohuk's prison and then to a military camp, located on the site of the violet-blue supermarket that I'd noticed on my arrival. His father, a guard at the prison, had been unable to help his son or express any sympathy when the boy was tortured. To do so would have been to risk arrest himself. After one week, the young Dr. Shawkat and the others were transferred to a prison in Mosul, Iraq's third-largest city, located just west of the semiautonomous zone.

Eighteen months later, the young Dr. Shawkat was released. He finished high school, studied veterinarian science at the Universities of Mosul and Baghdad, and got married. He was serving a required stint in the Iraqi military when he learned that he was about to be arrested again, due to his continuing underground activities. Escaping to Dohuk by car, he then fled at night on foot to Choman, a village high in the mountains near the Iranian border, where the KDP had established its headquarters. There, he set up a veterinary center, which would eventually grow to include fourteen vets and 150 technicians, operating in ten units throughout the liberated Kurdish areas. His wife joined him shortly thereafter, and gave birth to their third daughter, whom they named Choman.

In 1975, Dr. Shawkat and most of the KDP leadership was forced to flee from Iraq to Iran, due to the Algiers Accord. Dr. Shawkat first lived in a town near Lake Urumieh in western Iran, but in 1979, the KDP sent him to Karaj, just outside Tehran, which had become the party's new headquarters. There, he worked on behalf of Iraqi refugees and the party until 1995, when relations between Iran and the KDP soured, as Iran supported the PUK during the KDP–PUK internal war. Dr. Shawkat fled again, this time back to Iraq. It was then that he destroyed his personal letters.

Shortly thereafter, his daughter had a medical emergency, and he and his family traveled to Sweden to seek treatment. Following her recovery, his wife and children remained behind in Stockholm while Dr. Shawkat returned to Iraq.

"My children have a better chance for school in Sweden," Dr. Shawkat said. "And my wife must be with them. But I can't leave here. This is my life—I've been fighting for Kurdistan for forty years. What would I do in Sweden? Eat? Sit? What?"

Later, I learned that his was not an unusual arrangement or an unusual history. Many KDP officials had similar stories.

Dr. Shawkat now saw his wife and children only a few months a year, otherwise living alone with his aged mother in a big, chilly house provided for his use by the KDP. The house had a marble facade, spindly marble columns, and two lovely gardens—one originally built for men, the other for women. Visiting him at his home one day for lunch, I was shown around a dark living room packed with artifacts from the Kurdish resistance movement—photos, paintings, framed poems, the Kurdish flag—along with stuffed birds and foxes. We ate alone at a table large enough to seat at least a dozen. The room was completely silent except for the sounds of silverware clinking against plates and rain dripping off eaves.

"Life is a train—some people fall off, others climb on," Dr. Shawkat said lugubriously. It was a saying that he repeated often.

I HAD ARRIVED in the safe haven just in time for the Newroz festival. Believed to be Zoroastrian in origin, and thus over twenty-seven hundred years old, Newroz is celebrated on the vernal equinox in various parts of the Indo-Iranian world and lasts a week or more. Small bonfires are often lit on streets and hills, and young and old jump over the flames, in a symbolic leaving behind of the old and embracing of the new. All who can afford to do so dress in new clothes and exchange gifts, while everyone goes on picnics and visits with family and friends.

In Iran, Newroz is a national holiday, celebrated by all Iranians, no matter what their ethnicity or religion. But in Kurdistan, Newroz is *the* national holiday, celebrating not just New Year's, but also Kurdish identity, culture, and history. At times, it has served as a political flash point, especially in Turkey, where Newroz celebrations have turned into violent rallies pitting the Kurdish people against the Turkish authorities. In 1992, at least eighty civilians were killed in Newroz celebrations in three Turkish towns, after which the holiday was officially banned until 2000.

No one really knows how Newroz began, but one legend ties the festival to a Kurdish creation myth. It describes King Dehak—or Zahhak, as he's also called—as suffering from a curious affliction: two snakes grew out of his shoulders. The tremendous pain they caused him could be relieved only by feeding the snakes human brains each day. So every morning, the king had two young people killed. But the palace executioner soon took pity on his victims and killed only one person a day, mixing his or her brains with that of a sheep. He sent the second person away, to distant mountains. The rescued young people grew into a large community, marrying among themselves and giving birth to children. Evading other humankind, they developed a language of their own, built houses, grew crops, raised sheep, and called themselves Kurds. Among them was a poor blacksmith named

Kawa, who descended from the mountains one day to kill the cruel king, crushing his head with an anvil. Bonfires were lit all over the mountains in celebration.

The story of King Dehak and the greedy snakes is an ancient Persian myth, first recorded by the great Persian poet Ferdowsi in his *Shahnameh*, or Book of Kings, Iran's national epic, completed in A.D. 1010. Over five hundred years later, Sharaf Khan Bitlisi, prince of the Bitlis emirate, also recorded the myth in his *Sharafnameh*, or Book of Princes, a history of the Kurdish tribes.

Kurdish culture is closely related to Persian culture. Like the Persians, the Kurds are probably the descendants of the Indo-European tribes of central Asia, who settled and mixed with the original inhabitants of the region's Zagros and Taurus Mountains about four thousand years ago. The Kurdish language belongs to the Iranian branch of Indo-European languages. Like Persian, it is related to English, French, and German—not Arabic or Turkish.

The Kurds also have another creation myth, completely unrelated to Newroz, that tries to account for the high number of fair-haired, green- and blue-eyed Kurds among them, in an area of the world where most people have dark hair and eyes. "Invented on account of the fear and dread" that the Kurds inspire, according to one nineteenth-century traveler, the myth holds that centuries ago, King Solomon ordered five hundred of the magical spirits known as *jinn* to fly to Europe and bring back five hundred fair damsels for his royal harem. But on the way back, the *jinn* stopped in the Zagros Mountains, where they deflowered the damsels. Thereupon, an enraged King Solomon exiled the *jinn* and damsels to those same mountains, where they became known as Kurds.

I HAD AN introduction to Majed Sayyed Saleh, the mayor of Sumel, a subdistrict of Dohuk. Majed lived with his family on a quiet street not far from the Jiyan Hotel. Like Dr. Shawkat, he was a KDP man. His father had been a guerrilla, or *peshmerga*—literally, "those who face death"—who had died for the cause. As a teenager, Majed had also been exiled to Iran, along with his mother and siblings. Later, he studied engineering in Czechoslovakia. He spoke some English, and he and his sisters spoke Persian.

I visited Majed and his family on a rainy day near the end of the Newroz period. A dozen or so others were also there, including Majed's sisters and brothers, two cousins from Erbil, and two other cousins visiting from San Diego, California. Sitting stiffly on dark, velveteen couches, beneath photographs of Mulla Mustafa and Majed's martyred father, we exchanged pleasantries as rain poured down outside and round after round of treats went by. Orange juice served in golden-rimmed goblets. Sweet milky coffee served with brightly wrapped candy. A large platter of apples, grapes, and cucumbers, served with fragrant, amber-colored tea in tulip-shaped glasses.

Two days later, I received a call. Majed and his family had heard of my desire to stay with a Kurdish family, and they wanted to know if I'd like to stay with them.

And so began what would prove to be a monthlong stay with Majed and his family. More than once I wondered if I had perhaps overstayed my welcome, but the first few times I brought up the subject, it was waved away—if it's good for you, it's good for us, the family cried—and after a certain point, it wasn't possible to ask anymore.

Living in the family's large, two-story home were Majed and his immediate family: his wife, Huda, and their two young daughters; and his four younger siblings: his sister Zobayda, who worked in publishing; his sister Amal, an accountant; his brother Omran, who worked in the KDP government's treasury; and his brother Omeed, a college student. Also living with the family was their seventy-five-year-old mother, who'd suffered a debilitating stroke the year before. She needed round-the-clock care, which was provided during the day by Fakhriya, a cousin from the family village near the Turkish border.

The family house, protected by a high wall, boasted a pocket garden, balcony, marble facade, and small porch, upon which we left our shoes before entering, as is the Middle Eastern custom. Inside the front door was a tiny foyer with two doors—one leading to the formal reception room, the other to the family room. The formal side, where I'd first been received, and where the men usually sat, was furnished with sofas, coffee tables, a floor-to-ceiling cabinet, and a television and telephone, both served by satellite dish. The family side, where the women usually sat, was simpler and cozier, furnished only with rugs and a second television. But the rules governing who was received where were flexible. Mixed company, older company, and strangers of both sexes tended to be received in the more formal room, while younger company of both sexes was often entertained on the family side. Whenever both rooms were full, there was usually much traffic between them, while the closest family members were often whisked past the front altogether and into another room, by the kitchen.

At the front of the house was a room where Majed's bodyguards, provided by the KDP, ate and slept. He didn't really like having them there, he told me, and had never actually needed them but, between his political position and the region's general unrest, fears of Saddam Hussein and the Islamists, felt that they were necessary. The bodyguards were big, heavyset men, dressed in the military-style *khak* and red-and-white turbans. All also had thick mustaches, which are common among Kurdish men everywhere, and worn as a kind of badge of Kurdish honor. The guards' presence was both reassuring and unsettling.

In contrast to the guards, Majed and his brothers usually wore Western-style clothes—suits or jeans and sweaters—while the women dressed in a variety of styles. Majed's two sisters leaned toward knee-length skirts or dark pants, often worn with tight blouses or sweaters; Amal had a penchant for makeup and jewelry, Zobayda did not. Majed's wife, Huda, a beautiful woman with a luminous complexion and limpid brown eyes, usually wore flowing *dishdasha*, or caftans, as many Kurdish women do in the home, while the village cousin, Fakhriya, wore the long, traditional Dohuk-style dress, which features a long vest, balloon pants, and sleeves that tie behind the back. Except for Fakhriya, none of the women covered their heads either inside or outside the house.

My room was upstairs and held a Western-style bed, as did most of the other bedrooms. But the bathroom down the hall had an Eastern-style toilet—a hole in the floor—and when they were alone, the family usually ate around a tablecloth on the floor.

I soon settled into a pattern, leaving the house every morning with Majed, his guards, and five-year-old daughter Mina, on their way to work and school, to be dropped at the various places I wanted to visit. Whenever possible, I returned to the house by two P.M., in time for the main meal of the day and the typical Middle Eastern postprandial nap. In the late afternoon, I often went out again.

Like most civil servants in Kurdistan, Majed and his siblings worked only during the long mornings, and spent the afternoons with family and friends. This leisurely schedule was a holdover from the ruling days of the

Baath Party, which in the 1970s had instituted sweeping social change in Iraq, while also forming a close alliance with the former Soviet Union.

The Baath Party, whose name literally means "resurrection from the dead," was founded in Damascus, Syria, in 1940 by a Christian intellectual named Michel Aflaq. A socialist and secular party with a pan-Arab agenda, the Baath Party came to power in Iraq in 1968, following their second coup. Run by a small group of military and civilian officials at first, the regime only later developed into a ruthless totalitarian machine controlled by one man, Saddam Hussein.

In 1972, the Baath Party nationalized Iraq's oil industry, and used the revenues to construct a modern country, building infrastructure, instituting literacy campaigns, increasing the minimum wage, and greatly improving the status of women by revising outmoded Islamic laws. Women became college graduates, entered a wide variety of professions, and largely discarded the *hejab*, or veil. The Baathists also provided complete job security to large contingents of people—including acquiescent Kurds—and provided free education and health care, even while clamping down on dissent and human rights, in a campaign that would grow to horrific proportions. Some older Kurds I met rued the passing of those prosperous early Baathist days.

During the evenings, Majed and his family often entertained guests, who almost always dropped by unannounced, as is the Kurdish custom. Guests often stopped by during the day as well, and at least one woman of the house was always expected to be home to receive them, with tea, fruit, and candy at the ready.

Also in the evenings, the family and I often gathered in the formal living room, to talk and watch satellite television—Britain's BBC, Qatar's Al-Jazeera, and various Turkish, European, and Kurdish channels. Much of the Kurdish programming focused on music and dancing, and I watched endless hours of Kurds in traditional dress surging forward, ebbing back, bending, swaying, and jumping in tight, rainbow-colored line dances.

Every evening, the electricity would go out at least twice, as the long hand of Saddam Hussein reached toward us. Dohuk's energy supply did not meet its needs, and the Baath regime had agreed to provide the city with an additional thirty megawatts a day—at a hefty price, no doubt. But Saddam liked to play games, and often sent much of that power through in the early morning, when most people were asleep, leaving Dohuk constantly scrambling for light.

Whenever the power went out, Zobayda or Huda would leave the room to fetch a long fluorescent lamp powered by battery. The cold blue stick would cast pale sheets of illumination over those sitting nearest it, but leave the rest of us in darkness. A kerosene heater—in a country known for its oil—also warmed those sitting nearby, but left the rest of us shivering.

During those evenings, we would talk about the events of the day, personal histories, the weather, politics. Everything would seem to be quite ordinary, until suddenly it wasn't. A silence would fall, holding within it anxiety, depression, fear. But none of this was ever expressed, and a moment later the conversation would begin again as the electricity went on again, as ordinary and comforting as ever.

CHAPTER THREE

The Little Engine That Could

DOHUK CENTERED ON ONE LONG MAIN STREET THAT ROSE and fell as it ran from the more prosperous end of town, through the commercial center, to the poorer quarters. Much of its way was lined with small gray shops, some of which sported English-language signs: Havrest Hair Salon, Jzery Book Shop, Dohuk Center for Money Exchange, Titanec Hotel. Sparkling fruit juice stores, blenders whirling with bright swatches of color, beckoned from the occasional corner, along with a central bazaar, a few dusky Internet cafés, and several liquor stores, frequented by both Christians and liberal Muslims. Overhead, snarls of electricity wires drooped in the air, heavy black cobwebs.

At the traffic circles hulked bulky white statues commemorating the Kurdish revolution or a story from Kurdish folklore. Many had been sculpted after the 1991 uprising by art students under the supervision of their teachers, and were amateurish yet endearing, raw yet hopeful, embodying within them both the can-do attitude and the lack of sophistication of many Kurds, cut off from the rest of the world for generations.

DOMINATING PARTS OF the downtown was the University of Dohuk, housed in a scattered array of cold utilitarian edifices originally built by the Baath regime. The science faculty building had once been a prison; the administration building, a Baath Party headquarters; and the College of

Medicine, a Baath army outpost. The university had been founded only after the 1991 uprising, largely through the efforts of Dr. Asmat Muhammad Khalid, whom I went to visit one morning early in my stay. I wanted to learn more about how semiautonomous Kurdistan worked. The new university seemed a good place to start.

At the university, I found a burly, white-haired dynamo of energy waiting for me in a sunny, book-lined room, seemingly exorcised of its Baathist ghosts. Dr. Asmat spoke moderately good English and swiveled enthusiastically in his high-backed leather chair behind a shiny desk as he told me the university's story. Above him hung a photograph of Massoud Barzani, on another wall hung one of Mulla Mustafa.

Trained as an engineer, Dr. Asmat had first thought of establishing the university in 1970 while attending a conference, he said. But when he raised his hand and suggested it, everyone in the room, mostly Arabs, laughed in his face—"Dohuk is too backward for a university," they said. The Kurdish region did have one university at the time, but it was in Suleimaniyah, the Kurds' most sophisticated city. Dr. Asmat felt humiliated, but never forgot his idea.

The uprising and its aftermath provided Dr. Asmat with the opportunity he needed. He took his idea to Massoud Barzani, and on September 14, 1992, the Kurdish Parliament issued a decree establishing the University of Dohuk. It was to be composed of only two colleges at first: the College of Agriculture and the College of Medicine.

"Our start-up team was six persons," Dr. Asmat said. "But how to build a university from nothing? We had no money, no teachers, no classrooms, nothing. Everything was destroyed. And our campus—all these buildings— was occupied by refugees. We had lecture rooms filled with refugees. One time I entered a classroom between women making bread on one side, and women washing clothes on the other.

"We had to ask the people of Dohuk for help. We called to carpenters to repair the buildings, professionals to teach the classes, and farmers to teach farming. People cleaned, and gave furniture and books. All volunteer."

Now the university belonged to the International Association of Universities (IAU) and boasted nine colleges, various postgraduate programs, about two hundred professors, and over two thousand students. Tuition was free; its primary source of funding was the Kurdish government.

"But, wait—" I said as Dr. Asmat, apparently finished, stood up to usher me out the door. "I don't understand. . . ." The Kurdish government was far from flush, I knew, and I was puzzled as to how the university had grown so large so quickly.

But Dr. Asmat had no more time to talk—graduation was only two weeks away, and he had much to attend to. He passed me on to the dean of the College of Medicine, Dr. Farhad Sulayvani. A wiry, bespectacled man of erect military bearing, Dr. Sulayvani seemed tall when sitting down, but was of average height when standing up. He didn't look directly at me until well into our conversation—a mannerism that I often encountered in Iraq, where people also had the disconcerting habit of waiting, their faces expressionless, for me to fully explain myself before moving a muscle or saying a word. There's much wariness here, I often thought, at first attributing the trait to recent history and caution before foreigners. Only later did I realize that the Kurds are wary when confronting one another as well.

Also one of the university's founders, Dr. Sulayvani told me more about the school's earliest days, when the College of Medicine had had no decent facilities, equipment, books, or trained staff. Its adjoining teaching hospital, though in operation for years under the Baath regime, had also had little trained personnel. After the uprising, Saddam Hussein ordered all Arab professionals out of the region, thinking that without Baghdad brainpower, Kurdistan would collapse. "But the Kurds proved him wrong," Dr. Sulayvani said proudly, sitting up straighter than ever. Though improvement came only gradually, it did come—in the college's case, through the help of other universities, aid organizations, the United Nations, and the smuggling in of everything from books to secondhand microscopes.

So the university did have some other resources besides the government, I thought, while remembering the Kurds' well-known reputation for smuggling. They had been honing that expertise ever since their division between the Ottomans and Safavids. And who better to smuggle contraband across borders than a borders-divided people?

"In recent years, the Internet had also been very influential," Dr. Sulayvani continued. Before its arrival in the safe haven in the late 1990s, the university, along with everyplace else, had had virtually no contact with the outside world. There was no mail—Baghdad didn't let it in—and until only a few years before, phone calls had been prohibitively expensive. Now, though, thanks to satellite connections, international calls cost about 50 cents a minute, and the Internet, about $1 an hour. Those prices were still too high for many Kurds, but the middle class could afford it.

My next stop was the College of Arts, a new building housing the language and literature faculties, and a library filled with books that had been hand-carried into Kurdistan by travelers. Here, I met two young language teachers—an English-Moroccan woman from Yorkshire, England, and a French-Kurdish woman from Paris. Both had moved to Kurdistan only a year or two before. The English-Moroccan, a devout Muslim with a porcelain complexion, enveloped in a raincoat and headscarf, was married to a Kurd and had four children. The French Kurd, a single woman in a form-fitting black dress, with heels and curled hair, had originally come to Dohuk to visit relatives, but had liked it so much that she'd stayed, to become the university's only French teacher.

The two women shared an office, where they sang praises of the Iraqi Kurds to me. They're versatile people and, despite all the atrocities they've witnessed, very kind, said the English-Moroccan in her broad Yorkshire accent. They depend on themselves, they don't wait for outside help, said the French Kurd, in her lilting Parisian one. They take good care of their country, they're always cleaning, and are very well organized, both concurred. While silently agreeing with their first four points, I thought that, from a historical perspective at least, organization is not a Kurdish strong-point.

"The presentation of work here was terrible at first," said the French teacher. "Students would hand in homework written on dirty pieces of paper. They didn't know. But now they're getting better."

"Once I asked the students to write an essay about their most memorable moment," said the English teacher. "One student wrote that she came home one day when she was ten to find her whole family gone. She never saw any of them again." She sighed. "I can't seem to forget that story. But everyone here has stories like that. When my husband was six, he was playing in the garden when a bomb dropped and killed his brother."

While she was talking, a tall, soft-spoken man in his forties, dressed in a brown suit and tie, came in. A graduate student in the English department, he was writing his master's thesis on General Sherif Pasha, a Kurdish diplomat who'd been instrumental in negotiating the 1920 Treaty of Sèvres, the nonratified, post-WWI agreement that could have led to an independent

Kurdistan. The process was frustrating, as there were few books relating to his subject in Dohuk, and those were all in English or French. His English was serviceable, but for French, he had to rely completely on the French Kurdish teacher. She was happy to help, but spoke little Kurdish, and neither was completely fluent in English. Only bit by bit was his project progressing. Much like the university itself, I thought.

The soft-spoken man had spent many years as a *peshmerga* and as a refugee. He'd always dreamed of studying at a university, but had never before had the chance. Many of the students at the university were older. He didn't find studying at his age especially difficult, but "sitting with little boys" was hard. Nonetheless, he was hoping to get his Ph.D.

"Everything is now possible in Kurdistan," he said with a sigh.

A BELL RANG, and the threesome gathered their books for class. But before disappearing, they introduced me to a group of students who had just moved to Iraq from Iran. Like Dr. Shawkat, Majed, and his family, the students' parents had been forced to leave Iraq in 1975 due to the Algiers Accord. The accord had destroyed tens of thousands of Iraqi Kurds' lives, and every time I heard about it, my stomach churned, as the agreement had also marked the first great betrayal of the Kurds by the United States.

In 1974, following the breakdown of the 1970 March Manifesto that was to have granted the Kurds semiautonomy, war again broke out between Mulla Mustafa Barzani's forces and the Iraqi army. But this time, the Kurds were in a strong fighting position, as they'd accepted significant military aid from the Shah of Iran, who was in turn receiving partial funding for that aid from the United States—a critical point, as Barzani did not trust the shah, but did trust the United States. It was the height of the Cold War, and the Baath regime was aligned with Russia, whereas Iran under the shah was a prominent U.S. ally.

The shah hoped to destabilize Iraq by providing the Kurds with everything from U.S. Hawk missiles to fighting forces. However, the shah never intended the Kurds to win their war, and, in the Algiers Accord of March 1975, abruptly abandoned them. The accord gave Iran, with the tacit approval of the United States, what it had really wanted all along—control of half the strategic Shatt al Arab waterway, which separates the countries and leads to the Persian Gulf. In return, the shah withdrew Iran's aid to the Kurds.

Laying the groundwork for the Algiers Accord had been America's own Henry Kissinger, who encouraged the Kurds to escalate their revolution while knowing all the while that a Kurdish victory was not part of the plan. In the words of the 1975 Pike Report, commissioned by the congressional Select Committee on Intelligence, "It was a cynical enterprise, even in the context of a clandestine aid operation"; in the words of Henry Kissinger, "Covert action should not be confused with missionary work."

Within hours of signing the accord, Iran was withdrawing its forces and supplies from the Kurds. Mulla Mustafa Barzani was devastated. He was a passionate believer in the United States, having even once proposed, probably without really thinking it out, that all Kurds relocate to America. "I trust America," he said in one 1973 interview. "America is too great a power to betray a small people like the Kurds." In his disillusionment, Barzani decided to end the Kurdish national struggle, saying that its continuance would lead only to the massacre of his people. Many in the rank and file were eager to continue the fight, but Barzani stood firm—a decision for which he was later harshly criticized. Over one hundred thousand Kurds, including KDP leaders, fighters, and their families, fled to Iran, to join the over one hundred thousand Kurdish refugees already there. Thousands of others surrendered, and thousands more were slaughtered by the Iraqi forces.

Upon arriving in Iran, the Iraqi Kurds were first placed in refugee camps, and then parceled out to towns and villages far from the Iraq-Iran border. The shah did not want them in Iranian Kurdish territory, where a combined Iraqi-Iranian Kurdish population could stir up trouble, and he was careful to put only a few Iraqi families in each town so that they had little power. Not until Iran's Islamic Revolution of 1979 did the lives of the exiled Iraqi Kurds begin to improve, and later that same year, the KDP was allowed to hold its first post–Algiers Accord conference in Karaj, near Tehran, the KDP's new headquarters.

Thereafter, the children of the Iraqi refugees grew up in Iran, learning the Persian language and Iranian ways. Yet their parents never forgot their homeland and, after the establishment of the safe haven, began moving back in large numbers. By the time of my visit, there were approximately forty thousand recently returned refugees from Iran in the KDP's territory—all of whom had to be housed and fed, along with the many thousands who had lost their homes in the Anfal.

Most Iraqi Kurds I met felt that their people's exposure to Iran had been a good thing. The returning refugees were bringing with them the Iranians' love of learning, entrepreneurial spirit, organization, and sophistication, they said. Iran is considerably more developed than is northern Iraq.

At the College of Arts, the refugee students were ecstatic to learn that I, too, had been to Iran and spoke some Persian. Gathering around me, they ushered me into a sunny cafeteria, where they plied me with multiple rounds of soda, candy, and tea. Covering the wall across from us was an enormous poster of New York City, complete with the World Trade Center.

We're so, so happy to meet you, the students said over and over—you see, it's very difficult for us here, we were born in Iran, and we speak Persian and only a little Kurdish. Everything is so different here—the people, the clothes, the food. There are no shops. There are no movies or parks. There's no place to go for fun. We miss Iran!

"Do you want to go back?" I asked.

There was only a short moment of silence.

Oh, no! they replied. Yes, we miss Iran, but we had problems there. We were not free. People were prejudiced. Only here can we say we are Kurd without trouble.

AS I WANDERED around the university that day, I felt as if I had somehow landed in the middle of a giant jigsaw puzzle. The Kurds were trying to cobble together many odd-shaped bits and pieces—some half destroyed, others curious gems—to create something new out of the old. Some of the pieces weren't quite fitting yet—the refugee students from Iran still hadn't found their place, and the university's quality of teaching still needed much work, I guessed, an impression confirmed by others later. But the enormity of what had been accomplished in ten short years was impressive, as was the Kurds' courage to forge ahead with what had basically been an impossible task. No one had told the Kurds that a university couldn't be started from scratch without major funding, and so they had simply gone ahead and done it.

ON A SIDE STREET in downtown Dohuk squatted the Writers' Union, flanked by two oversized busts, one of Anwar Mai, a Kurdish historian, another of Saduq Bahaadin Amedi, a Kurdish classical poet. Dr. Shawkat had suggested I visit the union to meet others of my ilk, and I'd agreed. But I had no idea what to expect as I scurried into the building one late afternoon, fat raindrops spattering around me.

Inside a gloomy front hall, I bumped into an advance guard of five men—Dr. Shawkat had telephoned—who politely ushered me into a rectangular reception room, its perimeter lined with shiny baroque-style chairs. As we took our seats, at least a dozen other men also filed in and sat down. Most were middle-aged and dressed in neat dark suits. They looked at me expectantly, as a waiter bustled in with clinking glasses of tea, and my mind went blank. These men looked nothing like the scruffy bunch of writers I knew back in New York.

One of the men came to my rescue by delivering an introduction in broken English. Established in 1971 as a place for writers to work and congregate, the Writers' Union had somehow managed to survive through the difficult Baath regime years. But it was only since the uprising that the union had truly started flourishing. Before, writers had censored themselves or not written at all—they'd been afraid. Now, publications were everywhere, and even small Dohuk had its own Khani media center, which published a weekly paper and monthly magazine. The union's size had doubled, to over 130 writers, mostly professionals who worked during the day as doctors, accountants, lawyers, or teachers. To work full time as a writer in Kurdistan was impossible. Publications paid little, if anything, and most books were self-published.

"What about women writers?" I asked, looking around at my all-male companions. "Are there any?"

Of course, the men said, nodding proudly, the union had many excellent women writers—nine, to be exact.

"Why aren't they here?" I asked.

They are home, came the answer. As I was only just beginning to learn, most Kurdish women do not go out after about five P.M. unless in the company of their families, especially in a conservative city like Dohuk.

The introduction over, the men exchanged glances. Then, they looked at me appraisingly. How about a drink? they asked, a gleam in their eyes. Like many Kurdish men I met, they did not take the Muslim stricture against drinking alcohol too seriously. For a Kurdish woman to drink, however, was considered scandalous.

About a dozen of us then retired to the back of the building, the men talking in Kurdish, while I, suddenly acutely aware of being a woman out after dark in a culture where this was not done, self-consciously wondered what they were saying. The men had an easy, familiar air with one another, and I guessed that they met at the union often. Our retreat to the back had the feel of ritual.

We stopped outside a dismal room, furnished with stained sofas sagging around a scarred coffee table. Despite overhead fluorescent lights, every-thing in the room, including the air, seemed gray. "Women first," said one of the men, ushering me forward, and then chuckled—a reaction I encoun-tered often in Iraq, where men seemed to find the Western courtesy highly amusing. I called them on it once or twice, only to be met with even louder chuckles. "Yes, we do think it's funny," one man conceded once, "because women here come last, but perhaps this is our future!"

As beers, vodka, and pistachios arrived, I studied my companions more closely. One was a tall man with a big belly, bristling mustache, and thin-ning white hair. Another was a slight and dapper gentleman with fine fea-tures and a clipped mustache. A third was short and handsome with sparkling black eyes and black curls. In fact, each of the men around me was quite distinctive, and yet somehow, in their dark suits, in the grim room, they all seemed the same. It was partly the boxy cut of their jackets that did it, I thought, and partly something less tangible—the way they held themselves, perhaps, a shared assuredness, coupled with politeness and reserve. Neither that evening nor at virtually any other point during my trav-els did the Kurds I met ask me any personal questions—not even whether I was married or had children. To have done so, one Kurdish woman explained to me, would have been considered rude.

We talked about literature and writing for a while. Fyodor Dostoyevsky, Ernest Hemingway, and Jack London were among my companions' favorite authors. One man was working on a history of Kurdistan structured around the life of his father, and another on a novel about a young *peshmerga* who "had forgotten his humanity." A third wrote romance poems penned in a historical mode, and a fourth wrote poems about the Anfal.

The men started telling jokes in Kurdish, one of which they translated for me. One day, the *peshmerga* arrested some of Saddam's men. Holding them captive for months, the *peshmerga* fed them nothing but soup.

Negotiations took place, and the men were released. They went into a Kurdish town, entered a restaurant, and ordered soup.

At this, all the men laughed, while I looked blank.

"It's funny because they think soup is all the Kurds eat," someone explained.

I nodded as if I understood.

But the men saw through me, and they kindly tried again, this time with a joke that they said was very popular. A man in an airplane climbs out while in flight to fix the landing gear, which has jammed. He drops his wrench. One week later he goes back to his village. His father is dead. What happened? he asks. Oh, he was just sitting outside when a wrench fell out of the sky and killed him!

At this, all the men guffawed loudly, some slapping their knees, while I again tried to interpret what I had just heard. The jokes suddenly made the Kurdish world around me seem dense and impenetrable, and the Kurdish men, alien and remote.

The talk turned to politics, and the world became familiar again, with many men talking at once. Some cheeks, including mine, were flushed. The alcohol was taking effect.

"We want the United States to attack Saddam!"

"We don't care what it costs. Even if he bombs us again!"

"Our situation is not secure. He must go!"

I would encounter this same basic conversation everywhere I traveled in Iraqi Kurdistan. With memories of past atrocities all too fresh in people's minds, and an all-too-intimate understanding of Saddam Hussein's sadistic capabilities, most Iraqi Kurds had no doubts about where they stood regarding a possible war.

More surprising was their attitude toward Americans. Because the United States has let the Iraqi Kurds down on several significant occasions, with disastrous consequences, I had expected to find a fair amount of anti-American sentiment in Kurdistan. Yet most Iraqi Kurds I met not only seemed to regard those past betrayals as water under the bridge, but also viewed the United States as by far the greatest and most honorable country in the world. More than any other nation, the United States was protecting their no-fly zone and could be their possible future savior. I heard constant praise heaped upon the States, coupled with little skepticism about the

American way of life, and even met Kurdish babies dressed in snugglies with an American-flag design. "Kurdistan is a small country, so we need the help and protection of a bigger country," Majed explained to me one day. "And who will help us? Not the Muslim states, not Europe. Only the United States."

Such idealization of the United States can lead only to trouble in the long run, I thought. But I also recognized that given their precarious situation, the Iraqi Kurds had no patience for complexity. They needed a white knight in shining armor.

As an American, I was a prized visitor in Kurdistan. With the 2003 war then still a year away, there were only a handful of Americans of non-Iraqi origin in northern Iraq. Many Kurds viewed my visit as an indication that help would soon be on its way. Everywhere I went, people asked me not *if* but *when* I thought the United States would bomb Iraq.

The men at the Writers' Union fell to talking in Kurdish among themselves again, and I turned to the impeccably dressed gentleman sitting next to me. A doctor with an air of gentle sadness about him, he spoke good English.

"No one knows what the future hides," he said quietly. "And no one knows the effect of this situation now. People say that it has no effect, but I am a doctor, and I am sure that after eleven years of living this way, of not knowing the future . . . It is very hard to live your life without knowing the future. The psychological strain is very great."

His words trailed off. Although I was quite sure that no one else in the room had heard or understood his English, I thought I felt the bravado around me drain away. Everyone, myself included, seemed to be sinking deeper into the stained sofas as the air turned a darker gray.

Hasan Slevani, the short, handsome man with sparkling eyes and black curls, drove me home to Majed's. He worked in the governor's finance office and stopped by the Writers' Union every evening after work, staying until about nine P.M. He also had six children.

"Your wife must be very busy," I said, picturing the poor woman home alone with six children every evening while her husband was out socializing.

"Yes, she is," he said matter-of-factly, "but we have wonderful children. You must stay with us. My children are learning English and would love to practice with you."

I nodded but didn't commit myself. It had been a long day.

"What do you think of the life here?" Hasan asked as we turned onto a near empty street, the sky above us black crystal, the stars seemingly close enough to touch.

I struggled to respond, but before I could, he answered the question himself. "It is hard, but it is beautiful."

"What do you think of the Writers' Union?" he asked a moment later.

Again I struggled to respond, but again he answered the question himself. "Talk is something very small, but it is very beautiful."

EARLY ONE EVENING, Dr. Shawkat and I finally went to meet the governor of Dohuk, Nechirvan Ahmad. Arriving at his guesthouse just as the sun was setting, orange and pink splintering over black hills, we retired to a large reception room, where the governor immediately launched into a detailed but impressively succinct history of modern Iraqi Kurdistan, translated by an able interpreter. He ended with the implementation of the U.N. Security Council Resolution 986, the so-called "oil-for-food program."

First passed in December 1996 and aimed at relieving the suffering caused by the international economic sanctions imposed on Iraq for its refusal to disarm its nonconventional-weapons program post–Gulf War, the resolution allowed Iraq to export oil, but only in order to buy food and other humanitarian goods. The resolution further stated that 13 percent of the program's resources had to go directly to the northern no-fly zone. Baghdad decided how goods should be distributed there, but it was the United Nations that administered the north's program. Overall, 986 was the largest humanitarian assistance program in the world and in U.N. history.

It was the oil-for-food program, more than anything else, that had turned everyday life in the safe haven around, the governor said. Whereas before there had been hunger, now every denizen of the north automatically received a ten-item monthly rations basket that would otherwise have cost the average family its entire monthly income. Starvation had been eradicated, and child mortality rates were declining. According to a 2000 UNICEF report, the mortality rates for children under age five in northern Iraq had fallen to 72 per 1,000 in 1994 to 1999, as compared to 80 per 1,000 in 1984 to 1989, while they had more than doubled in Baath-controlled Iraq, to 131 per 1,000 in 1994 to 1999 as compared to 56 per 1,000 in 1984 to 1989. So how dare Saddam Hussein claim that it was economic sanctions that were causing Iraqi children to die of starvation? the governor asked. It was a question that I was to hear often in Iraqi Kurdistan and wondered about myself, though there were mitigating circumstances. The under-age-five child mortality rates in northern Iraq in 1984 to 1989 had probably been abnormally high due to the Anfal, and, after 1991, the safe haven began receiving far more humanitarian aid than did the rest of the country.

"You wouldn't believe the difference between 1992 and now," our host said. "We have many thousands of new housing units and hundreds of new kilometers of road. One example: ten years ago, Dohuk had only one secondary school. Now, we have twelve secondary schools, a technical school, Dohuk University, and an Institute of Fine Arts."

Later, I got the official statistics for all of Iraqi Kurdistan from the Ministry of Reconstruction and Development. Between 1992 and 2002, the Kurdistan Regional Government, with the support of the United Nations and other nongovernment agencies, had rebuilt an impressive 65 percent of what had been destroyed by the Baath regime. Well over half of the 4,000 or so ruined villages—out of an original 4,655—had been rebuilt, and more than 80,000 families had been resettled. However, about 140,000 displaced families, or 800,000 people, still awaited new homes.

COMMUNICATION WITH MAJED and his family was difficult. Only Majed spoke English, but he was far from fluent, and my Persian didn't extend beyond basic conversation. The women of the house and I spent much of our time communicating in gestures, often to the frustration of all involved, and to my discomfort, as I worried whether the family was regretting taking me in for such a long period. I didn't always know how to comport myself during the long evenings when they were socializing together. Would it be better for me to join them, perhaps making them feel forced to entertain me, or stay in my room, and perhaps offend them? But if the family tired of me, they didn't show it, as everyone took me under their wing, answering my questions, showing me around Dohuk, and introducing me to friends and neighbors.

Because of the language barrier, I spent more time talking to Majed than to anyone else in the family. A tall and reserved man in his early forties, with light brown, bristle-cut hair and the Kurdish mustache, he was the next-to-oldest son of his martyred father, Sayyed Saleh. A well-known *pesh-*

merga, Sayyed Saleh had joined the KDP in 1955, at age fifteen, only to be arrested and sentenced to death without trial a few years later. But the 1958 coup d'état of Brigadier Karim Qassem had saved him, and in 1961, he rejoined the Barzani revolution, to live and fight in the mountains, with only brief interruptions, for over thirty years, dying in battle in 1992.

Throughout Majed's childhood, Sayyed Saleh had come home when he could, sometimes staying for a few days, sometimes for a few hours, and occasionally for a few months. But sometimes, too, years would go by between visits, and Majed didn't always recognize his father when he arrived. How had Majed's mother endured it? I wondered.

After the Algiers Accord, Sayyed Saleh had not been able to come home to help his family escape to Iran. Majed, then age thirteen, his mother, and four siblings had gone on their own, making an eleven-day trek over the mountains with the help of other *peshmerga*. Upon arrival in Iran, they were placed in a refugee camp and, a short time later, sent to a small village where they and one other family were the only Kurds in town. Joined by Sayyed Saleh, they lived there until 1978, under constant surveillance, needing a police pass to leave the village. "We had a hard time," Majed said. "We were among strangers, and they were Shiites. In school, they would ask us, are you Muslim or are you Sunni? They didn't understand that Sunni is Muslim."

After the Islamic Revolution, the family was allowed to move to Iranian Kurdistan, and Sayyed Saleh returned to the mountains, while Majed and his older brother obtained scholarships to study in Europe, through the help of the KDP. Majed saw his father for the last time on January 4, 1985. Sayyed Saleh would live for another seven years, but between his *peshmerga* activities and Majed's studies, the two would not meet again.

"It doesn't matter how sad I get sometimes, remembering," Majed said to me one rainy afternoon while playing with his oldest daughter, whom he adored, lavishing on her the attention that his father had never been able to pay him. "Still I am happy, working for my nation and for my family."

MY COMMUNICATION WITH Majed and his family improved considerably whenever their cousins Yousif and Fatma, visiting from San Diego, were in the house. An outgoing brother and sister in their thirties, Yousif and Fatma had left the Middle East for California in 1992. As the oldest of nine siblings, Yousif had immediately gone to work and was still the family's primary breadwinner, employed as a taxi driver. Fatma, five years younger, had completed two years of community college and worked as a clerk. Both were now American citizens.

Like Majed, Yousif had a dramatic story. His father, Sayyed Rashid, Majed's father's younger brother, had also been a *peshmerga*, as had their two other full uncles—one killed in battle—and various half uncles. What a family, I thought as I listened to the history, though neither Yousif nor Majed seemed to find it particularly unusual. How many other Kurdish families had sacrificed an entire generation to the national struggle?

Sayyed Rashid, too, had fought in the mountains for years but, in 1985, had been imprisoned. Yousif, then eighteen and knowing that he would be next, went underground, keeping on the move, staying only with families he could trust. One time, while he was still at home, soldiers knocked on the door, but his mother told them that he had just left, and they believed her. Another time, he was at an aunt's house when a friend called to say that the soldiers were on their way. Yousif started out the door and was only part-way down the block when they appeared. But they didn't know what he looked like, and he passed by unnoticed, eventually to escape to Iran. Then in 1988, his father was released, and the whole family fled to Turkey during the Anfal. For one year, Yousif had no idea whether they were dead or alive. Finally, he located them in a refugee camp, but he was arrested several times by the Turks before being allowed to join them. In 1992, after four years in the camp, the family was offered asylum in the United States.

Yousif and Fatma were now in Kurdistan for a two-month visit. I found it a little curious that they could afford to take off so much time from work, but I didn't give it too much thought until one afternoon while I was socializing with other women in the family room. Neighbors had stopped by for tea and sweets and, in the course of conversation, I was startled to hear Fatma say that she hated Connecticut, the state in which I'd grown up.

"Why?" I asked, surprised. Connecticut isn't the sort of place to which people usually have visceral reactions.

"My husband was killed there," she said. "We were married on February 7, and twenty days later, he was killed in Bridgeport. He just went into a store, and two kids asked him for money. He had sixty-four dollars, but it wasn't enough. They shot him in the back. So I don't like Connecticut. San Diego is my favorite city."

She spoke in the same matter-of-fact tone that Kurds everywhere use when talking about personal tragedy. The kind of tone that doesn't allow for prolonged grieving or sentimentality, the kind of tone that says we have to be practical, be strong, move on.

Only twenty days, I thought. That would be tragic enough for an American woman, but I imagined it to be worse for a Kurdish one, as Kurdish culture holds virginity in high esteem. And how unfair it seemed that Fatma had lost her husband to violence in the United States, the country to which she'd fled for refuge.

"I'm so sorry," I said.

Fatma sighed, and toyed with her hands.

"But maybe I will find a new husband here," she said, with a glancing sparkle to her eye that disappeared again so quickly that I wasn't completely sure I'd seen it.

But I *had* seen it! So Fatma was in Kurdistan to find a husband. And Yousif was undoubtedly along to act as her protector and approve any prospective groom.

Many Kurds living in the diaspora return to Kurdistan when it comes time for them to marry. Most are men, who have often left the country illegally, established themselves abroad economically, and obtained a green card or its equivalent. Their mothers then line up a few marriage prospects, the men come home to look them over, and, after extensive negotiations and wedding ceremonies, take their new brides home—or, occasionally, have them shipped, sight unseen. And more than a few Kurdish women are quite willing to go along with this arrangement, if only to escape the economic and physical insecurity of life in Kurdistan.

Besides, the process isn't as cold as it sounds. In the close-knit Kurdish communities, families have usually known one another for generations, and the bride and groom often know of each other, even if they haven't actually met. As elsewhere in the Middle East, marriage between first cousins is preferred, followed by marriage between second cousins.

Fatma's case was unusual because she was a woman and a widow, come back to find a husband. But as a U.S. citizen and an attractive thirty-year-old, she had much to offer. So much so, I now realized, that in her case widowhood wouldn't be the slightest issue.

So I wasn't surprised to come home one day to find the house in a tizzy. A young man had asked for Fatma's hand. He had seen her at a family gathering where, as usual, men and women had scarcely mingled. But he'd nonetheless found a moment to speak to her privately, to say that he liked her and wanted to pay a visit. Why? she'd asked—surely disingenuously. Because I want to marry you, he'd said.

And so began a series of visits between the two families. Like many other Muslims, the Kurds have an elaborate marriage negotiation process. The week after the woman agrees to marry the man, his family comes to formally ask for her hand. Next comes a legal visit, in which the families agree on the conditions of the marriage and the bride-price, which the groom's family pays to the bride, usually in the form of gold, money, or property. Theoretically, the bride-price is for the woman to use in case of divorce, but it doesn't always work that way, as sometimes the estranged husband keeps the bride-price for himself.

I met Fatma's groom-to-be, his mother, and several women relatives one day as they were leaving the house and I was coming in. The women were dressed traditionally, with head coverings, but the young man wore a neatly pressed button-down shirt and pants. He was slim and pale, and seemed quiet and gentle.

After they had gone, Fatma grabbed my arm excitedly. "What do you think? He's nice, don't you think? He's a teacher in a college, and very intelligent." She blushed.

I agreed that he seemed nice, and asked how long it would be before they could marry.

"Oh, that will take a very long time," she said. "Maybe more than one year. We have much paperwork to do before he can come to the United States. We will have to meet often." She blushed again, more deeply. "That will be very embarrassing for me—Kurdish women do not meet with their husbands before they marry. We are very shy."

IN THE AMADIYA district, not far from Dohuk, rot the stumps of three castles that once belonged to Saddam Hussein. A mountainous region of great beauty, Amadiya has been a resort destination ever since the 1930s, when King Faisal built a Mediterranean-style palace in the village of Sarsing, and hotels sprouted up nearby.

One day, Majed, the family, Yousif, Fatma, and I set out in three cars to picnic and tour the sites of Saddam's former castles. Though it was no longer Newroz, thousands of other families were out picnicking—barbecuing, playing badminton, exploring the mountains, and dancing in motley lines that ranged in length from three people to forty or fifty. The longer lines were often wedding parties, with bands. Watching the many revelers, it was hard to imagine that only eleven years before, such activity had been strictly forbidden.

As we drove, Yousif told me about the castles. Before building them, Saddam had evicted all the local inhabitants, he said. But since the Iraqi president still needed local labor, he brought in workers blindfolded so that they wouldn't learn the approaches or layouts. The roads outside the palaces were completely off-limits, and any unauthorized person who trespassed was shot.

"One of our uncles was a famous wall builder who was called in to work on one of Saddam's airports," Yousif said. "Saddam came to the airport one day and said, 'This section must be finished by tomorrow.' It was a huge section, and the workers couldn't finish it by themselves. So they called in my uncle and hundreds of others, and they worked all night. Even the security men helped. They knew that if the section wasn't finished, they would all be killed."

Like most other Kurds I met, Yousif talked about Saddam Hussein in an intimate manner, as if he were an evil uncle or other close relative. It was always "Saddam," not "Saddam Hussein," and it was always Saddam, not the Baath forces, who was personally responsible for each and every cruel act. With Saddam at a safe distance, the Kurds could also joke about him and, at times, speak of his grim exploits as if they were tales out of Ripley's "Believe It or Not." Many Kurds were fascinated with Saddam, as was I. It was as if we were looking into a dark mirror, at the underbellies of ourselves, of what we might be capable of in the wrong time or place.

Our cavalcade reached the site of the first former castle, near Enishky village, but there wasn't much to see. After the uprising, Kurds had destroyed the edifice, pulverizing some parts, carrying others away for reuse, to leave nothing but a high brick wall behind. The site was now used by the KDP militia.

More interesting was an airstrip nearby, on which stood about a dozen Turkish tanks, neatly aligned in a row, their gun barrels glistening from a recent rain.

"What are they doing here?" I asked, shocked at the sight, but Majed and Yousif shrugged away my question, preferring not to talk politics. I would learn the answer later.

We drove on, to the second and third castle sites, which neighbored each other—one easily accessible near Ashawa village, the other out of reach atop Gara Mountain, a craggy black peak still patchy with snow. A road connected the two, but it was impassable at this time of year. Saddam had usually arrived at Gara by helicopter.

The Ashawa castle was also destroyed, but it had been built beside a series of lovely, landscaped waterfalls, and these remained. To one side, the waterfalls were shallow and wide, engineered to fall over a stepped-down series of rosy marble blocks. To the other, they were wild and natural, plashing against black boulders fringed with moss. Bridges arched here and there, and a small pool collected near the top, where a small zoo had once stood.

Parking our cars, we walked down to the wild side of the falls, along with dozens of other visiting families. Near the bottom was a stone patio with an oven built into a blackened rock wall. This had once been one of Saddam's favorite spots, Yousif said—he'd liked to come here for dinner and sit by the falls while his servants cooked. I could easily imagine the scene and even feel Saddam's mustachioed ghost, hovering nearby as it tried to take a seat at its invisible table. But the ghost kept getting shoved aside by groups of laughing Kurds taking pictures of one another. There was no room for him here.

CHAPTER FOUR

After al-Anfal

꜀꜀꜀꜀꜀

AL-ANFAL REFERS TO THE BAATH REGIME'S FINAL, GENOCIDAL attack on the Kurds, begun on a large scale in February 1988.* Blasphemously, and cynically, taken from the eighth *sura*, or chapter, of the Quran, "al-anfal" literally means "the spoils" of war. The *sura* tells the story of 319 newly converted Muslims who defeat three times their number in the A.D. 624 battle of Badr, and justifies the victors' pillage of the infidels' property.

During the Anfal campaign, about twelve hundred Kurdish villages were systematically destroyed by the Iraqi military through bombing and burning, mass evacuation, and execution. In the campaign's course, tens of thousands of Kurds—perhaps as many as one hundred eighty thousand— were murdered or disappeared. Ruined villages were bulldozed, wells capped with concrete, fields poisoned, and tens of thousands of civilians placed in refugee centers that were, in effect, concentration camps.

Though unique in its scope and aims, the Anfal was the culmination of decades of attacks against the Kurds by the Iraqi government. Many Iraqi Kurds have seen their villages destroyed numerous times; to rebuild one's house four or five times in a lifetime has been the norm, not the exception, in Kurdistan. From the British attacks in the 1920s to the Kurdish revolt of the early 1960s to the aftermath of the Algiers Accord, the Kurdish villagers

---

* A smaller version of the campaign began in spring, 1987.

have suffered the consequences of their leaders' actions. During the entire reign of the Baath Party, an estimated four thousand Kurdish villages were destroyed and perhaps three hundred thousand people perished.

However, the Anfal was an entirely different operation than the ones that had come before it, and one that went far beyond retaliations against a citizenry for supporting a war on the Iraqi government. According to a 1992 Human Rights Watch (HRW) report: "Anfal was a 'final solution,' implemented by the Iraqi government, the Baath party and the Iraqi army. It was intended to make the Kurds of Iraqi Kurdistan and their rural way of life disappear forever."

When the major operations of the Anfal began in February 1988, near the end of the Iran-Iraq War, Saddam Hussein was running scared of the increasing collaboration between the Iraqi *peshmerga* and Iran. In the previous few months, Iranian troops had captured strategic sites along the Iran-Iraq border and penetrated deep into Iraqi Kurdistan. But instead of retaliating with focused assaults against the Iranians and *peshmerga*, Hussein methodically began destroying Kurdistan. On February 23, he launched a colossal air and ground attack, using conventional and chemical weapons, against a *peshmerga*-held region to the east of Suleimaniyah. Seven other equally massive Anfal operations followed, each targeting a different area. The Dohuk region, farthest from Iran, was the last to be attacked, in the eighth and final Anfal of August 25 to September 6, 1988.

Most of the Anfal operations proceeded in more or less the same manner. After gaining control of a region, the Iraqi forces executed the captured *peshmerga*, herded the civilians into forts, and bulldozed the emptied villages. Virtually all surviving men and teenage boys, along with women and children at some sites, were handcuffed, loaded into convoys of trucks, and driven hundreds of miles to the southern Iraqi desert. There, often at dusk, they were forced out, their handcuffs removed (to be used again), and ordered to stand on the brink of shallow ditches where they were shot and bulldozed into mass graves.

The remaining civilians—tens of thousands of women, children, and old men—were dumped out into "camps" without shelter, food, water, health care, or sanitation. Usually, the only structures were guard towers and security buildings. Many of the camps were located in the barren plains surrounding Erbil, and the refugees survived only through the generosity of the city's citizens, who organized an enormous relief effort, bringing food, water, blankets, and tents to the camps.

Although technically not part of the Anfal, which targeted rural communities and left most large cities intact, the best-known and single most horrific of the 1988 operations occurred at Halabja, a city of fifty thousand near the Iran border. On March 15, the *peshmerga* helped Iranian forces enter Halabja—against the wishes of many of its citizens. The next day, Baath forces attacked the city with napalm and chemical bombs. About five thousand people died instantly, perhaps another seven thousand died over the next three days, and many thousands of others fled over the mountains into Iran.

The mastermind behind the carnage was Saddam Hussein's cousin, Ali Hassan al-Majid, nicknamed "Chemical Ali" by the Kurds—and captured about five months after the Iraq war of 2003. As the Baath Party Northern Bureau secretary-general, Chemical Ali had absolute powers over the region and the go-ahead to employ any means necessary to eradicate the "saboteurs." In one 1988 meeting regarding the Kurds, Chemical Ali boasted: "I will kill them all with chemical weapons! Who is going to say anything? The international community? Fuck them! The international community, and those who listen to them!"

Indeed, the international community did not listen. It was not politically expedient to do so; the United States and much of the West supported Saddam Hussein during the Iran-Iraq War. Even sympathetic listeners took little action, dismissing the Kurdish claims as wildly exaggerated, despite abundant evidence to the contrary. Only after the Gulf War, when the Kurds drew attention to their suffering through their uprising, and human rights organizations carefully documented the rampant atrocities, did the Kurdish story begin to be heard.

In his destruction of about 4,000 out of a total 4,655 Kurdish villages, Saddam not only destroyed the Kurds' communities, but the very fabric of their society. The Kurds had lived in largely self-sufficient villages for centuries; theirs was traditionally a rural existence centered on agriculture, animal husbandry, and family. By eradicating the villages, the Baathists destroyed the Kurds' economic base and weakened their societal ties, casting them into a chaotic modern world where many have been forced to rely on foreign humanitarian aid. Independence has been replaced by dependence.

Although al-Anfal refers specifically to the 1988 campaign, many Kurds now use the word generically, to refer to any massacre or large-scale attack. "To anfal" has also become a verb.

NIZARKEH IS AN ugly stone citadel on the outskirts of Dohuk. Though often referred to as a castle by Kurds speaking English, the word prison or fortress would be more appropriate. Like dozens of other buildings through-out northern Iraq, Nizarkeh was built by the Baath Party in the early 1980s to house the Iraqi army. But as the decade unfolded, the Baathists con-verted the buildings into refugee camps for displaced families.

During those years, Nizarkeh's perimeter was peppered with mines and patrolled by helicopters. Trespassers were shot on sight. And after the 1991 uprising, many Kurds were found still locked up in cells, their bodies ema-ciated, bruised, and broken. Some men had lost their minds; others couldn't remember their names. Women were discovered naked and cov-ered with sores.

One cold rainy day in April, I accompany a delegation of five women from the KDP's Women's Union into Nizarkeh, now occupied by homeless families. Along with other women's groups throughout Kurdistan, the union is working to improve women's lives through literacy and education programs, legal counseling, social services, political lobbying, and small economic projects, such as sewing cooperatives.

We pass through Nizarkeh's towering entrance gate and into its vast courtyard, encircled by a two-story building ringed with doors. A rusting water tank and battered pickup trucks stand to one side. Clusters of men, their depression apparent even from afar, huddle together near the trucks. Women crouch on concrete walkways, washing clothes.

Our van parks, and we climb out. Picking our way over the mud, we pass through an open doorway and into a dark hall piled high with metal drums, cardboard boxes, and bulky plastic bags. To one side is a makeshift shower, built of tin oil containers hammered flat, and a bare-chested man getting a shave. Upon seeing us, he lets out an embarrassed yelp and reaches for his shirt.

Down a shadowy circular hallway, our many footsteps echo. We enter a room—a former cell—where a woman named Bayan and two of her six children are waiting. Dressed in a green-print *dishdasha* and black head scarf, Bayan is in her thirties, with a drawn, careworn face.

The room is clean and well kept, with thin cushions lining three walls, and a refrigerator and cabinets lining a fourth. A television stands in one corner, near photos of family members and Mulla Mustafa.

We take seats on the floor as Bayan serves tea. Then she begins her story.

"My husband and I were married when we were in our teens," she says, "and twenty days after our wedding, he went to the mountains to become a *peshmerga*. Sometimes I didn't see him for two months, one time I didn't see him for two years. I raised my children by myself, but I didn't mind. People from villages are stronger than people from cities.

"One day in August 1988, the airplanes came to our village, and the next day, the soldiers also came. We ran away to the mountains and hid for fourteen days. But we became hungry, and so we surrendered. We were very frightened, we had no hope, we thought we would be executed.

"The soldiers took us to Beharkeh collective town near Erbil. It was hot, just like a desert, with no water. They gave us nothing. We only survived because the people from Erbil came secretly at night and helped us. Some of the guards also helped us. But we weren't allowed to leave Beharkeh unless we got permission—say, maybe if my son was sick—and then only for three hours a day. For two years, we lived just like prisoners.

"During the uprising, we went to Turkey, and when we came back, we had no place to live. Our village in the Sarsing area was destroyed. So we came here, the castle is free. There are about 140 families living here now. . . ."

A heavyset woman from the Women's Union leans forward. In her fifties and dressed in elegant black, with gold jewelry and a black head scarf striped with gold, she appears to have little in common with the residents of Nizarkeh. Appearances are deceiving; one person's story is everyone's story in Kurdistan.

"I am also from a village of Sarsing," she says, "and what happened to Bayan also happened to me. My husband was a *peshmerga*, and in 1985, I went to live with him and my three children in the mountains. There were many women living in the mountains, cooking and helping the *peshmerga*. But one day, the soldiers came and found us. They attacked us, and I still have two bullets in my leg from that time.

"After the attack, my children and I went back to our village. But then the chemical bombing came. I was pregnant, and when my child was born, he was not right in his head—he is fourteen now, but still like a two-year-old. On August 27, 1988, the airplanes began circling again, and we ran to the mountains. There was no place to hide. We thought we would be killed. The soldiers came and took us to Beharkeh at night and dumped us in the desert. When we woke up in the morning, we had nothing."

ZERKAH IS A reconstructed village typical of the many hundreds that dot the Kurdish countryside. Completely destroyed during the Anfal, it was rebuilt by the U.N. agency Habitat and the Kurdistan Reconstruction

Anfal widows Maryam (left) and friends

Organization (KRO). About 150 houses are neatly lined up along a few parallel streets. Painted bright white with blue trim, the houses seem doll-like, while the whole village feels a bit like a cruise ship washed up onto a foreign land.

Walking up a short walkway to one of the houses, our delegation is warmly received by Maryam, a small woman with a kind, round face made for smiling. Enveloped in a long black dress and head scarf, Maryam is about thirty-five and has five children. Beaming, she ushers us into her spic-and-span home, its main room furnished with carpets, cushions, a tall wall cabinet, and a large television. A born storyteller, Maryam serves tea and starts to talk, while two other women also enveloped in black slip in, to sit silently on either side of their friend like shrouded bookends, their expressions mirroring her expression, her sadness their own.

"It was winter when we left our house," Maryam says. "Saddam's forces had been marching in our area, and we knew something was about to happen. So we went to Gara Mountain, where we stayed for four months, living in caves. But in August the Anfal began, and we were captured.

"They took us to Aqra castle. We stayed there three days, and then they took us by truck to prison in Mosul. For sixteen days we had hardly any food. Some people fainted, some died. The guards came with music and said we had to dance for Saddam. But we were too weak because of hunger, and they beat us—children, women, men. They beat my husband very hard—I don't like to remember—and then one day they put us on buses again, men and women on different buses, and I never saw him again."

Tears roll down her cheeks, but she brushes them away impatiently and shrugs off the murmurs of sympathy around her.

"I memorized this history so it will never be forgotten," she says fiercely.

"They took us to a camp outside Erbil, and thirteen days later, they came and said, 'Oh, do you know what happened to your men? They have been killed, buried alive.' I had four children with me then, and I was pregnant with my last son. I named him 'Be Kas,' 'without anyone,' because I didn't have anyone then. I had already lost a daughter in earlier attacks.

"During the uprising, my children and I climbed the mountains to Iran. We walked on foot for eleven days. One man helped us for a few miles, but mostly we were alone with other women and children.

"After the uprising, we came back and lived in Nizarkeh castle for many years. The situation there was very bad, very dirty, and, in the beginning, there was blood everywhere. Two years ago, we came here. I am very thankful. We have two rooms, and a kitchen with a stove and refrigerator, and bathroom with a shower. I never had a bathroom before. I work a little in the fields, and I get a martyr's salary for my husband from the government. We get a food basket. We have peace. Our lives are very good."

IN THE AMADIYA district, about forty miles northeast of Dohuk, is the "village" of Gizeh. Before the Anfal, Gizeh stood on Gara Mountain, the towering black peak whose summit once held one of Saddam's castles. Security issues made Gizeh difficult to rebuild, however, and after the uprising, the villagers—almost all widows and children—were resettled on the outskirts of another mountain settlement, Kani, which is, technically speaking, their new address. Nonetheless, the villagers still call their new home "Gizeh." In Kurdistan, a village is as much a concept of community as it is a place.

From afar, Gizeh looks poorer than many villages, with huts built of clay and cement, and tall mounds of dark sticks—some animal huts, others, piles of firewood. But as our car turns off the main highway and enters the settlement, the place becomes cozy and welcoming in feel. Roosters and goats are strutting about, narrow paths are winding intimately between homes, and women are sitting on porches, gossiping. Fat clouds float like balloons through the air.

Parking the car, our driver wanders off for a smoke while my interpreter and I enter the house of the *mukhtar*, or village chief. On one wall hangs a mirror and several photos, including one of Mulla Mustafa. In a corner is a small, handmade cage holding a lovely gray *kau*, a plump bird of the partridge family. The Kurds keep *kaus* as pets, treasuring them for their melodious, full-throated song.

Smiling broadly at our request to speak alone with Anfal widows—a meeting only for women!—the *mukhtar* rounds up five women, all dressed entirely in black, and leaves the room. The widows sit down closely together. In the darkened room, in their dark clothes, their bright eyes flash like hot coals.

Pleasantries are exchanged, and I propose talking to the women one on one. They glance nervously at one another. They want to tell their story together.

Begi, Halimah, Fatma, Auminah, and Rakia all start talking at once. Teenage girls serve a simple lunch of flat bread, cheese, yogurt, and fresh honey still in its honeycomb.

"We were in our village when the airplanes came," the women say. "We ran away to the mountains. But the Iraqi army followed, surrounded, and captured us. They took our men away in closed trucks. We never saw them again.

"They separated the women into two groups, one to stay in Dohuk and one to go to Suleimaniyah, and then the soldiers said they would take away the girls. But we would die before we would let that happen. So we put a small child with each girl so it would seem as if she was married. . . .

"During the uprising, we climbed the mountains to Iran. We went all together, and when we came back, we settled here. We were just widows living alone at first, with no men, but then our children grew up and got married and now we have a village again.

"The organizations built our houses, and we took care of our children by ourselves. In the springtime, we went to the mountains to pick greens and sell them. We had no other work. But we helped one another. That is how we survive, by helping one another."

None of the women has remarried, and none wants to remarry. Their husbands might still be alive, they say. Then one of the women takes us to her home to show us a small shrine dedicated to her husband's safe return—one of hundreds of similar shrines all over Kurdistan. Candlelight flickers over a faded photograph of a man with a bushy, unkempt mustache. Tucked into the photo's corners are fresh wildflowers.

PEACE WINDS JAPAN (PWJ) is a small nongovernment relief organization that targets Kurdistan's most vulnerable groups, those whose needs are not being met by larger organizations. PWJ's core service is providing mobile medical care to isolated villages, usually on a two-week rotation basis. Except for one Japanese coordinator who shuttles between Dohuk and Suleimaniyah, all of the PWJ staff is Kurdish.

Heading one of Dohuk's mobile units is Dr. Saadi Namaste Bamerni, a compact man with alert black eyes and close-clipped dark hair. Compassionate and passionate, he is deeply committed to Kurdistan and its people. Several of his siblings live in Europe, but he has never considered leaving. "To be in one's own country is best," he says.

One day, I accompany Dr. Saadi into the Kurdish countryside. With us are several medical assistants and a young man in a dark, well-fitting suit. He resembles an upwardly mobile businessman but is a bodyguard, armed with an American-made pistol, for which he carries a permit—the law in Kurdistan.

Our spanking-white Land Cruiser sails through the Doski subdistrict, past one reconstructed village after another, some pastel in color, others white with bold-colored roofs and accents. Drifting out of the radio is the voice of Şivan Perwer, a Kurd from Turkey who is the most popular of all Kurdish singers. For years, his songs were banned in Iraq, Iran, and Turkey—which still bans all but his love songs—and one of his most famous songs is a haunting, unforgettable dirge about al-Anfal. "From the air comes the sound of planes, and everything is on fire, fog and dust. From the land comes the sound of crying children," Dr. Saadi translates.

We pass through Mangesh, an ancient Christian village and one of the two Doski villages—out of sixty-three—not destroyed by the Baathists. Mangesh, which means "touch" in Syriac, the language of the Assyrians, may be named after "Doubting Thomas." One of Jesus' twelve disciples, Thomas would not believe that Jesus had risen from the dead until he could touch Him for himself, and is said to have passed through the area on his way to teaching the Gospel in India.

Beyond Mangesh, we turn off onto a dirt road that bumps its way through wide valleys toward lemon-lime hills and a smoke blue mountain range. The landscape is devoid of people and villages, and the few trees in sight are all scrub oaks—small, black, and twisted. The Iraqi government destroyed most of Kurdistan's larger trees during the Anfal, as they once provided coverage for the *peshmerga*.

We arrive in Navashki, home to twenty-two families. Navashki was flattened in the Anfal, but the villagers rebuilt it themselves after the uprising, with materials provided by the KRO. To one side is a breeding pen of skinny black sticks, housing a half-dozen newborn lambs. To another are a neatly swept henhouse and traditional outdoor oven, where young women are baking *nane tanik*, a traditional flat bread. For each piece, they roll out a ball of dough into a circle large as a pizza, drape it over an iron mound, and place the mound on top of coals. They hand me one of the crisp breads, warm and delicious.

While Dr. Saadi treats his patients, a young man invites a PWJ assistant and me into his cozy home, complete with a television. Though too isolated to be on the country's electricity grid, the resourceful Navashki villagers combined their finances a few years before to purchase a small generator, which they turn on only at night.

"We are very happy to be back in our village," our host says as he pours out glasses of tea. "We lived in the city after the Anfal and never want to go back—life is ugly there. But I am worried about my children. There is only a primary school here, and I want them to study more. Maybe we will move to Dohuk in winter, so my children can go to school, and come back in spring to farm. It will be very expensive—we will have to rent a room. But I don't want my children to suffer, to have my kind of life. I want them to be part of the new Kurdistan."

BALAVA, GOHARZEH, AND BARCHI are three neighboring reconstructed villages near the city of Amadiya. Like all the forty-seven villages once surrounding Amadiya, they were destroyed in al-Anfal.

Balava-Goharzeh-Barchi is another regular stop for PWJ, and one that Dr. Saadi would prefer to make daily, rather than biweekly, as many of the villagers have serious medical problems. In 1988, the area was bombed with chemicals, and its citizens are still suffering the aftereffects. Dr. Saadi treats cases of heart disease, skin disease, thyroid toxikosis, and congenital malformations, mostly cleft palates, all unusual diseases in rural Kurdistan. He also encounters an abnormally high number of miscarriages.

We pull up in front of the Balava clinic, serving all three villages, where a long line of women are quietly waiting, their green-and-gold, red-and-gold, and blue-and-black *dishdasha* shimmering in the molten rays of the sun. Glued to many hips are small children. The PWJ team pulls a long wooden medicine box out of the van and hurries into the clinic, while the Balava *mukhtar*, Abdul Jelil Khalid Rashid, a trim, educated man in steel blue *khak* and turban, tells me his village's history.

"This is not the original site of Balava, the original site is on that hill." He points to a spot several miles away. "We moved here because after the Anfal and the chemical bombs, there was no life—no plants or animals—in the old village area.

"The first time our village was attacked was in 1975, after the Kurdish revolution collapsed. The Iraqi government forces surrounded the town, they shot and bombed, but we escaped and fled to Iran. We came back in 1981 and stayed until 1986. Then the government informed us we had to move to a collective town.

"The planes started flying over six times per day, each time two planes—Mirages, MiGs, helicopters. Then in 1988, ten planes came together, and we knew it was the last chance for us. At dawn, we moved the village to the mountains, and the TNT and chemical bombing began. People felt drowsiness, but only three died, I think because of good luck—the wind was blowing down from the mountains. But all the animals died, and the village was destroyed.

"After the uprising, the KRO helped us rebuild. We have thirty-four houses now, and a water project. Our children go to the new school in Goharzeh, one-two kilometers away. It is a good school with many classrooms and a basketball court. But we don't have enough teachers, and it is hard for the children to walk there in the snow."

Nahman Selim Othman, the director of the school, arrives and elaborates on the area's history. A heavyset, balding man in a tan Western suit, he appears to be much older than his forty years.

"In the beginning of the Anfal, helicopters would come and circle the area in the night," he says. "No one could sleep, there was panic. And some nights, we could hear bombing nearby. Then the bombing started in our area, and we fled the village. The first sign that the bombs were chemical was a shortness of breath, and we smelled a bad odor we couldn't identify. We fled higher up the mountains with just our clothes, we were very afraid.

"After some time, we started toward Turkey. On the way, we spent one night in a valley, and that night, that valley was bombed, again we were very afraid.

"When we reached the border, the Turkish government refused to let us enter. But the Kurds of Turkey helped us, and we forced our way in. The soldiers put us in a refugee camp, but there weren't enough tents, and they treated us very bad, kicking us, accusing us of being terrorists. So after one-two months, we fled to Iran and stayed there four-five years. Iran wasn't good, but it wasn't bad. All the village went together, around a hundred families. After the uprising, about forty families came back, and more are still coming.

"When the Iraqi forces occupied this area, they shot people first, asked questions later. One of my relatives was shot coming home from his fields in the evening. This happened all the time. We didn't have any rights. We couldn't travel between villages easily—checkpoints were everywhere. They took our crops and our animals. That's why we became revolutionaries."

ONE WEEK LATER, Dr. Saadi and I rendezvous again, to travel to Koreme, a village in the Doski subdistrict that was destroyed during the Anfal through massacre, deportation, and bulldozing. Human Rights Watch/Middle East conducted an early, in-depth case study of the Anfal here in 1992, which led to other studies elsewhere, and to the conclusion that the Anfal was a genocidal campaign. The HRW report initially brought some attention to Koreme, but now the small, reconstructed village feels isolated and forgotten, its moment in history passed. Accessible only by a poor dirt road, impassable in bad weather, it has no electricity or running water.

Entering Koreme in the pouring rain, the skies cracking apart with thunder and lightning, Dr. Saadi and I head to the home of *mukhtar* Hadji Mustafa Othman. Despite the tumultuous weather, he comes out on the front porch to welcome us. Dressed in baggy pants and a turban, he is one of the only middle-aged men left in the village, as he was in jail when the massacre occurred.

We enter a room furnished with thin carpets, a kerosene heater, and a picture of Mulla Mustafa. As we settle in, the front door begins creaking open and shut, open and shut. The room fills up with old men and young boys, all in traditional dress, and the men in red-and-white turbans, until it seems as if the whole village sans females is arriving. The old men's faces are tan, wrinkled, and worn, while the boys' cheeks shine pink with excitement—Koreme receives few visitors. One young boy pours out glasses of tea, another washes more glasses to accommodate the crowd, and the rest nudge one another and stare. Prayer beads go *click, click, click*.

"Since the Kurdish revolution began in 1961," the *mukhtar* says, "Koreme has been destroyed and rebuilt four times. The worst time was the Anfal on August 28, 1988.

"Before the Anfal started, the villagers knew something was going to happen. There were many soldiers in the area, and some of the villages nearby were being bombed. So on the morning of August 27, most of the Koreme families tried to flee to Turkey with their animals. But they couldn't get across. The Turkish soldiers closed the borders.

"The villagers started back to Koreme and reached the village early the next morning. It was surrounded by soldiers. The men and boys put their hands in the air, and everyone was arrested. The soldiers took the animals away, and divided the villagers into three groups—women and children, old men, and boys and men. The first two groups were taken to refugee camps. The third group was divided again, and thirty-three boys and men were taken to a field behind the village, where they were shot."

A few days later, I would speak to two of the survivors of the shooting, Qehar Khalil Muhammad and Abdul Kerim Naifhassen, who would describe being lined up and marched single file out of the village. Once in the field, they were ordered to stop, turn around, and kneel shoulder to shoulder. The Iraqi soldiers fired three rounds; none of the victims were blindfolded.

"When we returned to our village in 1993, there was nothing," the *mukhtar* goes on. "Everything was destroyed—the soldiers even poured cement over our springs. First, we lived in tents, but then the KRO brought us materials, and we rebuilt our houses.

"Before the Anfal, Koreme had more than one hundred families, or seven hundred people. Our soil is good, and we had many orchards and animals. Now we have only twelve families, or seventy-five people. Not all those people were killed, some didn't want to come back."

The tea glasses empty, the *mukhtar* offers to show us the place where the massacre occurred. Outside, we discover that the rain has stopped, dark clouds pulling back to reveal a glorious spring day. A half-dozen villagers accompany us as we traipse across a sloshy field to the edge of a gentle incline, now glistening with a velvety sheen. Quietly, the villagers point out the spots where the massacred once knelt, where the soldiers once stood, and where the bodies were once buried, before being moved to a cemetery. Everything is now overgrown with new grass. Birds are swooping, and rainwater drops are twinkling. Nothing indicates that anything out of the ordinary ever happened here.

CHAPTER FIVE

Disturbances

IN THE CENTER OF DOWNTOWN DOHUK STOOD THE INSTI-
tute of Fine Arts. From the outside, it was a forbidding-looking place with a
yawning entranceway manned by guards. Inside, the vestibule and corridors
were damp and dark, but then the building opened up to reveal a lovely
sun-dappled courtyard filled with flowering bushes, a vine-covered arbor,
dozens of students, and music. Brightly colored murals—of a Studebaker,
of fighters with flags—danced on the walls, and white sculptures stood here
and there. Three young women in long tight skirts were playing the violin,
their sheet music propped up on spindly stands. Two young men in leather
jackets were looking cool. Through an open practice room, another young
man was assiduously practicing Bach, his notes floating up to cup the scene
like a protective umbrella.

The artists Sirwan Shakir and Amin Yousif, and I were "taking a stroll."
Both men taught at the institute, and both spoke English. Amin, an intense,
dark-haired man in his mid-twenties, was fluent. Sirwan, a kindly looking
man with wavy hair just starting to gray, could make himself understood.
Both men effusively welcomed me. You cannot understand Kurdistan without talking to its artists, they said.

Like the University of Dohuk, the Institute of Fine Arts had been founded
after the 1991 uprising, and charged no tuition, scraping by each month on a
small stipend from the KDP government. The school offered classes in music, the visual arts, and theater, with most of its curriculum focused on the

Western artistic tradition. As we toured, we passed a drawing class sketching still lifes beneath reproductions of the old masters, and an orchestra class rehearsing Beethoven. Among the musical instruments that the students studied or had studied were the violin, piano, accordion, flute, and cello, although the school did offer a few Eastern music classes to juniors and seniors.

This lack of emphasis on Eastern music in general and Kurdish music in particular seemed to me a serious loss. The Kurds have an enormously rich musical tradition that differs from region to region. There are hundreds of Kurdish battle songs, love songs, children's songs, work songs, dance songs, wedding songs, religious songs, lullabies, and epics that tell heroic legends. Various instruments are used, including long-necked lutes (*saz, tambur*), short-necked lutes (*aud*), frame drums (*daf*), cylindrical drums (*dehol*), goblet drums (*dimbek*), oboes (*zirna, nerme ney, balaban*), flutes (*shimshal, shebbabe, dudik*), zithers (*qanun*), whistles (*pik*), and spike fiddles (*kemanche, richek*).

Was the institute's emphasis on Western art an attempt to validate its program to the outside world? Ironic, if so, as the world wasn't paying attention. Or did it have more to do with the Kurds' traditional attitude toward musicians? For centuries, Kurds regarded musicians as *chawash*, or low class, and in some regions, musicians were considered to be a separate, gypsylike caste who did not intermarry with others, despite often earning a decent living.

But with or without an Eastern music program, the mere existence of a fine arts institute in war-torn Kurdistan seemed remarkable—a sign that people do, after all, need more than food and drink, shelter and work, and even freedom to survive.

As we were touring, many students came up to me, wanting to know who I was and what I thought of Kurdistan. Two especially curious young artists pulled me aside. Don't believe everything people tell you here, they said. It is not true that we are free. The KDP controls everything, and they say we should not protest against two subjects—society and government. As artists, we must protest, it is our job, but they say, You are Kurdish; it is your national duty to make art that says only good things about the Kurds.

This was my first concrete validation that all was not precisely as it seemed in Kurdistan. As in every society, darker currents flowed beneath the shining, little-engine-that-could surface. The enormous power of the two governing Kurdish parties had already been making me nervous, as had

Dr. Shawkat's frequent phone calls, wanting to know where I was going, to whom I was talking. It is only for your own protection, you are free to do whatever you like, he always said. That was true, and I often operated without KDP—or, later, PUK—assistance, using taxicabs and independent translators. However, I was also growing slowly more aware of being loosely monitored, albeit in a friendly fashion. Dr. Shawkat, especially, seemed to regard my safety as his personal responsibility.

AS IT HAPPENED, the day of my visit to the institute was also the day of the school's graduation play. Though I was not especially interested in attending, Amin and Sirwan talked me into it. I returned to the institute that afternoon to find it mobbed with a well-dressed crowd of students, families, city officials, and a television crew. This student production was a major event, a place to see and be seen.

The small theater was crowded with fold-up chairs, the majority filled with men in dark suits. The far fewer women in attendance sat mostly in back. Four officious men reigned by the stage, kicking off the event with a moment of silence for the martyrs.

The play began. Called *Body Language*, and more a work of modern dance than a play, it starred three lithe young men in tight white bodysuits. Illuminated red fish and green mountains glowed on a backdrop, while music sounding suspiciously like Philip Glass drifted out. The young men stretched their limbs, from the fetal position into birth, war, suffering, death, and beyond. I could have been viewing a student dance performance in any cultural capital in the world. And in contrast to the Western music and painting classes I'd visited that morning, the performance seemed authentic and organic, a true melding of Kurdish experience and a contemporary art form.

After the performance, Amin led me down the street to two nearby exhibition halls—the Martyr Salman Gallery, named after a slain student, and the Dohuk Gallery. The Salman was filled with allegorical paintings of the Anfal that made me cringe, but the Dohuk Gallery was more interesting, with the works of dozens of artists, ranging in style from realistic to abstract. Some were simplistic and amateurish, but others, like the dance performance, felt authentically modern Kurdish. Sirwan's abstract, romantic landscapes—dark, with splashes of light—were there, as was Amin's work.

But I had to specifically ask to see the latter, which Amin showed me only after we had toured the rest of the museum. Then, and with some reluctance, he led me to two small paintings on a side wall that I hadn't noticed before.

I looked at the two appealing small dark nudes, and was struggling to find something insightful to say, when I noticed Amin staring at me, anxious and more intense than ever. Quiet and solemn, with a dark shock of hair and deep eyes, throughout the day, he had often seemed lost in his own thoughts.

"It is dangerous, but I can defend myself," he said.

I stared, having no idea what he was talking about.

"I am willing to make the sacrifice, I have nothing to lose," he said.

It dawned on me. In this Muslim society, this conservative city, the depiction of the nude was unusual, bold, and shocking.

"People are talking, even at the institute," Amin said. "They say I am a lustful man. I once made a nude sculpture, and they made me cover it. But the body is art."

AMIN AND SIRWAN had invited me to lunch. Since they lived separately, I assumed that meant going to one of their homes or the other, but when I arrived at the institute on the appointed day, I learned that the men had two lunches planned.

"First you will go to Sirwan's home, and then come to mine," Amin said.

"But you will eat so much at my house, you won't be able to eat at Amin's! My wife is an excellent cook," said Sirwan.

"What?" I said. "I can't eat two lunches."

"It's your own fault," Amin said. "Because you say you don't have enough time to come on different days."

It was true. I was making frequent day trips to villages outside Dohuk and, unsure of my schedule, was hesitant to make luncheon appointments. But my friends' double invitation, and their eagerness to host, saddened and embarrassed me. To think that so little happened in Kurdistan—aside from war and death—that my arrival was a major event. I wished I'd tried harder to visit them on different days.

Sirwan lived on an unpaved road not far from the institute. Beyond the house to one side was the White Mountain; beyond the house to another was one of Dohuk's newest housing developments. Built along hilly roads, it held huge marble homes, both mansions and caricatures of mansions. Not quite large enough to support their architectural elements, the strange edifices sported tall spindly columns framing normal-sized doors, gingerbread eaves, and turrets with too-tiny bay windows. The homes belonged to Dohuk's nouveau riche, who had made their money—how? Perhaps semi-legal trade?—such as the oil trade between Baath-controlled Iraq and Turkey, banned under international sanctions, but a major source of revenue for KDP Kurdistan. Or smuggling? No one could say, although everyone agreed that the homes belonged to families who'd had nothing before 1991.

Kurdistan, and especially Dohuk, also thronged with a surprisingly large number of expensive cars—BMWs and Mercedes, Land Cruisers and Jeep Cherokees. Most had arrived in the country only after 1997, when the oil-for-food agreement went into effect. Most were also refurbished seven- to ten-year-old models, purchased for $5,000 to $8,000. Still, to see so many expensive vehicles in a land of reconstructed villages, poverty, and much recent suffering was disconcerting, and it raised questions in my mind as to what exactly was happening behind closed doors.

The day of my luncheon visits was cold, wet, and miserable. I was shivering as we made our way through the muddy roads and fields surrounding Sirwan's home. Even after reaching our destination, it took me some time to feel at ease. Though spacious, Sirwan's house felt cold and dispirited, filled with aging furniture and faded photographs of a more prosperous era. Some depicted Sirwan's uncle, who had served as a minister in the Iraqi government.

"My uncle was very famous. When he died in Switzerland, Barzani shipped his body home," said Sirwan.

I nodded, trying to be appreciative, while wondering at the way in which so many people I'd met attributed everything positive directly to Barzani—father or son—much as they attributed everything negative directly to Saddam. Do the Kurds see the world much more personally than we do in the West? And, if so, is this due to their tribal heritage, with its emphasis on the community and *agha*, or tribal chief? How much of the Kurds' constant praise of the Barzanis was heartfelt, and how much pro forma?

Sirwan's wife's cooking was indeed outstanding—the same *biryani* rice, *tershick*, and other dishes I'd eaten elsewhere, but cooked to perfection, with unusual spices. The television was blaring throughout much of the meal, but no one seemed to notice until I brought it up, then Sirwan obligingly switched the channel to one broadcasting romantic vistas dubbed with the music of Celine Dion.

Sirwan and his family had stayed put during the 1991 uprising, when much of Dohuk had fled to Turkey, he told me over tea. His father had had a stroke and couldn't be moved. They'd been frightened, of course, but the Dohuk citizens had done nothing to antagonize the Iraqis and so stayed safe. I would remember his words later, in Erbil and Suleimaniyah, where some complained about the conservative, placid nature of Dohuk, which had played a feeble role in the revolution, they said.

While Sirwan was talking, the front door handle moved with a jerk. I jumped. Rain was pouring around the house. We were isolated by water and mud. Who knew what could happen here? The handle jerked again, accompanied by a thump.

"What was that?" I squeaked, heart racing, imagining armed men outside.

But it was only the family cats, who had learned to jump up to the door latch when they wanted to come in. I laughed, embarrassed. I don't know how to read this world yet, I thought.

But even many weeks later, near the end of my three months in Iraqi Kurdistan, I still didn't feel I had a true bead on the possible danger there. And neither, it seemed, did most of the populace. A few people chilled me with dire warnings, others seemed too cavalier, while most appeared to be as uncertain as I was about where things stood. Fear has little to do with reality, I learned in Kurdistan, largely because reality is so impossible to gauge.

How does prolonged fear affect the human psyche? I was in the country for only a short period, but the Kurds had lived with the suffocating weight of often indeterminate dangers their entire lives.

AMIN ARRIVED TO take me to my second lunch. The rain had let up somewhat, and we hurried to a ramshackle car parked about a hundred yards from Sirwan's house, where the road was still passable. Inside, his father waited.

"B'kher-hati," he said with a chuckle as we climbed in. Shorter and rounder than his son, he was dressed in a red sweater vest, tweed jacket, and fedora, cocked at a rakish angle. A former Communist who'd once been imprisoned for throwing a drink at Saddam's picture while drunk, he worked as a lawyer.

Driving down Dohuk's main street, we traveled into a part of town I hadn't seen before. Along the way, we passed various short commercial districts devoted to one product—refrigerators, TVs, carpets, sinks, couches. The buildings grew more decrepit.

"This is the poor part of Dohuk," Amin said as we finally parked. "Where you are staying is the rich part."

Entering a sullen apartment building, we climbed up crooked, uneven cement steps—typical of Kurdistan, where much has been built on the cheap and in a hurry—to a large but threadbare apartment. Amin's mother, a thin, dark woman who must once have been ravishing and still was beautiful, met us at the door in a knee-length skirt and blouse, a cigarette in her hand.

Amin and I moved into the main room, furnished with carpets, a television set, and a table at which lunch had been set up for two. Apparently, the rest of the family had already eaten.

Amin's mother glided in with various dishes, not saying a word. At first, Amin and I filled up the uncomfortable silence with idle chatter, but soon settled into what was a favorite topic among young Kurds: getting out of Kurdistan. Fed up with the region's high unemployment, insecurity, and sorrows, coupled with exposure to the West through the Internet and TV, many Kurds under thirty wanted out. But without passports, which were issued through Baghdad, most Kurds could leave the country only through the human smuggling "mafia" run by cooperating Kurds and Turks. Everyone knew about it, and when you were ready to go, you approached it like any other job—asking around, getting recommendations.

About $3,000 bought a third-class passage by truck and boat, first to Istanbul and then on to Greece or Italy. About $5,000 bought a second-class ticket, also by bus and boat; and $7,000, a first-class ticket, via airplane, to the European country of your choice. The cheapest option was the most dangerous, of course. People sometimes suffocated in the holds of the trucks or drowned in the boats.

A few days earlier, I had met one thirty-something woman who had been smuggled out on a third-class ticket two years before in order to marry, sight unseen, the brother of a colleague living in Austria. The woman, who spoke flawless English and German, was home visiting her mother when we met, and she told me about her dangerous ride. The first leg had been easy enough, she said, but from Istanbul to Athens, she and about thirty other Kurds had been tightly packed into a two-story hold hollowed into the center of a truck. The women had been in the top section, the men in the bottom. They squatted the whole way, for twelve hours. Once in Athens, they were placed in a refrigerator truck with the same two-story arrangement, and the truck boarded a ship en route to Italy. The truck had two fans, one blowing air in, the other pulling air out, but as the ten hours of the passage ticked by, the engine grew weaker, and the fans turned slower and slower. She thought it was the end.

I shuddered at the scene. Could I be as strong as she if I were in her shoes?

Amin's parents could perhaps afford to buy him a second-class ticket should he decide to emigrate, but he wasn't sure yet if he really did want to leave. He didn't know where to go or what to do when he arrived. Getting asylum in Europe was far more difficult now than it had been a few years before. The United States was out of the question: the long trip was too expensive, and visas virtually impossible to obtain.

"If I could get a good job here, I would stay," Amin said. "But to get a good job, you must belong to the party."

As I was learning, contacts and influence were key to success in Kurdistan, and helped to account for the schism I found between "can-do" Kurds on the one hand, and Kurds who seemed thoroughly exhausted, depressed, and without hope on the other. For Kurds with contacts, money, or education, the new Kurdistan had much to offer, as there was an enormous amount of challenging work to be done. But for the disenfranchised, as always, there was mostly hardship.

Amin and I moved on to other topics. Every week, he taught classes at the Juvenile and Women's Prison.

For the most part, street crime was a minor problem in Kurdistan. Theft and assault were rare, and drugs, still virtually unknown—so much so that the police often didn't recognize contraband when they saw it. The country also remained all but untouched by hepatitis and AIDS. But under Iraqi law, by which Kurdistan was still governed, children as young as eleven could be imprisoned for six months for stealing a pack of cigarettes, and women jailed for "sexual misconduct."

One young woman in Amin's class had been arrested at age fifteen for having sexual relations, he said. She'd gotten pregnant and gone to the hospital, where she told a doctor she wanted an abortion. But instead of helping her, the doctor reported her to the police, who placed her in jail, where she lost the baby. A Dohuk court then sentenced her to fifteen years in prison, of which she'd already served three. "It is better for her in prison," Amin said. "If she was free, her family might kill her."

Although I didn't know if all the details of Amin's story were correct, its overall thrust was. When it comes to sex, Kurdish culture is highly traditional. Women are expected to be virgins when they marry, and pre- or extramarital sex is strictly prohibited, as is flirting and "allowing" rape. Women who break the taboos are sometimes murdered by their own families, in so-called "honor killings"—a problem in various traditional tribal areas in the Middle East and southwestern Asia, but especially prevalent in parts of Pakistan, Jordan, Palestine, and Kurdistan.

Amin himself had once been arrested, at age 16. He'd had long hair then, which had led some to accuse him of being homosexual—another Kurdish taboo. One day a guard harassed him and Amin hit him back. He'd spent ten days in prison and afterward cut his hair.

The rebel is highly prized in Kurdish society, but only if he or she rebels against an outside authority such as the Iraqi government. Rebelling against the culture itself carries a heavy price.

BAYAN AHMED, AN INTERPRETER I'd met through the Women's Union, offered to show me around the Dohuk bazaar. A small woman in her mid-twenties, Bayan was always dressed from head to toe in dark-colored garments, with long-sleeved blouses, skirts brushing her ankles, and head scarves that revealed not a single strand of hair or inch of neck. When I'd first met her, I'd barely noticed her, as she had been one of many and had said few words. But after a few days together, spent interviewing Anfal victims in the villages surrounding Dohuk, I'd grown to greatly appreciate her eager intelligence, curiosity, open-mindedness, and streak of mischief.

On our first morning together, I had asked Bayan if I could pay her for her services. "No!" she'd said indignantly, straightening her already ramrod-straight back. "We Kurds are not like foreigners. We do not want money for helping people."

Bayan's dream was to work for the United Nations or another foreign aid organization in a country similar to Kurdistan. For the moment, however, she, like most young people in Kurdistan, was unemployed.

We rendezvoused that morning with Sosan, one of Bayan's best friends. In contrast to Bayan, Sosan wore makeup, large earrings, nail polish, and a V-neck sweater, and was bareheaded, with long curled hair. She also seemed more worldly than Bayan. I wondered at how two such apparently different women could be so close.

The twosome did have one thing in common, however: clunky black shoes with thick stacked heels, which in Bayan's case were about four inches high. I'd seen similar shoes all over Dohuk. They were the latest fashion craze among young women.

We entered the city's half-covered, half-open-air bazaar, which housed a typical Middle Eastern array of goods ranging from spices and vegetables to plastic products and makeup. Most interesting was the fabric market, holding dozens of shops bursting with bolts of mostly synthetic fabrics in all colors and designs, some very ornate, with gold and silver threads, sequins and brocade. Used in the making of the traditional Kurdish women's dresses, which could cost as much as $200, the fabric was imported from all over the region, the most expensive coming from Bahrain. Neither Bayan nor Sosan wore the traditional dress except on special occasions—only the older generations wore it every day, they said. Nonetheless, the fashion of the fabrics changed every few months, and the most stylish of Dohuk's matrons tried to keep up.

"Dohuk is a city that depends on appearance and gossip," Bayan said, "and clothes are very important."

Even in Kurdistan! How strange it is that the ordinary petty vices never lose their hold, even in the wake of extraordinary suffering. Vanity, jealousy, bickering—they're always there.

We stopped at a modern-looking restaurant for lunch. The airy downstairs was filled with many tables and chairs, but it was only for men. The upstairs, with far fewer tables and a ceiling so low that I had to duck my head, was for families and women.

"Sosan and I often come here for lunch," Bayan said, with such a gleeful look to her eye that I gathered that most women in Dohuk did not go out alone for lunch.

Bayan and Sosan had met at the University of Salahuddin in Erbil. It had been the best of times, they said, eyes shining. They'd loved being away from their families and living in a strange city. They'd shared a dorm room with three other young women and had learned so much—about their studies, about different kinds of people, about themselves. How we miss those days! they sighed. Bayan had earned a degree in English, and Sosan had graduated in law; but without jobs, both now spent most of their time at home and were bored.

I was surprised to hear that Bayan's family, whom I assumed were quite religious and thus conservative, had allowed her to go away to school. Traditional Kurdish families do not allow their daughters to spend the night away from home.

"Some families do not let their daughters go away," Bayan agreed when I asked, "but more and more are letting them go to the university because they know they will stay in a dormitory."

And Bayan's family was not particularly religious after all, it turned out. Except for two aunts who belonged to a moderate Islamic political party, Bayan was the only woman in her family who covered herself. She had decided to do so in college. "I thought it was right for me," she said simply.

Our kebabs arrived, along with large platters filled with rice, greens, and flat bread. A photographer wandered up to ask if we wanted our picture taken, reminding me that eating out was unusual in Kurdistan, where discretionary income was scarce.

I waited until we were almost through our meal before broaching what I knew would be a ticklish subject—boyfriends.

The women gasped.

"We cannot have boyfriends!" they half whispered, half giggled, glancing nervously around the restaurant, though we were the only upstairs diners, and the waiter was long gone.

"This is very dangerous for us!" Sosan said. "This is illegal."

"We know what is right and what is wrong," Bayan said. "And honor is very important to us. If we lose our honor, it is ninety-nine percent we will be killed."

"No," Sosan said, nudging her friend, "this is not right. The law does not allow killing."

The two women started urgently speaking in Kurdish. I got the sense that Sosan was telling Bayan to keep quiet. Like many Kurds I met, Sosan seemed reluctant to have me learn anything negative about Kurdish culture. Her liberal dress was as misleading as was Bayan's conservative.

"Do you hear about honor killings often?" I interrupted them.

"No," Sosan said.

"A few times a year." Bayan leaned forward confidentially. "One time, a woman was a little wrong in the head. She went to Zakho, she said she wanted to go to Turkey. She was there seven days, and she didn't do anything, but her family killed her."

"But this is illegal," Sosan said reproachfully. "It was, what do you say in English?—premeditated. Her killers were sent to prison. That is the law."

"It is a matter for the family and the clan to decide, not the law," Bayan countered.

"What about the man?" I asked. "Is he ever killed for having a girl-friend?"

"Everything depends on many things," Bayan said. "Often if the man and woman are young and unmarried, their families will talk, no one is killed, they will marry. But if they are older and it is adultery, the woman will ninety-nine percent be killed, and sometimes the man."

A FEW DAYS LATER, Bayan and I set off in a hired car to visit Aqra, about two hours east of Dohuk. Thought to date back to the 700s B.C., Aqra was developed by Prince Zayd, a Zoroastrian, who may have named the city after the Kurdish word for fire, *agir*, a sacred element to those of his faith. Probably founded in what is now Iran, Zoroastrianism is the first-known belief system to posit the concepts of life as a struggle between good and evil, individual responsibility for behavior, and life everlasting. Islam, Judaism, and Christianity all trace many articles of their faiths back to Zoroastrianism.

Aqra lay in a fertile valley surrounded by wheat and barley fields, and orchards of olives, figs, pomegranates, peaches, and plums. Kurdistan's famed mountains notwithstanding, it holds at least an equal area of flat lands, which, during the early 1980s, produced 35 percent of Iraq's cereals, 50 percent of its corn, 33 percent of its rice, and most of its tobacco.

The Aqra valley was also filled with picturesque villages built of clay and stone—a far cry from the crisp new village settlements almost everywhere else in the region. Unlike the vast majority of rural Iraqi Kurdistan, the Aqra valley had not been destroyed during the Anfal. It was largely occupied by the Surchi, Harki, and Zibari tribes, who had supported the Iraqi government during the Kurdish revolution. Traditional enemies of the Barzanis, these tribes and various others had wanted nothing to do with Mulla Mustafa, and provided the Baathists with small standing armies, in return for stipends, to help fight the rebels. Most of the tribes, however, were never so much pro-Baath as they were anti-Barzani, often treating the Iraqi government as if it were yet one more tribe to play off against the others.

Many Kurds call those who cooperated with the Iraqi government *jash*, or "little donkey." The first *jash* were recruited during the 1961 to 1963 Kurdish revolution, at which time they probably numbered about 10,000, but after 1983, their number grew exponentially, to reach as many as 150,000 by 1986. By that time, most Kurds were becoming *jash* as a way of evading service in the Iraqi army during the Iran-Iraq War. As *jash*, the Kurds' duties were light—guarding checkpoints, keeping the local peace—and they could remain at home, farming, herding their animals, protecting their families, and earning a small salary.

Many *jash* also remained secretly aligned with the *peshmerga* and, when the 1991 uprising began, quickly abandoned the Iraqis for the Kurds—though only after being granted amnesty by the Kurdish leadership. Shrewdly hedging their bets, the *jash* also helped the regular Iraqi forces who surrendered to withdraw safely behind enemy lines.

During my travels, most Kurds told me that the *jash* had been completely forgiven and melded back into Kurdish society. However, those who had not become *jash* were always quick to point out that status and to praise others who had done the same. Theoretically, tribes such as the Surchi, Harki, and Zibari were now equal partners in the new Kurdistan, but tensions simmered beneath the surface.

AQRA WAS BUILT up a mountainside, with houses stacked one on top of the other halfway to the summit. Roofs served as walkways and plazas, and narrow staircases led between homes. A large mosque was located at one end of the city, along with a religious library and school. Yellow KDP flags fluttered everywhere—undoubtedly to counter the region's anti-Barzani past. In the center of town sprawled an ancient courtyard with an open-air market where black-shrouded women silently examined the wares.

Bayan and I stopped at the mayor's office. Expected, we were enthusiastically received with multiple glasses of tea, served with fruit and candy, and given welcoming speeches by various officials. Then the mayor assigned us a guide to take us up the mountain to the ruins of a palace that apparently reigned on top.

Leaving from the central square, the guide led us up to one rooftop after another. Breathing hard, we passed women baking bread and washing clothes, children studying and playing ball. But our climb had only just begun: beyond the highest rooftop, a stony path continued zigzagging up the mountainside, heading first to three Zoroastrian caves. Said to be dug by hand, the caves contained arched doorways and ancient writings, along with blackened spots where sacred fires once burned.

Beyond the caves, the path continued ever steeper and stonier. I was wearing a long full skirt and city shoes that caused me to slip and slide, but they were nothing compared to Bayan's long, tight skirt and four-inch-high stacked heels. Nonetheless, she had perfect control, climbing far more easily than I. She laughed away my concern for her comfort.

Baking nane-tanik

"Don't worry," she said. "I am very happy here. This is a very great time for me. I have never been to Aqra before, and I love the mountains. Even during the uprising, when we were climbing to Turkey, I didn't mind."

Bayan had been raised in the city, but, like many Kurds I met, she had an intimate, comfortable relationship with the outdoors. Everywhere I went, I found many like her—people of all ages and backgrounds who clambered up and down mountains as if they were hills. Old men and women, children, and even the out-of-shape urban middle-aged—all moved at a remarkable pace, making me wonder at times if there is such a thing as a mountain-climbing gene.

Finally, Bayan, the guide, our guards, and I climbed up one last incline, onto the mountaintop. The world and time suddenly collapsed. All around us was a flat and silent plateau. To one side sat a lone *peshmerga* in a lookout post with a KDP flag dancing above his head. To the other side were the remains of what must have once been an enormous palace, spread out over hundreds of yards. Most of the ruins was now covered with sod, but a few walls were intact, while on the far side were the broken clay pipes of a sophisticated irrigation system.

Aqra, built up a mountainside

The guide told us that the palace had been built by the Romans. The *peshmerga* said that it had been built by the Kurds. Neither hypothesis seemed entirely credible to me, but it scarcely mattered. The palace felt like a tantalizing secret. It was invisible from down below.

On the way back to Dohuk, Bayan suggested that we take a short detour, and we turned off the main road to travel a scenic back route over a small mountain. I enjoyed the detour, but far more wonderful than the drive was Bayan's reaction. Her eyes were dancing. "This is not part of the program, we are traveling a forbidden way," she said, clapping her hands in excitement, and quoted a famous Arabic saying. "To do something forbidden is very delicious."

—

AMIN AND HIS FAMILY invited me to dinner and to spend the night at their house—a relatively common invitation in Kurdistan, where dinners often led to overnights, perhaps because of the region's general unrest. I accepted. I liked talking to Amin, who, along with Bayan, was one of the few people I'd met in Dohuk who wasn't trying to impress me with the accomplishments of the Kurds and their safe haven. In fact, the Kurds and their safe haven *were* impressive, but I wanted to draw that conclusion for myself.

We met at the Institute of Fine Arts, then wandered through the streets to the Mazi Supermarket, the violet-blue building that I'd noticed when first arriving in Dohuk. The biggest and most modern market in Kurdistan, the Mazi was stocked with everything from imported foods and cosmetics to German-made refrigerators and Sony video cameras. However, few Kurds could afford the Mazi's prices; the store catered mostly to foreign aid workers.

Which is not to say that Kurds did not frequent the market. Walking up and down the gleaming aisles, ogling the wares without any intention to buy, was a favorite form of entertainment in Kurdistan, especially in the evenings. There was little else to do in Dohuk at night—or anywhere in the safe haven for that matter. People visited the city from all over the region—including Baath-controlled Iraq—specifically to spend time at the Mazi.

As we neared the store, we ran into Amin's friend Farhad, who walked with us for a few blocks.

"What about the September 11 terrorist attacks on the World Trade Center?" Farhad asked when he learned where I was from. "Didn't they make you want to attack all Muslims?"

"No," I said. "That won't solve anything, and besides, most Muslims are innocent—I think the United States needs to reexamine its foreign policy instead. There has to be more dialogue between the East and the West."

Farhad was silent for a moment. "You are a humanitarian," he finally said. "And that is very beautiful. But I cannot think like you. If I were American, I would want to attack all Muslims. *I* myself want to kill Arabs and Turks. I hope there will be war so I can kill my enemies."

His face had darkened, and I shivered a little, wondering who he was.

But I also recognized that I had a luxury he did not have. As the citizen of a stable, powerful nation, surrounded by peaceful neighbors, I could afford to talk about a vague idealistic future filled with cultural exchange. But as the citizen of a fragile semiautonomous state, surrounded by hostile neighbors, Farhad had to worry about the immediate and very real problem of survival.

Over the next hour or so, Amin and I explored the Mazi market, wandering up and down every aisle several times. One section held fresh fruits, breads, and other local goods, but most shelves displayed hundreds of imported products, many from Turkey, the United States, France, Italy, Germany, Iran, India, and Oman.

Outside the store, we sat on benches and ate ice-cream bars. Night had fallen, and the sky was startlingly clear, white clouds passing before a full moon, sharp as a photograph in a developing tray. Strings of lights swooped up the sides of the White and Black Mountains framing Dohuk, while neon sunbursts advertising the market flashed overhead.

A large family passed by, the men swaggering in fine *shal u shapik* up front, the women struggling with children and packages behind.

"When I see that family, I remember a sad joke," Amin said. "A woman tells her friend, 'I know my husband loves me so much!' 'That's wonderful,' the friend says. 'He must be very generous and kind.' The first woman answers, 'No, that's not right. I know he loves me because he beats me all the time. . . .' "

A half hour later, we took a taxi to Amin's home. Shadows jumped back from the curb as we drove, melting into darkened buildings and blind alleyways. Black shapes skulked here and there.

When we arrived, Amin's teenage sister and mother were waiting. Delicious smells were wafting out of the kitchen. Beaming, Amin's sister sat me down on the living room floor, while her brother brought out small plates of pistachios and olives, along with twelve-ounce vodka cans—common in Kurdistan.

"First you will take a drink, then we will eat, then we will drink some more, and then you will tell us when you want to sleep!" Amin said, and disappeared again. Smiling shyly, his sister turned the television to the BBC.

But a moment later, Amin was back, his face sagging. A folded piece of paper was in his hand.

Somehow, although the family didn't have a phone, Dr. Shawkat had tracked me down. Apparently, he'd called someone who knew someone who brought the note.

"Christiane must go back to Sayyed Majed's house immediately," the note said. "Her life is in danger, and she will be better protected there."

"This note is like a dagger in my heart," Amin said.

"What does this mean?" I said. Had something happened—an Iraqi invasion perhaps—or was Dr. Shawkat just being overly protective?

I suspected the latter, but I didn't see how I could take the chance. Amin, his sister, and mother didn't want me to take the chance either.

You must go, they all agreed. Sayyed Majed has guards, and you will be safe there.

The taxi ride home seemed much longer than it had before, as I illogically imagined Saddam's agents suddenly pulling up, blocking our path, hauling us out.

But at Majed's, the family was surprised to see me. They knew nothing of Dr. Shawkat's note, though he had called for me earlier and been startled to learn that I wasn't coming home that night. He'd also taken Amin's name and particulars.

I knew it, I thought.

At the same time, I also realized that I was happy to be back. I did feel safer here, with the guards out front. Amin's neighborhood had been half lit and filled with shadowy doorways.

All that night, I pictured Amin back home, alone with his mother and sister, and wished that things had worked out differently. We'd been having an interesting conversation; I hadn't been ready to leave.

THE NEXT DAY, I telephoned Dr. Shawkat to complain.

"But you can't stay with just anyone!" he said angrily. "We don't know this family. Who is this family?"

"They're not just anyone—Amin works at the Institute of Fine Arts, and his father's a lawyer. Many people know them," I said, while noticing Dr. Shawkat's telling use of the word *we*.

"It doesn't matter—who are their neighbors? You don't know their neighbors," he said, while I silently thought that he'd made a good point. "You must be careful."

CHAPTER SIX

Balancing Acts

THE ROAD TO AMADIYA HEADS NORTHEAST OUT OF DOHUK through a land of red earth, tan clay, and granite. Bypassing the ruins of Saddam Hussein's old castles, it slips through rolling, jutting, jockeying hills, climbs up a steep crest, and points down again into a wide, fertile plain. Black and blue mountains with snowcaps tower in the distance.

Descending, the road enters a valley, flecked here and there with reconstructed villages and stone outposts guarded by *peshmerga* — sitting, watching, waiting. More black mountains arise from behind, as if sprouting out of the earth, and, suddenly, the whole world seems contained in the valley, the villages, the *peshmerga*, the mountains.

The sun pours silver dust down from the sky and the far wall of mountains moves closer, evolving as it does so from black to green. Diamond-necklace waterfalls appear, along with dark caves, hard to pick out at first, but then seemingly everywhere.

The road turns a corner, to abruptly reveal a mesa sitting alone in a valley, surrounded by shiny, lime-colored fields. Steep cliffs drop off the mesa's sides like a curtain, while scattered across the saddle on top are what look like broken pieces of rock: Amadiya, straight out of the *Arabian Nights*. Best known in Kurdistan today as the capital of the Bahdinan emirate, founded about A.D. 1200, Amadiya is one of the world's oldest continuously inhabited cities, dating back to the Assyrian Empire in the first millennium B.C.

The Bahdinan princes were among the most respected of the Kurdish rulers who reigned during the Ottoman Empire. Tracing their ancestry back to the early caliphs of Islam, they were honored as a near-saintly family, so much so that no person dared use the same dish or pipe that was used by a Bahdinan. Some Bahdinan rulers even "covered their heads with a veil whenever they rode out, that no profane eye could see their countenance."

Like other Kurdish princes in power during the Ottoman Empire, the Bahdinans reigned over a confederation of diverse tribes who were sometimes cooperative with their rulers, sometimes too busy at war with one another to heed the princely word. During periods of strength, the Bahdinans could intervene in tribal affairs, demanding taxes and military service, but during periods of weakness, the tribal *aghas* often stopped paying taxes and declined to lend the princes military aid.

One of the greatest princes of Amadiya was Bahram Pasha, who ruled from 1726 until 1767, to be succeeded by his son Ismail, who reigned for another thirty years. But upon his death, fierce fighting broke out within the Bahdinan family, and by the time it was over, the dependencies of Amadiya—the cities of Dohuk, Aqra, and Zakho—had been split up among various Bahdinan males.

One generation later, in 1833, the Bahdinan family fell from power altogether, thanks to the bloody work of Mir Muhammad, the ambitious, one-eyed "Blind Pasha" of the Soran emirate in nearby Rowanduz. After his father died under suspicious circumstances in 1826, Mir Muhammad seized the throne, immediately killing his father's old treasurer, both his uncles, and their sons. He next advanced ruthlessly and victoriously on his neighbors, including the Bahdinan emirate, and put most of Amadiya's leading citizens to death, including the entire princely line. However, the name "Bahdinan" is still applied to the northernmost area of today's Iraqi Kurdistan, which loosely corresponds to the Dohuk governorate.

The road curling up the mesa to Amadiya bypasses several lookout posts and occasional elderly men, crouched on skinny haunches atop boulders, a principality still at their feet. Near the top arches a flimsy modern gateway, painted with the names of the thirty-seven Kurdish princes who ruled Amadiya until Sultan Muhammad II consolidated all the principalities of the Ottoman Empire in the 1840s, thereby ending the Kurdish states.

The British archaeologist Austen Henry Layard, famous for excavating the ancient Assyrian capital of Nineveh, across the Tigris River from today's

Mosul, visited Amadiya in the early 1840s, not long after Mir Muhammad's rampage and the end of the Bahdinan emirate. "We found ourselves in the midst of a heap of ruins—porches, bazars, baths, habitations, all laid open to their inmost recesses," he writes. "Falling walls would have threatened passers-by, had there been any; but the place was a desert."

For all Amadiya's glorious setting, a similar unhappy atmosphere hovers over the town today, its population dwindled to about ten thousand. Amadiya has lost most of its antiquities and is poor and barren in feel— a jumble of cement-poured edifices, crooked buildings, and abandoned storefronts. Its streets throng with grizzled men, a sure sign of high unemployment.

Near the town center stands a statue of Ezzet Abdul Aziz, an Amadiya Kurd martyred for his role in the 1946 Kurdish Republic of Mahabad. A near-independent Kurdish state, Mahabad was established in Iran on January 22, 1946, by the Iranian leader Qazi Mohammed and his followers, with the support of the Russians, then occupying parts of northern Iran. Joining the republic one month later was Mulla Mustafa Barzani and twelve hundred of his fighters, forced out of Iraq after their failed early revolt. But the Mahabad Republic was short-lived. The Russians withdrew from Iran in late May, leading to internal conflicts within the new republic, and it fell to the Iranian army in December 1946, almost a year to the date of its founding.

THANKS TO AN introduction from a friend, I had an invitation to stay with a branch of Ezzet Abdul Aziz's family—his nephew, Muhsen Saleh Abdul Aziz, a representative in the Kurdish Parliament, and his grand-nephew, Hakar Muhsen Saleh, the commander of an elite group of *pesh-merga*. Another grandnephew—out of town during my visit—was the Amadiya mayor.

Hakar Muhsen Saleh lived with his wife and children in a second-story home overlooking the Ezzet Abdul statue. My taxi driver and I had some trouble finding the place, but when we did, I was warmly welcomed into a small room filled with ledgelike couches and about a half-dozen men.

Hickmat Mustafa Mahmoud arrived, a youngish man in a tan jacket. A high school teacher, and apparently one of Amadiya's only English speakers, he had been pressed into service as my translator—a role he greatly relished, he said, as it relieved him from his classroom duties. His job was difficult and exhausting; he taught weekdays from eight-thirty A.M. to nine-thirty P.M., for a total of eighty-eight classes and 500 *dinars* (about $30) a week.

With Hickmat was Muhammad Abdullah Amadi, the city historian, who had also taken the day off to introduce me to his city. A short, round-faced man dressed in a dark brown *shal u shapik* and red-and-white turban, Muhammad was the author of several books on Amadiya, copies of which he carried with him.

We settled down to talk, along with my hosts, the parliamentarian Muhsen Saleh, and his son Hakar. Muhsen Saleh was an elegant, older man with a long, tanned face, dressed in a steel blue *shal u shapik* and a black-and-white turban. His son Hakar, a handsome man with salt-and-pepper hair, wore a Western suit.

After a short general introduction to Amadiya's history, the historian zeroed in on the Bahdinan ruler Sultan Hussein Wali. In power from 1520 to 1561, at a time when much of Kurdistan was at war, Sultan Wali had succeeded in establishing a peaceful principality, envied by much of the land, he said. Enlightened and farsighted, the sultan had not only constructed many public buildings, mosques, bridges, roads, and hotels for travelers, but also built an extensive network of seventy-two religious schools. During Sultan Wali's reign, Amadiya had become one of the most educated emirates in the Ottoman Empire.

"Truly, it was the golden period for Bahdinan and the Kurds," Muhammad concluded, "and now we hope America will make another."

I couldn't help but wince at his optimism.

We set out to explore the city, in a BMW and two sport-utility vehicles, the latter filled with guards, friends, and neighbors—all male. As during many of my more formal visits in Iraqi Kurdistan, the women kept themselves strictly in the background, emerging only occasionally to join us for meals. Being in the large all-male groups was occasionally disconcerting to me, but usually I felt at ease, as I was treated as neither woman nor man, but as honored Westerner.

Hickmat, Muhammad, and I were assigned to the BMW, driven by the parliamentarian Muhsen Saleh, whom Hickmat addressed as "Mam," or "Uncle"—a term of respect in Kurdistan. The PUK president Jalal Talabani was often referred to as "Mam Jalal," while the KDP's Massoud Barzani was

"Kak Massoud," or "Brother Massoud"—more signs, I thought, of the intimate connection the Kurds feel with their leaders. A fine drizzle had
begun, and when Mam Muhsen opened his trunk to retrieve his parka, I
noticed a large pile of guns inside, covered with a plastic tarp.

Our first stop was the ruins of the Quba Khan school, outside the city at
the base of the mesa. We had to hike down a muddy hill to reach it. Leading
the way, going fast and sure, was the seventy-one-year-old Mam Muhsen.
He had spent many years as a *peshmerga* and was still in peak physical
condition.

Built by Sultan Hussein Wali in the mid-1500s, the Quba Khan school
had been in operation until the 1920s, drawing scholars from all over the
region, the historian said as we explored the romantic, overgrown ruins.
Famous for its library, the school had functioned much like a small university, offering classes in Islamic studies, science, math, medicine, philosophy, astronomy, and agriculture. Sultan Wali had also paid handsome
salaries to teachers, stipends to students, and grants to writers and scholars—my kind of ruler, I thought.

"When we have more peace, I would like to restore these ruins and
build a road down this hill so that tourists can visit," said Mam Muhsen,
bending to pick a flower.

I nodded. I could easily see tourists in Amadiya. In the early green of
spring, it was one of the most beautiful settings I'd ever seen.

BACK ATOP THE Amadiya mesa, we proceeded directly to the Mosul
Gate, once one of four ancient entrances to the city and the only one still
relatively intact. Built of large white stones, leaning heavily in upon one
another, the gate was engraved with pre-Islamic figures of a sun, eagle,
prince, and snake, along with four faint warriors marching along a wall.
Gazing down the steep mesa from the wall, I could just make out a path
that had once been a road leading up to the city from the valley below.

Not far from the Mosul Gate stood the minaret of the Amadiya mosque.
Twenty-seven meters tall, with 103 steps leading to its top, it was built of a
warm brown stone. Probably erected during the time of Sultan Wali, the
minaret had been partially destroyed by the Iraqis in 1961, but rebuilt by the
townspeople in 1965. They'd used the original stones, said to have come
from Gara Mountain, miles away, and transported across the plain and up

the Amadiya mesa one by one, through the work of hundreds of people in a queue.

On the eastern edge of the city stood the tomb of the Sultan Wali, looking like a simple gray igloo on the outside, but lovely within, with a graceful dome, coffin made of grape wood, and Kufi calligraphy script. A verse from the Quran on the tomb read: "Everything (that exists) will perish except His own Face."

THAT EVENING, OVER BEER, soft drinks, and nuts, Mam Muhsen told me his history. We were relaxing on the floor of a large front room with a kerosene heater and picture window overlooking the town; later that night, mattresses would be rolled out on the floor for the family's teenage daughter and myself.

We all stretched out, Mam Muhsen half reclining on his elbow as he rubbed his green stocking feet together. He was still in his *shal u shapik* and black-and-white turban, and looking as elegant as ever. He, his son, and I were the only ones drinking alcohol. Hickmat and Muhammad, as stricter Muslims, refrained.

A servant tiptoed in to discuss the dinner menu. Something simple perhaps, like chicken kebab and salad? We all agreed. We had feasted earlier, on the Amadiya specialty *dughabba,* which are wheat patties stuffed with ground lamb and served in a broth of goat's milk flavored with mint. I'd been skeptical, but they'd been delicious.

Mam Muhsen spoke about his childhood, when he and his family had fled to Iran following the first failed Barzani revolt of 1943–45—thirty years before the Algiers Accord. They had lived in the Kurdish Republic of Mahabad but, when it fell, were forced to return to Iraq. His uncle was executed, and his father was imprisoned for seven years.

As an adult, Mam Muhsen himself joined the Barzani movement. "I worked as a *peshmerga* from 1961 until 1975," he said. "All that time, except for the cease-fires, I was living in the mountains, with about one hundred men at my command.

"My most memorable battle was on Hindren Mountain, where I was in charge of three thousand *peshmerga*. There was constant shelling. We took positions in the openings in the rocks, but when the shelling started, we went into shelters. They were covered with thick branches and soil with two stones on top. One time in the shelter, I counted fifty-one explosions in one minute around me. But when the shelling stopped, we went back into position, and we were successful. We captured three Iraqi battalions, and took them prisoner.

"I was never taken prisoner or injured in the fighting, but in 1983, I was arrested by Iraqi intelligence. They took me to Mosul, blindfolded me, and put me in a room so small that I couldn't lie down. But my cousin Esmat Kattani was in the Iraqi ministry then, and he got me released. I came back to Amadiya.

"Later, Kattani was chosen to be an Iraqi representative to the United Nations. When I heard that news, I took a taxi straight to the mountains, and asked my family to join me. Without his protection, I was afraid that I or my family would be arrested again.

"That happened in 1987, and it was the first time our women and children joined us in the mountains. We dug a small shelter into the hillside. My grandchildren were very small, and they learned to run in there when they heard the airplanes.

"We stayed in the mountains until 1988, when we smelled chemical weapons and fled at night to Turkey. One of our dogs came with us to the border, but he wouldn't cross—he just sat down and howled. We saw him again when we returned. It was months later, and everything was destroyed, but the dog was still here, weak and thin. He recognized us, but he was very angry. He wouldn't come when we called."

Two or three days later, I was startled to hear this same story regarding a dog who refused to cross the border from another man in a different part of Kurdistan. Had the incident actually happened to both parties, or was something else going on—myths in the making, perhaps? Where does the line between myth and reality start? And does it matter? Either way, the story is emblematic.

WHEN I FIRST started learning about the *peshmerga*—themselves both mythic and real—I felt confused. To me, the term connotes armed fighters. But many Iraqis used the word, which is generally applied only to the Iraqi Kurds, much more loosely than that, to refer to any Kurd who fled to the mountains to resist or escape Iraqi repression.

When I first asked if there had been women *peshmerga*, the Iraqi Kurds often replied, "Oh, yes, many." But upon further questioning, it usually turned out that the women *peshmerga* had served primarily as support staff, cooking and caring for the men. Only a handful had actively borne arms; for that, I would have to wait until I reached Turkey, where the Kurdistan Workers' Party (PKK) included many women guerrillas.

Living in the mountains for years at a time, the *peshmerga*, like most soldiers, had spent only a fraction of their days in actual battle or preparation for battle; for the rest, they'd engaged in everyday activities. In some places and periods, the *peshmerga* had lived only among other men, sometimes isolated in inaccessible areas for many months at a stretch, other times serving in shifts, with perhaps two weeks on, two weeks off to visit their families. In other places and periods, the *peshmerga* had taken their families with them, sometimes living in small groups, sometimes in large makeshift mountain communities, complete with schools, hospitals, courts, and entertainment. I met teachers, doctors, lawyers, judges, and even actors who had all once plied their trades in the mountains and therefore described themselves as *peshmerga*, though they had never actually borne arms.

For most *peshmerga*, life in the mountains had been hard. They'd lived in caves and in small unobtrusive shelters built of stone and wood, sometimes sleeping under branches to keep warm. Free time was spent dancing, singing, telling stories, and watching Iraqi military movements. Food and other necessities were supplied by nearby villages. Without their help, the *peshmerga* could not have survived.

One *peshmerga* I met, Suleyman Hadji Badri Sindi of Zakho, explained to me how he had operated as a guerrilla leader in the early 1960s. In charge of overseeing villages in the then-government-controlled Sindi territory, he had known exactly how much wheat and barley, and how many horses and sheep, every family had, as well as who owned guns or had men of fighting age. Whenever the *peshmerga* needed wheat, he would contact those villagers with grain to spare, and they would hide the wheat in covered holes in the earth, to be retrieved by the guerrillas at night. Whenever Mulla Mustafa needed extra men, Suleyman Hadji would send out the word, and the Sindi men would appear, to fight for a day or two, and then return home as if nothing had happened.

At the time of my visit, the *peshmerga* were still a force in Iraq, although they were not as fierce as they once had been and functioned more like ordinary militias. The KDP had about thirty-five thousand *peshmerga* at its command, and the PUK, about twenty-five thousand. In addition, there were about forty thousand irregular *peshmerga* in reserve. During the 2003 war in Iraq, *peshmerga* enthusiastically joined the American forces, fighting with the same weaponry they had used for decades, and after the war, plans were to incorporate them into a new Iraqi army.

At the time of my visit, the PUK militia also had a new contingent, composed of about five hundred women *peshmerga*. Established on November 11, 1996, the unit had two main goals, its commander, Rezan Rashid, told me: one, to be a fighting force, and two, to change the "reactionary mentality of tradition and Islam" toward women in Kurdistan.

CLIMBING INTO THE BMW again the next morning, Mam Muhsen, Hickmat, a guard, and I drove down the mesa to the Christian village of Kani, to congratulate the Chaldean Bishop Raban. The bishop had been appointed to his position only two months before, Mam Muhsen said, and on this Easter morning—for it was Easter, I'd forgotten—people were coming from miles around to congratulate him and ask his blessing for the new year.

The village was located down a steep muddy hill, at the end of which stood a small church, an adjoining complex, and the bishop. A tall, thin, ascetic-looking man with long black robes, a fuchsia cap and belt, silver-rim glasses, and gray hair, he was mingling with his parishioners, kissing children on the head. But upon our arrival, he moved away from the throng to usher us into a huge reception room, its perimeter lined with dozens of cream-and-gold, Louis XIV-style chairs.

Moments later, a contingent of fifteen or twenty men and boys also arrived, all in traditional Kurdish dress. Some were Christian, some Muslim, but the bishop shook all hands with equal warmth and offered everyone candy, tea, and a seat. We had barely settled in when another group entered, causing everyone to rise, shake hands, and exchange good wishes. Then another group came in, and another, and as we rose and sat, rose and sat, the first group left. Except for a few girls under age ten and myself, everyone in the room was male.

Somehow, during a short break in all the coming and going, the bishop, who spoke some English, found a moment to tell me about himself. "In 1961, when I was ten and a half and the KDP had its headquarters here, the Iraqi government bombed Amadiya and all around Amadiya," he said. "A helicopter came down to my village, and I climbed in. I told the soldiers, 'I want to be a priest, I want to go to Mosul.' Then, like a miracle, the helicopter engine had trouble, and I had time to go home and get money and clothes."

"Weren't you afraid?" I asked, imagining him as a village boy surrounded by soldiers. But the bishop either didn't hear me or didn't understand.

"The helicopter took me to Mosul," he said. "And in all those hundreds of people, it was like a miracle again, I saw my uncle. He took me to a priest, and I started to study. I finished in 1973 and came back to my village. I have been a priest here for twenty-nine and a half years, and now, I am so honored, I have been made a bishop."

"Was this village bombed in the Anfal?" I asked, though I already all but knew the answer. Like the villages I had seen in the Aqra valley, Kani was largely built of clay and stone—not post-Anfal cement.

"No, God was with us," the bishop said.

As He was with many Christians during much of Saddam Hussein's regime. In the early years of Hussein's dictatorship especially, many Iraqi Christians—unlike the "traitor" Kurds—had enjoyed often-tolerable relations with the Baathists.

Christians in the Amadiya area had suffered a far worse time of it in the 1840s, not long after the Kurdish emirates had been abolished. Kurdistan had then become more accessible to Western missionaries, whose proselytizing activities led to a steep decline in relationships between the Muslims and the Assyrian and Chaldean Christians native to the region. The hostilities reached one horrific climax in 1843, when Kurds from the Botan emirate, north of Amadiya in what is now Turkey, brutally attacked their Assyrian neighbors, slaughtering around ten thousand men and abducting women and children as slaves.

Layard, the British archaeologist, blamed the attacks primarily on a fierce *shaikh* living in the court of the Botan prince, Bedir Khan. However, he also questioned the judgment of the American missionaries who had helped stir up trouble by building a large school and boardinghouse. "These buildings had been the cause of much jealousy and suspicion to the Kurds," he writes. "They stand upon the summit of an isolated hill, commanding the whole valley. A position less ostentatious and proportions more modest might certainly have been chosen."

Reading those words months later back in New York, along with daily missives advocating war against Iraq, but few words regarding the country's rebuilding, I angrily wondered why people hadn't yet learned to carefully consider the consequences of their actions before plunging into new environments. Like introducing a strange species or microorganism into an ecosystem, whole worlds could be turned upside down, with horrific consequences, by seemingly straightforward actions.

TO AND FROM Amadiya, Mam Muhsen pointed out various personal landmarks—a cave once used by his *peshmerga*, a valley where he'd lived in the 1970s, a ridge that led to Iran; he'd hiked that six-day trip too many times to count. And along one empty stretch of road, he slowed down the car until it stopped with a shudder.

"This is where I was almost killed by the PKK [Turkey's Kurdistan Workers' Party]," he said. "In all my years in the mountains, the Iraqis never wounded me, but here, the Kurds of Turkey almost killed me. They used an American-made gun, a BZK, and shot at the car from those mountains. The car started burning. I was unconscious, I don't remember. . . . Someone came and pulled me out."

We sat in silence. No other cars or villages were in sight, and I could hear nothing but the sounds of our breathing and the ticking of the cooling engine. Mam Muhsen had been extremely lucky.

"Amadiya has been tormented by the PKK," he said. "Their forces surrounded Amadiya. They forced us to defend ourselves. It's clear to us the PKK wants to destroy Kurdistan. It's all politics. The PKK is supported by Iraq and Iran, who are using them to hurt Turkey. The Kurds of Turkey don't understand this. They think they are fighting for their independence. But the PKK is the worst. They destroyed many of the villages we rebuilt after the Anfal."

He restarted the engine.

TO UNDERSTAND THE political situation in Iraqi Kurdistan today, it is also necessary to understand the political situation in Turkey's Kurdistan— something that I had not fully appreciated before departing for Iraq.

When it comes to the treatment of its Kurdish minority, Turkey has a

history that almost rivals that of Iraq. In its zeal to establish a national identity post–Ottoman Empire, Turkey even denied it had a Kurdish minority,
declaring Kurds to be "mountain Turks who have forgotten their language."
Kurds who did not call themselves Kurds could rise high in Turkish government and society, and often did. But to speak Kurdish in public places,
give Kurdish concerts, teach Kurdish language, and even at times wear
Kurdish dress—let alone talk Kurdish politics—was usually forbidden.

In the late 1970s, Abdullah Öcalan (pronounced "oh-jalan"), an Ankara
university student, and other young radicals secretly founded the Kurdistan
Workers' Party, or PKK. In 1980, Turkey suffered a military coup, which led
to brutal crackdowns on political dissidents. And in 1984, the PKK attacked
its first Turkish military outposts. Fed up with Turkish repression, an economic exploitation of the Kurdish southeast, and the overall failure of
democracy in Turkey, the PKK declared that the only solution for the Kurds
was to separate entirely from Turkey and form an independent nation.

Civil war began. Rather than addressing the Kurds' real grievances,
Turkey instituted a massive military buildup in the Southeast, torturing and
murdering suspected PKK members and supporters, and forcibly evacuat-
ing and destroying villages. The PKK reacted by slaughtering large numbers of Turkish soldiers and progovernment Kurdish civilians, quickly
garnering the group a reputation for terrorism. By the time the war ended,
with the arrest of Öcalan in 1999, about thirty-seven thousand people had
been killed, over three thousand Kurdish villages destroyed, and at least 1
million Kurds rendered homeless.

The Kurdish-Turkish conflict had a direct and immediate effect on Iraqi
Kurdistan. About ten years earlier, Baghdad had cleared villages in a
twenty-kilometer-wide stretch along its Turkish and Iranian borders, creating a no-man's-land where no guerrillas could hide. In the mid-1980s, Iraq
granted the Turks permission to enter Iraqi Kurdistan when in "hot pursuit"
of the PKK. The policy suited Iraq at the time; at war with Iran, it could not
afford to police its Turkish border. And the policy still suited Iraq over fifteen years later, at the time of my visit; Saddam Hussein welcomed the
Turkish presence in Kurdistan as a destabilizing influence. Hence the
Turkish tanks I'd seen on my outing with Majed, Yousif, and family. Hence,
also, the Turkish air attacks against PKK camps in Iraqi Kurdistan that had
started after the Gulf War and continued. Sometimes these air attacks had

destroyed Iraqi Kurdish villages, rather than PKK camps, leading the Iraqi Kurds to interpret them as warnings.

Initially, relations between the KDP and PKK had been good. In 1983, the two parties signed a cooperation agreement against any kind of imperialism, with American imperialism heading the list. But in 1987, the KDP broke with the PKK, largely because of the PKK's violent methods. Less than a year later, the PKK signed an alliance with the PUK, whose territory does not border Turkey, but it also soon fell apart.

After the 1991 Gulf War, the KDP, PUK, and other smaller parties successfully established a self-governing, semiautonomous Kurdistan. One of the fledging coalition's early acts was to declare its intention to "combat the PKK," as it understood that if Iraqi Kurdistan was to survive, it needed Turkey's help. Turkey was the only neighboring country that could provide the military bases needed for the Western allies' protective air patrols and offer the Iraqi Kurds an essential economic trade route to the West.

In July 1992 the PKK successfully cut off that trade route. Fighting broke out between the Kurds of Turkey and the Kurds of Iraq. In 1994, the internal fighting between the KDP and the PUK also began, enabling the PKK to play the two Iraqi parties against each other. "Öcalan is the enemy of Kurds," the KDP declared after one unfortunate incident in which the PKK took humanitarian aid workers hostage against possible KDP attacks.

In March 1995, some thirty-five thousand Turkish soldiers entered Iraqi Kurdistan in order to destroy PKK camps—only the largest of several similar expeditions throughout the 1990s. Officially, the KDP opposed the action. Privately, they condoned it; both they and the PUK worked with the Turks in various anti-PKK operations.

Öcalan was arrested in 1999, and the PKK abandoned its armed military struggle, saying that it would now fight for equal civil rights through peaceful means. However, about five thousand PKK *peshmerga* were believed to be still hiding in northern Iraq in the early 2000s, giving Turkey all the excuse it needed to cross the border—and to keep about fifteen hundred troops permanently stationed in Iraqi Kurdistan. Skirmishes between the PKK and the KDP also continued. I had already seen many buildings and a few villages now completely abandoned due to post-1991 PKK–KDP hostilities.

All of which set the stage for yet a new chapter in Iraqi-Turkish-Kurdish relations to begin with the Iraq war of 2003, when the United States proposed sending large numbers of Turkish troops into northern Iraq—supposedly for peace monitoring and humanitarian purposes. Not surprisingly, the Iraqi Kurds reacted with anger, outrage, and mass demonstrations. To allow some Turkish troops into Iraqi Kurdistan to pursue the PKK was one thing. But to allow a mass invasion by a military force that was brutally suppressing fellow Kurds and occasionally bombing Iraqi Kurdish villages—not to mention badly mistreating the Iraqi Kurds during the 1991 uprising—was unthinkable. Luckily, wiser heads prevailed, and the Turks were kept out of northern Iraq, though the issue was to come up again months after the war.

THE SHIFTING RELATIONSHIPS between the KDP, PUK, PKK, Iraq, and Turkey may seem Byzantine, but they are par for the course in Kurdistan. Throughout the centuries of the Ottoman-Safavid Empires and before, the Kurdish tribes were constantly forced to form new alliances, break old ones, join loose confederations, leave them, toy with friends, and two-time enemies in order to survive. And throughout the twentieth century, with little voice in their respective nation-states, the Kurds were again often forced to temporarily ally themselves with one strange bedfellow or another. An uncertain status in the world necessitates constant balancing acts.

LEAVING AMADIYA THAT AFTERNOON, I returned to Dohuk to find Majed and Yousif waiting for me. Like Mam Muhsen, they had Easter calls to make, and were eager to have me come along. It doesn't matter that we are Muslim and our friends Christian, they emphasized. The problems of the past are over; all religions as well as tribes get along well in the new Kurdistan.

Though nothing is ever quite so simple, many other Muslims, Christians, and members of other minority groups expressed similar sentiments to me in northern Iraq. The fledgling democracy was granting full religious and cultural rights to all minorities, and some citizens did seem to be developing what one scholar calls a "Kurdistani"—as opposed to a "Kurdish"—identity, apropos of the new pluralistic Kurdistan.

We made the rounds, starting with a visit to the big, modern Assyrian church, where we met several priests. Next came a stop at the home of Armenian neighbors, followed by visits to several Chaldean Christian families. At every stop, candy, nuts, colored Easter eggs, and tea were passed around, along with expressions of Christian-Muslim goodwill, and it was a heartwarming feeling to be enthusiastically welcomed into living room after living room by host after host. As at Bishop Raban's, other groups kept arriving and leaving as we made our calls, until I got the sense that the whole town of Dohuk was on the move. The whole male population of Dohuk, that is. Except in a few cases, there were no women guests—just hostesses.

Our last stop was the home of a Christian man originally from the Barwari region, also home to Majed and Yousif's family. The friendship between the two families went way back, to the days of their great-grandfathers. Back then, the Muslim great-grandfather had helped the Christian great-grandfather escape from an Ottoman massacre.

"They wouldn't give him up, and for this reason, we have always been close," the Christian said, ceremoniously laying out a pristine white table-cloth, upon which he placed assorted nuts, four tumblers, and a bottle of Scotch.

CHAPTER SEVEN

Questions of Honor

AT THE NORTHERN EDGE OF IRAQI KURDISTAN, NOT FAR from the Turkish border, is the city of Zakho, population about 150,000. Some historians believe that its name derives from the ancient Aramaic word *zakhota*, meaning "victory," and refers to a battle fought nearby between the victorious Romans and the defeated Persians. Xenophon the Greek mentions Zakho in *Anabasis*, written in 401 B.C., but the city is probably considerably older than that, perhaps dating back to the 2000s B.C.

Part of the Bahdinan emirate during much of the Ottoman Empire, Zakho hugs the banks of the Khabur River, which splits in two just before entering the city. A one-thousand-year-old bridge spans one of the channels, while the other circumnavigates the town to join up with the first branch by the ruined tower of the Zakho castle, built in the 1700s on the site of a much older fortress.

But none of this ancient history has much bearing on Zakho today. Like the rest of Kurdistan, its past has been burned and destroyed, submerged and trampled on so many times that it is but a blip in the city's collective memory. Most people in Zakho know almost nothing about its early history, just as most people in Kurdistan know little about what occurred in their lands prior to the 1960s, or even, among the younger generation, the 1980s. Ask the average Kurd to what era an ancient monument in town belongs, and he or she won't be able to say. Constant oppression and war allow no time for the contemplation of the past.

Continual upheaval has also meant that the Kurds have had little time to cultivate their traditional arts. Who can think of weaving carpets or spending hours cooking elaborate dishes taught by grandmothers when most of one's family is in the mountains or in jail, bombs are falling, and one may have to pack up—again—and leave soon?

Before the advent of radio and television, the Kurds preserved their history and culture through an unusually rich oral tradition—a treasure trove of folktales, epic poetry, songs, and proverbs. Especially on winter evenings, people gathered in homes and male-only guesthouses to gossip, exchange information, tell stories, and sing. Family and tribal histories, community legend and lore were preserved, created, and re-created through the authoritative voices of elders passing along their knowledge to the young. Some fortunate Kurds learned to read and write Arabic through village *mullahs*, and the upper crust learned Turkish and Persian in schools for the nobility, but for centuries, most villagers were nonliterate, and Kurdish remained an oral language. The first Kurdish newspaper did not appear until 1898, when it was published in Cairo, Egypt, of all places; pressure from the Ottomans made it impossible to publish in Kurdistan.

The Kurds' oral tradition was already breaking down by the 1960s, and would probably be in steep decline today even without the horrific events of the past four decades. But relentless war and oppression have hastened its demise. Only recently, with the start of a shaky peace, are the Iraqi Kurds fully opening their eyes and wondering at all they have lost, not just physically and emotionally, but also culturally.

Yet throughout it all, even in the worst of times, the surviving ancient sites of Kurdistan have never completely lost their power. Palpably drawing both the literate and the nonliterate to them, especially at the end of the day, when dusk brings with it the larger questions of life, the sites offer respite. They are places of forgetting as well as remembering, places in which to lose the pain and immediacy of the modern world in the imagined glories and mysteries of the past.

MY NEW FRIEND Arjin, who lived in Zakho, agreed to give me a tour of her city. Unmarried and in her early thirties, with a face filled with cheekbones and interesting angles, Arjin worked as an office assistant and had an excellent command of English. She was also extraordinarily astute.

Leaving her home shortly after my arrival, we headed downtown, picking up her friend Pelsin on the way. Pelsin worked with Arjin and was in her late twenties, with wide gray-green eyes. She also spoke some English and, like Arjin, wore a calf-length skirt and matching jacket, no head scarf.

Nearing the city center, we passed more of the strange marble houses that I knew from Dohuk—the ones with the spindly columns and odd-sized bay windows, built by the nouveau riche. And here and there stood a surprising number of drab, sullen hotels. As a gateway leading to Turkey, Zakho was a businessman's town and center for the illicit emigration trade.

We stopped into a tiny gold shop. Traditionally, gold and silver have played an important role in Kurdish culture—often part of the bride-price paid by the groom to the bride, and a way in which to store wealth, especially for women. A typically Kurdish style of jewelry is the *queesh* or *parang*, made of gold or silver coins on a chain hung around the neck or waist, or along the brim of a traditional hat or turban, once common among Kurdish women but much rarer now.

The storeowner was trained as a mechanical engineer, but he earned five or six times an engineer's salary by running his gold shop, he said. Nearly half of his business came from renting out his jewelry, usually to customers who were attending weddings—the single most important occasion in most Kurds' lives. One of his largest pieces, a flamboyant chest piece made of gold orbs, rented for 400 *dinars* a day, almost the equivalent of a civil servant's monthly salary.

Puffy white Western wedding dresses could also be rented at a shop down the street, next to a photographer's studio. Some Kurdish families rented the dresses, went next door to have their pictures taken, and then brought the dresses back. Others bought the "fake gold" that had recently become available. "This makes the rich people very angry," Arjin said with a sly smile.

Descending a few steps, we entered a dank vegetable market, its tables piled high with cucumbers, zucchini, onions, green almonds, and unripe pistachios in pink skins. Arjin and Pelsin greeted a friend while I looked around, trying not to stare at several women shrouded in black from head to toe, their faces covered with thin black cloths, lacking even slits for eyes. I'd seen a handful of similarly attired women in Aqra and Amadiya, but their dress was still strange for me, as it was unusual in Kurdistan.

Throughout Greater Kurdistan, women's clothing varies widely. In the villages of Iraq, Iran, and Turkey, many wear either the traditional colorful Kurdish costume—which differs from region to region—or a *dishdasha*, the caftan. When going to market, these women often cover their heads, but not their faces, and go uncovered in their homes and fields. The long black *abeyya* or *chador*, enveloping the entire body and head, but not the face, is worn mostly by urban Kurds. In Iran, such coverings are required on the urban streets—though not in the villages, or the home, where most anything goes. In Iraq, they are voluntary and usually worn only by traditional older women. In Turkey, they are rarely seen.

Few women anywhere in Greater Kurdistan cover their faces, and when they do, it is generally only in the smaller and more conservative cities, and only when visiting the market or other public spaces frequented by strangers. Most urban Iraqi Kurdish women, young and old, dress modestly in knee- or calf-length skirts and blouses, or sometimes pants, with occasional head scarves. Fashions are somewhat freer in the liberal Iraqi city of Suleimaniyah, where many women wear pants; freer still in the homes of urban Iranian Kurds, where many wear tight-fitting T-shirts and jeans; and freest of all in the cities of Turkey's Kurdistan, where women flaunt tight-fitting clothes on the streets. I scarcely saw a single young woman in Turkey's Kurdish cities in a skirt.

The face cloth is called the *kheli*, my new friends told me as we left the market, and the women could be wearing it because they were old and traditional, because they were shy, or because they came from a "high" or illustrious family. Pelsin herself came from a "high" family, and, though they no longer had much wealth or power, there was much consternation in her tribal community when she refused to wear the *kheli*.

"I told them, okay, maybe if I just went to the market once or twice a week, I would wear it," Pelsin said. "But I work in an office, I go out every day. And finally they accepted that. But they still don't like it that I wear jackets and skirts—they want me to be completely covered."

"I myself tried to wear the *kheli* to the market a few times," Arjin said with a mischievous grin, "but every time, I tripped and fell down."

As we walked, I learned more. Pelsin's neighbors were also peeved that she worked, was often not home to receive them, remained single, often refrained from gossip, and took taxis by herself—something few Iraqi Kurdish women do. As a member of an important family, she was expected to set impeccable standards by dressing ultraconservatively and comporting herself ultrademurely. Most of all, she was expected to keep herself well removed from the public eye; heaven forbid that she should ever think of taking a higher-profile job or a position in the government, as a handful of other Kurdish women had. And why in the world didn't she wear the *dish-dasha* around the house like everyone else?

Talk. Gossip. It is the oppressive bane of the Kurdish woman's existence. What is she wearing? Where is she going? How much did she pay for those shoes? How often has she spoken to that man?

In an earlier era, and in many parts of traditional Kurdistan today, Kurdish women drifted out of their homes in the late mornings or afternoons to sit in their doorways and talk. For many, it was the high point of an otherwise backbreaking day spent cleaning the house, preparing the meals, caring for the children, hauling the water and firewood, tilling the fields. Traditional Kurdish women worked—and work—far harder than the men. Times have changed, and people are changing, but the tradition of gossip is dying hard.

Arjin, Pelsin, and I meandered out of the downtown and down wide empty streets to the one-thousand-year-old Pira Dellal Bridge. Built of cut limestone blocks fit so tightly together that they appeared to be welded, the bridge rose to an arched peak about thirty feet above the Khabur River. The bridge's incline was so steep that it was hard not to imagine horses and people slipping and sliding over its smooth, guard-less sides in inclement weather.

"Do you notice that there are no other women alone together here?" Arjin said as we stepped onto the bridge.

She was right, although I did notice a few women together with their families.

"Women do not go out by themselves in Zakho, except to the market. Zakho is a very conservative city."

The Khabur River rushed below us, a churning brown current running high with the spring.

"After the uprising, some women *did* come here alone with other women," Arjin went on. "We had more freedom then, everyone was so happy Saddam was gone. But now that time is finished. Now is the same as before. Only men and families come here."

So the old order has reasserted itself, I thought dispiritedly. Throughout the traditional Muslim world, public spaces are dominated by men, while women are relegated to the private spaces of the home. Why had Kurdistan reverted to the old order? And why so soon? Was it simply because in the face of much upheaval, people needed familiar touchstones? Or had an early disillusionment already set in? When and how does change become permanent and true? How much of change comes from above and how much from below?

On the other side of the bridge, we walked along the riverbank. The bridge was more beautiful from this angle, with the late-afternoon rays of the sun warming the limestone into gentle pinks and tans. A wash had been thrown over the world.

The one-thousand-year-old Pira Dellal Bridge

"I never went to the bridge until I was fifteen or sixteen years old," Pelsin said, breaking into my reverie.

"What?" I said, startled. The bridge is Zakho's primary historic attraction, the focal point of an otherwise scraggly architectural landscape.

"As a high family, we never went out in public places."

I blinked hard. I didn't know what to say. To be of a "high" family in Kurdistan sounded like more of a curse than a blessing.

"Life must be very difficult for you here," I finally said, wishing that I could somehow change things. My new friends seemed so capable, so intelligent, so buried.

They shrugged, exhibiting the Kurdish stoicism that I noticed so often. "It is okay. Sometimes we are depressed, but little by little, things are changing."

BEHIND ZAKHO ROSE a range of dry, rugged, elephant-skin mountains, followed in the distance by the higher icy peaks of Turkey. Gazing out of Arjin's bedroom window later that day, I felt at the edge of existence, close to the land and the sky. Children were playing in streets nearly empty of traffic, and Arjin and I had just returned from visiting her sister, who lived next door. She had recently been ill and was receiving thirty or forty visitors a day, every day. The city around me notwithstanding, I was in a village.

Arjin's family home was big and dark and sparsely furnished, with an inviting garden lined with flower beds out back. In the house lived about a dozen people, including Arjin's frail mother, several siblings and cousins, and the wife of a brother who was living in England. Pale, silent, and pregnant after the brother's most recent visit, the wife had been waiting for five years to join her husband.

Arjin, one of her sisters, a teenage niece, and I had gathered in the small upstairs bedroom to talk and giggle, look at pictures, and munch on baklava. Arjin's sister spent a long time studying herself in a handheld mirror, while the teenage niece, who had just started covering herself, took time out to say her evening prayers. None of the other under-forty women in Arjin's family wore the head scarf.

"Many young women are starting to cover themselves more and more," Arjin said as we watched her niece, and I remembered Bayan, my bright-eyed, tightly covered translator in Dohuk. "I think because after the uprising, we went a little crazy. We were like teenagers, we did like Westerners do. So maybe now, without realizing, we want to return to our own culture. We are Muslim."

What parts of one's culture to keep and what to leave behind when moving from one era into the next? How to know what losses to mourn, what changes to embrace?

—

THE FOLLOWING MORNING, I awoke to the sounds of sheep baaing, birds singing, chickens cackling, people hammering, and men slapping loaves of bread into shape in a bakery down the street. On the rooftops around me, between satellite dishes, women were stringing laundry up on clotheslines.

Arjin and I breakfasted on typical Kurdish fare—the flat *nane tanik,* white cheese, yogurt, honey, tea—and then Arjin handed me the keys to the family car. We had places to visit, but Arjin couldn't drive and assumed that I could. Like many Iraqi Kurds with limited firsthand knowledge of the outside world, she imagined that Westerners, and especially Americans, were proficient at everything. If they only knew!

Arjin badly wanted to learn how to drive, but to do so would have meant undertaking a difficult and exhausting campaign against public opinion. Most women in traditional Kurdistan do not drive. Cars are regarded as the province of men, and women who trespass risk being viewed as immoral. Most traditional Kurdish women also do not travel by themselves or spend the night away from home unless in the company of male relatives.

However, these mores—which do not necessarily apply to urban Kurdish women, especially in Iran and Turkey—are changing. Many in Iraqi Kurdistan told me that women's lives have greatly improved over the last two decades. And I had already met several women from traditional families who drove, lived in school dorms, or held jobs that involved extensive unaccompanied travel.

Whether or not a woman was allowed to drive, travel, or spend nights away from home without a male escort all depended on her family and where it stood vis-à-vis the hoary question of honor.

Honor is a central value in Kurdish society, affecting everyone, but it is women who are the most burdened. It is they who must maintain their family's reputation by keeping both their behavior and all perceptions of their behavior above reproach, especially in poorer communities, where a young girl's virginity may be her family's only commodity. Women must therefore not only refrain from pre- and extramarital sex, flirting, and seductive dress, but they must also take care not to be spotted with an unrelated man once too often, spend too many unaccountable hours away from home, or go out without family after a certain hour. Such strictures lead to women keeping unnaturally tight reins on themselves. Yet they can scarcely afford to do otherwise, as the price for mistakes is extraordinarily high. The specter of honor killings is always lurking.

Many Kurds I met were quick to blame honor killings on fundamentalist Islam, but the practice is feudal and patriarchal in origin, not Islamic. *Sharia*, or Islamic law, calls for the stoning of both men and women for adultery, but only when there are four witnesses and when the punishment is carried out by the authorities. Taking the law into one's own hands, as some Kurdish families do, is not condoned by Islam, and sex between an unmarried man and unmarried woman is not a capital offense under *sharia*.

As elsewhere in the traditional Muslim world, most Kurdish women live under many other strictures as well. Women must marry, preferably before age thirty, if they wish to gain respect and a three-dimensional, quasi-independent life. Unmarried women usually live with their parents or married siblings, where they are expected to shoulder much of the housework, and remain virgins until they die. Divorced women are usually forced to return to their parents' or a sibling's home, as they have no other means of economic support, and they are often treated as objects of great shame by their family.

Men are also expected to marry. A bachelor garners little respect in traditional Kurdish society, where a man needs a wife to provide him with everything from food to sex. Prostitution was almost unknown in the strongly family-oriented Kurdish communities until recent decades, and is still often regarded with unmitigated horror, as I learned for myself one evening, when a male friend of Arjin's family took us up a mountaintop for a scenic view of Zakho. Dusk was settling in, a blue haze descending, and bushes were jumping out of the darkening landscape like fat black sheep. From one spot on the mountain, the friend pointed out the site of a former "casino," once filled with Egyptian prostitutes imported by the Baathists to distract the Kurds from their cause, he said. But the *peshmerga* had successfully bombed the casino one day, killing all the "evil" women inside. He beamed proudly, seemingly not suspecting that there might be another way to view the matter.

Once married, Kurdish women were traditionally expected to produce as many children as possible. Many middle-aged Kurds I met throughout

Greater Kurdistan had ten, twelve, or even more siblings. But today's families are considerably smaller, with many younger village families raising only three or four children, and educated families, only two or three. However, especially among villagers, boy children still tend to be more prized than girl children, and, as elsewhere in the Muslim world, if a wife does not bear a son, her husband has grounds to take a second wife.

As Muslims, Kurdish men are allowed to have four spouses, while Kurdish women can have only one. But a man can take another wife only if he is financially able to do so. "Marry of the women, who seem good to you, two or three or four; and if ye fear that ye cannot do justice (to so many) then one only," reads the Quran (4:3).

Not surprisingly, the taking of second wives was not a subject about which most Kurds felt comfortable talking to me. And many insisted that with modernization and the deterioration of their agricultural society, in which many children were needed to harvest the crops, the practice is dying out. But in the absence of any hard data, I remain unconvinced, at least as far as Iraqi Kurdistan is concerned. I met a number of powerful men under age forty-five who had two wives, and some women told me that they believed the custom was becoming more, rather than less, common, due to the shortage of eligible men post-Anfal, coupled with Kurdistan's increased oil-for-food wealth.

In Iraqi Kurdistan, both men and women were always pointing out to me how liberal their society is, compared to other Muslim societies, in its treatment of women. Educated Kurds often referred to the writings of early Western travelers and scholars—most male—who commented on the relative freedom of Kurdish women. And in some ways, the early visitors' observations hold true: many Kurdish village women cover only their heads, many have much authority in the home, men and women mix somewhat in social settings, and Kurdish women are often much more outspoken than are their Arab counterparts. Throughout history, too, Kurdish women have occasionally held high positions in politics and the military.

But from what I saw, the typical Iraqi Kurdish woman's so-called "greater freedoms" were limited and far from widespread. Though change is under way, most traditional Kurdish women's lives remain highly circumscribed, sometimes in ways that are more extreme than in some other parts of the Islamic world. While in Iran in 1998, for example, I met many women who, despite the mandatory covering, drove cars, took taxicabs by

themselves, owned businesses, served in government, worked as professionals, and went out alone with other women at night, at least in the larger
cities, without anyone blinking an eye. Honor killings are also rarer in Iran,
as it is a more sophisticated society, further removed from its tribal past. But
many Iraqi Kurds I met did not want to hear this; they were too intent on
proving their moral superiority over their hostile neighbors. To them, Iran
was an enemy state and, ipso facto, more antifemale.

LEAVING ZAKHO, ARJIN and I headed west through a dry, flat land
bordered to the immediate north by the elephant-skin mountains that I had
seen from her window. We were traveling on a well-paved, four-lane highway and at first encountered little traffic.

As we drove, I tentatively asked Arjin about the tribal affiliations of
Zakho's citizens. Despite my interest in the topic, I'd learned to approach it
with caution. Some people reacted quite defensively to the subject, saying
that there was no such thing as tribes in Kurdistan anymore and that the old
tribal names—Barwari, Zibari, Doski—now referred more to geography
than to groups of people. "Is New York a tribe? Is California a tribe? No!
They are places, and it is the same in Kurdistan!" one man said to me, shut-
ting me up. But other Kurds I met were as interested in their tribal heritage
as was I, and Arjin—I should have known—fell into the latter category.

Although the once-paramount power of the tribe is no more—in that
sense, my defensive friend was right—tribal affiliations are still central to
Iraqi Kurdish identity, a fact I first learned from anthropologist Diane King,
who lived in northern Iraq for a year in 1997–98. However, as King points
out, the tribes differ considerably in age, form, and degree of influence over
their members. Some tribes are centuries old, others relatively new. Many
are based on genuine kinship links, others share a more fictive sense of family. Some number in the tens of thousands, others in the hundreds. A few
still wield considerable power, most do not. Many Kurds are also completely nontribal, having either lost their affiliations centuries ago or else
descendant from a once-separate group that was never organized into tribes.
I would find even more nontribal Kurds in Turkey and Iran, where many
have been assimilated into large, non-Kurdish cities such as Istanbul and
Tehran.

Even the word *tribe* means different things to different Kurds. Some

Iraqi Kurds, for example, consider the Barzanis, despite their enormous power, to be a confederation rather than a tribe, as they were only formed in the nineteenth century, by a *shaikhly* family and peasants who defected from neighboring tribes.

The city of Zakho, said Arjin, was a mix of many people. "Most people in Zakho are from the Sindi, Suleyvani, or Guli tribes, or they are Zakholi or Kocher," she said. By "Zakholi," she meant people who had lived in the city for several generations and who'd forgotten, or pretended to have forgotten, their tribal affiliations. By "Kocher," she meant the former nomads of various tribes, settled now for generations, who lived scattered all over Iraq and Turkey. The Sindi were a conservative mountain tribe known for making mistakes—"I would never marry one," Arjin laughed—and the Suleyvani, a more modern plains tribe known for paying too much attention to appearances. The Suleyvani were more modern than the Sindi because the Iraqi government had conquered their flat lands some twenty years earlier than they'd subjugated the Sindi, who were able to put up a fiercer fight from the mountains.

"What about you?" I asked Arjin. "What's your family's history?"

Arjin had been born in Mosul, now in Iraqi government territory, as had all her siblings, she said. Her father had died when she was young, and an older brother joined the *peshmerga*. Then one day in the 1980s, the Iraqi forces arrested her mother. "You must go to the mountains and tell your son to give himself up," they said—a common tactic used to pressure the Kurds. Her mother refused and was promptly imprisoned. She'd had brain surgery a few years before and was not in the best of health. But through bribery, Arjin's uncles managed to smuggle the drugs she needed into her cell.

Some months later, the Iraqis rounded up all the *peshmerga* mothers in the prison, took them to an isolated region in the mountains, and dumped them out with nothing but the clothes on their backs. "Now, go find your sons and bring them back," they said.

"How did she survive?" I asked, flabbergasted at the extent of the Iraqis' harassment and at the thought of Arjin's fragile mother wandering in the mountains.

"The villagers helped her," Arjin said, almost nonchalantly, perhaps because she couldn't bear to remember. "And we hired someone to go look for her. He found her and brought her back."

I braked suddenly. Intent on listening to Arjin, I had scarcely registered the traffic that was thickening around us. For the past few miles, we had been driving beside a long line of parked oil trucks heading toward the Iraqi-Turkish border. The trucks were transporting diesel fuel and crude oil from Baathist-controlled Iraq through Kurdistan to Turkey. Such trade was illegal under international sanctions, but Turkey was averting its gaze. There was money to be made. Up to $600 million a year, in fact, with Saddam Hussein also profiting by as much as $120 million a year. The United States had objected to the trade but hadn't forced the issue. After all, the economic sanctions were being erratically implemented throughout the region—another blatant example of noncompliance being the Iraq-to-Syria pipeline, illegally transporting up to two hundred thousand barrels of crude oil a day in the early 2000s.

As one KDP minister later informed me, the illegal smuggling of diesel fuel between Iraq and Turkey had at times provided the KDP government with up to 97 percent of its annual operating budget of $150 million. That put the KDP in a much stronger economic position than the PUK, whose neighbor was Iran, not Turkey, and helped account for the many wealthy denizens of Dohuk, whose province bordered Turkey. However, about a year before I arrived in Kurdistan, Turkey had cut the number of diesel fuel trucks that it was allowing through its border to one hundred a day from one thousand a day. And in the fall of 2002, Turkey formally shut down the illegal trade altogether, claiming that an oversupply of diesel fuel was hurting the country's economy, already in deep recession. But privately, Turkish officials all but admitted that there was another reason for the shutdown. With war drums beating louder, Turkey no longer wanted to help enrich the Iraqi Kurds, who they feared would encourage the Kurds of Turkey to push for their own independence post-Saddam.

Skirting the congested border crossing, Arjin and I traveled on, into a landscape that grew wilder and emptier as we went. The trucks disappeared, and the asphalt road turned to dirt. In the distance, at the base of a sheer brown mountain, sprouted a lush grove of trees. "That's where the sister of Nur is buried," Arjin said as we sailed by.

Only later did I realize that by Nur she meant Noah, of Noah's Ark fame, and kicked myself for not stopping and finding out more. The story of the Great Flood is still very much alive all over Kurdistan today, with some Kurds believing that the ark came to rest on Mount Ararat in northeastern

Turkey, and some believing that it landed on Mount Cudi in southern Turkey, just across the border from Zakho.

According to many historians, an unusually severe flood of Mesopotamia and its environs did occur, sometime around 3500 B.C. The region's ancient Sumerians obsessively recorded the event, writing of one man, Utnapishtim, who survived the flood, along with his family and the animals and plants that he took on his ark, as instructed by a god. When the prophet Abraham left Mesopotamia for Turkey, he took the Sumerian legend with him, and, in all probability, it later became the prototype for all Near Eastern deluge stories, including those recorded in the Torah, Bible, and Quran.

The most famous of the Sumerian tales is the Epic of Gilgamesh, the world's oldest surviving epic, which tells the story of King Uruk, who ruled around 2700 B.C. Shortly before the flood, Uruk's good friend Enkidu is killed, and the devastated king sets out to search for immortality, voicing the oldest lament of humankind:

Fearing death I roam over the steppe;
The matter of my friend rests heavy upon me.
How can I be silent? How can I be still?
My friend whom I loved, has turned to clay.
Must I, too, like him, lay me down
Not to rise again for ever and ever?

THE NEXT DAY, Imad came by Arjin's to pick me up. One of Majed and Yousif's younger cousins, he lived and worked in Zakho but had agreed to take me to the family village of Chamsaida in the Barwari district, about two hours away. Arjin had hoped to come, too, but she had family obligations; I sensed that she often had family obligations.

Instead, Imad and I took along another companion—a plainclothes bodyguard. Dr. Shawkat had insisted that I stop at the Zakho mayor's office to request one, as the PKK was active in the Barwari area. He had also nixed my original plan to spend the night in Chamsaida—it wasn't safe, he said. Once again, I wasn't altogether sure how seriously to take his warnings, but once again, I decided to err on the side of caution. Arjin refused to express any opinion regarding the matter, but I saw her repress an amused grin as she watched the three of us drive off.

The bodyguard was a hefty young man who didn't seem at all eager to be spending the day in the country, and I wondered how much help he would be should anything happen. He seemed slow and lethargic, and I had my doubts as to whether he actually knew how to use the pistol fastened to his belt. Imad, slimmer and quicker, seemed the better protector—and also came armed with a pistol.

"Thank you for taking me to Chamsaida," I said to Imad as we set out.

"It is my duty to help you," he said, and I squirmed at the words. Other Kurds had also used them, and I didn't know how to interpret them. For all the generous hospitality I encountered in Kurdistan, treating guests well is one of the tenets of Islam, and I hoped my hosts weren't acting by that precept alone.

We headed east, on a road that ran parallel to the Turkish border and the mountains. With hazy peaks to one side, flat lands to the other, we passed through miles of fertile farmland, peppered with women workers in reds, yellows, and blues—and few men. Then we entered a sea of hills, descended into a valley filled with fruit trees, and came to Batufa, a huge collective town built well before the Anfal. During the early 1970s, this northernmost part of Iraqi Kurdistan had been a stronghold of the KDP, with the road we were traveling along marking the dividing line between KDP-controlled territory and Iraqi-controlled territory. And after the Algiers Accord, the Baath Party had been ruthless, destroying all the area's villages and forcedly relocating thousands of people into Batufa, where many still lived. Batufa had become their home, and they could see little advantage in returning to reconstructed villages that might or might not have all the services to which they'd become accustomed. Besides, the villagers were older now, and they had no desire to tend to crops, orchards, or animals. And neither did their children, who, in any case, didn't know how. Saddam Hussein had won, at least for the moment.

Near Batufa was a small walled cemetery, where we stopped. Inside fluttered two faded green flags, marking the graves of Zembil Firosh and his would-be lover.

Zembil Firosh, whose name means "basketseller," is the hero of a famous Kurdish folktale. The son of a powerful ruler, Zembil Firosh leaves his comfortable home to seek a spiritual life. Transforming himself into a poor dervish, he wanders the countryside with his faithful wife, surviving by making and selling baskets. One day they arrive in the capital of a Kurdish emirate, where the prince's wife sees Zembil Firosh and falls in love. Summoning him to the castle, she declares her love and proposes consummation. Zembil Firosh declines, but she presses, offering him many riches. Still, he refuses, and she locks him in the castle tower, from which he escapes. Heartbroken, she dons a disguise and wanders through the town until she finds his home. Lying to his wife, she convinces her to lend her her clothes and leave the house. When Zembil Firosh returns that night, it is dark, and the prince's wife welcomes him into bed. But a silver ankle bracelet gives her away, and he runs off, closely followed by his would-be lover. When he sees that escape is impossible, he prays to God, asking Him to release him from this world of misery, and God complies. Reaching Zembil Firosh's lifeless body, the prince's wife is so heartbroken that she, too, dies. The townspeople bury them side by side.

What a strange and marvelous story, and how different it is from Western folktales, I thought. Kurdologists point out that the story has Sufi overtones, with both protagonists leaving their comfortable lives in order to search for the Beloved.

But how odd, I also thought, that it is the prince's wife, and not Zembil Firosh's own faithful spouse, who is buried beside him, as if passion carried more heft than fidelity among the Kurds, when the opposite is so powerfully the case in everyday life. I puzzled over the conundrum for months before coming across an explanation. In a seminal 1954 article, folklorist William R. Bascom writes: "the basic paradox of folklore [is] that while it plays a vital role in transmitting and maintaining the institutions of a culture . . . at the same time it provides socially approved outlets for the repressions which these same institutions impose."

BEYOND BATUFA, THE landscape grew wilder, with hills turning into mountains, and fields into cliffs of granite, red, and tan. Each bend of the road, rising ever steeper, revealed new vistas. Snowcapped peaks overhead. A hawk circling in a valley below. The curve of a far-off river. Turkish tanks on a mountainside.

"What are they doing here?" I muttered angrily, mostly to myself.

"Don't ask *me*," Imad said. "*I* am not political. Ask the KDP or the U.S.

government. As the English say, if you eat with the devil, you must have a long spoon."

Back in the valley again, we crossed the Khabur River and passed a half-dozen signs announcing new villages built or being built by the United Nation's Habitat or other aid organizations. Similar signs were posted all over Iraqi Kurdistan, neatly painted plaques that included dates of construction, number of units, and other figures, in a sort of cool assessment of death and rebirth, sans personal stories and suffering.

Turning off, we bumped down a dirt road, over potholes and patches as ridged as a washing board. We passed more of the black, twisted scrub oaks I'd seen everywhere and a strapping young Kurd wearing a General DataComm T-shirt that read: "The future shines so bright, I gotta wear shades." A battered truck hung with pots and pans careened by—a sort of modern Zembil Firosh without Sufi overtones.

Coming to a flooded patch, we stopped. Beyond, a clutch of houses beckoned.

"Welcome to my village." Imad turned off the engine, and I grinned. I loved the way almost everyone I met in Iraq spoke of "my village." Whether he or she lived in a village now or not—or perhaps had never lived in a village—everyone had one, a place of his or her parents and grandparents, a place distinctly his or her own. And even decades after leaving their villages, many Kurds said that they still dreamed of their old communities. We were happiest in our villages, out in the open air, away from the cities, they said, in an idyllic re-creation of a past that for many was now irretrievably lost, as much through modernization as through Saddam Hussein.

Imad and I walked through Chamsaida, the bored guard trailing behind. Before the Anfal, the village had housed about seventy families, but now held only fourteen or fifteen. Imad pointed out a new schoolhouse and showed me several new houses. All had electricity and looked comfortable. But like many other villages I'd visited, the place felt too empty, too unlived in, too new. Like all reconstructed rural Kurdistan, it needed time.

"I lived here until I was six, and then my family moved to Zakho," Imad said as we walked on. "But in 1984, the central government put my father in prison, took away our house in Zakho, and told us to return here. My father's cousin—Majed's father—was an important *peshmerga*, that's why they bothered us." He shrugged. "This is the life," he said, using an expression that Kurds speaking English use often.

Imad showed me the ruins of his family's home, destroyed during the Anfal. Built on a hilltop with splendid views of the valley, dotted with apple orchards, the house had once included a lush garden with flowers imported from Holland and Iran. Imad remembered climbing up a tree that was now a stump, and running down the hill at age six to tell his grandmother that he had a new baby brother.

It had been a different world, and one to which I, too, longed to return.

Climbing the path that led to the orchards, the guard huffing and puffing behind, we passed a steady stream of people returning to the village for lunch. The first was a man in a turban with a donkey, coming back from pruning apple trees. The second was a woman in a green-and-gold *dishdasha* herding a half-dozen lambs who were too young to join the adult flock. The third was a man in extra-baggy pants with a scythe, who had to work alone because all his children were in school.

As each person stopped to talk, I suddenly felt as if I'd fallen into a fable. I was ensconced in a beautiful valley, on a beautiful day, with a stone bridge, a rushing stream, shady walnut trees, and people in fantastic dress. Each person who stopped could tell me something wise and wonderful, drawn from the depths of lives lived close to the earth and to suffering, I thought, if only I could find the right questions to ask.

CHAPTER EIGHT

The Cult of the Angels

I FIRST MET KAMERIN KHAIRY BEG IN THE RESTAURANT OF the Lomana Hotel, next door to the Writers' Union. Majed and Yousif had invited me to lunch, asking me first where I wanted to go. But when I'd suggested finding a popular restaurant serving typical Kurdish food, they'd looked blank—for that kind of meal, they could just stay home. Going out to eat for them meant going somewhere where alcohol was served, and that meant a hotel.

We passed through the Lomana's dark, silent lobby and into its restaurant, lit only by the diffuse natural light of a rainy spring day. A clutch of bored-looking waiters ushered us past a round table at which six men, dressed entirely in white, were seated.

I barely noticed them because directly behind them, at the only other occupied table in the place, sat an extraordinary-looking man. He had a frizzy white beard with a wide dark streak down its middle, a red-and-white-checked head cloth flowing regally around his shoulders, and dazzling white robes whose fine quality was apparent even from afar. Absorbed in his own thoughts, he looked up only briefly as we came in, and then returned to his meal. His face was deeply tanned.

Majed, Yousif, and I sat down at a nearby table, and ordered beers and lunch. I kept stealing glances at the bearded man. Sitting impassively chewing in the darkened restaurant, his face sealed with privacy, he looked utterly unapproachable.

Our beers came, followed by platters of chicken kebab, broiled toma-toes, rice, and greens. Majed and Yousif told me about several buildings vis-ible from the restaurant. Yousif's father had been imprisoned in the basement of one for over a year, during which time no one in the family had known where he was.

Then Majed nodded a hello at the bearded man, who nodded back.

I started. "Who is he?" I asked.

"Kamerin Khairy Beg," Majed said. "He's the son of the prince of the Yezidis."

I was in luck! I had heard much about the Yezidis, often erroneously referred to as "devil worshipers," and felt hungry to learn more about them.

"Can you ask him if I could come visit him sometime?" I asked.

"Ask him yourself," Majed said, grinning. "He speaks some English."

I made my request, and Kamerin Khairy Beg nodded.

"Yes, of course, with great pleasure, I would be honored to welcome you in my home," he said slowly. His unapproachable veneer had completely vanished. Before me sat a gentle and somewhat shy-seeming man with kind, brown eyes.

As it happened, Kamerin Khairy Beg lived in Baadri, the historic home of the Yezidi princes, located in a remote area about two hours from Dohuk. I'd been hoping to travel there for Sarisal, the Yezidi New Year, coming up in mid-April—would it be possible for me to visit then?

Absolutely, Kamerin Khairy Beg replied, the festival would be an excellent time for me to come. I would be his guest, of course—he would send a car for me—and could stay with him and his family as long as I liked.

MOST NON-MUSLIM KURDS belong to one of three religions, which have no direct connection with one another, but which some scholars refer to collectively as the "cult of the angels." Drawing on precepts from both pre-Islamic faiths and Islam, the cult consists of the Yezidis, who live mostly in northern Iraq; the Ahl-e Haqq, or Kakais, who live primarily near the Iran-Iraq border; and the Alevis, who live mostly in Turkey. Scholars dis-agree as to the number of believers in the religions, but estimates range from one-tenth to a probably exaggerated one-quarter of all Kurds, with the largest group being the Alevis and the smallest being the Yezidis. The Alevi

Kurds may number about 1.5 million, the Ahl-e Haqq about 700,000, and the Yezidis about 300,000.

All three religions believe in one God, and in seven divine angels who protect the universe from seven dark forces. Good and evil were both present at creation, the cult holds, and are equally important in the continuation of the material world. A belief in the transmigration of souls through reincarnation is also central to the religious group, which is a universalist one, meaning that it regards all other religions as legitimate.

Both the Ahl-e Haqq and the Alevis worship Imam Ali, the son-in-law of the Prophet Muhammad, and the main prophet of Shiite Islam, and Ismail of the Safavid dynasty, who first spread Shiism across Iran in the sixteenth century. The groups are therefore sometimes classified as being on the extreme edge of Shiism, although for the Ahl-e Haqq, their founder Soltan Sahak is far more important than are Ali and Ismail.

Only the Yezidis are exclusively Kurdish. Over one-half of Alevis are Turk, while some Ahl-e Haqq are Turcoman. The Alevi religion contains Turkic shaman elements, as well as Shiite and Zoroastrian ideas, while the Ahl-e Haqq draw on Shiism, Zoroastrianism, and Manichaeism, a gnostic sect that began in the A.D. 200s. The Yezidi religion is a mix of pagan, Zoroastrian, and Manichaean beliefs, overlaid with Christian, Jewish, and Sufi Muslim elements.

The Yezidis' reputation for devil worship is based on their veneration of Melek Tawus, the Peacock Angel, who is the chief of the seven angels. As in Judaism, Christianity, and Islam, the religion holds that after God created man, one angel refused to bow down before the mortal, as God ordered, and was thereupon cast out of heaven. In the three major monotheisms, this angel — Satan — remains forever damned, but in Yezidism, God forgives the angel, named Melek Tawus, and reinstates him.

Melek Tawus's emblem is the peacock, and the religion's most revered object is a life-sized bronze figure known as the Great Peacock. One ceremonial practice, begun in the nineteenth century, involves taking one of six brass replicas of the Great Peacock to every single Yezidi community, no matter how small, for the collection of alms. Over the last fifty years, however, due to wars and repression, some replicas have been "retired."

A persecuted group within a persecuted group, the followers of the three religions have suffered repeated violence at the hands of Muslim neighbors. During the Ottoman regime, at least twenty pogroms were waged by Turks against Yezidis, resulting in mass migrations to the Russian Caucasus. In the early 1500s, tens of thousands of Alevis were slaughtered by Sultan the Grim for suspected pro-Persian sympathies. Throughout Persian history, the Ahl-e Haqq have been shunned, vilified, and, as late as the 1920s, cruci-fied and lynched by Muslims. All three groups have been repeatedly and falsely accused of sexual promiscuity.

In Iraq, the Yezidis are often referred to as the "original Kurds." The reference is an odd one, seemingly based more in politics than in fact. The phrase is often used by Kurds with a dislike for Islam, by Kurds who want to see Yezidism more closely associated with Zoroastrianism, an "Aryan" religion, and by Kurds eager to place the Yezidis squarely in the Kurdish political camp. In fact, most Yezidis, who are Kurds, do actively support the Kurdish cause. But the Baath regime declared them to be Arab, and the Kurdish leadership, cognizant of the group's strategic position on the Iraqi-Kurdistan border, fought back by publicly honoring the Yezidis as "original Kurds," and using the pre-Islamic elements of their religion to promote a secular Kurdish nationalism.

SHORTLY AFTER MEETING Kamerin Khairy Beg, I visited the Yezidi Cultural Center, not far from Majed's house. A broad walkway led to its front door, where I was ceremoniously received by about ten men who swept me down a dark and drafty hallway, into an equally dark and drafty room. Most of the men wore red-and-white turbans, and many sported the walruslike mustaches for which the Yezidi are famed.

Sitting upon dilapidated sofas and chairs, we nodded hellos. Cans of soda were popped, and we nodded some more. Then we waited. Though they were obviously expecting me—Dr. Shawkat had called—no one spoke English.

One hour later, Dr. Khairy and Mr. Fadhil arrived. Dr. Khairy came in first—a small, gaunt man in a formal black suit with cheekbones that seemed sharp enough to cut through the lucent pallor of his skin. Mr. Fadhil followed. Though somewhat taller and bigger than Dr. Khairy, he was equally thin, with a broad and creased brow, worn brown suit, and rum-pled white shirt. Between the two of them—one a medical doctor, the other an English teacher—they spoke passable English. They were also close friends.

"What can we do for you?" Dr. Khairy said.

I explained that I wanted to learn more about Yezidi culture and history.

"Yes, well, we don't know much about our culture or history ourselves," he said. "We're trying to learn that now. This is the first time in many years that we can have our own religion. We couldn't do it before. The Iraqi regime didn't accept it."

"We don't know what it means to be Yezidi," Mr. Fadhil added.

"But don't you have a museum?" I asked, feeling disappointed. "Or hold concerts or lectures?" To me, a cultural center connoted some sort of cultural activity, though from what I'd seen so far, the place did seem to be nothing more than a dilapidated social club.

"We're trying to make one now," Dr. Khairy said. "Do you want to see?"

The two men led me down the hall to a small room. Inside were a few dusty exhibits showcasing traditional dress, household items, and farm implements.

"The center was only founded in 1992, after the uprising," Dr. Khairy said apologetically. "We have no money."

Of course, I thought, embarrassed at my own obtuseness.

"Many of our villages were destroyed, especially in Shaikhan and Sinjar," Dr. Khairy said, mentioning the two areas, still under Baathist control, where most Yezidis live.

"But they didn't destroy Lalish," Mr. Fadhil said, with a nod of satisfaction.

My ears pricked up at the mention of the holy shrine of the Yezidis, located in a valley enclosed by mountains, about an hour and a half from Dohuk. Lalish contains the tomb of the mystic Shaikh Adi ibn Musafir, the great prophet of the Yezidi religion. The son of a Muslim holy man, Adi was born in a Lebanese village around A.D. 1075, and studied in Baghdad with Sufi masters, before retreating to the remote Lalish valley. Discovering a region of great beauty, he remained there the rest of his life. A man emaciated with fasting, renowned for his piety and miraculous powers, he was said to recite the entire Quran twice every night. Pilgrims came from far and wide to see him.

Yezidi legend has it a bit differently, saying that Shaikh Adi was miraculously born to an elderly couple, and left home at age fifteen to seek his fortune. Five years later, riding across a plain bathed in moonlight, he passed a tomb, where an apparition arose before him. Terrified, Adi knocked over a jug of water nearby. The apparition turned into a boy with a peacock's tail who told him to fear not, he was Melek Tawus, come to reveal to him the religion of the true world. The Peacock Angel took Adi's soul to heaven for seven years, where God taught him the truth of everything while he slept. When his soul was returned to his body, Adi awoke to find the water still running out of the overturned jug.

"I would like to go to Lalish," I said to the two men. "Can you help me?"

"Yes, yes, of course, we can take you," Dr. Khairy said, with some enthusiasm.

"It's our job to introduce our religion to foreigners," Mr. Fadhil added, with considerably less enthusiasm.

LEAVING DOHUK A FEW days later, we passed a simple checkpoint of the type that guarded all towns in northern Iraq, and turned onto a road zigzagging up a rocky mountain. Though it was only midmorning, families were already out, setting up tents and building bonfires for picnics. A pickup truck packed with goats passed, followed by flocks of jogging sheep, their plump, wooly bodies swaying to and fro above short, stubby legs. The voice of Ibrahim Tatlis, a popular Kurdish singer from Turkey, drifted out.

We stopped to pick wildflowers—mostly the scarlet, purple, or yellow *sheqayiq* (ranunculus) that were everywhere, but also red *gulale* (poppies) and tall stately *hero* (hollyhocks). Both the Kurdish men and women love flowers, and will stop to pick them when given the chance.

The final approach to Lalish was narrow and hilly, bracketed with trees and boulders, and more picnicking families. Three men dancing merrily together, one chubby face beaming, caught my eye. Then I spotted the tops of two fluted cones—the signature architecture of the Yezidi tombs—and we arrived at an enclave of cream-colored buildings, cars parked in a large lot out front. Sitting atop a nearby wall were dozens of men and boys in traditional dress, talking, nudging, and nibbling on seeds and nuts.

Before getting out of the car, Dr. Khairy and Mr. Fadhil removed their shoes. All Yezidis must go without shoes in the holy city, they said. As a visitor, I could wear mine until we entered the temple. I shivered on their behalf. The spring day was cold and wet.

Several round old women in voluminous dress greeted Dr. Khairy. He kissed their gnarled hands, and they kissed the top of his head in an age-old gesture that seemed straight out of a medieval world.

Climbing up a few wide steps, we reached a paved courtyard where cross-legged vendors were sitting before neat piles of seeds and nuts. A bare-

Outside Shaikh Adi's shrine

foot woman in a plain white sheath and head scarf appeared, lugging buckets brimming with water. Seeing my camera, she stared fixedly down at her feet and hurried by, water slopping around her.

"She is *faqriyat*—like a nun," Dr. Khairy said.

To the right of the courtyard stood a gateway with heavy wooden doors that marked the entrance to the sanctuary. *Don't step on the threshold!* Dr. Khairy and Mr. Fadhil warned me repeatedly as we approached; as soon as we crossed over, they ordered me to remove my shoes.

We were at the top of a flight of stairs leading down into a second paved courtyard, shaded with mulberry trees. To the right was a maze of living quarters and reception areas where we would later eat lunch, while straight ahead was another doorway, this one marked with ancient inscriptions, geometric designs, and a six-foot-tall vertical figure of a snake. Blackened with soot or shoe polish, the dark reptile seemed to jump out of its dull stone background with an immediacy that made me shiver.

"Yezidis respect all black snakes," Dr. Khairy said. "Because during the great flood, when Noah's Ark hit a mountain and made a hole in the ark, the black snake put himself in the hole and saved humanity. For this, we never kill black snakes."

Crossing the second threshold, made smooth by pilgrims' kisses, we passed into a dark, cavernous room—the shrine's main hall. The floor was black and wet, and my socks immediately became soaked and icy. I could hear water plashing somewhere to my right, while straight ahead were five pillars draped with red and green cloths. Dirty chandeliers hung from the ceilings and crooked prayer rugs from the walls.

We headed to the sound of the water—a deep cistern whose source was the holy White Spring. All Yezidi temples must be built over a spring, Dr. Khairy said, as a portly *faqir*, or pious man, with a wandering eye arrived. Dressed in elegant black pajama-like garments edged with red and a black-and-red head cloth, he took care of the temple, living out back. He pointed out several sticky charred spots. On every Tuesday night, 366 fires were lit all over Lalish, he said. The fires marked the eve of the Yezidis' holy day, Wednesday, and were fueled by olive oil and wool wicks spun by the *faqriyat*. As he spoke, I longed to return to see these lights—flicking, licking up all over, like fireflies, like tongues.

Passing from the main room, we entered a large chamber containing the chest-high tomb of Shaikh Adi, draped with more red and green cloths. A marble facade covered the lower part of the room, while higher up were broken pieces of mirrored mosaic and a conical dome—the interior of a fluted cone I'd seen outside.

Near Shaikh Adi's chamber began the "caves," a series of natural underground rooms with rounded stone walls and flagstone floors. Some contained dozens of waist-high clay urns once filled with olive oil, others contained more tombs. We had to duck our heads lower and lower as we passed between the rooms until, finally, we dropped almost to our knees to crawl through the last doorway and descend a short stairway into a cavern housing the Yezidis' sacred Zamzam Spring.

"This is our holiest area, we don't let Muslims visit," Dr. Khairy said as I looked around the small enclosed space, water gushing out of the wall and into a stone channel. The water is said to cure all ailments.

"You are Christian, and so you are our friend," the *faqir* said.

"You are only here because you are our guest," Mr. Fadhil added pointedly.

Historically, the Yezidis have maintained the utmost secrecy regarding their faith, believing that secrets protected them. Only in the last few years have some come to the realization that exposure can help rather than harm them, by providing outsiders with a better understanding of their religion and culture.

As we left the main shrine to tour various smaller ones nearby, Dr. Khairy and Mr. Fadhil told me more about the customs and beliefs of the Yezidis. We pray three times a day, and when we pray we face the sun, they said. Mecca has no significance for us, but we respect it because it is Abraham's house, and Abraham came before every religion. We do not get married in April—it is the month of the angels. Traditional Yezidis do not eat lettuce—they say it is the hiding place of evil—or wear the color blue. It is the color of Islam. We prefer to wear white.

"What about the mustache?" I said. "Why do Yezidi men have such big mustaches?"

"It makes us better listeners," Dr. Khairy said.

"It keeps secrets in," Mr. Fadhil said with a grin.

WHEN I ARRIVED in Baadri, the historic home of the Yezidi princes, about two weeks later, I was surprised to find myself in what looked like any other northern Iraqi town, swollen with refugees and squat concrete buildings. The Baadri that I'd read about had been small, dominated by an elite class of Yezidis, some living in castles. I'd also expected Baadri to be in the mountains, like Lalish, but it sat exposed in a shallow valley, surrounded by rolling brown fields.

Kamerin Khairy Beg and a clutch of armed guards waited for me outside his home, near a front gate adorned with peacocks. The Yezidi leader was again dressed all in white, but today his robes were of simple muslin.

From atop his sprawling, single-story house fluttered the yellow flag of the KDP.

Solicitously ushering me into his home, my host seated me in a long reception room and promptly disappeared. I breathed in deeply, luxuriating. The room was unremarkably furnished with heavy armchairs, couches, and coffee tables, with a pastel mural of Lalish covering the entire far wall. Nonetheless, the place had a magical, out-of-time feel. I could easily imagine Yezidi tribal chiefs meeting here.

Kamerin Beg reappeared, now dressed in a tawny, finely woven *shal u shapik* with very thin, widely spaced, red and green stripes.

"I am very, very happy you have come," he said. "Thank you for visiting me."

I returned the compliment, honored that he had changed on my behalf, as a servant glided in with steaming glasses of tea.

Kamerin Beg's English was basic, but we could communicate. Despite his bushy white beard, with its wide streak of dark gray, he was also younger than I'd previously thought—early fifties rather than mid-sixties.

Kamerin Beg's father had been the leading Yezidi prince in Iraqi Kurdistan and a member of the Kurdish Parliament until his death in 1997, my host said. He himself was the oldest son and had studied law in Egypt, graduating in 1979, before working as a lawyer in Mosul for seventeen years. After his father's death, he'd returned to Baadri to take his father's place and help his people.

I listened with surprise. My initial impression of Kamerin Beg as an unsophisticated tribal leader with little experience of the outside world had been way off the mark.

Despite the stature of Kamerin Beg's father, he had not been *mir*, or the supreme Yezidi prince; that honor belonged to Kamerin Beg's uncle, Tahsin Beg, who lived in Shaikhan, in Baathist-controlled Iraq. Later, others told me that there'd been a rift in the princely family, with Tahsin Beg coerced into cooperating with the Baath regime. But Kamerin Beg told me only that he himself couldn't travel to the Iraqi side because of his close connections with the Kurdistan government.

"We have had much trouble in our history," he said. "We say there have been seventy-two genocide attacks against the Yezidis. These were all Muslim attacks, most by Turks."

"What about Muslim Kurds?" I asked.

He shrugged. "In the past, sometimes. But we have no trouble now."

A servant entered with a tray of colored eggs, and offered it to me. It was the day before the Yezidi New Year, held on the first Wednesday in April of the Yezidi calendar, which begins thirteen days later than the Christian one. During the festival, the Yezidis paste nosegays of red flowers over doorways and give and receive colored eggs.

"Why colored eggs?" I asked. Raised in a Protestant family, I'd colored Easter eggs as a child, but it had never occurred to me that the ritual might have ancient roots, shared with other religions.

"Eggs because God had a jewel, which, when it exploded, became gases and the earth," he said. "And the same thing happens when an egg is opened. Colors because with the spring comes the colors of plants, and eggs and plants are the beginning of life."

Kamerin Beg's wife entered. Dressed in multiple long layers, she was small and round—"like a Hindi," Kamerin Beg said. It was time to go to the graves, he added—I had requested going to the graves, hadn't I?

We climbed into a waiting Land Cruiser, Kamerin Beg's oldest son behind the wheel, his father beside him, and his mother, younger siblings, and I in back. I had asked to see the graves of Ali Beg and his wife Mayan Khatoun, renowned figures in Yezidi history. Ali Beg had ruled as *mir* from 1899 until 1913, endured torture rather than change his religion, and been found murdered in his bed one morning.

But it was Mayan Khatoun who really interested me. Born in 1874, and also of the princely family, she had been beautiful, intelligent, bold, sly, deceitful, and ruthless. Some had even accused her of masterminding her husband's murder. Whatever the facts, Mayan Khatoun claimed to have solved the crime, and had a family of suspected usurpers—husband, wife, four sons, and two daughters—arrested and sentenced. Wearing a red dress as a symbol of revenge, she watched as her guard shot all the family except the two girls, whom she later adopted. She then rose calmly from her chair, walked over to the bodies, touched their still-warm blood, and licked her finger. And the next morning, she reputedly replaced her red dress with the black one traditionally worn by Yezidi widows.

After Ali Beg's death, the Yezidi leaders agreed that Said Beg, Ali and Mayan's son, should be the next *mir*. As he was still too young to rule, Mayan was appointed his guardian and administrator of the princely revenues, a role she did not relinquish until her death at age eighty-three in

1957. Serving first as regent for her son, a weak man whom she despised, and then her grandson, it was she and not they who ruled over the Yezidis throughout the demise of the Ottoman Empire, the establishment of Iraq, and World War II.

At the Baadri cemetery, Mayan Khatoun and Ali Beg were buried beneath fluted, cone-shaped spires of the type I'd seen at Lalish. We had to traipse past other overgrown graves to reach them, and when we entered, we found a dozen men seated in a circle on the floor before Ali Beg's walk-in tomb. Most were dressed in *shal u shapik* and red-and-white turbans, and had huge white mustaches. Several were astonishingly fat.

Everyone lumbered to their feet to kiss the hands of Kamerin Beg and his wife. She responded by kissing their heads, and a few women material-ized out of nowhere, one wearing the traditional red-and-green dress and silver-and-black turban of the Yezidi women. Candy was passed in honor of the New Year. Two women supplicants entered to visit Ali Beg's tomb, care-ful not to step on its threshold, covered with a thick layer of *dinar* bills.

"Where is Mayan Khatoun's grave?" I asked, and was pointed toward a flat and disappointingly nondescript grave near the door, marked only by an inscription on the wall. With death, the patriarchal order had reestablished itself.

The ruins of Ali Beg and Mayan Khatoun's palace still stood on a small hill. As we stopped to visit, the owners of a nearby house rushed out to kiss hands and invite us into their garden for tea. I could sense their excitement when we accepted, and there was much running to and fro as chairs were set up in a semicircle overlooking the town.

We sat down, birdsongs weaving around us. A man came out with a pitcher of water and a single glass that he refilled for each person in turn, followed by a woman carrying a silver-colored tray, about three feet in diam-eter and piled high with fruit. Both the single water glass and the silver tray were trademarks of Kurdistan. I encountered them everywhere, and mar-veled at the way the women could hoist the huge platters, often loaded with dishes, from the floor to above their shoulders in a single smooth swoop.

After the fruit came "chicklets," meaning candy, followed by more col-ored eggs, orange juice, and tea. Kamerin Beg instructed me how to take a colored egg, hold it in my fist, and tap the end of his egg while he tapped back. It was a New Year's game, and there was a knack to it; whoever cracked the other's egg first, won.

"Three things are special for the Yezidi men." Kamerin Beg fumbled around inside his shirt, pulling out a small pouch, which he opened to reveal a pebble. "One is the Lalish pebble, made from the dust of Shaikh Adi's tomb. It brings us good luck, and we give it to our enemies to make peace. It can pass from men to men, but not from men to women. My wife also has one, which can pass only to women."

He said something in Kurdish to her, and she smiled, but didn't oblige by pulling out her own pebble. She had been smoking steadily since our arrival, and each time she reached for her cigarettes, one of our hosts hurried over with a light, which she languidly accepted without a word of thanks.

"Another is our mustache," Kamerin Beg said. "It is our duty to wear a mustache. And a third is our white undershirt."

Kamerin Beg then offered to show me Shaikhan, still under Baathist control, and led me to the end of the hill beyond the palace ruins. We gazed west, over a rolling brown plain peppered with darker brown settlements—all in Saddam Hussein's territory, only two or three miles away, with no real barricades between.

"My uncle and brother live there—that's Shaikhan," Kamerin Beg said, pointing to one of the larger settlements, as I suddenly realized with a shock that his uncle, Tahsin Beg, the current Yezidi *mir*, must be Mayan Khatoun's grandson. As otherworldly as the Yezidi history seemed to me, it was no fairy tale.

KAMERIN BEG AND I continued our conversation later, in the garden behind his house. Dusk had fallen, and a bulldozer moved through town below us, its hungry mouth raised in the air, as if to catch the emerging stars. Giggling children peeked at us from behind a nearby wall until a man with a yellowing mustache big as a kitchen brush appeared to chase them away.

Kamerin Beg began to list for me the dozens of Yezidi villages that had been destroyed, partially destroyed, or moved by the Iraqi government— some before Saddam Hussein came to power, but most afterward. I tried to write them down at first, but finally gave up, confused by the seemingly endless litany of strange names.

A man in a turban and slippers approached, carrying a small silver urn and two handle-less ceramic cups. He poured Kamerin Beg a swallow of coffee, and then offered one to me, before wiping out the cups and serving a second round.

I would encounter the same ritual later in the homes of other Kurdish *aghas*, but it wasn't until I reached Turkey and saw a museum exhibit on *mirra*, meaning "bitter coffee," that I understood how widespread the practice is—or was, as it is dying out. The coffee brewer, who holds a privileged position in his employer's household, must always carry the urn in the right hand, the two special cups in his left. He must serve the eldest or most respected guests first, then, after serving everyone once, begin a second round. Only important personages can serve *mirra*, and should a poor man become wealthy, he must invite the elite of his village to a feast, where he asks permission to serve the brew.

"Saddam Hussein tried to enter Baadri one year ago," Kamerin said. "When there was no Bush, no Clinton."

"During the presidential inauguration, you mean?" I said, startled.

He nodded. "They came and surrounded the town for three days."

"What did you do?" I couldn't imagine the scenario. Baadri didn't seem capable of defending itself for more than ten minutes.

"I telephoned to Dohuk for *peshmerga*, and they came. They prevented the Iraqis from entering. There was some firing, but no one was hurt. The United Nations interfered."

Why had that mini invasion taken place, and why had it ended? The Iraqis could easily have taken Baadri if they'd wanted. And how many other mini invasions of Kurdistan had occurred?, invasions we public heard nothing about in the United States.

THE NEXT MORNING, Kamerin Beg excused himself after a light breakfast, saying that it was time for him to go to the "house of the old men." By this, he meant a dark building next door, housing a long hall and small kitchen. The "old men" were the villagers who dropped by every morning to ask for his advice or blessing. Today, there would be many of them, paying their respects for the New Year.

I followed my host about a half hour later, assuming that since it was still early, the hall would be half empty. But by the door of the building nested dozens upon dozens of black shoes, many made of plastic and edged with drying mud. My heart sank a little—so many strangers' eyes lay ahead.

Entering, I found the hall packed with even more men than the empty shoes had prepared me for. Numbering about seventy or eighty, they rimmed the entire room—talking, smoking—with Kamerin Beg sitting in the center of one long wall, near the wood stove that was the hall's only furnishing.

He beckoned to me, putting me more at ease, and made room for me beside him, dislodging a young, heavyset man in the process. I sat down on the thin carpet, my mind swirling, unable to take it all in.

Before me sat an astonishing array of faces, heads, and bodies, most well worn with age and the elements, and clothed in striking costumes. There were turbans of red and white, black and white, pale pink, and solid white, some piled high on the head in a double spiral, some just a modest ring, and some draping down around the shoulders. There were flowing white gowns of the kind usually worn by Arabs, bulky woolen jackets, and hand-woven *shal u shapik* with wide brown-and-white stripes. One younger man was in starched, pale green *khak* worn with an electric green shirt and burnt orange sash. Another older man was entirely in white, from his socks to his turban, except for a richly textured black cape.

A few men had old-fashioned pistols, a few had tobacco pouches, and many had prayer beads. And whenever there was a lull in the conversation, the *click-click-click* of the beads was all that was heard.

The men in the flowing white gowns were Yezidis originally from the Sinjar region in Baathist-occupied Iraq, Kamerin Beg explained to me. That was the style there, due to Arab influence, and even though the men had been forced out of their homes following the Algiers Accord in 1975, they had never changed their dress. The brown-and-white-striped *shal u shapik* were typical of Dohuk province, and the heavyset man whom I'd displaced was now a citizen of Norway, back to collect his wife and children.

Every time a new man entered, *"b'kher-hati"* came from all sides, as the man crossed the room to kiss Kamerin Beg's hand. And occasionally, when the guest was very old or distinguished-looking, our host stood up, to embrace him or kiss his head. Others then cleared a space for the new man on the floor, and servants proffered him a tray laid with open packets of cigarettes—Kent, Victory, Craven—followed by a tray of colored eggs, and a splash of bitter coffee from the silver urn. Kamerin Beg oversaw these proceedings carefully, making sure no man was slighted.

By ten-thirty or eleven, the crowd was thinning out, and we moved to the reception room of the main house. I naively thought that the visiting was nearly done. But almost immediately, it started all over again, this time with mostly younger guests, some dressed in *khak*, some in pants and crisp shirts, and some in suits and ties.

Throughout, I was the only woman in the room. The Yezidi women, I thought I was told at one point, were visiting in the back, but when I went to investigate, I found only Kamerin Beg's wife, daughter-in-law, and children, looking bored.

Two English-speaking doctors from Mosul arrived. They had crossed the Iraq-Kurdistan border secretly at night, traveling the back roads, taking a chance, in order to be in Baadri for the New Year. Kurds from apolitical families, which often meant uneducated, poor villagers, could usually cross the border in either direction without incident. Kurds from political families, which usually meant better-educated urban folk, could not. Heading either way, they would be subject to interrogation and perhaps worse.

A half hour later, a local official appeared with an entourage that included a TV cameraman, causing the two doctors to rise abruptly. We're sorry to be so rude, they said to me as they slipped away, but we don't want to run the risk of being seen on television.

Car doors started slamming on the driveway outside, and, a moment later, in swept two Chaldean bishops and a group of Assyrians, arriving together "by chance," someone whispered to me, while explaining that the two Christian groups didn't always get along. Like Bishop Raban of Amadiya, the Chaldean bishops were dressed in long black robes with fuchsia caps and belts, while the Assyrians wore black suits.

Both groups had come to wish the Yezidis a happy and prosperous New Year. Both had their contingent of guards, and photographers, including two Assyrian visitors from Australia, who snapped dozens of shots as the religious leaders drank tea together. Unable to understand Kurdish, Arabic, or Syriac, I wondered how much of all this goodwill was political.

Then, suddenly, we were all rising and crossing the yard, back to the "house of the old men." Apparently, it was time for lunch. Reentering the hall, men flowing around me, I saw a long skinny cloth on the floor, stretching the entire length of the room. Place settings for about fifty rimmed its edge, while in its middle rose heaping platters of rice and lamb, wheat and chicken, broiled whole fish, flat bread, and fresh greens. A Pepsi or Fanta soda can stood at each setting.

The men sat down quickly and began digging in, eating with spoons and fingers made slick with grease. From the head of the table, Kamerin Beg beckoned, and I sat down beside him and the older Chaldean bishop, who was gingerly balancing himself atop two cushions. But I had barely started eating when many of the men started rising again, already finished, to leave the room as abruptly as they'd entered.

We returned to the reception room for fruit and glasses of tea. Then it was time to go. The Chaldeans left first, followed by the Assyrians. Finally, only Kamerin Beg, a few neighbors, and I were left.

"I am sorry you are leaving," Kamerin Beg said, his kind eyes tired. "I wish you could stay."

He looked as if he meant it. The room felt cold and deserted, the chilly wind of an uncertain future brushing against our necks. The Baathists were only a few miles away. Anything could happen here.

A FEW MONTHS later, I visited the shrine of Soltan Sahak, the founder of the Ahl-e Haqq religion, in Iranian Kurdistan. The shrine was located in Perdiwar, an isolated spot between the southwestern Iranian city of Paveh and the Iran-Iraq border. With me was a high school student who spoke moderately good English, and one of his relatives, who was our driver.

The late-afternoon sun was pouring gold over our windshield by the time we pulled off the main road and onto the circuitous dirt lane that led to the shrine. Bumping our way along, we crisscrossed slopes bristling with bleached grasses, while below meandered the Sirwan River, shining with a strange, bright, dark green color—perhaps the effect of algae. No other person or vehicle was in sight.

As we pulled up to the compound that enclosed the shrine, I wondered for a moment if it was closed—it was so still and quiet. But then I noticed a souvenir shop where a vendor with a bushy mustache was lounging, half asleep.

Another mustachioed man wearing a loose shirt and sandals came out to greet us. As the guardian of the shrine, he, Taher Naderi, would be happy to give us a tour, he said. His family had protected Soltan Sahak's tomb for over eight hundred years, ever since the Soltan's death, when a Naderi ancestor had been by his side and pledged to take care of his body.

The Soltan's shrine was divided into two small rooms, with a tall marble tomb in the second chamber. Dozens of prayer rugs and photos hung on the walls, most depicting a doe-eyed man with a green mantle draped over his head. This was Imam Ali, founder of Shiism and a prophet for the Ahl-e Haqq.

Soltan Sahak had been born in the holy town of Barzinja, in Iraq, Taher told us as we left the tomb, and had come to Iran only later. When he first arrived, the sound of the river had been very loud, but Soltan prayed and now—*listen!*—the river was very quiet.

I had read about Soltan Sahak. As the story goes, before his birth, three dervishes visited his father, Shaikh Ise, then an old man, and urged him to marry again. The *shaikh*, who already had three sons, tried to excuse himself, but the dervishes insisted, and he finally gave in, saying that he fancied the daughter of a local *agha*. Upon hearing the proposal, the *agha* was outraged—he would never marry his daughter to such an old man!—and ordered the dervishes torn to pieces. But no sooner had they been killed than they came to life again. This happened two more times, until the *agha* finally agreed to allow the marriage if the dervishes carpeted the road leading to his door with expensive rugs, brought him a thousand mules loaded with gold, and awarded him ten thousand camels and the same number of horses and sheep. The threesome went away and came back in the morning with all that he had requested. The couple was wed, and, a year later, in 1272 or 1273, Soltan Sahak was born.

"Why are mustaches so important to the Ahl-e Haqq?" I asked Taher, remembering the Yezidis' mustaches. The Ahl-e Haqq wore theirs equally thick and long.

We were walking back to the front of the complex. To one side were dormitories for pilgrims; to another, a white-tiled room with meat hooks, where worshipers brought their sheep and goats to be sacrificed.

"So we can recognize each other; it's a sign of our faith," he said. "And when someone comes here whose mustache is too short, I don't let him in."

It took me a moment to realize that he was joking.

"Do you know why Muslims fast for thirty days, but Ahl-e Haqq fast for only three?" he asked.

I shook my head, though I had heard that the Ahl-e Haqq, along with the Yezidis and Alevis, did not observe Ramadan, the Muslim month of fasting.

"Because the Holy Prophet Muhammad's hearing was not so good! And when God said you must fast three days, he thought he said thirty!"

I tried to ask more questions about the Ahl-e Haqq, but Taher declined to answer, saying he was no expert. I suspected there was more to it than that. Like the Yezidis, too many painful memories of persecution have taught the Ahl-e Haqq to keep their beliefs deeply hidden.

Nearing the front of the complex, Taher invited us into his home for tea, and we entered a spare room where his wife was already heating water and preparing plates of fruit and fresh white cheese. Made from curdled milk flavored with herbs, the cheese is a staple throughout Greater Kurdistan.

In one corner of the room lay a *tambur*, a kind of long-necked lute. One of the world's oldest instruments, originating thousands of years ago, the *tambur* far predates the Ahl-e Haqq faith and is popular throughout Iran. But the instrument has become central to the religion, so much so that a *tambur* can be found in virtually every Ahl-e Haqq home, and most of Iran's best *tambur* players are Ahl-e Haqq.

The Ahl-e Haqq believe that when God created Adam and Eve, God wanted to put a piece of His soul inside Adam, but the soul didn't want to go, a musician told me later in Tehran. So God said to Gabriel, "Go inside Adam's body and play the *tambur*." Gabriel obeyed and played a beautiful song called "Tarz," which is still played today. The piece of God's soul became bewildered. He liked the song very much, but where was it coming from? He approached Adam, and the music pulled and pulled, finally pulling the piece of soul inside.

I asked Taher and his wife if it was difficult for them to live so far away from any settlement, at the end of a road that would become impassable with snow in the winter, mud in the spring. Taher looked confused at my question, then shrugged. Sometimes it was lonely in winter, he said, but in spring, summer, and fall, the shrine was always busy. Didn't I know that the Soltan's shrine was as important to the Ahl-e Haqq as Mecca was to Muslims? Pilgrims came from all over, and on major holy days, the place was so crowded that you couldn't even find a place to sit! Even Shiites and Sunnis believed in Soltan Sahak, and came here when they were sick, leaving a few hours later, miraculously cured.

As he spoke, I suspected that I was talking to a happy man.

———

ONE SUNDAY IN Istanbul, my new friends Ali, an economist, and Sheri, an architect, took me to a *cem*—an Alevi religious ceremony. Ali and Sheri were both Alevi Kurds, but they had never attended a *cem* before and were going only on my behalf. Like many younger urban Kurds in Turkey, and Americans, organized religion did not play much of a role in their lives. They could answer few of my questions about the Alevi faith, and they had as little curiosity about it as I have about Christianity.

Of Turkey's perhaps 3.5 million Alevis, almost half are Kurdish. Their heartland is Tunceli, known as Dersim in Kurdish, a hardscrabble city some distance north of southeast Turkey, where most Sunni Kurds live. The Alevis have a strong humanist tradition, celebrating their religion with song and dance, and often educating their daughters as well as their sons. The Alevis are also known for their leftist politics, which have often pitted them against Turkey's rightist government, with disastrous consequences.

The Alevi Turks and Alevi Kurds are two separate groups, in frequent disagreement with each other. Historically, however, the chasm between the Alevi Kurds and the Sunni Kurds has been far greater. Traditionally, the Sunni Kurds have viewed the Alevis as irreligious and unclean, abhorring their lack of mosques, ritual ablutions, and prayer. And the Alevi Kurds in turn have often viewed the Sunni Kurds as ignorant and backward. God is in the heart, not in ritual and prayer, they say, and ridicule the Sunnis for "hitting the ground with their heads five times a days."

Only in the modern era have the Alevi Kurds and Sunni Kurds become more closely aligned—and largely because of the Kurdish-Turkish civil war. Whatever his faults, PKK leader Abdullah Öcalan succeeded in uniting various disparate Kurdish elements, and many Alevi Kurds joined with Sunni Kurds in their armed struggle against the Turkish state.

Ali, Sheri, and I arrived at the Shakulu Sultan Cemevi around midday. The large, whitewashed complex was filled with inviting gardens, cobblestone courtyards, towering leafy trees, and hundreds of men, women, and children. Near the entrance was a modern bookshop, tables loaded with books and CDs, and an animal pen crowded with sheep. The sheep were available for purchase and sacrifice.

Following a voice drifting out of loudspeakers overhead, we entered a twelve-sided room filled with worshipers. Most of the women sat on one side, most of the men on the other, but there was some intermingling and much informality, as children came and went and adults whispered to one another. Some of the women were covered in head scarves and long dresses, others wore tight blue jeans and T-shirts. By the door, directing traffic, reigned a portly man with a cane.

At the front of the room sat a frail old man with a full white beard, three-piece olive green suit, dapper hat, and dark sunglasses, swaying gently. He was known as a "grandfather," or *dede*, Sheri whispered. Beside him sat another bearded old man, this one wearing a cap, and a somewhat younger man in a suit, with a beard and mustache.

The *dede* started chanting through a microphone, "Allah, Allah, Allah," while the other old man joined in with words of prayer. All of the supplicants sat up on their knees and bent their heads, while a man on a *saz*, or lute, started a disjointed strumming. "Ya Allah, Ya Allah," the worshipers prayed.

As I enjoyed the peaceful scene, I contrasted it in my mind with the Alevis' difficult history, beginning with the rise of the Ottoman Empire in 1514, when Sultan the Grim massacred about forty thousand Alevis, whom he suspected of supporting the Safavids. Ever afterward, the Ottoman Sunnis treated the Alevis with utmost contempt, an attitude that lingers among some in the modern era. Throughout the twentieth century, the Alevis were the frequent targets of violence, with the most brutal campaign occurring in 1937–38, when Turkey's President Atatürk used poison gas and heavy artillery to quash an incipient rebellion. Perhaps forty thousand Alevis died in the attack. And in 1978, at least 109 Alevis were massacred and 176 badly injured during a rampage by the right-wing Grey Wolves, who ripped children from the bellies of pregnant mothers and hung up dead men on electricity poles, saying that it was their duty to wipe out "the enemy within."

The most recent large-scale Alevi tragedy occurred only ten years ago in the ancient Turkish town of Sivas. Here dozens of intellectuals gathered one July 1993 day for an Alevi literary festival honoring Pir Sultan Abdal, a sixteenth-century poet, mystic, and social rebel, executed by the Ottomans. The Alevis have long likened the *pir*'s struggle with the Alevi one, while, in more recent decades, many Alevi Kurds—and the Turkish authorities—see a connection between him and the Kurdish struggle. Among the festival's honored guests was the noted satirist and leftist Aziz Nesin, a Turkish Alevi, who opened the celebration with a passionate speech filled with anti-

Islamic overtones. The next day, an angry Islamist crowd surrounded the hotel in which the intellectuals were staying. Frantically, the Alevis telephoned for help from the local police, the security forces, and the capital of Ankara, but no response came. Finally, shouting *"Allah-u Akbar,"* God is Great, the frenzied crowd set fire to the hotel. Thirty-seven writers, artists, and thinkers perished in a tragedy that the Alevis blame as much on the authorities as they do on the perpetrators.

Ironically, Aziz Nesin survived the inferno. He was mistaken for the police chief and rescued by a fire engine ladder.

CHAPTER NINE

From Kings to Parliamentarians

ﾞﾞﾞﾞﾞ

FROM DOHUK TO ERBIL, THE HEADQUARTERS OF THE KDP
and seat of the Kurdish Parliament, was a five-hour drive. I had been planning on hiring a car to make the trip, but, at the last minute, Dr. Shawkat
put me in touch with a KDP official on his way to Erbil. He had his own car
and driver, and offered to give me a ride.

I said good-bye to Majed and his family, and to Dr. Shawkat, whose
attentions were no longer annoying me—I would miss him and all my
friends in Dohuk. And I wondered, as I often did when departing from people in Kurdistan, what the status of their world would be the next time we
were in touch. The specter of war hung over everything.

Around midday, the KDP official and I came to the wide expanse of the
Greater Zab River, the main tributary of the Tigris. The river's waters
churned in ropes of brown and white as it raced alongside us, toward snowcapped Qandil Mountain. Passing over a small bridge, we entered a pas-
sageway bordered by rock cliffs to one side. And as we did so, we passed out
of Bahdinani Kurdistan and into Sorani Kurdistan, where Kurds speak a different dialect.

The Greater Zab marks the dividing line between the two main dialects
of the Kurdish language. North of the river, including northern Iraqi
Kurdistan and much of Turkey, Kurds speak Kermanji. South of the river,
in southern Iraqi Kurdistan and much of Iran, they speak Sorani. Sub-
dialects also exist, including Zaza, spoken primarily in central-eastern

Turkey, and Gurani and Kermanshahi, spoken in Iranian Kurdistan. Interestingly, Zaza and Gurani are closely related, even though they are at the opposite geographic ends of Kurdistan. Many Kurds are also bilingual, speaking Arabic, Persian, or Turkish in addition to Kurdish.

All Kurdish dialects belong to one of two branches of the Iranian languages and are related to Persian. Nonetheless, they differ considerably from one another, so much so that many Kermanji speakers cannot understand Sorani speakers, and vice versa. Lacking a standard language has been yet another barrier to Kurdish political and social unification.

Tents of the seminomads

However, this barrier is breaking down, largely because of television, and partly because of war and upheaval. Perhaps two-thirds of Iraqi Kurds now have access to satellite dishes, as do many Kurds in Iran and Turkey, with which they watch the KDP's Kurdish Satellite TV, where announcers speak in both Kermanji and Sorani; the PUK's Kurd Sat, usually broadcast in Sorani; and the PKK's Med TV, a Kermanji station broadcast from Europe. War and upheaval has also meant more intermingling between speakers of Kermanji and Sorani, both within Kurdistan and the diaspora.

Complications remain, most notably that of written Kurdish. Iraqi and Iranian Kurds, like their compatriots, use the Arabic alphabet, while Kurds in Turkey, like the Turks, use the Roman.

In the safe haven, Kurdish was the primary language being taught in the schools, where a "Kurdicized" curriculum was also being developed. Parents who learned their lessons in Arabic were delighting in children learning theirs in Kurdish. But the practice has dangers. Many of today's younger generation cannot speak Arabic, a considerable liability in a land with many Arabic-speaking neighbors.

A similar understandable but nonetheless irrational distaste for Arabic also runs deep in Iran, where many Kurds feel oppressed by their Islamic government. One intelligent, ambitious high school student I met there recoiled in horror when I asked him if he spoke Arabic. "I have to learn some in school, but I will never *speak* it, it is *evil*," he said.

The teaching of Kurdish in the Iraqi schools has enormous resonance for the Kurds of Iran and Turkey, where Kurdish-language schools scarcely exist. A few universities and private institutes in Iranian Kurdistan do offer courses in Kurdish language, history, and culture, but the language is not taught at the lower public school levels. And in Turkey, the teaching of Kurdish has been a red-hot political issue—only very recently easing—with Kurds at times arrested and imprisoned for promoting Kurdish language rights. In late 2001 and early 2002, for example, students at twenty-five Turkish universities signed 11,837 petitions arguing for optional Kurdish lessons. In response, 1,359 students were arrested, 143 imprisoned, and 46 suspended.

FROM THE GREATER ZAB, we continued south, passing through Harir, once ruled by a seventeenth-century woman warrior named Princess Zad, and Shaqlawa, a leafy Christian town. Behind Shaqlawa rose brooding Sefin Mountain, the site of a decisive *peshmerga* victory over the Iraqi army that paved the way for semiautonomous Kurdistan.

Later in my stay, I would be invited to a picnic on Sefin and was surprised to find a broad grassy plateau on top, sprinkled with daisies, purple thistles, and big red wild tulips with pointy leaves. All around Sefin bobbed hills of dark red and gray, resembling giant clam shells, due to prominent vertical ridges, and hillocks streaked with bright yellow, white, and green— as if cans of paint were spilled down their sides.

Beyond Shaqlawa, the road zigzagged up a steep, distinctive ridge to Salahuddin. Visible from miles around, Salahuddin had been a resort pre-1991, but since the uprising, had served as the headquarters of the KDP. A huge party seal, dominated by a fierce-eyed eagle, stood at a central cross-roads on the mountain's top. To both sides stretched the offices and homes of top officials, including KDP President Massoud Barzani and Prime Minister Nechirvan Barzani. The massif was also an important meeting site. In October 2002, after the Gulf War, various disparate elements of the Iraqi opposition first met here to form the Iraqi National Congress (INC), a major anti-Baath coalition. In February 2003, one month before the Iraq war, the 65-seat Iraqi opposition committee convened on the summit to dis-cuss plans for post-Saddam Iraq.

Visible from Salahuddin, and accessible via another zigzagging road, was Erbil, or Hawler, as it is known in Kurdish. The two towns were less than a half hour apart, and closely connected, with politicians and bureau-crats often traveling between them several times a day. Traffic jams along the interconnecting road were common, as were traffic jams in Erbil itself. I was many miles away from sleepy Dohuk.

LIKE AMADIYA, ERBIL is another of the world's oldest continuously inhabited cities, dating back about eight thousand years. The Sumerians called it "Urbilum" in their cuneiform tablets of the 3000s B.C.; while under the Assyrians, the city became known as Arbailu, or "Four Gods," as it served as the empire's religious capital and home to the shrine of the goddess Ishtar.

It was to Erbil that Sennacherib, perhaps the most famous of all Assyrian kings, made a pilgrimage in 692 B.C. to pray to Ishtar for his com-ing battle with the Babylonians; his prayers were answered. It was also to Erbil that the supporters of Teumman, a would-be usurper to the Assyrian throne, were brought and brutally flayed alive in the mid-600s B.C. In 608 B.C., the Medes conquered the city, followed over the next six centuries by the Persians, Greeks, and Parthians, under whose rule Erbil became Christian. Mentioned in the Bible as Arbela, the city was also an important crossroads for caravan routes.

However, it was the famous 331 B.C. battle between the Greeks and the Persians for which ancient Erbil is most known. One of the most decisive battles of all time, pitting Alexander the Great against the Great King Darius III, the battle caused all of Asia as far east as the Hindu Kush to fall under Greek rule, thereby ending the powerful Achaemenian Persian dynasty. The battle of Arbela was also a brilliant military achievement in which Alexander and his army defeated a force many times their size, losing about twelve hundred men to the Persians' loss of perhaps forty thousand.

Despite its name, the battle of Arbela was actually fought on the plain of Gaugamela, meaning the "Camel's Grazing Place," about fifty miles northwest of Erbil. The Great King Darius had reached Gaugamela well before Alexander, but made critical tactical errors, such as neglecting to occupy hills that could have been used as lookout posts. A few days before the battle, Darius also learned that his wife, a prisoner in Alexander's camp, had fallen ill and died. He tried to make a last-minute peace settlement, offering a huge ransom for his other, still-captive family members. Alexander refused, and the battle began, with the Persians finding themselves in more and more desperate circumstances as the day wore on.

When the battle reached a crescendo, Darius and his immediate followers fled to their base camp in Arbela, from which they continued north into the Kurdish mountains and Iran. Alexander entered Arbela the next morning, to find the Great King gone, but he seized his chariot and weapons, and proclaimed himself King of Asia. The Greeks then buried their dead and marched on to Babylon and the Persian capitals of Susa and Persepolis. Thousands of Persian corpses were left to rot on the battlefield.

In A.D. 196, the Romans conquered Erbil, only to succumb to the Persian Sassanians thirty years later. Under their enlightened rule, however, the city's Christian community continued to flourish. Erbil was the see of a bishopric until the ninth century, two hundred years after the arrival of Islam, when it was moved to Mosul.

Erbil rose to importance again in 1167, when it became the capital of the powerful Kurdish prince, Zayn al-Din Ali Kucuk Begtegin. His descendant Muzaffer al-Din Kokburi built a major Sufi center and *madrassa*, or religious school, whose tile-studded minaret still stands. Muzaffer may have also been the first to officially celebrate the birthday of the Prophet Muhammad, in 1207—a festival that has since spread throughout the Muslim world.

Like much of Kurdistan, Erbil was viciously attacked by the Mongol armies of Hulagu Khan in the thirteenth century, but the city put up an impressive resistance and fell only after a long siege. And under the Ottomans, Erbil served as a cultural and administrative hub, home to many poets, scholars, and bureaucrats.

———

UPON REACHING ERBIL, I went directly to the home of Nesreen Mustafa Siddeek Berwari, Kurdistan's minister of Reconstruction and Development, who had invited me to stay with her. Nesreen and I had been in frequent touch by e-mail before I left the United States, thanks to a mutual contact, and we had already met in Dohuk. It was Nesreen who had introduced me to her cousins Majed and his siblings, and Nesreen who had helped arrange my stay in Amadiya. Nesreen had also answered many of my basic questions regarding Kurdistan and helped me navigate its societal mores.

In her mid-thirties, Nesreen lived with her father and an unmarried brother in a large house that had been provided for her use by the KDP. Running the household were relatives from the family village of Chamsaida, while out front was a guardhouse manned by *peshmerga,* most also from Chamsaida. Kurdish families are loose structures, often numbering in the hundreds, and those in positions of power often hire relatives.

Nesreen was waiting for me when I arrived, and we soon settled down for a glass of tea. Confident and direct, with shiny dark hair and eyes, Nesreen was one of the most unusual women in Iraqi Kurdistan, and emblematic, I hoped, of better things to come for all Kurdish women. One of two women ministers and four women parliamentarians serving in the KDP government, she was single, traveled extensively by herself, oversaw a ministry of about fifteen hundred employees, and held a masters' degree in public administration from Harvard University's Kennedy School of Government.

She owed a large part of her success to her father. An uneducated but open-minded man who'd grown up in Chamsaida, he had moved his family to Baghdad in 1958, understanding that his children—eight sons and one daughter—would have little future if they stayed in rural Kurdistan. His foresight had paid off extraordinarily well. Among Nesreen's brothers were a geologist who was also a successful painter, an engineer, a businessman who specialized in computers, and the director of Brayati, one of Kurdistan's foremost newspaper and media companies.

Born in Baghdad in 1967, Nesreen was the next-to-youngest child. Her oldest brother joined the Kurdish revolution in 1974, when she was seven, and thereafter, the Baathists periodically harassed her father. Then in 1981, they imprisoned the entire family for one year, along with hundreds of other *peshmerga* families. Nesreen took her schoolbooks with her into jail, and the guards let her out to take her final exams.

"I didn't want to give up my chance for an education," she said as we sipped our tea. "This is what Saddam wanted, for the Kurds to have no education, to be nobodies. But because of Saddam, I and many other Kurds have always pushed ourselves harder, to prove we could do it." She passed me a box of imported chocolates.

After the family was released from prison, they moved to Dohuk, but Nesreen stayed behind to attend the University of Baghdad, where she studied architectural engineering and urban planning. She was in her final year when the Gulf War broke out and the uprising began, forcing her and much of her family to flee to Turkey. But after living in a Turkish refugee camp for two months, she heard that the University of Baghdad was reopening and decided to go back to finish her degree. The move took courage; as a Kurd, she hadn't known how she would be received. Yet once again, she hadn't wanted to give up her chance for an education, and had graduated without incident.

Back in Kurdistan after the creation of the safe haven, Nesreen first found work as an administrative officer for the United Nations High Commission for Refugees. She steadily rose in the U.N. organization, eventually becoming head of the Habitat field office in Dohuk. Like all U.N. workers, she was paid far more than ordinary Kurds, and at that time, when most of her brothers were unemployed, she was her family's main source of economic support.

Through the help of an American working for the United Nations, Nesreen began requesting catalogues from graduate schools in the West. Setting her sights on Harvard's Kennedy School, she took the required entrance interview by phone, was accepted, and flew to Boston to become the school's first Iraqi Kurdish student. Fifteen months later, she graduated. Half of her tuition was paid by the Kurdistan government, half by a Kennedy School scholarship. Her father had attended her graduation, a scene I loved imagining.

When Nesreen had first left Iraq to study in the United States, there had, of course, been much gossip. She's going alone—for over a year!—the community tittered. She's going to get married; she'll never come back.

Yet Nesreen did return, to initially be offered the position of deputy minister of Reconstruction and Development, which she turned down. All too familiar with her culture, she knew that as a woman deputy minister, she would have little power. Then in 1999, to the credit of the KDP leadership, often criticized for its traditional tribal politics, Nesreen was appointed minister of Reconstruction and Development. It had worked out well.

"I can honestly say that I've had no real problems as a woman in government," she said. "My age and lack of government experience have been the greater obstacles."

But those, too, had been dealt with and overcome. The KDP had gone so far as to say that of its twenty ministers, the best were its two women. More important, much of the Kurdish community had grown both accustomed to and proud of Nesreen's accomplishments, so much so that younger women often spoke of hoping to follow in her footsteps.

OVER THE NEXT few days, I explored Erbil with Rezan, a pretty and giggly young translator, recently graduated from the University of Salahuddin. We started with a tour of the many indoor-outdoor markets surrounding the Citadel, Erbil's oldest district, rising about twenty-five yards above the rest of the city. All of the expected items were for sale—carpets, clothing, CDs, computers, fruits, and vegetables—and I was only half listening to my guide's patter when she suggested we stop to visit her "milk brother." Thereupon, I met a beaming young man who ran a carpet store. His mother had died when he was an infant, and Rezan's mother had suckled him. This meant that he and Rezan were related by milk and so looked out for each other and could not marry.

Within Erbil was a huge Turkish-style mosque being built by the city's Turcomans—a people with whom Kurds have a fractious relationship, though there is no real history of violence between them. Related to the Turks, the Turcomans live primarily in Iraq's northern cities and in Baghdad. No reliable population figures exist, but they probably number between 350,000 and 750,000. Among Kurds, the Turcomans have a reputation for being extremely conservative, wealthy, haughty, standoffish, and passive—a view that the Turcomans I met basically agreed with, although they preferred the words "conservative, wealthy, proud, private, and peaceful." Many Turcomans work as artisans, especially carpenters and tailors, and for centuries, they controlled the northern cities' gold markets.

Although brutally mistreated by the Baath regime, the Turcomans boy-cotted Kurdistan's 1992 elections and turned down the chance to participate in the reunited 2002 Kurdish Parliament. Many observers believed, how-ever, that those policies had less to do with the Turcomans' hostility toward the Kurds than with their unwillingness to anger Turkey by appearing to endorse Kurdish autonomy. Turkey kept a protective eye on its related com-munity and often complained of the Turcomans' second-class status in the safe haven—an accusation the Kurds denied.

That afternoon, Rezan and I stopped by the Faili Cultural Center, home to another minority group in Kurdistan. Numbering perhaps 150,000, the Faili are Shiite Kurds who settled during Ottoman times in various parts of Iraq, including Baghdad, and yet were denied Iraqi citizenship. The Baath regime had proclaimed them to be Iranians and, on two separate occasions, cruelly expelled them to Iran, forcing out about fifty thousand in 1971 and an even larger group in the early 1980s. Over seven thousand Faili had also been arrested in the early 1980s, never to be seen again, said the center's director, Shawker Faili, as he showed us a long, sad wall, lined with photographs of the missing. Within his extended family alone, eighteen people had disappeared after arrest, while eleven others had been executed.

Another morning Rezan and I attended a session of the Kurdish Parliament in what had once been the Baathist security district. From the outside, the concrete-and-stone parliament building glowered, dark and forbidding. Inside, a new era had begun. In the entrance hall, floors pol-ished to a high gleam, hung an enormous portrait of Mulla Mustafa, flanked by two guards in Kurdish costume, both standing disconcertingly motionless and expressionless, à la Buckingham Palace.

Heading straight to the visitors' gallery, Rezan and I took seats above a wood-paneled room filled with semicircular rows of green-upholstered seats. About fifty or sixty representatives and cabinet ministers were filing in, with the ministers—including my friend Nesreen—taking seats in the front row. Mam Muhsen, my host from Amadiya, was also there, along with a half-dozen other representatives in traditional Kurdish dress and a Christian in black robes etched with gold. Most of the other men wore Western-style clothes, as did the half-dozen women among them.

The parliament president, Dr. Rowsch Shaways, took the podium, and the session began with the traditional Muslim benediction, *"Besmellah, al-rahman al-rahim"*—In the Name of Allah, the Magnificent, the Merciful.

As the words rang out, I marveled at how familiar it all seemed, and how small. With a slight change in the religious message, I could have been in the capitol building of one of the smaller U.S. states.

To one side of Dr. Rowsch sat a KDP representative, but the chair to his other side was empty, as were over half of the seats in the assembly hall. Since the 1994–97 internal war, almost all of the PUK representatives had left Erbil, and their absence was yawningly apparent. The parliament still had a quorum—fifty-three members—but whatever laws it passed now applied only to the KDP-controlled side. The PUK governed its territory through a separate cabinet of ministers and the party's politburo.

For many Kurds I met, the hostility between the KPD and PUK was a painful and embarrassing subject, best avoided. Memories of the internal war were still raw, especially in Erbil. The conflict had displaced tens of thousands of people and resulted in thousands of deaths. It had also brought out the worst in both ordinary citizens, some of whom took to looting and murder, and politicians.

The first clashes between the KDP and PUK after Kurdistan's 1992 elections took place in December 1993 and by 1995, the death toll was already in the thousands. Unable to reconcile their differences, the parties sought the help of outside allies, with the KDP turning first to Turkey and the PUK cultivating Iran. But both parties also kept communications open with Baghdad, and Saddam Hussein adroitly manipulated the hostilities between them until tensions rose to the breaking point.

In August 1996, the PUK allowed Iranian forces to enter Kurdistan, allegedly in pursuit of the Iranian version of the KDP (KDPI). Panicking, the KDP turned to Baghdad for assistance. Horrified civilians watched as thirty thousand Baath troops entered the region and immediately captured Erbil. The forces also tracked down several hundred rebels who had supported a failed 1995 CIA-backed coup attempt to oust Saddam, leading the United States to airlift out of the region about five thousand Americans, Kurds, and other Iraqis deemed at risk. The maneuvers gave Hussein back some of the prestige he had lost following the 1991 Gulf War and undermined the legitimacy of the Kurdish safe haven.

International pressure forced the Baathists to withdraw from Kurdistan within weeks. Subsequently, the KDP took full control of Erbil and the PUK retreated to Suleimaniyah. Not until September 1998, with the help of American mediation, did the two parties sign the Washington Agreement, which established a permanent cease-fire between them and paved the way for future negotiations.

I shuddered as I remembered this history, wondering at the fragility of emerging nations, so easily swayed as they take two steps forward, one step back. Another serious misstep and semiautonomous Kurdistan could have been gone for good.

AFTER THE PARLIAMENT session was over, Rezan and I toured the building with Fawzia Eziddin Rashid, one of the KDP's four women parliamentarians. A warm and round middle-aged woman with short black brushed-back hair, Fawzia had started working for the KDP when she was still a student. As one of the few single women then working for the party, she had taken care to spend every night in a different home, to diminish the chances of being arrested. Especially back then, the community treated women who'd been imprisoned as "very little things," as the assumption was that they had been raped by the guards and, thus, had lost their honor.

Fawzia had also been one of fifty-nine representatives who had holed up in the parliament building for 101 days from late 1994 to early 1995, frantically negotiating to save their splintering government. With her husband working in Salahuddin, and her children safe with relatives, she had watched with deep despair as Iraqi tanks rolled past the parliament and the rival *peshmerga* fought each other street by street, building by building.

After a tour through the parliament library—filled with law books in Arabic and Kurdish—we headed to Fawzia's office to speak about the women's rights committee on which she served. The committee had recently succeeded in changing seven laws that affected women. One made it illegal for a man to beat his wife; another stated that if a man took a second wife without the permission of the first, he could be sentenced to three years in prison. These changes sounded sadly limited in scope to me, but they brought home how painstakingly slow change can be. As one Kurdish politician said to me later, "Of course, we can pass all sorts of admirable laws, but what good will they do us if they can't be implemented? The trick is to pass laws that our society is ready to accept."

The Kurdish Parliament also had to take care to pass only laws that fell within the Iraqi legal framework. Kurdistan was still governed by Iraqi law, albeit with some alterations, and, if the Kurds departed too far from

Baghdad's authority, a post-Saddam federation would be harder to establish. They could also be accused of separatism, which would lead to a whole host of other problems.

Down the hall from Fawzia were the offices of other parliamentarians, some of whom I spoke with on subsequent visits. I also met with the Kurdish Parliament president, various cabinet ministers, and other officials. Some had nothing but praise for their new government, but others frankly admitted that it still had some way to go before achieving true democracy.

Interestingly, when I asked the politicians what they felt was the biggest problem confronting Kurdistan, aside from Saddam Hussein and the surrounding enemy states, many answered, "People don't understand their rights." By this they meant that the Kurds, like all Iraqis, had lived under a strong-armed regime for so long that they didn't know they could object to mistreatment or otherwise stand up for themselves. Women didn't know that they had any recourse against cruel husbands; men didn't know they could protest illegal arrest or torture; families didn't know that they could refuse to kill their "wayward" daughters in the face of societal pressure.

Many in government and the media were now working hard to spread the word in this arena. Through television and articles, conferences, and classes in democracy held in the schools, police departments, and militia centers, the Kurds were gradually becoming aware that just because certain things had been handled in certain ways in the past, that didn't mean such practices had to continue. "We are still very new to democracy," said one deputy minister. "But we are a humble people, and we learn quickly. Even five years from now, things will be very different. Look at all the change that happened in the last ten years."

ONE OF THE first women to work for the KDP in a leadership capacity, elected to the party's Central Committee in 1959, was Nahida Shaikh Salaam Ahmad. Now in her eighties, Nahida had first become involved in politics in 1937, when she'd worked for the Hewa party, a forerunner to the KDP. Her father, Shaikh Salaam, had been a famous poet, her husband an influential KPD member, and one of her eight sons, Dr. Rowsch Shaways, was president of the Kurdistan Parliament.

My translator Rezan and I went to visit Nahida one morning, to find a charismatic woman with bright white hair and a strong, weathered face waiting for us. She wore a magnificent blue dress with a floral design, a sheer black head scarf, numerous gold and coral bracelets, and a turquoise ring reaching almost to her knuckle. Despite her age, her voice rang deep and strong, and she spoke with dramatic gestures, which I felt sure must once have commandeered the Central Committee.

Nahida told us about working for the KDP in its earliest years, in the mid-1940s. Back then, she said, she was one of few women among many men, and so always carefully covered herself in her *abeyya*. The party was poor, and one of her jobs was to write out its newsletter by hand, making multiple copies. Until, that is, she had a brainstorm. Through her work as a teacher, she knew that Suleimaniyah's Department of Education had a typewriter. She decided to steal it for the KDP. With the help of the door-keeper, she made a copy of the office key and returned late one night in her *abeyya*. Picking up the typewriter—far heavier than she'd anticipated—she hid it under her garment and slipped away.

The next day, the city was in an uproar. Where was the missing type-writer? The doorkeeper was questioned, but swore—honestly—that he'd never opened the office door. Nahida and her colleagues then made a wooden box with a handle in which to keep the machine, which they moved from house to house, to ensure its safety.

Imagine a typewriter having so much value, I thought as she spoke. Less than sixty years had elapsed since then, but even in "backward" Kurdistan, the typewriter was all but obsolete.

Nahida also spoke about the many times she had successfully deceived the Iraqi authorities, who, in the 1940s and 1950s, were representatives of the Hashemite monarchy or various military dictators, not the Baathists. Frequently, the police hauled her down to their stations for interrogation, and one time in the 1960s, the guards said they would release her if she gave up the names of two party members. You promise? she asked. Yes, they answered, and she gave them the names of Mulla Mustafa Barzani and Jalal Talabani, already known leaders. The guards kept their promise and let her go.

On another occasion, Nahida had delivered a high-ranking KDP offi-cial to an important meeting in a heavily guarded town by disguising him in old patched clothes, and traveling with him and two other women. Upon

reaching the town, the foursome were stopped at a checkpoint and interro-
gated by an army commander. We are only three poor sisters who have
come to see our family and this man is our village cousin, here to help us
with our travels, Nahida said. The army commander, saying that he had six
sisters himself, offered them a cup of tea, which Nahida asked the disguised
KDP official to serve. Being unaccustomed to such tasks, he dropped the
tray. You idiot! Nahida said, thinking quickly. I don't know why we bothered bringing you along.

Listening to Nahida tell her stories, I was struck by their "big adventure"
quality, which gave them an almost innocuous character. Had that been a
less-dangerous time? I wondered for a moment, and then decided against it.
Rather, it was the stories' high-adrenaline quality that gave them their feel.
I'd heard others tell of near escapes from the Baathists with similar glee.
Something light to hang on to in all the darkness.

WHILE IN ERBIL, I often came home at the end of the day to visit with
Nesreen. Sometimes, there was a certain stiffness between us, as she, in her
official capacity as minister of Reconstruction and Development, wished to
represent Kurdistan in its most positive light, and I, as a writer, instinctively
wanted to see what lay in the shadows, good or bad. More often, we had an
easy give and take as I tried to make sense of the world around me.

Nesreen and I usually caught up on our days over a simple dinner in the
kitchen, shared with her father and brother, neither of whom spoke
English. Both dressed traditionally, while Nesreen wore stylish Western
clothes and spoke of how much she'd enjoyed shopping while in the United
States. It was comments like these that reminded me that Nesreen's life was
not just like mine, a fact I sometimes forgot, as her English was excellent
and she was well informed about many things American. She was also one
of a growing number of Kurds with Internet access at home; her Internet
provider was AOL.

Despite all that Nesreen had seen and the many humanitarian crises that
she tackled daily, her outlook was overwhelmingly positive and optimistic in
a way that also struck me as very American. She did not dwell on current
problems as much as plot routes around them, seeing the possibility of wide-
ranging improvements just ahead. And her outlook was not unrealistic. In

the previous ten years, and especially in the last five, Kurdistan had successfully transformed itself from a war-ravaged region into a functioning quasi-
modern society, with 65 percent of its countryside rebuilt.

One day I traveled with Nesreen, her guards, and staff on one of their
weekly field trips to inspect newly reconstructed villages. In various stages of
completion, the projects were overseen by serious-faced foremen and engi-
neers in hard hats who rushed to greet us when we arrived. Watching the
men as they consulted with Nesreen and her staff, and their wiry workers
laboring hard, I was struck by everyone's earnestness, energy, and drive—so
different from the lethargy often found at U.S. construction sites. These
people weren't just doing a job, they were building the country they'd never
before been allowed to have, while also providing for their dispossessed.

According to the United Nations, a total of about 140,000 displaced families, or 815,000 displaced people—the most anywhere in the Middle
East—were living in northern Iraq at the time of my visit. And they came in
many different types. The newer refugees had the most urgent needs, and
they were given resettlement priority, which created some resentment, of
course, as did the fact that the newer homes were of better quality than
those built just after the uprising.

When the Ministry of Reconstruction and Development was first established in 1992, it had operated with limited funds provided by various relief
organizations and the Kurdistan government. But, starting in early 1997,
with the implementation of the United Nation's oil-for-food program,
money had been steadily flowing into the ministry's account. Nasreen and
her colleagues had an annual budget of $60 million to $70 million for project implementation—in stark contrast to most of Kurdistan's ministries,
which did not directly benefit from the U.N. resolution, as they were not
involved with humanitarian issues and so were often barely scraping by.

Everywhere I went in Kurdistan, the oil-for-food program was a topic of
much heated discussion. Despite all the humanitarian relief that the program was undeniably providing, it was fraught with problems. Some policies that had made sense when the program was first implemented had
outlived their usefulness, while others needed drastic revision.

Security Council Resolution 986 was originally developed to help
relieve some of the civilian suffering caused by the economic sanctions
imposed on Iraq following the Gulf War. The program allowed Iraq to

export its state-owned oil and use much of the revenue earned, kept in a U.N. bank account, to buy food and other basic goods. As such, the program was not humanitarian aid, but rather, the directed use of Iraq's own revenue toward humanitarian purposes. The program was organized in six-month phases, with the Baath government submitting a proposal for each new phase to the United Nations for its approval.

Under the resolution, 13 percent of the program's resources had to go directly to the northern no-fly zone. Baghdad decided how goods should be distributed there, but the United Nations administered the program—a complex process with many sticking points. First and foremost, Baghdad effectively stonewalled many of Kurdistan's most urgent requests, ranging from medicines to the visas required for foreign experts to enter the country. Second, the enormous program suffered from endless bureaucracy.

So much money was flowing into the United Nation's Kurdistan coffers that it couldn't be spent fast enough. As of January 10, 2003, according to the Kurdistan Regional Government, $4 billion of the Kurds' share of oil-for-food funds was sitting unused in a French bank account, where it remained months after the war. The United Nations disputed the figure, saying that the unspent sum by May 22, 2003, when the United Nations ended sanctions on Iraq, was only $1.6 billion. Either way, the unspent sum was serious money.

Central to the oil-for-food program, and emblematic of its problems, was the monthly ten-item ration basket provided to all Iraqi residents over age one, no matter what their economic status; infants received a monthly four-item ration basket. Without these food rations, an estimated 60 percent of Kurdistan would be going hungry, and so, in one essential way, the program worked very well.

But in addition to wastefully supplying even the wealthy with rations, the food basket wreaked havoc with the local economy. Kurdistan is a fertile agricultural region. Before the Anfal, most Kurds were farmers. But with every adult receiving nine kilograms of wheat flour every month, along with other foodstuffs, those Kurds who were still farming were unable to sell their crops profitably. Others had no incentive to begin farming again.

By creating a lack of incentive to farm and a dependence on handouts, the oil-for-food program was in effect continuing Saddam Hussein's campaign to transform the Kurds from active producers into passive consumers.

And there were other disturbing repercussions. As much as the refugees needed adequate housing, some now balked at moving back into the countryside out of fear that they would be unable to make a living.

"One of our biggest problems is sustainability," Nesreen said on the day of our tour. "We build the villagers new homes, but then leave them there with no means of support. A few projects have even failed because of this — after all this investment."

Nesreen's ministry, along with the Ministry of Agriculture and various aid organizations, tried to tackle the problem by providing villages with supplies to create small businesses such as aviaries and poultry farms, but the real answer lay in convincing the United Nations to change its policies. During my visit, Kurdish officials were in constant discussion with the international organization, trying to effect such change, but little progress had been made. Central to the problem was the fact that Resolution 986 was conceived to deliver short-term humanitarian and reconstruction relief, not bring about long-term development. Thus, the United Nations saw the building of the Kurdish economy as falling outside its mandate. However, the organization also seemed to have little interest in reexamining that mandate, perhaps because it was collecting a 2.2 percent commission on all Iraqi oil sales for operational costs. Between 1997 and early 2003, the oil-for-food program had generated over $1 billion for the United Nations.

The Kurdish officials sometimes tried to get around the resolution's limitations by claiming that a new project — such as a tomato paste factory or road — wasn't really new, and thus "long-term development," but rather an older project that needed rehabilitation. Sometimes the ploy worked, sometimes not. Either way, it was a ridiculous game to be forced to play in a land where aid was sorely needed — and theoretically available.

Another important piece of the Kurdish economic puzzle was its bloated civil servant population, numbering well over three hundred thousand. Like all civil servants in Iraq, these well-educated Kurds — most of whom had also served under the Baath regime — were accustomed to taking orders rather than initiative, and to their government providing them with everything from free health care to education. But be that as it may, the civil servants were also earning the ridiculously low salary of 500 *dinars* a month, about $30 at the time of my visit — as compared to $500 to $2,000 for Kurds employed by the United Nations. Yet to raise the civil servants' salaries was apparently impossible. The Kurdish government did not have the money, and the oil-for-food funds could not be used to pay civil servant salaries or for any other aspect of the Kurdish government's operating costs.

The more I learned about the oil-for-food program, the more it made my head spin and bile rise. Indeed, the program had done much good: no Kurds were going hungry, many worthwhile projects had been implemented, and much of the country had been rebuilt. But the Kurdistan of 2002 was not the Kurdistan of 1996. Much change had taken place, and the program was in dire need of aggressive reform. In addition to granting Saddam Hussein far too much decision-making power—a separate and noxious issue in itself—Resolution 986 was treating the Kurds like children. The oil-for-food money wasn't charity; it was the Kurds' share of their country's income. Yet they had little say in how it was spent.

One year later, after the fall of Saddam Hussein, I would remember all this and wonder about what was to happen in Kurdistan and the rest of Iraq when other perhaps well-meaning but nonetheless often bungling outsiders arrived. On November 21, 2003, the oil-for-food program was officially terminated; how to replace it and the previously fostered culture of dependency posed major challenges for the new country.

Invitations

IN THE CENTER OF ERBIL, RISING LIKE AN EERIE LUMP OUT OF the world's collective subconscious, was the Citadel. At about seventy-five feet in height and one hundred thousand square yards in area, the massive brown mound was built on layers upon layers of consecutive ruins, with the bottommost ones dating back to the sixth century B.C., when the first village was built on the spot. Over the centuries, the Citadel has been ruled by some of history's greatest civilizations: the Sumerians, Babylonians, Assyrians, Persians, Greeks, Romans, Sassanians, and early Islamic dynasties. All undoubtedly left their marks somewhere deep within the Citadel's mysterious layers, but no serious archaeological exploration of the mound has ever been conducted.

In the modern era, prior to the 1960s, the Citadel was home to many of Erbil's oldest and wealthiest families, who lived in the five hundred or so houses on top, many of which still stand. The Citadel was also home to coffeehouses, government offices, mosques, religious schools, and a jail. Most of the Citadel's residents were Muslim, but there was a Christian community and—before the establishment of Israel—a small Jewish one.

About forty years ago, however, the wealthy started moving out of the Citadel. Many of their houses were too old to be updated, and city services were poor. As the old families abandoned their homes, villagers escaping the destroyed countryside moved in. Five or six impoverished families crowded into homes that had formerly belonged to one, and the upkeep of the

Citadel declined. Today, the site is a hodgepodge of divided old homes, dilapidated newer ones, and piles of rubble. Only a handful of well-preserved historic buildings still stand, one a romantic turn-of-the-twentieth-century home, now holding a folklore museum.

WHILE VISITING THE Citadel, I was introduced to Yassim Muhammad Wossou, the keeper of a small vegetable shop. A burly, one-eyed man in his thirties, Yassim lived with his eight children and wife in a single room bordering a grassy plot near the edge of the Citadel—twenty-five yards straight down from their home honked and flowed city traffic. Three other rooms also bordered the plot, and in each lived other members of Yassim's family and their families: his brother and his wife and three children, his sister and her husband and seven children, his father and mother and four younger unmarried siblings.

The extended family numbered thirty in all, Yassim said, and on behalf of everyone, he would like to invite me to spend a night with them at their home. "*Ser chaow,*" he said, and touched his eye in a lovely gesture that literally means "on my eyes," and figuratively means "I am at your service." It was a gesture that traditional Kurds used often, along with the even lovelier one of placing the right hand over the heart, meaning either "I am honored," or "I am honored, but no thank you," depending on the situation.

I accepted the invitation. I felt eager to escape the privileged circles in which I'd been moving and had been told that spending the night at the Citadel presented no security risk.

Invitations such as Yassim's greeted me everywhere I went in Kurdistan. Sometimes, they seemed pro forma, as it is the thing to do in Muslim society, but more often, they seemed genuine.

When I arrived at Yassim's home a few afternoons later, I found him and his younger brother, both dressed in *khak* with cummerbunds, and many of their children waiting for me. "*B'kher-hati, b'kher-hati,*" they cried. A Mr. Ibrahim, dressed in a jacket and yellow polo shirt, was also there. An educated man and friend of the family, he spoke some English and Persian, and had come to help with translation.

Yassim and Mr. Ibrahim gave me a tour through the four family rooms and up onto their rooftops. Two of the rooms were built of clay bricks perhaps eighty years old, another room was about twenty years old, and the fourth felt cool, dark, and ancient, with rounded corners, high ceilings, and uneven walls. All the rooms had the standard TV, clock, mirror, and framed photos that I'd come to expect in poorer Kurdish homes; one room was as brightly luxuriant as a sultana's jewelry box, enveloped with multicolored wall coverings, rugs, and cushions. Birds had built nests in the rafters outside, and they swooped in and out of the rooms with equanimity.

Up on the roof, the sun was setting on one side and the moon rising on the other, while calls to prayer drifted up from the mosques below. Minarets, domes, and rusting water tanks dotted the flat-as-a-pancake cityscape all the way to its abrupt edge at a brown plain.

Descending again, we entered the grassy plot and sat on cushions of bright orange, green, and purple. Other men, teenage boys, one elderly woman, and children of both sexes joined us, but all the other women and teenage girls remained standing in the doorways, watching. From somewhere rasped a sweeping broom, and a few honks rose from the traffic below.

"I am a poor man, but I have a rich heart," Yassim said, and, indeed, it seemed to be so. His younger children lingered around him, waiting for him to grab them and smother them with kisses and tickles.

Yassim and his family had moved to the castle in 1979, after five years of exile in southern Iraq, he told me. They were of the Khoshnaw tribe, and they had originally lived in valleys to the north of Erbil. But they'd been forced to flee to Iran because of his father's *peshmerga* activities, and when they'd returned, they had been captured, shipped south, and placed in a camp with about fifty other Kurdish families. Not until the Iran-Iraq War were the families allowed to return north.

"Tell me more about the Khoshnaw," I said. "How are you different from other tribes?"

"The Khoshnaw know how to forgive," Yassim said. "If someone kills a member of our family and comes to ask for forgiveness, we will say okay. We also give safe haven to others. Even if a Turk has killed another Turk, if he comes to us, we will support him until his problem is solved. And if we make a promise, we don't break it—

"Before the Anfal, the Khoshnaw had more than three hundred villages, and we were famous for our tobacco and fruits, especially apples and nuts. In the past, in the springtime, all the girls and boys went to the mountains to bring back vegetables. They stayed two, three weeks, and when they came back, they told their families who they wanted to marry. The boys went to the girls' families to ask for their hands, and in the autumn, they got married. We always got married in the autumn, because we sold our crops and had money. The wedding festival lasted three days. We had dancing and racing, and each village gave a gift to the bride. We don't do that anymore. Now we get married in the cities, and the wedding is just one day."

While we were speaking, my hosts took turns saying their evening prayers, each retreating to one side of the garden for a few minutes, where a prayer mat had been laid out. Then, as night descended, we retired into Yassim's room for dinner. About two dozen of us crowded around a plastic tablecloth on the floor covered with platters piled high with rice and wheat dishes, flat bread, yogurt, and mountain greens—no meat. Everything looked delicious, but the rice and wheat dishes were hard for me to eat, as they'd been prepared with generous helpings of the saturated oil that was part of the monthly U.N. food basket.

Yassim's *peshmerga* father arrived. A slight man dressed in olive green *khak* and a turban, he had a long, striking face crisscrossed with wrinkles and scars, and deeply expressive eyes—a face created by decades spent fighting, suffering, and dreaming in the mountains, I thought. *B'kher-hati*, he said again and again, his eyes shining, every time our eyes met.

Mr. Ibrahim and Yassim left to visit a sick friend, and Yassim's father led me to his home to watch television. An American game show was on, and four teenage boys were playing dominoes. Yassim's mother, a round woman in a black-and-white traditional dress, was gossiping with a friend wearing a purple-and-gold dress, while both clicked prayer beads.

Yassim's mother and I spoke a little in Persian. She had been with her husband in the mountains when he'd been in Haj Omran, near the Iran border, she said. It had been a terrible time. She'd had four children then— all under age eight—and they'd had no shoes, few clothes, and little food. The bombs fell all the time—in the day, in the night. A family of seven living next door had been killed.

Canned laughter blasted out of the television, and Yassim's mother turned her attention away from me. Her husband had fallen asleep at her side, and as she stared, rapt, at the TV, prayer beads clicking, I longed to have been in Kurdistan fifty years earlier, in the age of storytelling, not electronics.

That night, I slept in a room with only Yassim's wife and oldest daughter, thereby displacing at least seven people, who must have been parceled out to the other rooms. I tried to convince the family that I wouldn't mind sleeping with more people, but they wouldn't hear of it, and I soon gave up, knowing it was hopeless.

The next morning, Yassim and I explored more of the Citadel. We passed by turbaned men crouched on haunches in shop doorways and pushcarts piled high with vegetables and sundries. Bands of boys played soccer, and groups of younger children called out "hello" in English as I walked by, doubling over with giggles when I replied. Women and girls over the age of puberty were nowhere in sight.

Turning off the main thoroughfare, we snaked back through narrow alleyways. Yassim seemed to know everyone, his kind, one-eyed face wreathing with smiles at every turn. Then we entered a small compound to visit Yassim's sick friend. Passing through a listless garden, we walked into a dark room filled with several women, a person on a rickety bed, and metal basins on a cement floor. It took a few moments for my eyes to adjust, but when they did, my stomach flip-flopped. The woman on the bed had almost no face. It had been eaten away, leaving only raw flesh and bone behind. Her eyes flashed in the darkness, and, although she made no sound, I could hear her screams, spiraling into the void that had opened up around us.

"Take a picture," Yassim said, but I couldn't.

We went back outside.

"What happened to her?" I asked, my heart pounding.

"It's from the chemical bombs," Yassim said. "Until two years ago, she had no trouble, but now she will die, I think."

"Is she seeing a doctor?" I felt appalled—by the woman's face, by her living conditions, by the isolation of the Citadel. At the same time, I thought—this is nothing for Kurdistan, perhaps Yassim has witnessed this sort of thing a hundred times.

"They took her to doctors in Erbil and Baghdad," Yassim said. "There is no cure, only a drug from Tehran for the pain."

Back at Yassim's garden, with Mr. Ibrahim to help with translation, I learned more. Like Yassim and his family, almost everyone on the Citadel was of the Khoshnaw tribe, whose Balisan Valley had been bombed with chemical weapons on April 16, 1987, nearly one year before the start of the Anfal. According to Human Rights Watch, the attack killed about 125 civilians outright, and scores of others disappeared after the Iraqi forces removed them at gunpoint from an Erbil hospital to which they'd fled for treatment.

Neither Yassim nor Mr. Ibrahim, nor anyone else I spoke with later, could tell me anything more about the woman with the disintegrating face. To be affected in such a way so many years after the attacks was highly unusual, one doctor told me, but he speculated that perhaps the woman's immune system had been weakened and that she suffered from a virulent infection left untreated for too long.

FAWZIA EZIDDIN RASHID, the woman representative who had shown me around the parliament building, invited me to spend a few days with her and her family. Fawzia's husband, Zahir Ali Mustafa Rozhbayani, was director of the Gulan Cultural Foundation, one of Kurdistan's foremost publishing centers. A feminist, he strongly supported his wife's right to work. Neither Fawzia nor Zahir spoke English, but their two university-age sons, Zhila and Hozak, spoke well and were happy to serve as my translators. Rounding out the family was Kurdonia, age fourteen.

The family lived in one of Erbil's nicer and quieter neighborhoods, in a house that reflected their cultural and intellectual interests. Reproductions of Gustav Klimt and Vincent van Gogh hung on the walls, and their library was packed with a wide array of books by authors from around the world, as well as copies of the Bible, Torah, Quran, and Avesta, the holy book of the Zoroastrians.

The family's clan, the Rozhbayanis, was known for its poets and intellectuals. Among them was Muhammad Jamil Bandi Rozhbayani, who had been murdered with an ax, screwdriver, and knife on March 26, 2001, in his home in Baghdad at age eighty-nine. A writer, journalist, and scholar, Rozhbayani had been visited by three men from Iraqi intelligence a few days before his death, who warned him about his recent critiques of the regime. Later, when his body was found, his finished but unpublished memoirs and other manuscripts were missing. Muhammad Jamil Bandi Rozhbayani was just one of an estimated five hundred intellectuals murdered by the Baath regime between 1968 and 2003.

Despite my hosts' influential positions in Erbil, they were originally from Kirkuk, a city of about 1 million just outside the semiautonomous zone. As ancient as Erbil, Kirkuk presides over a vast oil field, with proven reserves of 10 billion barrels. In the late 1990s and early 2000s, the Kirkuk wells were pumping between five hundred thousand and nine hundred thousand barrels a day, and exporting over one-third of Iraq's highest-quality oil, despite a shortage of investment due to economic sanctions.

With oil has come suffering. Kirkuk has been the cause of bitter conflict between the Arabs, Kurds, Assyrians, and Turcomans ever since 1927, when its oil fields were first discovered. All four groups lay historical claim to the city, but during most of the twentieth century, Kirkuk was predominantly Kurdish and, thus, a violent flash point between the Kurds and the Iraqi government. It was largely Kirkuk that caused the failure of the 1970 March Manifesto, which in effect would have granted the Kurds a federated state, as Mulla Mustafa demanded that Kirkuk be included in the Kurds' territory and the Baath regime refused. And a similar scenario began after the 2003 Iraq war, as Kurds demanded that Kirkuk be included in a future federated Kurdish state, and Arabs heatedly disagreed.

During the 1970s, the Baathists began an "Arabization" process, initiated by earlier regimes, designed to transform the city's ethnic makeup. To force the Kurds and other minorities out of Kirkuk, the Baathists barred the ethnic groups from owning property—revoking their deeds of ownership—and from registering businesses, marriages, and births unless the children were given Arabic names. The teaching of Kurdish was banned and Kurdish teachers expelled. Arbitrary arrests became frequent. Streets and districts were renamed in Arabic, and Arabs from elsewhere were enticed to move into Kirkuk with offers of free housing and other rewards.

Most of the expelled Kurds and others resettled in the semiautonomous safe haven. Between 1991 and early 2003, an estimated 120,000 displaced Iraqis arrived in Kurdistan, many entering only with the clothes on their backs. Some had even been robbed of their identity papers and U.N. ration cards, creating a humanitarian and bureaucratic nightmare.

My hosts had been driven out of Kirkuk after the 1991 uprising. Zahir, a towering and introspective man with a furrowed brow, told me the story over several consecutive evenings, while his handsome sons took turns translating, and Fawzia served multiple rounds of tea, cookies, and fruit. She also did most of the family's cooking and cleaning. Feminism in Kurdistan has yet to extend to housework.

In early March 1991, as the post–Gulf War uprising began, the Iraqis preemptively rounded up every male Kurd in Kirkuk between the ages of sixteen and sixty, eventually to arrest over five thousand. Zahir was caught at seven A.M. on March 11 by men in red masks and taken with hundreds of others to Maidan Amalah, or Workers' Square. Here Ali "Chemical" Hassan al-Majid, the mastermind behind the Anfal, and his brother were waiting. Arbitrarily, the two selected thirty-four men from the crowd and shot them.

Back at the house, Fawzia and the children heard the shots. "Everyone in the neighborhood was crying," she said, "and later in the square, we saw fingers, money, parts of people stuck to the wall by blood. They'd been splattered all over by the machine guns."

Zahir and the other prisoners were herded into buses and taken to Topzawa, an army camp south of Kirkuk. There, they were packed into standing-room-only, eight-by-fifty-meter cells for forty-eight hours without food or water.

"On the third day, the soldiers released two hundred or three hundred mostly old and sick men," Zahir said. "And on the fourth day, the special security forces of Saddam's son Qusay put us on buses again. Each one called the other 'sir,' and they were all very young, under eighteen. They were like a gang, like the Khmer Rouge, and they commanded even the older Iraqi officers who first arrested us. . . . On the bus, they killed one epileptic because he was shaking. They said he was making trouble."

At two A.M., the buses arrived at a second prison, this one outside Tikrit and surrounded by barbed wire and mines. The men were divided into groups of about fifty each and shoved into pitch-black four-by-six-meter cells, with no windows and thick doors. Some of the men in Zahir's cell started crying, but he began talking, urging the others to introduce themselves.

"I was thinking of All Quiet on the Western Front by Erich Maria Remarque," he said, "and I said to them, it will be better if we know who we are, especially if some of us survive, to tell the others' families."

About twelve hours later, the prisoners convinced the guards to give them a lightbulb, which both eased and heightened their fears. Their cell walls were covered with graffiti and blood from the Kuwaiti prisoners who had been captured not long before them, during the Gulf War. Where were those prisoners now?

After one week in the prison, most of the men had dysentery. But Zahir was still healthy. He had not eaten the food provided, surviving only on the dried apricots that he had with him at the time of capture. The apricots had been given to him by his daughter Kurdonia, and he vowed not to eat them all until he saw his family again.

Finally, after twenty days of imprisonment, the men were taken to their third and last prison, Warrar, where they remained until May 20, when they were released, following post-uprising negotiations. During the men's imprisonment, no one had registered their names, and their families had had no idea whether they were alive or dead.

At this point, Fawzia and the rest of the family took up the story.

After Zahir's arrest, they stayed in Kirkuk at first, hoping for his return. But when the uprising reached the city on March 18, they fled to the safety of their relatives in Chemchemal. The *peshmerga* captured Kirkuk for a few days, but on March 21, the Iraqi forces bombed the city, and hundreds of civilians were killed.

The bombing spread to Chemchemal. Out picnicking, the family saw a helicopter circling overhead and knew that the Iraqi warplanes were coming. "We ran for our cars, with thirty-six people crowding into one Land Cruiser," Fawzia said. "We went to Suleimaniyah and stayed in a school overnight. There were explosions everywhere. And the next day, we ran to Iran, escaping over the border on foot."

The trek took five days, through much rain and mud. The children were ages thirteen, ten, and three. Hozak fainted, Kurdonia had allergy attacks, and they all slept on wet cushions in the cold and often pouring rain. The worst danger were the land mines. But they crossed safely and, with the help of Iranian Kurds, found their way to a refugee camp.

Fourteen days later, through much searching and several lucky accidents, Zahir arrived. "We heard our names over the loudspeaker, and we ran and saw our father," Zhila said. "Up until then, we thought he was dead. He looked like another person. He had a beard and was thin and sunburned." And he still had dried apricots in his pocket.

NOT ALL OF my discussions with the Rozhbayani family were so serious. Thanks to the sons Hozak and Zhila, I finally learned a few Kurdish jokes that I could understand. Many of them concerned the citizens of Erbil, known as Hawler among Kurds, who have a reputation for simplemindedness.

"A man from Hawler buys a mobile telephone," said Hozak. "The phone rings and he answers it, very surprised. 'How did you know where I was?' he asks."

"A Kurd from Hawler and an Arab are friends," said Zhila. "They are visiting one day when someone writes a slogan on the wall below them. The Kurd lowers the Arab out the window by a rope to see what it says. 'It says, long live Mulla Mustafa,' the Arab says. The Kurd claps his hands and the Arab falls."

Other jokes concerned Saddam Hussein or the Arabs.

"Saddam's daughter is in an accident," said Zhila. "She calls her father and gives the phone to the man who hit her. 'Do you know who I am?' Saddam asks. 'Yes,' the man says. 'Do you know who I am?' 'No,' Saddam says. 'Thank God,' the man says, and hangs up."

"After an election, the Americans are very slow, they take twenty-four hours to count the votes. The British are better, they take only four hours. But the Arabs are the best—they know the results before the election!"

Another joke concerned one of Kurdistan's most popular singers, a heartthrob named Zakaria, whose face was plastered all over the CD shops in downtown Erbil. Zakaria had given a concert in Erbil the year before my visit, during which several young women had kissed him, much to the outrage of conservative Kurdistan.

"After the concert, a *mullah* gives a sermon," Hozak said. "He says, 'There is too much adoration of this man Zakaria, the one that sings, I can't remember exactly what—' And the whole mosque starts to sing one of Zakaria's most famous songs."

WHILE STAYING WITH the Rozhbayani family, I went to visit some less fortunate Kirkukis living in the Beneslawa refugee camp outside Erbil—one of many such camps all over the Kurdish countryside. Part bedraggled white tents, part mud huts with straw roofs, the makeshift settlement sat in a muddy field pushed up close to a road. Here and there stood outdoor beehive-shaped ovens and one or two satellite dishes. Even in their misery, the refugees knew about American sitcoms and the NBA.

One tiny lady with huge sorrowful eyes invited me into her home, a neatly kept, hobbitlike hut with a ceiling so low I could barely stand up, miniature yard, cement floor, pile of bedding, and baby asleep in a corner. Once happily married, the woman had divorced her husband after he took a second wife, even though she was pregnant at the time. But then she lost her job—cleaning floors for a school—and the Iraqi government told her that she must call herself Arab or leave. She left, and now survived only on her U.N. rations, some of which she sold.

A few yards away, in a flimsy tent with a dirt floor, plastic bags and

Outside Erbil

raggedy clothes everywhere, lived a wiry man in his thirties with his pregnant wife, two young sons, and an older, dazed-looking woman relative who was missing her front teeth. They had left Kirkuk because the man refused to join the Baath Party and was afraid of being imprisoned. The older woman *had* been imprisoned, for allegedly planning to bomb a police station—at her age! the man said—and refusing to say she was Arab. I can't speak Arabic, so how can I say I am Arab? the woman mumbled. Good point, I thought.

The third refugee home I entered was a well-kept, two-room, cement-block house with whitewashed walls, a neat fence of black sticks, a gate built from flattened tin containers fastened together, and a garden with flowers. Here, I met a refined lady in a tweed suit whose family had once been successful Kirkuk businesspeople. But she and her husband, both teachers, had been expelled in 1989 for teaching the Kurdish language and refusing to call themselves Arab. Upon arriving in Erbil, they rented a house, which they paid for by selling their possessions one by one, year by year. Then her husband became seriously ill, and they had nothing left to sell. She, her husband, and their teenager daughters were just scraping by on her teacher's salary.

To be forced to deny one's ethnicity is a strange thing. In some ways, it seems relatively benign, at least compared to imprisonment, torture, and death. But in other ways, it is the ultimate cruel act, to be fought against at all costs, as it denies not only one's existence but also one's right to exist.

I would learn much more about the practice, and its repercussions, in Turkey.

HIMDAD ABDUL-QAHHAR, an English professor at the University of Salahuddin, invited me to speak to some of his classes. We had exchanged e-mails before I left New York, thanks to a mutual contact, and by the time we met one afternoon in a dimly lit university corridor, I found him brimming with plans for my visit.

It was through Himdad and others at the University of Salahuddin that the intense hunger of the Iraqi Kurds hit home to me. This was a people desperate to learn more about the world, to devour knowledge that had so long been denied them. Every time I stepped foot on the campus, I was instantly besieged with throngs of students and teachers, all of whom wanted to talk. It had nothing to do with me personally, and everything to do with my foreignness: I represented a conduit to the wider world.

One popular topic of discussion among the students and teachers was how democracy was affecting Kurdistan.

"After the uprising, when people first were free, some threw litter on the street and said, 'I am free, I can do what I want!' " said a teacher. "They didn't understand what freedom is. They didn't understand that freedom means responsibility. We still need much education."

"Our society is changing too fast, and this is a danger," said a student. "Some who are younger than us have lost themselves. They don't care about Kurdistan. They only care about material things, like people in the West."

"We still have many problems," said another. "The parties have too much power. We don't have real democracy yet. But these problems seem like nothing to us because of our history."

Others wanted to discuss the role of the United States in the developing world.

"We like what America stands for—freedom and democracy—and the way that politics are run inside your country," said one student, whose beard gave away his political Islamic leanings. "And we hope to one day have a system like yours. But we don't like what America is doing to the rest of the world. You are trying to control everything, and make every society like you. But we are not Western, we are Muslim."

"Religion is a strength for us, and we must use it," said another student. "Islam is very important to our future."

"There are some who abuse our religion, like Iran—they say they are good Muslims but they are not," said a woman in a head scarf. "Others have lost their religion, like Turkey, and still not joined the West. We don't want to be like them."

The students' comments surprised me. I'd grown accustomed to speaking with Kurds who couldn't praise the United States highly enough, while often blaming political Islam for Kurdistan's woes. I wondered how much of the students' opinions were due to their more contemporary education, how much to the resurgent interest in Islam among the young everywhere, and how much to the fighting between the KDP and PUK, which had caused some disillusioned Kurds, and especially young Kurds, to give up on traditional Kurdish politics. I also thought, both then and after the 2003 Iraq war, that for all the pro-U.S. sentiment running rampant in Iraqi Kurdistan, it could not be taken for granted.

ONE DAY, HOZAK, the younger Rozhbayani son, took me on a tour of the College of Dentistry, at which he was a student. Only seven years old, the college was housed in one of the university's more run-down buildings—though a new home was in the works—and, like many faculties, had a shortage of instructors and up-to-date periodicals and books. Of the college's 170 students, over half were women.

As we toured the campus, Hozak pointed out that most of the university's male students "don't know how to dress." By this he meant that most were too formally attired, in dark suits and ties, or well-pressed pants and shirts. Only Hozak and a handful of others wore the Western uniform of jeans and sneakers. And as for the women, could I tell the difference in their *hejab*, or Islamic covering? he asked. I shook my head, though I was aware of a wide variety of clothing styles, including many in Western dress.

The women wearing the formal suits with calf-long skirts came from religious families and, though conservative, could usually be approached by male students, Hozak said. But the women in the ankle-length dresses and tight head scarves were more Islamic and couldn't be approached. Those attired in loose head scarves and Western-style clothes wore the *hejab* just for fashion, while those in tight pants, flattering coats, and loose head scarves were refugees from Iran. These last two groups could also be approached by men, but the students from Iran tended to stick to themselves.

Hozak's comments fascinated me. As I'd been told in Dohuk, gender relations did seem to be slightly less rigid in Erbil than they were farther north, but still, the whole area was a minefield through which both men and women moved with extraordinary caution. Many were also quite circumspect in what they said to me.

A few students at the University of Salahuddin, and at the University of Suleimaniyah, which I visited a few weeks later, did have a boyfriend or girlfriend. All the other students knew about these couples and watched them with what seemed to be a mix of jealousy and protective surveillance; the university felt like a hideaway apart from the harsher gaze of Kurdish society at large. However, even within the university, these young couples were bound to certain codes. Their relationships were expected to be platonic and to lead to marriage. If a relationship did not lead to marriage, a girl might be able to escape condemnation the first time around, but not the second, and the boy's reputation could also suffer.

The year before my visit, a "great catastrophe" had occurred at the school, a medical student told me. A student caught a couple kissing and reported them to the dean, who wanted them expelled. Talk and protest erupted all over campus, until the issue was finally resolved with the suspension of the "guilty" students for three days.

"The whole thing was very stupid," the medical student said. "Our dean is very conservative. But even among married people in Kurdistan, there is no kissing or hugging in public. It is shameful. Only holding hands is okay. But if a boy and girl are not married, they cannot touch at all. Not even with the finger. It's something very bad. The boy will feel guilty and feel for the girl. So a boy will not approach a girl unless he thinks it is serious. It's too much trouble, and when he approaches, he approaches very slowly.

"In a relationship, a boy and girl can talk about everything, even sexual things. But if they kiss, they must marry. If not, it's a disgrace, and the girl will not have another chance."

"There's much sexual repression in Kurdish society," a well-educated thirty-something woman told me a week or so later, "but some of it comes out in talk—and in our songs, which are very sexual, maybe the most sexual in the Middle East. And once women are married, they talk about sex a lot—they love to tell dirty jokes on the telephone and send dirty e-mails. It's as if they've joined a secret club."

One that men have undoubtedly entered at a far earlier age, I thought, wondering, as I often did, at all in Kurdish society that was hidden to me, and would remain hidden.

Yours is a pair of perfect pears;
Your bosom is a garden in Merivan.
Those two pears on your bosom, I am afraid of touching them.
I fervently wish I could be a button on your dress
So that I could watch your bosom and breast.

—*Kurdish folk song from Erbil region*

ONE OF MY FAVORITE STUDENTS at the university was Sherin, who drew me aside one day to tell me a secret, although I never quite figured out what it was. Mostly, she seemed simply to want to talk, and we met on several occasions. Delicate and very pretty, with streaked hair, Sherin usually wore neatly pressed blue jeans, feminine blouses, and open-toed sandals. She also spoke much better English than most of her peers. She'd learned by watching American movies—her favorite actors were Kevin Costner and Bruce Willis. In fact, she loved all things American, and sometimes seemed beside herself with excitement when with me, simply by virtue of my nationality.

But despite her modern clothes and Western interests, Sherin came from what sounded like quite a traditional family. She had originally hoped to become a translator, but couldn't because of her father, who didn't want her meeting so many foreigners. She also couldn't talk with boys at school, let alone have a boyfriend, as it might get back to her father. In fact, once when she and I were alone in a taxi together, she refused even to talk to the driver, as it was against her father's precepts. Sherin said she was interested in creative writing, but she never wrote about love—her father might find out.

Still, Sherin loved her father "so much," she told me on many occasions. "He is very strict, but he is very good," she said. "And I am not the owner of myself. Everything I do, I must think of my sisters, I must think of my family, I cannot act alone. Sometimes this makes me nervous because I am not free psychologically. But it is necessary."

And this, I thought, was an important crux to understanding the relationship between the sexes and much else in Kurdistan. Having a love affair wasn't about following one's heart, or even about lust. Having, or rather not having, a love affair was about loyalty, both to the family and, by extension, to all Kurdish society. Acting inappropriately meant deeply betraying the family and perhaps causing its ruin. To follow one's heart had the potential to destroy all that one loved most.

LEYLA, A SLENDER, athletic-looking woman in pants and a black jacket, had invited me to spend the night at her dormitory, one of a half-dozen cheery utilitarian buildings clustered around walkways and gardens, enclosed by a high wall. Leyla's friends joined us in the gardens soon after my arrival, and we spoke about many topics, including Saddam, American music, and the possibility of a U.S. attack on Iraq, which everyone favored. Then we focused in on personal stories. As usual, everyone had one.

One woman with curled hair and eyes framed with mascara said that she had been promised "from the cradle" to a grown man of a neighboring tribe because her uncle had killed one of the man's family—a common practice in tribal Kurdistan. But by the time she reached puberty, the man was forty-six, and she refused to marry him. He agreed to let her go if she paid him 100,000 *dinars*—an enormous sum. But then she got lucky. The man ran into financial difficulties and agreed to let her go for only 15,000 *dinars*. "Now I am studying to be a teacher and every day I thank God for my good fortune," she said.

Another woman, dressed in a tight black sweater, had also been promised "from the cradle" to an older man. But when she was in her second year of high school, she told her family that she would never marry him. She wanted to continue her studies, perhaps become a doctor or journalist, and although "the man was beautiful, he was empty in the head." Her father had been angry at first, but he loved her and eventually relented.

A third woman pulled me aside to tell me privately that she was the daughter of a man who had two wives. "My friends don't know, please, please don't tell," she said urgently, making me promise. Her mother was the unfortunate first wife, who had borne only five daughters, no sons, and so her father had married again, to a woman who'd given him three sons and two daughters. As a businessman, he was rarely home, but when he was, he stayed exclusively with his second family—the student hadn't seen him in years. Why did the man bother having so many children if he wasn't going to stick around? I wondered, moved by the student's distress and need to tell me her story.

That evening, after a simple dinner of cracked wheat, yogurt, and tea, Leyla took me around the dormitory to collect more stories. I spoke with students whose villages had been destroyed in the Anfal, students whose fathers and brothers had disappeared, students who'd been forced out of Kirkuk, and students who'd survived the devastating chemical bombing of Halabja. I listened and took notes until I couldn't listen or take notes anymore. There were just too many stories, and after a certain point, they all sounded the same. I felt weighted down, to perversely—and guiltily—perk up only when a story was especially gruesome.

At the same time, I felt in awe. Here were all these hundreds of young women—just a tiny fraction of young Kurds everywhere—who were not only putting their indescribable past behind them, but gamely moving forward into a modern and, to them, completely foreign new world. Who knew what these women could do, where they might go, what Kurdistan might become?

CHAPTER ELEVEN

Along the Hamilton Road, with Side Trips

ı ı ı ı ı

IN 1928, A BRITISH ENGINEER NAMED ARCHIBALD M. HAMILTON set out to build a road through one of Kurdistan's wildest and most inaccessible regions—a land about an hour north of Erbil, filled with jagged mountains, deep-cut gorges, rushing rivers, and sheer rock cliffs. The ostensible purpose of the road was to enable trade between Iraq and Iran, hitherto difficult because of the many mountains. But an equally important by-product of the project was to gain control over the fiercely independent Kurdish tribes who lived in the region. As Hamilton writes in *Road Through Kurdistan*, quoting the director of the project, " 'You know that all great nations, past and present, have found roads essential for maintaining law and order. Once highways have penetrated a region the wildest people are pretty sure to become peaceful simply by copying civilised modes of life. . . .' "

Hamilton Road, as it became known, begins at Spilik Pass, just east of the town of Harir. When Hamilton started work, Spilik Pass was infamous for its marauding brigands, who for centuries used the lookout point to watch out for caravans traveling between Arabia and Persia. The engineering party was itself under constant threat of attack.

Beyond the pass, Hamilton Road turns a bend to reveal a blinding vista of blue-white peaks marching toward the horizon, before starting a twisting descent into dark, mysterious Gali Ali Beg, a skinny, ten-mile-long chasm. Canyon walls rise on both sides, as slopes striated with diagonal slabs of rock flash by, turning the world into a tilting whirligig. Glittering patches of streams appear, to end in a thick, fast gush of water—Gali Ali Beg waterfall—shooting out of the mountainside like a fat tongue.

From the falls, Hamilton Road enters the valley proper, its entrance marked by a twenty-foot-high column of twisting orange-and-white rock. With sheer walls rising on both sides, the road nudges its way forward, winding in and out of shadows. Alongside rushes the chasm's river, above which hide caves once used by the *peshmerga*, and small waterfalls bursting out of rock, silver sunflowers. High above, striated cliffs resemble castle battlements, keeping watch over all who pass below.

In the spring, grasses and wildflowers erupt all over the gorge, dashing drops of color everywhere. "When spring comes to Gali Ali Beg," writes Hamilton, "the barren country of Kurdistan, with its rugged mountains and grey rocks, bursts suddenly into extraordinary beauty. . . . The mists lift, and it is as if a veil that for months past had hung over the eyes of the beholder, were suddenly withdrawn. . . . One realizes then why men have fought and slain each other during so many centuries for possession of these apparently useless lands."

JUST BEYOND GALI ALI BEG was a turnoff for Diana, where I had an invitation to stay with an Assyrian family. Perhaps descendants of the ancient Assyrian Empire—a subject of much debate among scholars—the Assyrians are not Kurds, but a separate Christian people, also known as Nestorians, who broke with the Western church in A.D. 431. Their community once extended as far east as China and Siberia, but they suffered horrific slaughter at the hands of the Mongols, shrinking to a tiny population centered in southeastern Turkey and northwestern Iran until after World War I, when many moved to northern Iraq. From the 1920s until the Anfal, Diana was predominantly Assyrian, but now housed only about eighty Assyrian families amid a much larger Kurdish refugee population.

The road into town meandered past a marketplace selling carpets, couches, and cabinets, all sitting outside in the dust. At one end was the Diana Prosthetic Limbs Center, and at the other, a bridge leading into the older, quieter, prettier part of town, where the Assyrians lived. Passing over the bridge, the atmosphere on the streets immediately felt strikingly different from anything I'd yet experienced in Kurdistan, though I would encounter it again in Ainkawa, a Christian town just outside Erbil. People were dressed in T-shirts and jeans, men and women were casually socializing, and inviting cafés were open for business. It was the freer Christian culture that did it, some Muslim Kurds later ruefully told me.

In a walled compound across from Diana's main church lived my hosts—Guergis Yalda, his wife, Wargin Issa, and their three children. Out front stretched a garden and porch, while inside, their home was spacious and airy, furnished with Persian carpets and baroque-style chairs. On the walls hung several religious plaques and photographs of Guergis as a *peshmerga*. A tall man dressed in *khak* and a turban, he had joined the Barzani revolution in 1968, at age seventeen.

Like Guergis, many rural Assyrians joined the Kurdish resistance early on, fought alongside them for decades, and passionately supported the current Kurdish leadership. In contrast, many urban Assyrians kept well away from the revolution, and harbored deep resentment toward the Kurds, both for historical reasons and for more recent grievances, primarily over land claims. When setting up the semiautonomous zone, the Kurdish government made equal rights of minorities a founding principle, and the Christians had five representatives in parliament, many more than their small population warranted. Nonetheless, relationships between the two groups were often strained.

One of the most famous of the Assyrian *peshmerga* was a woman commander named Margaret George, whose name was frequently mentioned to me as an example of Kurdish tolerance toward both women and Christians. But Margaret George, much distinguished in battle in the early 1960s, was a poor and ironic exemplary choice. Not only had she been one of few women fighters in the Iraqi Kurdish revolution, she had also been murdered in 1966, probably by a jealous lover.

Guergis had joined the Kurdish revolution "to protect my family from the Iraqi government," he said. "And because I liked Mulla Mustafa. All Assyrians liked Mulla Mustafa, and he liked Assyrians. He trusted us more than he trusted his own Kurds."

As a *peshmerga*, Guergis's expertise lay in land mines. He advanced ahead of the regular forces to deactivate the mines, or followed behind to lay mines for the enemy. The Russian-made mines were the easiest to find, as they were stuck into the ground on nails. American-made ones, buried in the earth, were more problematic.

From 1968 to 1974, Guergis fought in the mountains, and, after the Algiers Accord, fled to Iran. But he never forgot his childhood sweetheart Wargin. For twelve years, they kept in touch by phone and finally, in 1981, married. "Even when we weren't in contact, I always knew she was waiting for me and never looked at another," Guergis said, gazing fondly at his wife. As I was discovering, the people of northern Iraq are highly romantic.

Also living with the family was Guergis's father Yalda, to whom everyone was eager to introduce me. He's almost one hundred years old, but speaks excellent English, they said—a claim in which I didn't place much stock. I was always being introduced to people who allegedly spoke excellent English, only to find that their grasp of the language was fair at best.

A tiny man paralyzed from the waist down, Yalda, I soon realized, spent his days sitting largely alone on big, puffy cushions in his sunny bedroom. Blind and almost deaf, he wore a sweater and dapper fedora throughout my visit and kept himself company by praying and singing for hours at a time, his lilting voice rising and falling as the world swirled by. The family was accustomed to the sound, eating and talking in other rooms to its background, but to me it was extraordinary, a harmony to the melody of life.

To talk to Yalda was to interrupt his inner dialogue and penetrate through hoary shades of old age—a challenging task I didn't undertake until the second day of my visit. Yet when I did, I was astonished to discover that the family was right—Yalda spoke a near perfect British English, using a sophisticated vocabulary far larger than almost anyone else I'd met in Kurdistan. He hadn't spoken English in many years, but easily fell back into the language. I sensed his excitement at the chance to speak it again. "You came back!" he said to me at one point after I'd left him for several hours.

Born in 1907, Yalda had served with the British levy forces, or conscripted troops, composed of mostly Assyrian soldiers under British officers, employed to help control the unruly Iraqi countryside after World War I. Later, he'd worked intermittently as an interpreter in various military and civilian capacities, including a stint at the front during World War II. Between jobs, he came home to till the soil in Diana.

Yalda was filled with stories of battles and betrayals, which I had a hard time following at first, as I thought he was telling me his personal history. But then it dawned on me that he was reciting the whole sorry twentieth-century history of the Assyrian people, including their 1920s resettlement in northern Iraq from Turkey and Iran, following much harassment by the

Turks and Persians, and their betrayal at the hands of the British. The Assyrians had supplied the British with most of their troops during the 1920 to 1932 British Mandate, creating bitter antagonisms between them and their Muslim neighbors. So when the British Mandate ended, the Assyrians requested special protection from Britain or permission from the League of Nations to migrate to Syria en masse. But the British saw no reason to reward their loyalty and left them to fend for themselves under the newly instated Hashemite monarchy. Thereupon the Arab rulers deemed the Assyrian community, despite its small size, to be a threat to national unity. In August 1933, Iraqi armed forces massacred many hundreds of Assyrian villagers. Joining in the fray against the Christians were the Kurds.

Not surprisingly, Yalda had little good to say about his Kurdish compatriots. But, echoing his son Guergis, he made one major exception. "The best Kurds are the Barzanis," he said. "They are not Christian, but they are kind people, they are educated people. We can work and live with the Barzanis."

GUERGIS AND I could communicate in Persian and English, but for more serious conversations, we depended on the help of a neighbor, Susan. A pretty and vivacious woman in her thirties, Susan had recently returned from many years spent living in Canada. She had married a Canadian but was now divorced and back to see if she could make a place for herself in the new Kurdistan—although I sometimes wondered why exactly she had returned, as she, too, had little good to say about the Kurds.

One morning, Guergis, Susan, and I set out to explore the Hamilton Road east of Gali Ali Beg. But first, we returned to the dramatic gorge to take a narrow, zigzagging detour up a mountainside to the fortress town of Rowanduz. Diagonal shafts of brown and red fell in striated cliffs around us as we climbed, while on the earth's floor below, at the junction of the rivers of Gali Ali Beg and a smaller gorge, waters boiled.

We entered Rowanduz, once the thriving capital of the Soran emirate, built on sheer rock cliffs between two chasms and flanked by eight thousand-foot-high peaks. To one side rose gray-faced Hindren Mountain, the site of a decisive 1966 battle in which a few thousand *peshmerga* had held off ten thousand Iraqis, forcing the government to negotiate with Mulla Mustafa. To another side dropped Kharand Valley, into which we gazed to see birds floating on the winds and a green snake of a river blinking far below. During World War I, when the Russians were fighting the Turks in the area, a squadron of Russian Cossacks charged toward Rowanduz at dusk, unaware of the gorge, and fell to their deaths, Guergis said.

Rowanduz itself, for all its splendid setting, felt poverty-stricken and neglected. In its center lay a bereft square equipped with a cannon, which had been made by one Wastah Rajab for his emir, Mir Muhammad, the one-eyed prince who ruthlessly captured Amadiya and much of the sur- rounding region in the 1820s and early 1830s, slaughtering thousands along the way.

Rejoining the Hamilton Road, Guergis, Susan, and I continued east. The way was dotted with poppies and caves, some of which Guergis had lived in as a *peshmerga*. He told war stories as the landscape flashed by—the Iraqis had bombed here, a KDP hospital had stood there—and seemed to know everyone manning the checkpoints we passed. Watching him wave to the grizzled guards, their baggy pants flapping in the wind, I got the sense of a huge net laid over the land, with everyone and everything connected.

Here and there erupted the occasional dark brown tents of the semi- nomads. Usually, two or three were clustered together—rectangular shapes with open sides and whipped peaks, supported by sticks. Goats and sheep and children sometimes gamboled about out front.

The tents were made by women, who wove strips of goat's hair, each about three feet wide by fifteen or more feet long, and sewed them together. The goat's hair was waterproof, but it still let in the light, and the average tent lasted six or seven years. There were both winter tents, which were per- manently pitched near towns and villages, and much smaller summer tents, made for carting up mountains.

We reached the village of Berserin, marking the end of Gali Berserini, another steep, shadowy ravine. On the lam somewhere within it had once lived Ismail Simko Agha, the handsome, daring, and ruthless chief of Iran's Shikak tribe, from the Urumieh plains in northwest Iran. In 1921, Simko led a successful revolt against the Persians, proclaiming autonomy, and was subsequently driven over the border, into Iraq.

Simko had been a notoriously cruel leader, of the kind that has given Kurds a bad name. He once obtained the surrender of rebellious under- lings by promising to spare their lives and grant them their freedom. He then had their right wrists smashed and neck tendons slashed, leaving them technically free, but with their heads rolling.

Not being as familiar with Simko's history as I could have been, I made the mistake of mentioning his name to Susan, who responded with a rush of invectives. One of Simko's most treacherous acts had been to invite a delegation of Assyrians, including their spiritual leader Mar Shimum Benyamin, then over ninety, to meet to discuss a possible alliance during World War I. Simko then ambushed the party, killing every one of its members, and drank Benyamin's blood in a rage.

Hamilton Road continued, with snowcapped mountains rearing to the right and the left. At times, high hills hemmed us in on both sides; at other times, we shot up inclines to see waves of green and blue ridges lapping in all directions. We were nearing the Iranian border, a wild region that had often been entirely under *peshmerga* control. We passed the small towns of Nowperdan, once a KDP political center, and Choman, where my lugubrious friend Dr. Shawkat had spent his early revolutionary years. Thereafter soared Halgurd Mountain, the highest mountain in Iraq, a 12,250-foot-high peak standing in magnificent isolation, wrapped in a mantle of snow.

As we drove, Guergis continued telling his *peshmerga* stories, praising the valorous Kurdish movement at every turn. Susan was telling stories now, too—about how the brutal and ignorant Kurds had ruined the country. Guergis could not understand Susan's English, and she paid little attention to what she was translating, making me feel like a Ping-Pong ball bouncing back and forth between two widely divergent opinions. And in the end, though my sympathies lay with the Kurds, all that mattered were the heart-stopping mountains.

On the slopes beyond Halgurd Mountain, red flags flashed. Between them crawled space-age men in heavy helmets and plastic face shields. The flags marked land mines, which the men were defusing. An estimated 12 to 15 million mines riddle Iraqi Kurdistan, especially near its borders, making it one of the most heavily mined regions in the world. Most of the mines were laid in the 1970s, when the Iraqi army used them against the Kurds, and during the Iran-Iraq War, when they were laid by both countries. Between 1991 and 2002, over thirty-six hundred people had been killed and over six thousand maimed by the mines, and civilian casualties continued at the rate of ten to twenty people per month. Between 1993, when demining began, and 2002, only about a hundred thousand mines, or less than 1 percent, had been destroyed.

Hamilton Road ended in Haj Omran, a scruffy border town where Mulla Mustafa had once had his headquarters. Clinging to a mountainside, the town overlooked a wide valley, making it a strategic lookout point that the Iraqis had been furious to lose to the Iranians, with the help of the KDP, at one point during the Iran-Iraq War.

"Mulla Mustafa's house was down there near that spring," Guergis said.

"Tourists used to come here to ski before the Kurds destroyed it," Susan said.

Haj Omran centered on one windswept street lined with dusky storefronts and dingy eateries. Jostling shoulders in the thoroughfare were dozens of dark men in bulky jackets and straight-legged trousers, few baggy pants and no turbans. There were also no women, or, at least, none in sight. Haj Omran existed for trade, not for living.

The tradesmen in town operated legally, Guergis said—though I had my doubts—while smugglers operated down below. He pointed to a spot in the valley far away where I could just make out dozens of men and horses moving about in a square-shaped camp.

I remembered a popular joke I had heard. God pushed the Kurdish people out of heaven and into hell because they were making too much noise with their dancing. But Satan didn't like the noise either, so he sent the Kurds to purgatory. Passing by one day, God noticed that things were suspiciously quiet. What's happening? Why isn't anyone dancing? he asked a young boy. Oh, everyone is too busy to be dancing! the boy said. They are all out smuggling people between heaven and hell.

NORTH OF HAMILTON ROAD lay the valley and village of Barzan, the heart of Barzani tribal territory and birthplace of Mulla Mustafa. The region was best explored with a member of the Barzani confederation, as they are a notoriously insular and private people. I headed north with Mr. Saleh Mahmoud Barzani and Jula, a translator. Mr. Saleh was an impeccably dressed older gentleman in crisp *khak* crisscrossed with a shiny leather pistol harness, a double-tiered red-and-white turban, and a soot black mustache that I suspected was dyed. Many Kurdish men are quite vain, and to dye one's hair or mustache is not at all unusual. Jula was a slender young woman who'd recently returned to Iraq from Iran. She was not happy to be back. Previously pursuing a career as a filmmaker in Iran, a country known for its many fine directors, she saw no future for herself in Iraq.

When we reached Barzan, I was surprised to find myself in a wide valley dotted with dark green scrub bushes and trees. I'd heard Barzan described as "hardscrabble" and "rocky," but in the late spring at least, the region was an idyllic retreat, with the village clinging to a slope at one end, the Greater Zab River roaring with melted snows at the other, and brightly colored birds flitting between. More birds, wild animals, and plants can be found in the Barzan valley than almost anywhere else in Kurdistan, as Mulla Mustafa's older brother, Shaikh Ahmad, outlawed hunting and the use of vegetation

Heading north to Barzan

for firewood in the 1920s—one of the many unusual actions of the Barzani family.

The village of Barzan was surprisingly small, with less than two thousand people. The valley seemed to echo with emptiness. More than any other region in Kurdistan, Barzan has suffered endless assault. Only one house in the village dated back to before 1991, and the village center was not a square or marketplace, but a prominent graveyard in which Mulla Mustafa, his son Idris, and other famed Kurdish revolutionaries were buried.

The origins of the Barzani confederation are unclear, but it probably dates back only to the early nineteenth century when a newcomer to the valley, a man named Taj ad-Din, was initiated into the Naqshbandi Sufi order. This first Barzan *shaikh* and his successors soon acquired many followers in the isolated region, then inhabited by a simple but fierce pastoral people living on the edge of Zibari tribal territory. The *shaikhs* had a reputation for utmost piety and integrity, and, by the late 1800s, believers were touting the Barzan valley as a quasi-utopian community in which land was held collectively, and refugees of all tribes and religions were welcome.

Mulla Mustafa was born in 1904, the son of Shaikh Muhammad, known for his religious mysticism, and younger brother of Shaikh Ahmad, an eccentric and rebellious religious leader at least thirteen years his senior. The Ottomans imprisoned Mulla Mustafa and his mother for nine months when he was less than two years old, and hanged his oldest brother Abd Al-Salam II in 1914. His father may also have been hanged by religious fanatics in 1908. Mulla Mustafa studied for ten years in Barzan, and later furthered his education in Suleimaniyah. Always a secular leader, "Mulla" was his proper name, not a religious title.

In 1931, Shaikh Ahmad apparently instructed his followers to eat pork, perhaps to symbolize the link between Christians and Naqshbandis, infuriating a powerful neighbor, Shaikh Rashid of Baradost, who attacked the Barzani villages. The Iraqi government, already soured on Shaikh Ahmad for his refusal to obey various decrees and pay taxes, used the violent outbreak as an excuse to march on Barzan, only to be soundly defeated by the small and poor, but tough and valiant Barzani confederation. The government then called on the help of the British Royal Air Force, who bombed seventy-nine Barzani villages, destroying over thirteen hundred homes. Shaikh Ahmad and Mulla Mustafa escaped to the mountains, but they were eventually caught and exiled, first to southern Iraq and then to Suleimaniyah.

When his exile ended in 1943, Mulla Mustafa returned to Barzan and began building the Kurdish resistance movement in earnest. His first revolt failed, forcing him and about twelve hundred fighters into exile in Iran, where they joined the Kurdish Republic of Mahabad. When Mahabad was defeated in December 1946, Barzani was offered the chance to surrender, but refused. Instead, he and his forces, hotly pursued by the Iranians, fled to Iraq, Turkey, back to Iran, and finally to Russia, in a heroic retreat legendary among Kurds. "We marched for fifty-two days," Barzani once said.

"In the high mountain passes the late spring snow was six to twelve feet deep. We fought nine encounters, lost four killed and had seven wounded."

Living in exile in the Soviet Union for almost twelve years, Barzani learned Russian and studied economics and science, but never became a Communist, saying that good Muslims could not become Communists. Returning to Iraq in 1958, after Brigadier Qassem's coup d'état, he fiercely continued the Kurdish struggle until 1975, when the Algiers Accord forced him into exile again—at first in Iran, but later in the United States, where he was diagnosed with lung cancer. By then a defeated man, stranded far from his aerie in the land that had betrayed him, he spent his last years writing letters to Washington politicians, trying to raise interest in the Kurdish cause. He died on March 1, 1979.

UPON OUR ARRIVAL in Barzan, we were met by Dr. Abdullah Loqman, a tall and lanky man with salt-and-pepper hair, originally from Dohuk, who had moved to Barzan in 1991 to provide humanitarian medical aid. At that time, there had been almost nothing left standing in the entire region, he said to me in good English as we walked through the village. Only in 1997, with the help of the oil-for-food program, had relief come to the valley, in the form of reconstructed villages, paved roads, schools, and a comprehensive health program. Dr. Loqman now oversaw the region's health services and worked with a German aid organization that had built a nursing school in the valley.

Dr. Loqman took us to visit a half-dozen Barzan widows, living in reconstructed homes interspersed with animal huts on the edge of the village. Greeting us with wide smiles, the women ushered us into a spare, whitewashed room, with thin rugs and cushions, where a teenage girl prepared tea. All of the women appeared to be in their late forties and fifties, and were dressed in a distinctive style, with long black dresses and two hennaed locks of hair framing their faces. The rest of their hair was tucked away, under two thin black scarves, one of which was tightly drawn and tied in back, and the other of which was looser, its skinny ends knotted together and either thrown over the back or left to hang in front.

In 1975, after the Algiers Accord, not all of the Barzanis and their followers fled to Iran. Many remained behind in their villages, or returned home from Iran a few months later after a general amnesty. That fall, while they were out collecting their harvest, thousands of Iraqi soldiers arrived to surround and eventually destroy some eighteen hundred mostly Barzani villages. Helicopters whirling overhead to prevent escape, the soldiers brutally shoved the villagers into vehicles and bused them to the southern deserts, where they lived in desperate conditions for almost five years.

"Kissinger," Mr. Saleh spat out as the women related this story. He then glared around the room, his hawklike features catching the light from the window.

In 1980, the women went on, a convoy of army trucks rolled up to their camp to take them away again—this time to the collective town of Qushtapa, near Erbil. Qushtapa had no real facilities either, but at least it was in Kurdistan, for which they were grateful—until, that is, about three-thirty A.M. on July 30, 1983. Hundreds of soldiers surrounded the camp. Moving in a tightening band from house to house, rooftop to rooftop, they arrested all men and boys over age twelve.

"It was just before daybreak when I saw the soldiers on the roofs, in the helicopters, everywhere," said one woman. "My husband looked at them and said, 'Now is our end, these are not ordinary soldiers.' They shot everyone who tried to run away, and they searched every house, every cupboard, every WC."

The other women and we listeners sighed deeply—a reaction that I had noticed often before during the telling of tragic tales. The sighs seemed to alleviate some of the stress building up inside the room.

By noon, about nine hours after the operation had begun, it was over. Between five thousand and eight thousand Barzani men and boys had been captured in Qushtapa and three other collective towns, to be loaded onto buses and driven away. Like those who disappeared five years later during the Anfal, they were never seen again. A decade later, Saddam Hussein left little doubt as to their whereabouts. "They betrayed the country and they betrayed the covenant," he said in 1993, "and we meted out a stern punishment to them, and they went to hell."

In accusing the Barzanis of betrayal, Hussein was referring to a specific event. Shortly before the Barzani men were abducted, the KDP had helped the Iranians capture Haj Omran, the scruffy border town I had visited earlier. The men were taken in retribution. The absence of any international outcry following their disappearance may well have encouraged Hussein to use the same technique again, on a larger scale, during the Anfal.

After the buses rolled away, the Qushtapa camp was sealed and its electricity and water supply cut off. "We remained alone, only women," said a younger woman, starting to cry. The room fell silent. "We had no more men, we had lost them all. We went to the river to try to get water, but the soldiers chased us and hit us with stones. And at night, we were very afraid, maybe they would come back to rape us. We didn't dare sleep alone, we always slept six or seven together, with big knives."

Everyone was crying now, even Mr. Saleh and perhaps, I thought, Dr. Loqman. Though they had all lived and relived this story thousands of times, it was impossible not to.

"Others have cried, too, hearing our story," a woman said, watching me, "but why is the world listening only now? This happened many years ago."

THAT AFTERNOON AND the next day, Dr. Loqman took Mr. Saleh, Jula, and myself on a driving tour. We visited a small carpet factory and drove along the Greater Zab, lush with poplar trees and flanked by jagged peaks, in which once had roamed a kind of leopard and still roamed wild boar, wolves, and bear. Reaching the top of one crest, we came upon a tiny village of twenty-two families recently returned from Iran. The village had no electricity or running water, but it did have the kind of views that would cost millions many places in the world. The village *mukhtar* was a handsome, educated young man with a fashionable haircut and leather jacket.

Northeast of Barzan was Bedial, an ancient Christian settlement. Driving along a well-paved mountain road, we saw it sitting by itself on a grassy mountaintop across a valley, surrounded by red peaks. Reaching the village was a different story altogether, however, as we had to drive down one steep mountain and up another, on rocky dirt roads pockmarked with deep muddy holes. It was astonishing to hear that after Bedial was bombed in 1975, the villagers rebuilt their beloved church—sixteen hundred years old, they said—entirely by hand and on foot, hiking up and down the surrounding slopes with the necessary building materials. There had been no road then.

We traveled on, to an even more ancient site, the Shanidar Cave.

Between 1951 and 1960, an American archaeologist named Ralph Solecki excavated the cave, to find nine Neanderthal skeletons, the oldest dating back forty-six thousand years. One of Solecki's more startling discoveries were the flowers that he found buried with the bodies. "With the finding of flowers . . ." he writes, "we are brought suddenly to the realization that the universality of mankind and love of beauty go beyond the boundary of our own species. No longer can we deny the early men the full range of human feelings and emotions."

Solecki's discovery reminded me of the Kurds' own love of flowers—and dance, song, poetry, and love stories. Despite a relentlessly cruel history, at times self-inflicted, the Kurds are in many ways a gentle people.

To reach Shanidar from the road was a forty-minute walk along a trail that headed up a small crest, dipped, and swung up again to the dark triangular cave. Along the way was evidence of an old Assyrian road, built by King Sargon II to carry out expeditions against the Kurds—an earlier version of the Hamilton Road.

The mouth of the cave was about eighty feet wide by twenty-five feet high. Inside, the shelter expanded out to about twice that size, with dust motes spinning in the air and black soot hanging in thick threads from the ceiling. During the winter months, villagers kept their sheep and goats in the cave, much as they had done for centuries. Padding about on the loamy dark earth, hidden from sunlight, I wondered about all the generations that had once lived, loved, and had dreams and secrets here. The only evidence of Solecki's dig, which had descended some fifteen feet, was a shallow indentation in the floor.

THAT EVENING, AFTER a multicourse meal served by a bevy of Barzan widows, Dr. Loqman, Jula, and myself settled down in the living room to interview Mr. Saleh. Born in Barzan, he knew and had experienced much, or so I'd been told, and I wanted to hear his personal story. But that proved to be all but impossible. Although Mr. Saleh had enthusiastically agreed to be interviewed, he did not want to talk about his life, but rather about the larger Kurdish story. No matter how much I, with the help of Dr. Loqman, tried to encourage him to talk about himself, he forged ahead with a detailed and accurate impersonal history of the Iraqi Kurds. I had had other similar encounters, especially with older Kurdish men, and I

wondered how much of it had to do with the Kurds' emphasis on the communal rather than the individual. I couldn't imagine interviewing any
American about his or her life, and hearing details about U.S. foreign and
domestic policy rather than about careers, families, personal highpoints,
and low points.

Interviewing was often tricky in Kurdistan. Sometimes, as with Mr.
Saleh, there were gender- and age-difference issues. Often, as with many
villagers, there was the literacy issue. Before traveling to Iraq, I had thought
of literacy primarily in terms of whether a person could read or write, but,
in Kurdistan, I realized that it extends further than that. Literacy gives a
person reference points, the ability to reach beyond his or her immediate
world, and an acquaintance with the logic inherent in reading and writing.
During my early interviews with villagers, especially, conducted with the
help of eager but inexperienced translators, who often added yet another
layer of obfuscation to things, I frequently came away befuddled by stories
that followed no timeline, had murkily related causes and effects, and
names that meant nothing to me. It wasn't a matter of the villagers' intelligence, but their way of ordering the world.

Furthermore, there were cultural issues. Although I'd read as much as I
could before traveling to Kurdistan, in-depth anthropological studies of the
Kurds, as opposed to political ones, are limited in number, especially in
English, and I had few guidelines to go by when formulating certain kinds
of questions. How to find out about centuries-old customs and rituals when
I didn't even know exactly where to look? Much of traditional Kurdish culture was dying fast, I knew, as the younger generation was more interested
in the Internet and satellite TV than in their grandparents' old-fashioned
ways, but reaching out to record some of it was no simple matter.

I was able to coax a few personal facts out of Mr. Saleh that evening,
however. Mulla Mustafa had been his uncle, and after his own father had
been killed when he was very young, Mr. Saleh had been raised by Mulla
Mustafa's family. Later, he had worked for the Kurdish leader, serving in his
guesthouse and looking after his children while they were all living in the
mountains.

"What was Mulla Mustafa like?" I asked.

"He was a simple man, he never thought about anything but the
Kurdish cause," Mr. Saleh said. "He would say, 'I am only the servant of this
nation.' "

What little Mr. Saleh told me corresponded to what I'd read. Mulla Mustafa was said to have focused all his energies on the Kurdish struggle. A man of average height but imposing build, he was reputedly tough, charismatic, and courageous, of quick intelligence, shrewd instincts, and good judgment, despite a limited education. Usually dressed in *shal u shapik* and a two-tiered red-and-white turban, with a double cartridge belt around his waist, he liked to talk cryptically and often conveyed his ideas through fables. He regularly found the time to pray and to receive all kinds of visitors, from diplomats to peasants. However, he was also said to have been autocratic, egotistical, shortsighted, and naive in the ways of the outside world, and to have had a ruthless side.

Mr. Saleh had been with Mulla Mustafa in Haj Omran in 1971, during a famous attempt on his life. The Baath regime's head of security had sent five *imams*, or religious men, to negotiate with Mulla Mustafa, giving one of them a tape recorder, which, unbeknownst to them, was also an explosive device.

"Mulla Mustafa welcomed the *imams*, and they took seats and a servant came in with tea," Mr. Saleh said. "The *imam* turned on the tape recorder, and it exploded, but Mulla Mustafa was not killed because the servant was between him and the *imam*."

The *imams'* cars were also rigged with explosives—the men were not meant to return alive. In those days, the Baath Party did little to hide its disdain for Islam.

RETURNING TO ERBIL the following evening, I went directly to the family home of Othman and Kanan Rashad Mufti, two brothers in their fifties whose father, Rashad Mufti, had been a famous Qadiri religious leader and judge. Othman and I had a date to attend a ritual ceremony in a local *tekiye*, or religious meeting place, an excursion that he had already prepared me for by showing me graphic photographs of long-haired dervishes plunging swords and daggers into their bodies.

The Qadiris and Naqshbandis, to which the Barzanis belonged, are the two great Sufi orders of Kurdistan. Like all Sufi orders, they are mystical Islamic sects whose members work to achieve a personal, ecstatic communion with God. The Naqshbandis do so through quiet meditation, the Qadiris through ritual ceremony. Both orders' spiritual leaders, the *shaikhs*, have at times played extremely powerful roles in Kurdistan, forming alliances with wealthy *aghas* and leading mass rebellions. Kurdistan's earliest nationalist movements were led by *shaikhs*, and the Barzani family could not have reached the prominence that it did without its standing in the Naqshbandi order. Jalal Talabani, leader of the PUK party, also came from a *shaikhly* family, of the Qadiri order. Both orders transcend tribal loyalties, however, and once counted many tens of thousands of Kurds from many different tribes among their followers.

The Qadiri order arrived first in Kurdistan. Founded in the twelfth century by Shaikh Abd al-Qadir, originally of Gilan in Persia but later of Baghdad, it spread to southern Kurdistan around 1360. The Naqshbandi order, founded in the fourteenth century by Baha ad-Din Naqshband in Bukhara, in today's Uzbekistan, arrived in Kurdistan only in the early nineteenth century, but spread with much greater rapidity, largely because of its charismatic Kurdish leader, Mawlana Khalid. However, since the rise of the modern nation-states and the Kurds' growing awareness of the outside world, the influence of both sects has precipitously declined. Today, many educated Kurds scoff at the old-fashioned ways of the *shaikhs*, whose most dedicated followers remain the uneducated, powerless, and poor.

Arriving at the Mufti family home at about eight P.M., I found its front porch crowded with visitors, most older men in baggy pants and turbans, visiting in a carryover tradition from the former Rashad Mufti's religious leadership days. Neither of Rashad's sons was a religious leader—Kanan ran Erbil's archaeological museum, and Othman was director of the Ministry of Islamic and Religious Affairs—but because of their family's notable standing, dating back centuries, many believers still visited their home every evening, some coming for advice, others to socialize. The crowd made me wonder when the two brothers ever got a chance to rest.

Joining me at the Mufti family home were my English professor friend Himdad, and several of his friends. Himdad had agreed to serve as my translator that evening, and his friends had asked to come along. None of them had ever been to a Qadiri religious meeting before, and there was an escalating buzz of excitement among us as we waited to depart. Rezan, the woman translator who had shown me around Erbil, had also wanted to come, but because the ceremony was held at night, her attendance was impossible.

Finally, it was time to go. Othman's wife lent me her *abeyya*, the black tentlike garment that covers everything but the face, and we set off, heading to the Kesnazan *tekiye* in one of the darker and older sections of town. As we drove, Othman expressed some last-minute reservations about bringing me along. I would be the only woman there, he said, as the ceremony was only for men, and although he'd cleared my attendance with the local *shaikh*, some believers might resent my presence. I didn't take his words to heart; I'd been hoping to attend a Qadiri ceremony ever since arriving in Kurdistan.

As we neared the *tekiye*, the street around us became crowded with cars and men, while, at the end of the block, an entrance door blazed silver-white in the darkness. Parking, we headed toward the sound of drums and a chanted prayer, or *zikr*, which is a recitation of the divine name. The sea of men parted neatly, chanting all the while, and we passed into a foyer, where we took off our shoes, to add them to the hundreds already puddled all over the floor.

We entered a well-lit, rectangular room, where lines of men in baggy pants or caftans sat cross-legged against the walls and in a neat double row in the center. Some wore white or embroidered caps, and all were chanting "*Ya, Allah*" over and over. On the walls above hung banners embroidered with the names of Allah and the Prophet Muhammad, while up front sat a round, white-bearded *shaikh* in a bright green turban, a dagger at his waist, leading the *zikr* through a microphone. We joined the *shaikh* at the front and watched as believers filed steadily in until every inch of the floor was covered with perhaps three hundred cross-legged men. "You are the strongest, You are Almighty, stop this oppression," said the *shaikh* in a prayer as the chanting continued.

The men stood up, and recited the Islamic *shahada*, or confession of faith, "*La elaha ella Allah*"—There is no God but God. As they chanted, the men rhythmically moved their heads up and down, slowly at first but then faster and faster, as their breaths became shorter and punchier, and the *shahada* gave way to *Allah, Allah, Allah*. Three men entered thumping *dafs*—large tambourines—and some of the chanters took off their caps to let loose long cascading hair that they swung up and down with ever increasing speed until I could hear them crack. One man pointed at the sky, shouting "*Allah, Allah*," then collapsed into a faint, to be pulled out of harm's way by his colleagues.

Another *shaikh* entered, this one dressed in a green-and-gold cape and turban, followed by a dozen believers. The *shaikh* beside us took a few angry steps forward. This was his *tekiye!*, the new *shaikh* was intruding!—perhaps, Othman said, because he'd heard of my presence, which seemed to be eliciting more curiosity than disapproval. Someone brandished a sword, sending a ripple of fear and excitement through me, and the first *shaikh* became angrier than ever. Apparently, he had commanded his followers to refrain from using swords that night—at Othman's urging for my sake, I suspected. But the new *shaikh* was protesting that decision, with my secret encouragement.

The lights went out, and we all sat down while the *shaikhs* negotiated. The room grew hotter, the chanting louder. A man came up to me in the semidarkness, munching on a tea glass and pointing at my camera, and I dutifully took a picture of his mouth, miraculously devoid of cuts. Then the believers stood up again, and suddenly the swords and skewerlike daggers came out, by the dozens it seemed. The first *shaikh* had lost the battle, and the men were in a frenzy to begin. The chanting and drumming grew louder, more men pointed at the ceiling and collapsed, hair flashed. One man approached me with a dagger, crouched down, and pushed the skewer through one cheek and out the other, followed by another man who did the same with a skewer pushed through his lower jaw. The men walked around the crowd for several minutes, making sure I took their pictures, before pulling the skewers out again and pressing their thumbs against the wounds.

Other men took off their shirts and, one by one, plunged long gleaming swords through the sides of their torsos with no apparent pain or blood, although another man felt for soft spots first and pressed the wounds with his thumb afterward. Initially, the men performed their feats slowly, giving me time to take photos. Then, all at once, skewered male torsos seemed everywhere. Someone directed me to climb onto a low table, where I began clicking so fast that all I could see of the darkened room was what lay directly before my camera's lens. The chanting rose to a crescendo, and arms and hair whipped through the air as I turned left to right to left, trying to control my awkward *abeyya*, suddenly aware that the frenzied believers might decide to initiate me into their rite with a dagger or sword thrust. Still, I felt no real fear until Othman pulled me down off the table. He firmly held my hand as he rapidly escorted me out of the room and into the car without stopping for my shoes. "You are not safe," was all he said as we climbed inside, then he sent our companions back to look for my shoes.

Driving away, Himdad, his colleagues, and I talked at a feverish pitch. How had the men done it, why had they felt no pain, who was that handsome man with the waist-length hair, what had really been going on between the two *shaikhs*? And Himdad and his friends applauded my performance—you were so brave, you never hesitated, no Kurdish woman would have behaved the way you did, they said. But I didn't feel at all brave,

At the Kesnazan tekiye

just wildly elated and a little foolish. Had I really been in danger? Had I behaved naively? And what exactly had my friends meant by their comparison of me with Kurdish women? Was it a compliment, or not?

In contrast to the rest of us, Othman was almost silent. He had close ties to the *tekiye*, and had seen the ceremony hundreds if not thousands of times before. "In the morning I am on the Internet with my daughter, and in the afternoon, I talk with my wife, who is a biologist," he said gloomily.

"But in the night, I must come here, into this superstitious world. I wish for it to end. The time for such things is past." I understood what he meant, and guessed that he might be feeling defensive, but I also thought that when the time of the Qadiri ceremony is truly past, something astonishing will have gone out of the world.

CHAPTER TWELVE

In the Land of the Babans

EVERYWHERE I WENT IN IRAQI KURDISTAN, PEOPLE RAVED
about Suleimaniyah. It is the most liberal and open of Iraqi Kurdish cities,
with a long tradition of arts and culture, they said. It is filled with gracious,
charming people who love to socialize, but who are also tough and always
at the forefront of the Kurdish struggle, they said. And for the most part,
they were right. In Suleimaniyah, I felt the urge to stroll the streets, poke
into shops, go out at night—an urge that had been lacking in Dohuk and
Erbil. In Suleimaniyah, troubling subjects such as honor killings, the power
of the parties, and the lingering strength of tribal law were discussed more
frankly. Suleimaniyah also had an intangible romantic quality, though I was
hard put to say exactly why. It wasn't an especially beautiful or well-planned
city, or even an old city, as its famed Baban princes had moved their capital
to its present location only around 1785. At the time of my visit, it wasn't an
especially safe city either. Islamists had tried to assassinate Barham Salih,
the PUK prime minister, one month earlier, and although he had survived,
five of his bodyguards had been killed. *Peshmerga* also periodically blocked
off strategic streets, in response to Islamist bomb scares.

Suleimaniyah was anchored on a major thoroughfare that ran from the
outskirts of the city into the downtown, past a straggly line of offices, hotels,
Internet cafés, a large Shiite mosque said to have been built to please neighboring Iran, and a towering silo begun by the Russians before the uprising
but never completed. At the city center was a park with the busts of four

Kurds martyred after the fall of the Kurdish Republic of Mahabad, a traffic circle flanked by a mural of the 1920s rebel Shaikh Mahmoud, a bazaar selling everything from live chickens to tourist handicrafts, and the luxury marble-and-glass Palace Hotel. On par with upscale hostelry elsewhere in the world, the Palace was booked solid throughout my stay with Iranian businessmen, conventioneers, a few fellow Western journalists, and, at one point, some of my writer friends from Dohuk, in the city for—what else?— a writers conference, which had attracted about eighty Kurdish scribblers, including twenty-odd women, many from Iran. As I bumped into my old friends in the lobby, I felt as if I were somehow being woven into the warp and weft of Kurdish society, that I was indeed a "friend of the Kurds," that warm phrase by which many introduced me. Whenever I heard those words, they both heartened and saddened me, as they seemed to connote a people so neglected by history that any outsider who bothered visiting was, ipso facto, a friend.

In Suleimaniyah, many women wore slacks, fewer men wore baggy pants and turbans, and the sexes socialized together a bit more easily than they did farther north. But the difference between the regions was far less than I'd been led to expect; what looms large in the eyes of local citizenry is often much less distinct to the outsider.

Only on the outskirts of Suleimaniyah did some of the reason for its magic became apparent. The city sat in a gentle bowl, once the floor of a primordial lake, which in the early summer seemed to be bathed in a near-luminescent light, protected on two sides by mountain spurs.

At one end of the city beckoned Sarchinar, a leafy pleasure land built around a natural spring lake. Sarchinar held dozens of open-air restaurants and teahouses, some catering to families and some only to men, in which patrons dined on kebabs and rice dishes, drank beer and *araq* (a kind of anisette), and smoked the hubble-bubble, the large water pipes made of candy-colored ceramic and glass. At night, the park blazed with hundreds of globes of colored lights, bobbing gently between eaves and trees, as laughter, gossip, singing, and political discussions rang out.

I joined one such celebration one evening, a weekly gathering of a group of middle-aged professional men, no women, though all were married. A table had been set up in an isolated area, well away from the restaurants, and the men brought along appetizers and libations, with kebabs delivered later. One of the men also had a *daf*, a tambourine, and midway through the evening brought it out, as the others joined in to recite dramatic poems and sing haunting songs. Looking around at my pot-bellied, gray-haired companions, singing with longing about unrequited love, youth, and loss, I felt astonished and moved by the endless surprises of the human heart.

On the western edge of the city, near a refugee camp, rose Hero's Rock, an unimpressive black stump where the legendary Shaikh Mahmoud had been wounded. Of the Qadiri Sufi order, Shaikh Mahmoud had been appointed governor of Suleimaniyah by the British in 1918. As *shaikh*, he

Shaikh Mahmoud overlooks Suleimaniyah

had widespread influence over many different tribes, and the British awarded him the position in expectation of receiving loyalty in return.

But Shaikh Mahmoud believed himself to be the region's rightful ruler with or without the British. In 1919, with the help of tribal followers, he raised a Kurdish flag—green, with a red crescent in the middle—and imprisoned all British personnel. The British responded with an attack that left the *shaikh* defeated and exiled. Three years later, however, as the Turks gained influence in the region, the British called their old enemy back to unite the Kurds against the intruders. Again Shaikh Mahmoud lost no time in asserting independence, this time forming a Kurdish government, issuing postage stamps, publishing a Kurdish newspaper, and declaring himself King of Kurdistan. The British then bombed Suleimaniyah, forcing Shaikh Mahmoud and his forces to retreat to the mountains, from where they carried out raids against the British until 1927.

During his lifetime, Shaikh Mahmoud did not have overwhelming Kurdish support. Many of the Suleimaniyah townspeople resented his rule, other powerful tribes offered to help the British suppress him, and he was accused by some of surrounding himself with sycophants and incompetent relatives. But the *shaikh* was an early proponent of Kurdish nationalism and, as such, has since metamorphosed into a full-blown hero, his shortcomings faded into the wash of time.

Tucked high into the mountains above the other end of Suleimaniyah reigned Qala Cholan, or "Castle of Green Almonds." The headquarters of the Patriotic Union of Kurdistan, Qala Cholan had been the first home of the Baban princes. One of the most influential of Kurdish families, the dynasty was founded in the seventeenth century by Baba Suleiman, said to have been the son of a young "Frank" woman warrior named Keghan, captured during battle by the Ottomans but saved from death by the Baba's father, Fakih Ahmad. As the story goes, Fakih Ahmad took Keghan to Kurdistan, where she bore him two children and, one day when he was away, single-handedly defeated an enemy tribe, putting four or five hundred to flight and killing many others. Thereupon, Keghan declared her debt to Fakih Ahmad for saving her life repaid, and she returned to her city. But lovelorn Fakih Ahmad followed her there, to rescue her once again, this time from marriage to a brute who beat her for being "dishonored," and the twosome happily returned to Kurdistan.

A fractious family, the Babans were often at war with each other and with their rivals, the Ardalans, who lived on the other side of the Zagros Mountains in today's Sanandaj, Iran. Yet the Babans were also responsible for transforming Suleimaniyah into a cultural capital, thanks to Abd al-Rahman, who ascended to the Baban throne in 1789—to be deposed by various usurpers five times before his death in 1813. Abd al-Rahman had spent much time in the Ardalan court, where he greatly admired his rival's cultural patronage system. Importing architects, scientists, and religious scholars from Persia, he built mosques and schools, and he encouraged poets and minstrels to compose in the region's Sorani dialect, as opposed to the Gurani dialect encouraged by the Ardalans. Sorani then rose to become the Kurds' literary and intellectual language. The first Kurdish press was established in Suleimaniyah in 1920, and over 80 percent of all Kurdish books published in the twentieth century were in Sorani. The city's cultural history was a source of great pride to its citizens and to all Iraqi Kurdish intellectuals. One major reason why many early intellectual revolutionaries looked down on Mulla Mustafa was because he spoke Kermanji, not Sorani.

In 1850, the Ottomans dismissed the Babans from power, and the Kurdish emirate system came to an end. But the Babans live on in the imagination of the Suleimaniyah people. Writes the nineteenth-century poet Shaikh Reza Talabani in "The Baban Land":

I remember Sulaimani when it was the Capital of the Babans;
It was neither subject to the Persians nor slave-driven by the House
    of Usman.
Before the palace gate Shaikhs, Mullas and Ascetics stood in line;
The place of pilgrimage for those with business was the Gird-i
    Seywan . . .
Arabs! I do not deny your excellence; you are the most excellent; but
Saladin who took the world was of Baban-Kurdish stock.

SULEIMANIYAH WAS ALSO HOME to Jalal Talabani, the round, talkative, and charismatic president of the PUK. Involved in Kurdish politics since the late 1950s, Talabani, like Massoud Barzani and his father before him, had near-total control over his party. He and the PUK central committee made all the territory's regulations and approved the appointment of its cabinet of ministers. Talabani's photograph, like the Barzanis' farther north, was prominently displayed everywhere.

Serving directly under Talabani, and appointed by him, was PUK Prime Minister Barham Salih, whom everyone called "Dr. Barham." An urbane and well-spoken man who had never fought with the *peshmerga*, Dr. Barham represented a new generation of Kurdish leaders. Born in 1960, he had been arrested twice in his youth but had left Iraq in 1979 to study in England, where he received a Ph.D. in statistics and computer modeling from the University of Liverpool. After graduation, he served as a PUK spokesman, first in London until 1991, and then in Washington, D.C., until 2000. He became PUK prime minister in January 2001.

On the day of my arrival in Suleimaniyah, I was invited to an intimate cocktail party at Dr. Barham's home, along with other foreign journalists who had started arriving in the region to investigate reports of possible links between Al Qaeda and the Baath regime. This was followed by more invitations to join Dr. Barham and his entourage at more functions, including an all-day excursion into the countryside.

On the morning of our outing, dozens of politicians in neat dark suits, *peshmerga* in crisp *khak*, and two other American journalists and I in wrinkled T-shirts and pants, piled into waiting Land Cruisers, Jeeps, and sedans—a cavalcade that would wax and wane as the day wore on, sometimes growing to over twenty vehicles, sometimes shrinking to five or six. We headed south to the Qara Dagh or "Black Mountain," a region of extraordinary beauty, bordered to the southeast by a straight-as-an-arrow chain of sharp, serrated peaks, framing valleys plush with vegetables and grain. The region was also known for its ancient history, with Assyrian carvings sprinkling its mountains, and for its modern tragedy. The Qara Dagh was the site of the second major Anfal campaign, waged March 22 to April 1, 1988.

Throughout the morning, our cavalcade made many stops, to be greeted by enthusiastic crowds and groups of schoolchildren singing Kurdish folksongs. Dr. Barham, tall and balding, with a round and open face, large glasses, and the Kurdish mustache, gave speeches, met with mayors and *shaikhs*, listened to citizens' complaints, and posed for photo ops. Then we wended our way through miles of increasingly isolated farm country, cloud shadows drifting around us, to arrive at a sleek knoll-top guesthouse owned by Diller Mustafa Ali. One of the region's wealthiest landlords, he had invited our whole party—now numbering well over one hundred—to lunch.

An imposing-looking man in traditional dress, Diller welcomed everyone at his door—our removed shoes swelling into a dark pool around him—and then joined us in an octagonal, air-conditioned room complete with a marble fireplace and a twinkling chandelier. Cold drinks were served, and our host took a few moments to tell us foreign guests his family's story.

His forefathers had been *shaikhs* and wealthy landowners for generations, he said, while his father, Mustafa, had been a PUK martyr and man of vision who'd built the region's first school. In that year, 1951, the king had promised every village three kilos of tea and three hundred meters of cloth, as the country had been suffering from severe economic depression and many villagers were going hungry. But Mustafa, as the region's *agha*, refused the offer, requesting a school instead. The impressed king complied, while also awarding the village five kilos of tea and four hundred

Our host, Diller Mustafa Ali

meters of cloth. The new school had educated both boys and girls; Diller himself had a daughter now studying law.

Diller was trying to follow in his father's footsteps, he said. He'd forbidden villagers to cut down trees, kill animals, and smoke indoors. This last decree, which he'd issued five years before, had been met with widespread resentment at first, but now the villagers were thanking him, telling him that their health had improved. An interesting mix of feudal lord and modern health advocate, I thought.

Dr. Barham came over to check on us and to answer a few questions. We asked first about the recent Islamist attack on his life. It had taken place outside his home, and he had survived only because he stepped back inside at the last minute to take a phone call. He acknowledged that Kurdistan still had some way to go before becoming a full democracy, but he also spoke about the Kurds' hope to be at the forefront of building a more perfectly democratic federated Iraq. When asked about an Islamic school that we had visited that morning, Dr. Barham replied, "We need these schools to help us counter the influence of the extremists. Their graduates can help us build the kind of tolerant society we want."

As Dr. Barham spoke, rarely stumbling over his words, I was struck by his ease, apparent openness, and charm—both genuine and calculated, I thought. As an astute politician who had spent many years in the West, he knew the advantage that lay in courting journalists—and most especially at this juncture, American journalists. The Iraq war of 2003 was then still ten months away, and the PUK desperately wanted the United States to attack the Baath regime.

Lunch was laid out in several adjoining rooms, with our guards assigned to the back rooms, the rest of us up front. Long tables groaned with kebabs, stews, and rice dishes, some delicately flavored with pomegranate juice, a popular Kurdish ingredient. Afterward, we all retired outdoors to sit on a rug-covered cement platform, almost as big as a basketball court, beneath a roof of thatched grape leaves. Servants padded about pouring tea, and a soft breeze blew as Dr. Barham, his entourage, and our host bantered about this and that, all the while keeping a close eye on their foreign guests to make sure that our every need was being met. I could only be in the Middle East, I thought as I luxuriated in the gracious mix of ancient and modern hospitality, and in the seamless sense of peace that our hosts had created in their troubled land.

IN DOWNTOWN SULEIMANIYAH stood the old Central Security Headquarters, a monstrous gray compound of four or five cavernous, empty edifices pockmarked with artillery fire. The compound had once housed Iraqi intelligence and a secret prison, into which an untold number of

Kurdish civilians had disappeared. And although overall the Kurds had exercised surprising restraint during their 1991 uprising, allowing most Baathists to retreat from Kurdistan unharmed, a mob of civilians had slaughtered some four hundred Baath party members and intelligence officers there, purportedly using everything from knives to iron saws.

Several other visitors and I toured the compound one afternoon with Jemal Aziz Amin, a small and elegant man with a raspy voice, bright eyes that twinkled behind thick rimless glasses, and an irrepressible smile. Jemal Aziz walked with a limp, due to a 1994 assassination attempt by Baathist agents. Though he had never been a major politician or military leader, as head of the PUK's foreign bureau in the early 1990s, he had escorted many foreign delegations through Kurdistan, thus enraging Saddam.

Jemal had also been imprisoned in the Central Security Headquarters for ten months in 1990. Then working as a teacher, he had been preparing to leave his school one day when several men seized him, threw him into a car, and pulled his jacket up over his head, blindfolding him. Taking him into an interrogation room in the security building, they punched and kicked him, handcuffed his hands behind his back, hung him up by the handcuffs on a meat hook, and applied electric shock to his toes, tongue, ears, and "other places."

"I decided then that even if they killed me, I would not confess about how I helped the *peshmerga*," Jemal said in crisp, British-inflected English as he escorted us into the compound. "If I confessed, I would have to give them names and then I would be lost." His voice caught. "I prefer my own death to this, to bringing friends of mine into this kind of hell."

Entering one of the deserted buildings, Jemal led us into the former interrogation room. All the room's furnishings and lighting were gone, but three rusting and surprisingly small meat hooks still hung from the ceiling. "Sometimes they tortured three men at once." Jemal nodded at the hooks. "To torture one man was not enough for them. . . . They had a technique, to take us right to the moment of death, but not to cross over. They regarded it as an art."

He led us deeper into the dark, cold, miserable building, showing us the communal cell in which he had been imprisoned with ninety other men, and the solitary confinement cells, each measuring about four by six feet. The communal cell had only one tiny window high up near the ceiling, the solitary confinement cells no windows at all. We passed by a midsized room in which women and their young children had been imprisoned, and by the site of a shed, since torn down—by the irate mob? I wondered—in which women had reputedly been raped and thereafter killed.

"I was luckier than most." Jemal paused in one of the dark hallways. "Because at least my family knew where I was. A student recognized me when the guards took me to the hospital one night. . . . The Iraqis never told the families when they arrested someone. And no one was allowed to approach the security building to ask about a person who'd disappeared. Sometimes people tried to bribe the soldiers for information. Sometimes they sold everything they had for that little bit of information."

As we toured the complex, Jemal's eyes were leaden and at times filled with tears, but as soon as we left, they started dancing again, and his irrepressible smile returned.

AT THE UNIVERSITY of Suleimaniyah, I met with professors who told me more about life under the Baath regime. Saddam Hussein was especially harsh on the city because of its rebellious history and many *peshmerga* supporters, they said. In Suleimaniyah, more than Dohuk and Erbil, the Baathists frequently cut off public services, imposed curfews, arrested civilians, and killed "saboteurs" in cold blood on the street, often burying them where they fell and making their families pay for the bullets. "It became a familiar sight to see a group of officers standing in a circle with a shovel," English professor Kawan Arif told me. "The families had no right to claim the bodies. They had to come back for them secretly at night."

Kawan's stories reminded me of another I'd heard, from a thirty-something Suleimaniyan named Zerrin Ibrahim. When Zerrin was in intermediate school, she had a teacher who tried to "brainwash" the children with constant tales about the greatness of Saddam Hussein, she said. The *peshmerga* warned him many times to tone down his message, but when he persisted, they murdered him. The Baathists responded by gathering the children in a circle in the playground, arbitrarily choosing eight or ten boys, putting bags over their heads, and killing them on the spot. "I was sick for a week," Zerrin said.

In contrast to the older generation, most of the students at the University of Suleimaniyah, who had been children when the Baath forces withdrew from Kurdistan, spoke to me not about atrocities, but about their desperation to leave Iraq. Kurdistan offered no jobs, no physical security, and few social freedoms, they said. "I want to go to a nightclub—there are no nightclubs here," one male student elaborated. "And I want to go to the beach and ride a bicycle, wearing shorts and listening to a headset. But you can't do that here. People will say you are not normal, you are rude and crazy, they will call you bad names."

How difficult it must be to live bombarded with images of the pleasure-seeking West while being confined to a boxed-in, traditional country like Kurdistan. It was no surprise that many young people were emigrating illegally, and often under dangerous conditions; the students told me of one friend who drowned in the Aegean Sea and of another who lost both legs to frostbite crossing snow-covered mountains. But how terrifying the whole process must be for their parents, left behind with no news of their children for months. And how different these young Kurds' concerns were from those of many older Kurds. All it takes to forget is one generation.

THE WOULD-BE BICYCLE rider's worry about being thought "rude and crazy" echoed other sentiments I'd heard. Kurds of various ages and both sexes had told me that they avoided drawing undue attention to themselves because others might make fun. It had something to do with *sherim*, which translates into "shame" but is more akin to stage fright, I learned months later. A group-created concept that children learn at an early age, *sherim* is a powerful form of social control that helps to hold the communal society intact. *Sherim* contrasted sharply with the image of the Kurds that I'd had for years—that of a courageous and rebellious people willing to risk all they had for freedom and independence. But, in fact, both sets of attributes applied, and now that I thought about it, there was really no reason why they should be mutually exclusive. Perhaps only in the Western mind are the words "rebel" and "loner" regarded as synonymous.

SHALAW ALI ASKARI was a tall, lithe man with a deep tan dressed in a cream-colored *shal u shapik*, black button-down shirt, and dark cummerbund, no turban. His father, Ali Askari, had been among the first to restart the Kurdish revolution in 1976, post–Algiers Accord, and Shalaw himself was a member of the PUK high command, overseeing the *peshmerga* in the

Suleimaniyah region. He was also one of the few Iraqi Kurds I met who did not favor a U.S. attack on Saddam. "I think the status quo is best for the Kurds," he said. "In this situation, we are getting stronger and Saddam is getting weaker, because of sanctions. But if Saddam goes, things might get worse. A weak Saddam is better than many other alternatives."

One morning Shalaw took me to a narrow valley beneath the grim, awesome Pira Magrun mountain range, a wall of seemingly impenetrable rock, with many peaks leaning far in one direction as if being blown by a fierce wind. Here, his father and a group of *peshmerga* had lived in a large cave — Shalaw pointed it out — from which they conducted clandestine operations between 1976 and 1978, when they and eight hundred other men headed north to the Turkish border to pick up an arms delivery. Tensions between the KDP and PUK were then at a high, and the PUK leader Talabani gave Ali Askari written instructions to wipe out any KDP bases he encountered along the way. Askari apparently intended to ignore the order, as he had a working relationship with the KDP, but a copy of Talabani's instructions fell into KDP hands, and the PUK force was ambushed by seventy-five hundred KDP troops. After suffering heavy losses, Askari surrendered, to be shown no mercy. He and his commanders were summarily executed, on the order of Sami Abdul Rahman, who at the time of my visit was deputy prime minister of the KDP-controlled zone.

It is upon hundreds of such incidents, carried out with equal intensity by both sides, that the bitter animosity between the KDP and PUK is built. "You don't forget such things," Shalaw said wearily, as I studied the cave, wondering how I would react if my father were killed under similar circumstances. It is easy for outsiders to condemn the Kurds for their inter-tribal and political violence, but quite another to be a victim of that violence, and still another to rise above its murderous cycle.

Behind the valley in which Ali Askari had once lived, on the other side of the Pira Magrun range, spiraled the hauntingly beautiful Jafati Valley, an isolated hideaway of terraced fields and goat paths winding around jade slopes, villages nestled in the ravines below. With mountains protecting it on all sides, the Jafati Valley had served as a natural fortress for the PUK in the 1980s, and so had suffered the first major Anfal attack, waged between February 23 and March 19, 1988. The PUK region suffered seven of the eight major Anfal attacks; it bordered Iran, and its *peshmerga* had been pre-eminent in aiding the Iranians during the Iran-Iraq War.

Shalaw's family had deep roots in the Jafati Valley region, and, from Pira Magrun, we traveled on to the village of Shadala, where his ancestor, Shaikh Abdul Kerim, had founded the Haqqa religion around 1930. A small splinter sect of the Naqshbandi order, now all but died out, the Haqqa had attempted to create a semi-utopian community based on social equality, communal ownership, and greater freedom for women, some of whom became religious leaders. "But the Haqqa do *not* believe in free sexual relations, as some of our enemies have claimed," Shalaw's cousin, Abdul Kerim Hadji, informed me soon after we arrived at the sect's humble headquarters.

A sect of the poor and oppressed, the religious movement had grown rapidly, spreading to about three hundred villages in just a few years. Anyone could join, including the wealthy, and several powerful *aghas* had done so, but only after burning their fine clothes and "putting ropes around their necks and running like donkeys" to prove their new humility, Abdul Kerim said.

The Haqqa's growing power, nonconformity, and refusal to pay taxes led the British to arrest Shaikh Abdul Kerim and imprison him in Kirkuk in 1934. In response, thousands of Haqqa believers put on burlap sacks, emblematic of their vow of poverty, took up walking sticks, and marched on the city, forcing his release. "It was like Gandhi," Abdul Hadji said. "Our demonstration was completely peaceful, but we frightened the British and they let the Shaikh go."

If only such an approach could work today, I thought, while also remembering the quasi-utopian community reputedly established by Shaikh Ahmad of Barzan and the once-widespread popularity of the non-worldly Naqshbandi and Qadiri Sufi orders. Was there something in the Kurds' character that had attracted them to such idealism, or had they turned to it more as a means of escape from a difficult world?

SHALAW AND I traveled on to Goktapa, largely built by his grandfather, an influential man with four wives. Perched on a high bluff, the village boasted a splendid setting overlooking the cobalt blue Lesser Zab River, hills neatly terraced with orchards, and a valley patchworked with light and dark fields. But to one side of Goktapa stood the empty ruins of Shalaw's grandfather's former mansion, while to the other rose a steep hill topped by a mass grave and a white sculpture of screaming human and animal forms entitled *Shouting*.

Saddam's attack on Goktapa had come at about five-thirty P.M. on May 3, 1988, during Ramadan, the Muslim month of fasting. The women were outside baking bread for the evening's meal, the children playing in the river, and the men, socializing or working in the orchards. Four or five planes appeared, but the villagers paid little attention—the region was always being bombed. The first plane dropped pieces of paper, to see which way the wind was blowing. Then the bombs fell, softer than usual and releasing a strange odor of garlic and apples—the smell of chemicals. One bomb fell in the river, instantly killing all the fish for miles upstream and down, and others hit the orchards and fields. The panicking villagers fled in all directions, some collapsing as they ran, others expiring days later, and the rest were herded off into camps and prisons. About 150 people died in the attack, including forty-nine of Shalaw's cousins.

ONE EVENING, I MET with Safwat Rashid Sidqi, a lawyer affiliated with the Kurdish Human Rights Organization. Founded by a group of Kurdish intellectuals in 1991, the organization was almost unique in Kurdistan; it was independent of all political parties, with what little funding it had provided by its members. The group's aim was to monitor human rights abuses committed against Kurdistan by its surrounding states, and to look into abuses within Kurdistan itself, first by contacting the accused party, in the hopes of redress, and then, if that was not successful, through legal investigation.

In a dark, upstairs office, Safwat filled me in on the human rights record of the semiautonomous state. On the positive side, the 1992 elections had for the most part been democratic and fair, and since then, both the KDP and PUK had succeeded in establishing police and court systems that worked relatively well. His organization had unrestricted access to officials, and a moderately good relationship with both Barzani and Talabani, who sometimes responded to their concerns, sometimes not.

During the internal war, from 1994 to 1997, both parties had committed every atrocity in the human rights book—"killing POWs, confiscating property, firing each other's employees, even mutilation, you name it," Safwat said. "The only thing we didn't hear a single incident of was rape." However, over the last five years, with the growing peace between the parties, the situation had much improved.

Nonetheless, both the KDP and PUK were still missing *peshmerga* from the internal fighting, who were perhaps being held secretly as POWs. Under Iraqi law, the governments could legally arrest suspected spies through a "special investigation judge," and hold them in isolated prisons. Each party also had its own internal intelligence apparatus and talked more about human rights abuses than they took action against them.

In addition, tribal law still reigned in the more remote villages, with even murders often settled within the tribes. "The parties encourage this," Safwat said. "They each have Social Bureaus that try to solve things outside the courts. . . . Why? Because it allows them to gain strength with the tribal leaders and be in control."

Safwat's words reminded me of *Agha, Shaikh and State* by Martin van Bruinessen, a classic work in Kurdish studies, based largely on fieldwork conducted in the 1970s. One of van Bruinessen's central arguments was that the Kurdish tribe was sustained by the state, with the state aiding and using the power of the *aghas* to control huge segments of Kurdish society. The Ottomans and Saddam Hussein had been experts in this arena, and now it appeared that the PUK and KDP were following suit.

Safwat went no further in discussing human rights abuses, but one week later, I met with other professionals who expressed a more negative outlook. Speaking off the record, out of fear of repercussions—"rightly or wrongly," they said—the professionals described a land in which "whoever is not with the party [the KDP or PUK], is against it." Employees who protested party decisions too strongly were fired; nonparty members had virtually no chance of reaching senior civil service positions or landing government business contracts, and even the United Nations consulted with the parties before hiring employees, they said. Great distrust between the KDP and PUK continued, the possibility of fresh violence between them was still very real, and neither party wanted to hold another election, as they were afraid of losing power. Underneath, too, both sides were opposed to independent human rights groups, and many Kurds thought twice before joining the Kurdistan Human Rights Organization. Concluded one of the professionals, "On the surface, we are free and democratic, but in the details, we are not."

Many of these inbred political problems could be solved if Kurdistan had a serious free press, I thought. But it did not. Although a free press was in principle encouraged by the semiautonomous state, all publications that existed were directly or indirectly supported or controlled by the parties; there were few sources of independent financing in Kurdistan.

Several Kurdish journalists told me that, over the last two years, they had been speaking out with increasing openness about various social problems, including the formerly taboo subject of honor killings. However, when it came to criticizing politicians or the parties, they still proceeded with caution. "There are some red lines that we cannot cross," said Asos Hardi, editor-in-chief of *Hawlati*, the region's most independent paper at the time of my visit. "Usually, we can find a way to talk about everything, but we don't do so directly," and the paper seldom named names.

Many Kurds I met, including some party officials, openly acknowledged the daunting power of the KDP and PUK—a good sign, I thought. Yet many also partially excused that power, saying that the vulnerable position of Kurdistan, coupled with its lack of a civil rights tradition, made the problem a thorny one to solve. The parties had to watch their backs at every minute, they said—threats from the Baath regime, the Islamists, and the surrounding states were constant and very real, and the parties could not afford to be infiltrated with spies or otherwise lose power or control. In addition, the Kurdish people themselves, so new to democracy, were still inept at using their new institutions for the common good. Building a civil society took time.

The arguments made sense. Perhaps it was still too early to expect full-fledged human rights, watchdog organizations, and a free press to operate in Kurdistan. Abuses of power had ravaged the country for centuries; to end them was no simple matter. On the other hand, if a system of accountability was not established now, then when? "I think when Kurdistan and Iraq are free of Saddam Hussein, we will solve all these problems," said the *Hawlati* editor. I fervently hoped he was right. Against all odds, and to the Kurds' great credit, democracy had taken root in Kurdistan, but its shoots were still tender and green.

CHAPTER THIRTEEN

Judgment Day

AS IF THE CITY OF HALABJA HAD NOT SUFFERED ENOUGH in 1988, losing over five thousand souls in a single day of chemical bombing, it was now under threat of attack by an Islamist terror group, Ansar al-Islam, or Supporters of Islam. Thought to number about five hundred or six hundred, Ansar al-Islam had seized control of about a dozen villages in the valley between Halabja and Iran, and controlled the main highway east of the military road. Ansar al-Islam had killed at least forty-two PUK *pesh-merga* in one incident the previous September, massacring over half in cold blood after they'd surrendered, and attacked the PUK's Halabja headquarters several times that same fall. Ansar al-Islam was hostile to Westerners, and the PUK always provided foreign journalists visiting Halabja with a heavily armed escort, while most foreign aid workers had ceased to visit the city altogether, saying that the risk was not worth it.

Journeying with me to Halabja one early June day were the two American journalists I had traveled with to the Qara Dagh, Kevin McKiernan and Ginny Durrin. They were in Kurdistan to film a documentary on weapons of mass destruction that Ginny was producing for Ted Turner Documentaries. Kevin, who was working as her cameraman, was a journalist and documentary filmmaker in his own right, best known for his award-winning film *Good Kurds, Bad Kurds*; he had been covering the Kurds since 1991. Accompanying us was our translator, Dildar Majeed Kittani, a strong, outspoken woman of about forty who had lived in the mountains with her *peshmerga* husband in the 1980s.

Ansar al-Islam was a young organization, formed only about eight months earlier, in September 2001, from several splinter groups that had previously broken away from the more moderate but still fundamentalist Islamic Movement in Kurdistan (IMK). Once the third-largest political party in Kurdistan,* the IMK had received 5 percent of the vote in the 1992 parliamentary elections. After unsuccessfully contesting that vote, the party split off from the Kurdish regional government to operate largely independently in an area bordering Iran. Headquartered in Halabja, where it received strong support from Iran, the IMK had its own separate administrative and political infra-

Our escorts en route to Halabja

structure, and its own militia. For most of the period between 1992 and 2001, the IMK ran Halabja—enforcing the veil, building religious schools, banning cinema and music, and requiring mosque attendance, but not publicly endorsing terrorism or the harshest strictures of *sharia*. Then in late September 2001, the PUK stormed the city, forcing the clerics from power, and reinstituted secular control—much to the anger of the city's more radical Islamists.

* By 2002, the third-largest party was the considerably more moderate Kurdistan Islamic Union, which traces its roots to the Muslim Brotherhood movement.

The militant Ansar al-Islam was fiercely opposed to the IMK's more moderate approach and policy of cooperating with the secular PUK and KDP. The splinter group called for the strictest application of *sharia*, including the barring of women from education and employment, and for harshly punishing those who failed to comply. Among its members were Arabs and Kurds who had fought in Afghanistan in the 1980s and the early 2000s, fleeing to Kurdistan after the Taliban's defeat. The PUK accused the group of having links with Osama bin Laden's Al Qaeda network. Prior to the Iraq war of 2003, the United States contended that Ansar al-Islam was also the connecting link between the Baath regime and Al Qaeda, thus necessitating invasion. But this claim was never credibly proven, and the unsophisticated nature of the group's recovered documents call the allegation into serious question. Ansar al-Islam was routed from Kurdistan, as least temporarily, during the Iraq war of 2003, when about two-thirds of its members were killed or captured and the rest escaped into the mountains.

At the time of our visit, however, the Islamist group was still a significant threat, and *peshmerga*-filled Jeeps, one with a mounted antiaircraft gun, protectively flanked our sedan at either end as we drove toward the city. Around us were low hills patched with blond fields, pink wildflowers, and flocks of sheep. All was silent, with the promise of a hot day on its way.

Descending the hills, we came to a bright blue river, where we climbed out to wait for a flatbed ferry, now on the other side. The river flowed south to the Darbandikhan Lake and Dam, a strategic point much fought over in recent years, as it provided Baghdad with most of its water supply. While we waited, I snapped photos of our *peshmerga*, all impeccably dressed in pressed camouflage uniforms, despite hours spent traveling in dusty open Jeeps. The men carried a large assortment of weapons, including Kalashnikovs, AK-47s, hand grenades, and a thirty-plus-year-old rocket-propelled grenade, or RPG—an antique anyplace else in the world. But in the hot morning sunlight, in a land of blond fields and plump sheep, none of the weapons seemed quite real.

The ferry came, and we crossed, to arrive a short time later at Halabja, its entrance marked with a statue of a prone man in traditional dress lying protectively over a small child. The figures were based on one of the most famous photographs of the March 16–18, 1988, attacks, when Halabja was smothered with a concoction of mustard gas and the nerve agents sarin, tabun, and perhaps VX. The man's gesture had proved futile; both he and his grandson were already dead when photographed.

Downtown Halabja centered on a few commercial blocks. Men and a handful of women, their heads tightly covered, wandered from shop to shop, but the atmosphere felt guarded and subdued, as if everyone was waiting for disaster to strike again at any moment. A Land Cruiser packed with bearded men sailed by, making me wonder about the citizenry we were passing. Although Halabja was now ruled by the PUK, it remained a conservative, religious city. If there were any Islamist spies among the ordinary believers—waiting, perhaps, for an unforgivable breach in Islamic law— they would be hard to pick out.

Outside the immediate downtown reigned a large new green-and-white mosque with a wide dome, followed by neglected street after neglected street, all flanked with blank walls, half-destroyed homes, and piles of rubble. Fourteen years after the bombings, much of the city still lay in ruins, due to a lack of funds and to inertia caused by depression and fear. Although the city had received some foreign aid in the early 1990s, that aid had ended abruptly in 1994 when the internal fighting began, with the IMK siding with the KDP. Then had come problems with Iran and the rise of the Islamists. One or two aid organizations had returned to Halabja in 1999, but their activities were limited.

I tried to imagine the city as it once had been. For Halabja, and the surrounding Shahrizur, one of the world's richest agricultural regions, had no ordinary history. Throughout the Shahrizur rose hundreds of unexcavated mounds, some dating back to the Assyrians, others to the Sassanian Persians, who developed trade in the area from the 200s until 637, when Islam arrived. The Arabs associated the Shahrizur with Saul and David of the Bible, suggesting an early Jewish presence, while the Ahl-e Haqq—the "cult of the angels" faith—believe that the valley will be the site of the Last Judgment; "on the threshing floor of the Shahrazur, all the faithful will receive their due," say their holy scriptures.

In the 1700s, about fifty thousand Jaf, one of the largest, oldest, and most powerful of Kurdish tribes, moved into the Shahrizur from Persia. Known for their fierce independence, arrogance, and un-Kurdish-like ability to work together, the Jaf had had a violent falling out with their Ardalan rulers, who had slain their *agha*. The Suleimaniyah pasha offered the Jaf protection and the right to graze their animals in the region, while the Jaf chieftains took up residence in the area's villages and towns, including Halabja.

During much of the twentieth century, Halabja was a center of trade, learning, and enlightenment, home to many merchants, poets, scientists, and religious scholars, and a by-then thriving Jewish community. One elderly Halabja native I met remembered that in his boyhood, the city boasted near-weekly celebrations and festivals, large public gardens encircling the entire town, and many intellectual gatherings, during which the literate had read fat histories to the nonliterate on long winter evenings. Some of Kurdistan's most famous twentieth-century poets were from Halabja.

Much of the credit for Halabja's cultural flowering goes to Adela Khanoum, or Lady Adela. Born into the Ardalan dynasty, Adela Khanoum moved to Halabja around the turn of the twentieth century, after her marriage to Osman Pasha, a Jaf chieftain and the Ottoman-appointed governor of the Shahrizur. Halabja was then still a dusty, unsophisticated town, but the well-cultured, aristocratic Adela Khanoum set about re-creating the life she was accustomed to in Persia. She built two fine mansions, many woodsy Persian-style gardens, and a large bazaar of her own design, then invited old Persian friends to come for extended visits. Halabja's fame spread, attracting both merchants and learned Kurds to the growing town.

Adela Khanoum also built a new prison, instituted a court of law over which she ruled, and, after her husband's death in 1909, governed the entire Shahrizur district, to reign until her own death in 1924. She hired the Englishman Ely Bannister Soane, traveling through the region disguised as a Persian, as a scribe for six months in 1909. Perhaps because of his influence, she sided with the British against the rebel Shaikh Mahmoud in 1919.

What exactly Soane was doing in the region disguised as a Persian is not known. He had worked for a British bank in Iran for some years, but then set out on his odd journey, described in his memoir, *To Mesopotamia and Kurdistan in Disguise*. It is possible that his trip had some official purpose (the British did hire him six years later for his expertise in Kurdish affairs), but he had a deep love for the Middle East, living there most of his life and converting to Islam. I prefer to think that he undertook his trip purely out of curiosity and the desire to lose himself utterly and completely in another world. I also marvel at his linguistic skills, as almost everyone he met, including Adela Khanoum, took him to be what he claimed: a Persian from Shiraz.

Soane described Adela Khanoum as being strong willed, urbane, and "of pure Kurdish origin," with a "narrow, oval face, rather large mouth, small black and shining eyes, [and] a narrow slightly aquiline hooked nose"—a description borne out by his photos of her. When the two of them first met, she was wearing a skullcap smothered with gold coins, gold wrist and ankle bracelets, seventeen rings, and a necklace of large pearls alternating with gold fishes. Soane admired her greatly, and she remains a legend in Kurdistan today.

The last of Adela Khanoum's mansions was destroyed in the 1988 attacks, and Halabja has no more public or Persian-styled gardens, or historic Jaf monuments. But miles away, beyond the southwestern edge of the Shahrizur, rises a grand castle built in the 1860s by the last paramount Jaf leader, Muhammad Pasha, father of Adela Khanoum's husband. Perched on a hill outside the town of Kalar, with sweeping views of the surrounding plains, the palace is one of the few remaining physical testaments to the once-widespread power of the Kurdish tribes.

KEVIN, GINNY, DILDAR, and I went to visit Aras Abid Akram, a tall and thin man in his early thirties, who was dressed entirely in black. Given to quick, jerky movements, Aras was a sort of celebrity in Halabja, as he had lost twenty-two family members, including ten siblings, in the chemical attacks. He had been interviewed over a thousand times, or so he said. None of the interviews had done much good, he shrugged, as the foreign journalists, human rights workers, and aid organizations had all come and gone, doing nothing to alleviate Halabja's suffering. In fact, it had gotten to the point where most people in the town didn't even want to speak to foreigners anymore.

We would be three more guilty parties, I thought, with a pang of helplessness.

Aras lived on a quiet street, in a solid old family home with thick walls, stone floors, and a small garden filled with flowering rosebushes and a huge satellite dish. In his living room hung photos of his handsome parents and a romanticized shot of his many brothers and sisters, the latter wearing long white dresses that seemed straight out of the 1920s. Another photo, also of

Aras's family, showed about a dozen disheveled bodies strewn haphazardly down a dirt alley.

The morning of March 16, 1988, had begun calmly enough, Aras said, as his wife served tea. He had gone to a neighborhood hospital to help bury dead soldiers, victims of the Iran-Iraq War then raging around the city. But since the *peshmerga* had helped the Iranians enter Halabja the day before, he, like most residents, was expecting an Iraqi counterattack. At about ten A.M., he noticed two Iraqi planes circling overhead, and around noon, five more planes arrived, flying low and dropping small conventional bombs. One landed near the hospital, injuring Aras in the leg, and he limped out to take refuge in a neighbor's basement, along with his mother, one sister, and others.

The bombing continued unabated for hours. Then, at about three P.M., a vaguely pleasant smell of garlic and apples drifted into the basement, causing immediate panic, as many knew what it meant and rushed toward the door. Some were vomiting, some felt sharp pains in their eyes as they stepped outside to see animal and human bodies already slumped every-where. White clouds of chemicals clung to the ground, and people streamed out of basements. Because of his injured leg, Aras stayed behind, along with a few neighbors, one of whom gave him a wet turban to wrap around his face. He hugged his mother and sister tightly before they left, certain that he would not leave the basement alive.

But hours passed without further incident, and around eight P.M., Aras and a neighbor wrapped their turbans tightly around their mouths and stepped outside. The neighbor immediately went blind—temporary blind-ness being one of the effects of mustard gas. Stumbling in the dusk, they slowly made their way forward, tripping over bodies every few feet. Some alleys were so packed with bodies that they couldn't pass; they had to back up to try another way. They headed toward a village on the outskirts of the city, a trip that usually took fifteen minutes. On that night, it took five hours. Around them bumped other blind people and disoriented animals. Finally, at about one A.M., they reached the village and rested for a few hours, des-perately hungry and thirsty. At five A.M., the Iraqi planes returned, flying low and dropping more chemical bombs.

Later, Saddam Hussein would claim that it was the Iranians who had dropped the chemical bombs, a claim initially bolstered by U.S. intelli-gence reports, which accused both sides of using chemical weapons. But

Iran's alleged involvement has never been substantiated, and the thousands of Halabja survivors—like Aras—speak only of seeing Iraqi warplanes over-head.

Hours later, Aras and fourteen other injured civilians were loaded into a car by *peshmerga* and Iranian soldiers and transported to Iran. He was taken to a hospital where he awoke to hear a baby crying. "That sound was like a shock to me," he said. "I thought, Where are my mother and father? Where are my sisters and brothers? I had to go back."

Leaving the hospital that same day, and back in Halabja the next, he found hundreds of bodies still lying in the street. His house—the same house we were in now—was completely empty, with plates and silverware laid out as if for a meal. A neighbor directed him to a nearby basement. There Aras found his grandmother dead on the stairs, two other family members dead down below. He blacked out and, when he came to again, found himself back in Iran.

Aras couldn't go on. His wife, a large and pretty woman with a big maroon bow perched at the back of her head, had been watching him intently. How can they go through this over and over again, I wondered, as Aras abruptly asked, "Is that enough?" Without waiting for an answer, he left the room.

The silence left in his wake seemed unbearable. As during many inter-views in Kurdistan, I didn't know where to put my eyes, or what to do with my limbs.

Later, I asked Aras why he kept submitting himself to the painful process of remembering. "People are scared here, I'm scared here," he said. "I'm wanted by the Iraqi government for talking so much. But I want the pain of Halabja to be heard around the world."

While Kevin and Ginny continued filming Aras and his wife, and our *peshmerga* picked roses from the garden, happily sticking the big pink puffs into their cummerbunds, I went out into the street and gazed up and down the dirt thoroughfare. The only signs of life were two bony cows ambling along and a few women gossiping in doorways, their covered heads bent closely together. Keeping a damper on things was the boxy, well-guarded headquarters of the IMK on the corner. Our translator Dildar had pointed it out upon our arrival, and implored us not to make too much noise or oth-erwise call attention to ourselves. Unhappy that so many foreigners were visiting Aras, the IMK could make trouble for him later.

Taking two *peshmerga* with me, I went to explore a nearby street that had been especially hard hit in the bombing attacks. Half-destroyed houses filled the otherwise empty blocks—great piles of rubble in which children were playing, amid possible lingering contamination. One of the buildings housed a semi-intact basement, and as I peered down into the claustrophobic space, filled with rubble and plastic bags blown in by the wind, I felt as if I would gag. It was easy enough to imagine suffocating inside the room now, let alone back then.

BEFORE AND AFTER meeting Aras, I talked to dozens of other Halabja survivors and read a sheaf of autobiographical stories compiled by a doctor some years before. Their accounts of the attacks differed in small ways regarding the timing and sequencing of events, but all described the strange smells, the difficult breathing, the vomiting, the panic, the squealing animals, the mass exodus, and the countless, countless bodies. One woman spoke of hearing no noise at all when she emerged from her shelter. Another spoke of seeing her entire family blown to bits en route to Iran. A third described seeing dozens of screaming people trapped in a basement, their faces pressed hard against the windows, afraid to come out. "It was like judgment day in the Quran," she said. And many told of losing their sight for three or four weeks, or more, and of losing loved ones to the noxious fumes. "I saw people lying on the ground, fluttering their legs and hands and dying," wrote one man. "And I saw people laughing hysterically," the effect of the nerve gas.

TO LEARN MORE about the long-term effects of the chemical bombings, I visited Dr. Fouad Baban, a pulmonary and cardiac specialist, and one of Kurdistan's best-known doctors. A reserved and thoughtful man of about sixty, Dr. Baban was the Kurdish coordinator of the Halabja Post-Graduate Medical Institute (HMI), which was founded in 1999 by a coalition of Kurdish doctors, Dr. Christine Gosden of the University of Liverpool, and the Washington Kurdish Institute, an advocacy group based in Washington, D.C. With initial funds provided by the U.S. State Department, U.K. Department for International Development, and other sources, the institute was working to document cases and treat patients affected by the chemical bombs dropped not only on Halabja—by far the most devastated site—but also on about 280 smaller targets in Iraqi Kurdistan. For the Kurdish doctors, such a liaison prior to the Iraq war of 2003 had taken much courage, as they were involved in a project whose findings could be used against Saddam Hussein in a war-crimes tribunal, and his agents could be anywhere.

Welcoming me into his Suleimaniyah home, Dr. Baban spread out a raft of papers on a coffee table, the results of a one-year study, undertaken with funding from the HMI. Traveling by car, bicycle, mule, and foot, about twenty doctors and paramedics had fanned out over the Kurdish countryside, to survey two thousand households. And in those areas where chemical bombing had occurred, the medical team found increased incidents of: (1) eye disorders such as blindness, conjunctivitis, and continuous watering of the eye; (2) skin damage such as constant irritation and patches of deeper or lighter pigmentation; (3) respiratory disorders, including asthma, shortness of breath, and chronic lung fibrosis; (4) gastrointestinal disorders; (5) heart attacks and strokes; (6) neuromuscular disorders; and (7) cancers, including skin, colon, and stomach cancers, and leukemia and lymphoma. In addition, the medical team found increased rates of congenital abnormalities in children born to parents who had been exposed to the chemicals, and increased rates of infertility, sterility, and miscarriages.

"So from this last evidence, it seems that chemical weapons affect DNA, carrying over into the next generation," Dr. Baban said. "These disorders have led to a distortion of the structure of our entire population. Men are divorcing their wives because they can't give birth. The number of our young people is decreasing."

Nearly one-third of the deaths in Halabja were now caused by cancers and less than 10 percent by infectious diseases, figures more in line with industrialized nations than with a rural society, Dr. Baban said. Halabja had fourteen times the rate of miscarriage and five times the rate of colon cancer of Chemchemal, a comparable city nearby that had not been bombed by chemicals. Congenital abnormalities in Halabja were also four to five times greater than in the postatomic populations of Hiroshima and Nagasaki.

Dr. Baban estimated that about forty thousand adults and children in Iraqi Kurdistan were in need of prioritized health care due to exposure to chemical weapons and perhaps biological agents, which may also have been used in some attacks. However, little of that prioritized care was being delivered, largely because of the dual constraints of international and Iraqi economic sanctions. The United Nations did not allow Iraq to import advanced diagnostic equipment, as its parts could be used for more nefarious purposes, and Hussein effectively blocked many of the Kurds' medical supply requests, such as surgical gloves and cancer medicines.

"The U.N. is providing all communities with the same medicines, and making no extra provisions for areas with widespread diseases," Dr. Baban said. "It's very disappointing."

Dr. Baban was also disappointed that the Kurdish doctors' study had thus far failed to be published in final form or given the sort of worldwide attention that he felt it warranted. He'd sent the completed research to Dr. Gosman at the University of Liverpool in early 2000, but she was having trouble getting it published, for reasons that were unclear. Perhaps it wasn't rigorous enough? I wondered.

Yet even if that were the case, why weren't more studies being conducted? The paltry amount of international attention being paid to the effects of Iraq's chemical attacks was appalling. After the Halabja bombing, thousands of victims had received immediate treatment in Iran, a nation seldom given credit in the West for that humanitarian aid, self-interested though it undoubtedly was. The Iranians ferried the Iraqi victims across the border, gave them atropine injections to counter the effects of nerve gas, and cared for the sickest in hospitals. But upon returning to Iraq, most of the chemical victims received no advanced health care at all. Until the Halabja Medical Institute began its study, no large international research or aid organization had collected data on the bombings' effects or tried to address the medical needs of its survivors. Fourteen years after the fact, the West had finally conceded that the attacks had indeed taken place, but few soil or water samples had ever been taken, and no investigations conducted to determine exactly which weapons had been used or whether harmful agents still lingered in the environment. If for no other reason, such research should be conducted for the world's self-interest, to gain knowledge in the event of possible future chemical attacks.

LEAVING ARAS ABID AKRAM and his wife, Kevin, Ginny, Dildar, and I traveled on to the Halabja Hospital, where we met Dr. Adil Karem Fatah.

A naturally elegant man with a gentle if nervous manner, long tanned face, and prematurely graying hair, Dr. Adil had been helping to publicize the city's high incidence of disease since 1996. His efforts had carried a stiff personal price—because of his frequent contacts with foreigners, extremists were accusing him of spying for the United States and threatening his life. Shortly after I left Iraq, the threats got so bad that Dr. Adil fled to Syria to seek asylum, not returning until after the war.

Dr. Adil took us on a tour of the hospital. Built by a Swedish aid organization in 1999, it was simple but multistoried and very clean, painted in greens and whites with shiny floors. It was also surprisingly empty. I had steeled myself for the visit, expecting to see dozens of heartbreaking cases, but for the most part, the victims of the chemical attacks weren't there. They had chronic illnesses that were best treated on an out-patient basis, Dr. Adil explained, reminding me that we were visiting fourteen years after the fact—a detail that I sometimes forgot, as Halabja's suffering still felt so palpable.

We did see one man with painful patches of an angry red skin disease and a young child with a severe cleft palate, who probably wouldn't live out the month. And outside the hospital, we met an older child with a cleft palate who had already had seven operations and still needed two more. His young mother, whose first child had died of the same malformation, hugged her son close as she spoke of neighbors who had advised her not to bother trying to save her child, as he would never make it, they said.

While Kevin and Ginny filmed the patients, Dr. Adil took me to see a different kind of Anfal victim—a young woman whose chest and arms were covered with third-degree burns. She'd tried to commit suicide by setting herself on fire.

"She's luckier than many because she didn't burn her face," Dr. Adil said as he gave her an injection to ease her pain. "But there will be many complications. She will have a hard life—with internal problems, with social ones. Her family might abandon her. Her skin will contract. We have very few plastic surgeons here."

In the last six or seven years, suicide through burning had become alarmingly widespread in Iraqi Kurdistan, he went on. One study, conducted by the Women's Information and Cultural Center in Suleimaniyah, estimated that between 1991 and 2000, about fourteen hundred women had tried to burn themselves to death. The victims were usually young village women suffering from depression, perhaps over forced marriages, cruel husbands, or desperate economic situations—in other words, from traditional tribal customs, coupled with the general breakdown of Kurdish society post-Anfal. And treating burn patients, a long and costly process anywhere, was especially difficult in Iraq. Dressings, ointments, and the mesh necessary for skin grafts weren't readily available, and hospital salaries were too low to retain the dedicated staff needed to care for the victims.

Will it never end? I thought dejectedly. Here it was, fourteen years after the Anfal, and yet the campaign of death was still continuing.

ON A HILL just above Halabja sloped the city cemetery, offering magnificent views of the surrounding plains, valleys, and mountains. Straddling the Iran-Iraq border to the east rose the great wall of the Hawraman range, home to the Hawraman people, known for their distinctive dialect and handicrafts, whom I would visit in Iran.

Ansar al-Islam had seized two Iraqi Hawraman villages, Biyara and Tawela, to use as their headquarters, and desecrated the region's centuries-old Naqhsbandi Sufi tombs and shrines. Especially in the late nineteenth and early twentieth centuries, Biyara had served as an important religious center, attracting believers from all over the Islamic world. Then, as now, bearded men had congregated in this isolated, stunning land in the name of religion. But the first group had come for peace, the second, for war.

Many of the victims of the chemical attacks were buried in the cemetery, in mass graves amid thistles and wildflowers, with a never-completed commemorative arch falling apart in the background. One mass grave, created out of a napalm bomb crater, contained fourteen hundred bodies, and another, eight hundred, of which only two had been identified—Jalal Hussein and Bahar Hussein. Aras Abid Akram's family had its own mass grave as well, with twenty-two names neatly handwritten in white on black.

BY A LUCKY COINCIDENCE, I ran into British journalist Gwynne Roberts a few days later at the Palace Hotel. An award-winning documentary filmmaker, Gwynne had been covering Kurdistan since 1974. In fact, it was his reporting on Halabja that had first brought Dr. Gosden to Kurdistan, which in turn led to the founding of the Halabja Medical Institute. Gwynne had also secretly entered Iraqi Kurdistan in 1988, when it was still under Baathist rule, to collect soil samples, which had been analyzed by Porton Down, Britain's armed forces chemical weapons laboratory, to less than conclusive results. He had collected more soil and water samples from Halabja in 2000—a complex process necessitating the help of many others—but these had never been analyzed. To do so was wildly expensive, ranging in cost from $1,000 to $50,000 per sample, and only governments had equipment sensitive enough to measure small amounts of chemical weapons agents. Gwynne had approached the Swedes, the Dutch, the British, and the U.N. Organization for the Prohibition of Chemical Weapons in the Hague for help, but all had turned him down.

Why that was, he and I could only speculate. Did it have to do with the United Nation's refusal to release the names of companies that had supplied chemicals to Iraq—many during the Iran-Iraq War—on the grounds that this would end the cooperation they got from the companies in tracking down Saddam's weapons supplies? Was there perhaps intensive lobbying going on to prevent potential political embarrassment?

By the time the Iraq war of 2003 began, the names of the chemical companies were no longer secret. In December 2002, Iraq delivered a twelve-thousand-page weapons declaration to the United Nation's Security Council that included the names of dozens of foreign companies that provided most of the chemicals and equipment for Iraq's chemical weapons program prior to the 1991 Gulf War. The United Nations insisted that it would not make the list public, but it was leaked to the press. On it were thirty-one foreign major suppliers, including fourteen from Germany, three each from the Netherlands and Switzerland, and two each from the France, Austria, and the United States (Alcolac International of Maryland and the Al Haddad trading company of Tennessee, both now defunct).

CHAPTER FOURTEEN

Safe Havens

KARIM AGHA, TRIBAL CHIEF, SAT AT ONE END OF HIS LONG summer guesthouse, surrounded by an oval of empty Louis XIV–style chairs. A tall, thin, and slightly stooped man in his seventies, he was dressed in a dark gray *shal u shapik* and a black-and-white turban. Prominently hanging behind him was a glossy, poster-sized photograph of PUK president Jalal Talabani.

Jumping up as we arrived, Karim Agha greeted us warmly and escorted us to chairs beside his own. Servants glided in with tea in tulip-shaped glasses, followed by platters piled high with fruit. One of Karim Agha's sons hovered in the background, to ensure that all went smoothly. As is the custom in many powerful Kurdish families, he never sat down in his father's presence.

"Each tribe has its own way of life," Karim Agha said, settling in contentedly after the initial pleasantries were over. "Each tribe is like a family."

His tribe was the Hamawands, who until about 1925 were the most famous fighting tribe of southern Kurdistan, despite also being one of the smallest. Originally from Persia, they settled in the Suleimaniyah area in the early eighteenth century, where they supported the Babans against the Ottomans until the emirate ended in 1850, and then terrorized the entire region between Baghdad, Mosul, and Kermanshah, Iran.

E. B. Soane, the Englishman who traveled in disguise through Kurdistan in 1909, gives a vivid account of meeting the tribe:

[F]rom every gully in the hill-sides horsemen came galloping down. Handsome men these Hamavands. As they rushed along, their silk head handkerchiefs of many colours streamed behind them; their long tunics, covering even their feet, rose and fell with the horses' action. The stirrups of many were inlaid with silver, contrasting with the scarlet upturned shoes. . . . As they approached near, each one ostentatiously opened the breech of his rifle and emptied it of cartridges, then slung it on his back, thereby announcing at once their friendly intentions.

Soane also writes of the Hamawands' alert dark eyes, directness, haughty pride, and "hostile manner that even among friends they cannot always control." All but the latter still applied to the Hamawands today as represented by Karim Agha.

"In 1847, the Ottoman Empire occupied our land, they controlled the whole area," Karim Agha began his history. "We were the only tribe that did not bow down to them—we fought them. But after losing many people, the Turks with the support of other tribes made a large attack against us and we fled to Iran. But still we considered this our land, and we came back in groups of fifteen on horseback to fight them. We disrupted many caravans, we inflicted heavy losses. Finally they sent delegates to make peace, and we came back. But then the fighting began again, and we went to Iran again. Four times we went to Iran and four times we came back.

"A representative of the Sultan came to negotiate. We sent two hundred horsemen to greet him, and after five days of entertaining them, he captured all two hundred. He said, 'All this year, you have broken negotiations, now we will break you.' The families of the two hundred horsemen surrendered—seven hundred people—and they sent some to Adana in Turkey and some to Libya in North Africa. Many became sick and died on the way. . . . The year was 1889.

"My father and his family were sent to Libya. They sent them there to become farmers. But they refused to become farmers. They said, 'We are going back to Kurdistan,' and they escaped from the desert to the mountains.

"The Arab tribes helped them get to Egypt and across the Suez Canal, through the Sinai Desert and Syria. They went mostly at night, by the stars, and fought many battles. It took them nine months, most going on foot. Women and children on foot walking through the desert—Rommel needed tanks and airplanes to make it through! And in 1896, after seven years in Libya, they came back to Kurdistan."

Documented by historians, this astonishing story summed up the Kurds' doggedness. Nothing could keep them from the land they loved, which was so central to their identity. As one well-educated Kurdish deputy minister said to me, "Whenever we Kurds leave our land, we are lost. Without it, the Kurds are nothing."

Coffee is served to Karim Agha

Translating Karim Agha's story for me was Nizar Ghafur Agha Said, a disheveled-looking man in a rumpled brown suit. An old friend of Karim Agha, Nizar spoke good English, as he had lived in the United States for over twenty years. He was now in Kurdistan to test the waters for a possible move back. In the United States, Nizar was just one more struggling foreign-born businessman, but in Iraq, he was a member of a distinguished family, with many connections. His grandfather was Piramerd, a beloved Kurdish poet famed for his originality and long life, dying in 1950 at age eighty-seven. Piramerd had written a well-known poem about the Hamawands and their earlier marauding ways: "Terror of highwaymen, bribes to the escort, pilfering at night. . . ."

KARIM AGHA WAS not the first *agha* I had met. In the Dohuk governorate, my host Majed had introduced me to Muhammad Agha, chieftain of the Sharifani, a subtribe of the Kocher, and to two Yezidi *aghas*. The Sharifani *agha*, an educated man of about forty, wearing *khak*, a turban, and ultrashiny leather shoes, had hoped to study medicine, but was forced to become *agha* at age sixteen, because of his father's untimely death. His *agha* responsibilities were twofold, he said—working as the representative of his clan, and as an adviser to his people.

The two Yezidi *aghas* could not have been more different. Nejem Agha Qaidi, chieftain of Al-Qaidi, was an uneducated older man with a grizzled face, thick glasses, ratty red cardigan, and baggy pants. He seemed deeply depressed. His tribe had been forcibly moved out of their eight villages and into the small, poverty-ridden collective town of Sharia during the Anfal, losing not only their homes and farmlands, but also their holy shrine, which could not be rebuilt elsewhere, as it had to be erected over sacred graves.

In contrast, Shaikh Shamo, *agha* of a Haveri subtribe, was a buoyant, round-faced man who ran several successful businesses, including hotels and lotteries, and had two wives and many children. He reigned over the much larger collective town of Khanik, population about three thousand, and invited me to a sumptuous lunch, which we ate standing up, together with about a dozen other men, all of us crowded around a table groaning with heaping platters of food. Everyone except my translator and I wore a red-and-white turban and ate with his fingers.

In Diana, off the Hamilton Road, I met Delawar Muhammad Ali, the big and friendly *agha* of the Majel tribe, who hated to be addressed by his title; he felt it distanced him from people. Uneducated but perceptive, Delawar struggled to understand the changing world around him. "In some ways, being an *agha* is easier for me than it was for my father because people have more money now," he said. "But in some ways, it is harder because there are many more people, more problems, and bigger problems. My father did not have an Anfal."

The *agha* was once the all-powerful Kurdish leader. Whether in charge of a small clan of a few hundred or a large tribe of many thousands, he made all major decisions for his group, while often extracting oppressive taxes. He usually had multiple wives and many children, and owned vast tracts of land and many thousands of animals. Sometimes the *aghas'* greed and cruelty created much deep resentment among their followers, but many *aghas* were greatly respected. Some were loved.

The authority of the *agha* in Iraq began to decline in the 1950s, due to the growing power of the central government, agrarian reform laws, and the mechanization of agriculture, which made the chieftains and their villagers less interdependent. Nonetheless, and despite what many people told me, the time of the *agha,* like the time of the tribe, was far from over in Iraqi Kurdistan. Though many *aghas* no longer had any real power, even the weakest among them still garnered much respect and brokered disputes, both between members and between members and the state. Some *aghas* also retained considerable wealth and sizable militias, meaning that they were heavily courted by the powers-that-be.

By far the most impressive *agha* I met in Iraq was Ako Abba Mamand Agha, chieftain of the Ako tribe, who lived in and around Raniya, a town surrounded by craggy peaks about an hour and a half north of Suleimaniyah. One of the most tribal regions left in Kurdistan, the Raniya area was also home to the Bilbas people, allies of the Ako. Next door lived the Pizhdar, a once-fierce but now much weakened tribe, who were the Akos' traditional enemy. The town of Raniya was also where the 1991 uprising began, on March 5, triggering a revolt that almost overnight swept throughout Kurdistan.

Ako Agha lived in a simple compound of new, low-slung buildings on the edge of Raniya. Dildar, the translator who had traveled with my companions and me to Halabja, first took me to meet him one night at about eleven P.M., after our drive up from Suleimaniyah, dinner, and a nap. I wondered about the wisdom of arriving at such a late hour, but Dildar, whose husband was from Raniya, assured me that she knew Ako Agha well and that it would be no problem. We arrived to find him sitting outdoors on a cement patio splashed with yellow light, surrounded by about twenty other men and teenage boys in baggy pants. A tall, charismatic, and powerfully built man in his mid-forties, with a thick black mustache and dark observant eyes, Ako Agha was himself dressed in a resplendent white *shal u shapik* and a black-and-white turban.

He did not smile when we were introduced. For a moment, I wondered if Dildar had misjudged things and he resented our intrusion: two women breaking into this comradely all-male gathering. I also doubted that he would say much of interest. Most *aghas* I met seemed guarded, perhaps unsure of their footing with a foreign woman. Ako Agha surprised me.

Two of the men vacated their seats, and Dildar and I sat beside our host. She and he caught up for a few moments, while I looked around, suddenly realizing that we had arrived in the middle of a traditional evening at a *diwan*, or guesthouse. I had been in many *diwans*—most recently with Karim Agha—but never at night.

The *diwan* was a quintessential element of traditional Kurdish life. At one time, every leading family had one, a special room or house to which male villagers went to socialize, do business, and consult their *agha* regarding social and legal matters. Women sometimes went to the *diwan* for advice during the day as well, but the guesthouse was a predominantly male preserve. Boys began attending the *diwan* in their early teens, and it was here that the traditional tribal ways were passed from one generation to the next. All men were expected to attend the *diwan* every evening.

In earlier eras, many *diwans* also functioned as inns for travelers, and in return, the travelers provided the villagers with a much-hungered-for commodity—news of the outside world. The most famous of *diwans* were celebrated in Kurdish folksongs and folktales, while many wealthier *aghas* had their own residential minstrels. Wandering dervishes and *dengbej*, or traveling storytellers, stopped by from time to time as well.

Like most of the *aghas* I met, Ako Agha maintained a formal indoors *diwan*, furnished with spotless white armchairs and couches, in which he and his visitors usually convened. But during the summer, he moved his court outdoors, onto the patio, where fireflies danced arabesques over the lawn in front and black mountains hulked protectively behind.

"The Ako have lived in Raniya for more than nine hundred years," Ako Agha said, turning his attention to me. "Our territory stretches north into the Erbil governorate and east to Iran. We are a strong and powerful tribe, with many subtribes. . . ."

At this, he reeled off twenty-five names without hesitation and without repeating himself, and said that he, like all Ako *aghas* before him, was of the Bash-aghayi subtribe. His father had owned tens of thousands of acres of land pre–land reform, but Ako owned less than forty, and supported his family mostly through business contracts and trade.

"The Ako are famous for offering refuge," he went on. After the fall of the Kurdish Republic of Mahabad in 1946, some Iranian Kurds had escaped to Raniya, while both Mulla Mustafa Barzani and Jalal Talabani had at times hidden in the inaccessible Ako mountains. In fact, during the "thick-headed" internal war, Ako Agha himself had tried to reconcile the two par-ties. At the height of the hostilities, he and Dildar's husband, who I now learned to my surprise was a Bilbas leader, made sure that "not one shot was fired in Raniya."

To offer refuge, especially to those fleeing the wrath of their own *aghas*, was an important role of many traditional tribal leaders. But the host *agha's* hospitality was not altogether altruistic. In return for providing the fleeing refugees with protection, land for a new home, and other necessities, he expected labor and loyalty.

A servant brought out large glasses of chilled *du*, the Middle Eastern drink made of yogurt, followed by trays heaped high with ripe apricots, watermelon, and small sweet cucumbers. Served with the cucumbers were plastic salt shakers, one neatly parceled out to every two people.

"Because I am *agha*," Ako Agha said as we munched on the fruit, water-melon pits flying around us, "I also help the poor and resolve many differ-ent kinds of conflicts." One constant source of trouble was the arena of love and marriage, of course—about which I would learn more the following day—and another concerned land disputes. "But the most difficult problem to resolve is murder," he said.

"How often does that happen?" I asked, startled that he had voluntarily brought up the subject.

Ako Agha shrugged. "Sometimes I resolve two or three killings a month, sometimes only one a year. The people come to me, and I try to reconcile their two families, with offers of money, or land, or women. I try to find a link between them, so that they will settle and no more blood will flow."

"So you don't go to the police or courts?" I asked

He laughed. "No. We love our government, but we don't want to tire them out."

Many *aghas* preferred to settle killings intertribally, and the process did make some sense, the Kurdish Human Rights Organization notwithstand-ing. The legal system in Kurdistan was still slow, and many villagers, remembering the Baath regime, feared dealing with state authorities. The *agha* was the power that they knew, trusted, and obeyed.

The killings were often resolved with "blood money," usually ranging from 100,000 to 300,000 *dinars* (about $5,000 to $15,000), with accidental deaths costing less, and premeditated ones more. Promising an eligible daughter in marriage to a man in the victim's family was also a common solution, especially among the poor. And when no eligible daughter was available, a younger child was sometimes promised instead.

To be avoided at all costs was a "blood feud," which began between the two families when no peaceful solution could be found. Once a serious problem in the region, the blood feuds could last for generations. In earlier decades, it scarcely mattered whether the original murderer was killed or not, what mattered was that the collective honor of the group be restored by killing an enemy of at least a comparable social status. In the modern era, the prevalence of blood feuds has greatly diminished, but I did meet one man in Suleimaniyah who had fled his village because of a blood feud.

"To resolve a killing takes much time and patience," Ako Agha said. "One killing took me six years, another eight years. The killing that took eight years happened between two subtribes, and before it was finished, eight people were killed and five people injured."

THE NEXT MORNING, Dildar, Ako Agha, and I climbed into his shiny Land Cruiser for a tour of the Ako valley, a narrow opening between two mountain ranges. With us were two armed *peshmerga*, and Ako Agha brought along a video camera.

Quickly leaving Raniya behind, we headed west and then north along a flat dirt road, lined with pretty clay homes, neat stone walls, symmetrical piles of firewood, and gardens beaming with sunflowers. Many of the homes had electricity, harnessed from a river below, but nowhere in sight were the ugly electrical wires that blighted other parts of Kurdistan. The region had a settled and peaceful feel.

"Was the Ako valley attacked in the Anfal?" I asked Ako Agha, already all but knowing the answer.

"No, we were with the government at that time," he said, and my stomach sank a little. "But before that, we were in the mountains. I spent most of my first twenty-five years in the mountains. Our valley was bombed in the 1960s, because my father supported Barzani, and again in 1976, when they destroyed our family's house and the only Ako school."

The road stopped abruptly. The Ako valley had ended, while to either side extended two new valleys, one leading to Rowanduz, the other to Haj Omran. We climbed up a small hill to view the countryside.

"Why did you support the Baath regime?" I asked our host, summoning up my courage.

"We didn't really support them," Ako said. "We were really helping the *peshmerga* by letting them pass through our mountains. The Kurds needed a few tribes to be with the government in this way."

"So you were a kind of double agent?"

"Yes." Dildar answered the question herself, without translating. "And there were no hard feelings because of this. Everybody loves this man."

"During the Anfal, the Iraqis controlled all the area around our mountains," Ako Agha said. "But over eight hundred *peshmerga* were hiding in safety here. Some stayed in my house, and some I took in my car through enemy lines."

"And the Iraqi government didn't know?"

"Not for a long time. But on January 31, 1990, the Iraqis finally arrested me and thirty-three others. They'd heard some reports. They held me ten months and twenty days, and I was taken to the Revolutionary Court in Baghdad three times. Six among us were executed, twelve sentenced to life, and the rest freed."

On our way back to Raniya, I asked Ako Agha what he thought would be the future of the tribes and *aghas* in Iraqi Kurdistan.

"It will depend on the situation of the government," he said. "If there is conflict between the parties, the *aghas* will still have much power. During the internal fighting, the *aghas* grew stronger. But if the government is settled, the *aghas* will lose power, and then I think the power of the tribes will be finished in another fifteen, sixteen years."

"Would that be good or bad for you?" I wondered what it felt like to contemplate losing the powerful position that one's family has held for generations.

"I would prefer for the government to be settled," he said. "Because if the government is settled, then my life will be settled, too."

—

BACK AT AKO AGHA'S compound, we were met by two strutting male peacocks, fanning their shimmery tails, and by the younger of our host's two wives, a tall and handsome woman of about thirty, who whisked Dildar and me behind the winter *diwan* to the women's quarters.

Like the rest of the compound, the women's quarters were spartan, composed of several large rooms furnished only with red carpets and thin green-and-gold cushions. In one corner stood a traditional Kurdish cradle, covered with a floral sheet, under which the youngest of Ako Agha's nine children slept. Built in a style that dates back to the thirteenth century, and still widely used in Kurdistan, the traditional cradle is made of wood, with rockers on the bottom and a handle for carrying spanning the top. The child is strapped in with cloth strips, with a urine pipe attached, so that the mother can go about her chores, but cannot flex its legs, which can lead to medical problems. Hip dislocation is common among young Kurdish children.

As Dildar and I took seats, a wizened but still beautiful woman with round dark eyes joined us. Dressed in black from head to toe, she looked to be over seventy years old, but her hair was still dark and shiny, thanks to dye and henna, and woven into five or six braids in back, with open tresses framing her face, as was the Bilbas custom. The tresses reminded me of the ones worn by the Barzani women I'd met earlier, and when I commented on this, the woman agreed, but said that the braids were exclusively Bilbas.

The woman was Maryam Swara Hammad Agha, Ako Agha's mother and a local legend. Although the lowly fifth and last wife of Ako's father, Ako Abbas Mamand Agha, whom she married when she was a teenager and he middle-aged, Maryam had garnered the utmost respect in his household, often serving in his place when he was away. "Abbas Agha loved her a lot, she could do what she wanted, and he never did anything without asking her first," Dildar told me.

When Maryam and Abbas Agha fell in love, their tribes, though usually allies, were feuding. And her father, the Bilbas chieftain, had promised her to another. But Maryam refused to obey her father's wishes and after years of stubborn resistance and admiring Abbas Agha from afar, finally got her way in 1951, when they wed. "My husband was the most handsome and most powerful man I ever met," she told me, still much in love though Abbas Agha had passed away decades earlier. "He was taller than Ako—over two meters—and had big and beautiful eyes. He couldn't read or write, but he was very wise."

One of Maryam's main duties as a wife had been caring for her husband's many guests. In those days, much more than now, throngs of people were always stopping by. One time, during the Barzani revolution, she fed nine hundred people on only a few hours' notice.

However, the most strenuous part of her job had been caring for the many couples who took refuge in the *diwan*. As her son Ako Agha had told me the night before, the guesthouse was not just a meeting place and inn, but also a hideaway for runaway lovers. Young men and women who had fallen in love against their family's wishes came to the *diwan*, where no one dared touch them, to live until their case was resolved. The couples stayed in the *diwan* for as long as it took to negotiate peace, sleeping strictly separately, of course, until they were married. Ako Agha himself had a perfect track record, never failing to reconcile the lovers' families.

So here is a much-needed safety valve, I thought as I heard of the custom—a way for at least some lucky lovers to escape the horror of honor killings.

"We have two couples staying here now," Maryam said. "One has been here for two years."

"Two years!" I said.

"Two years is nothing!" Maryam said. "Two couples is nothing! Sometimes, we had ten, twenty couples staying here. Some got married and still stayed here. Some were married when they came and had to wait to get a divorce and get married again. One stayed five years."

"Five years!" I said.

"Yes, it was like a free hotel," Maryam said, with a smirk. "And sometimes, those who came didn't listen, they didn't help, they didn't work. They just took advantage."

Shaking her head in exasperation, Maryam rose to say her midday prayers, while Dildar and I went out back to find the runaway couple who had been at the *diwan* for two years. The wife, Adiba, was too busy cooking to talk, but her husband, Khalid, agreed to take a stroll with us around the garden, now wilting in the noonday sun.

"We come from a village near Koya, many miles away," he said. "I first saw Adiba when I was seventeen and she was fifteen, and we loved each other right away and wanted to marry. I asked her family, but they refused, and so we ran away. We don't have any tribes or *diwans* in Koya, but we knew about Ako Agha and how he helps people, and so we came here."

As we were talking, I realized that Khalid had, in Kurdish terminology, "kidnapped" Adiba. Throughout my travels, many Kurds had mentioned the "kidnapping" of women to me, a phenomenon that seemed to happen quite often. Until now, I had never really understood what it meant, as further questioning usually revealed not a true kidnapping, but a kind of elopement in which a woman voluntarily leaves her home to follow a man.

Though not always. In the past especially, some women had been kidnapped against their will, sometimes by rival tribes. I would meet one such woman in Turkey. She had been abducted at age fourteen, while out in the fields, and had cried herself to sleep at night for years. But over time . . . She shrugged. She was middle-aged now, with a comfortable home and four children of her own.

"Adiba and I married last year, and have a son, but still we cannot go back," Khalid said. "Maybe in another one, two years . . . I talk to my family sometimes, but Adiba still has not talked to hers. They are still very angry, even though I paid them 50,000 *dinars* [about $2,500]."

How ridiculous of Adiba's parents, I thought. Khalid seemed like an honest, hardworking man who sincerely loved their daughter. And he had already paid them a significant amount of money. What more did they want?

BACK INSIDE THE women's quarters, Ako Agha, freshly returned from brokering a settlement over a traffic accident, and Hamid Kak Amin Bilbas, Dildar's husband, had arrived for lunch. A compact, gray-haired man of about fifty, dressed in baggy Kurdish trousers and a button-down shirt, Hamid was a lawyer, a profession that ran in the family.

Hamid's stepfather and Dildar's father had gone to law school together, which was how Dildar and Hamid had met. Yet throughout their courtship, Hamid had never told her about his deep involvement with the PUK, and in 1986, she was astonished to find herself fleeing with him to the mountains to join the *peshmerga*. "I couldn't believe it!" she said, shaking her head and laughing.

"Dildar is a very brave woman," Hamid said. "During the chemical attacks, she was the only one who went out of the shelter to get wet blankets to cover our faces."

"I was always sticking my head out, trying to see what was going on," Dildar laughed, amazing but not surprising me.

As it turned out, Hamid and Dildar had survived not one, but two, chemical attacks. And twice, Dildar had been forced to travel through enemy territory almost completely on her own. One trip was due to a medical emergency that necessitated treatment in Baghdad. The other was the death of her father in Dohuk. For four days, she traveled by mule and foot from Suleimaniyah to Raniya, where, with the help of Ako Agha, she slipped secretly through enemy lines and over mountains to her father's home. On her way back, she collapsed in Ako Agha's *diwan* for a week or two, numb with grief and exhaustion.

"I told you I knew Ako Agha well," Dildar said as the two of them exchanged glances, and I wondered about all the other possible personal interconnections swirling around me in Kurdistan.

A servant came in to spread out a plastic tablecloth on the floor for lunch. The conversation turned to Hamid and the Bilbas. A confederation of six tribes that straddled the Iraq-Iran border, the Bilbas were at least as numerous as the Ako.

But the Bilbas no longer had a paramount powerful *agha*. Maryam's father had been the last.

"We went the other way, the educated way, and left the tribal behind," Hamid said in passable English, thanks to several years spent in London. "My stepfather started this when he graduated in law from the University of Baghdad in 1948. Now we still have some small *aghas*, to help with small problems, but for killings and other big problems, we go to the courts. We believe in the justice of the courts."

I looked from Hamid to Ako Agha and back again. Both were about the same age and of high standing within their respective tribal groups. But one had stuck to the traditional ways, and the other had been modernized through education. Ako Agha was by far the more romantic character, but Hamid personified the inevitable way of the future. Earlier, Ako Agha had told me that he was planning to send his children to college. He was, in effect, the end of the traditional Ako *agha* line. I was witnessing the twilight of an era.

—

THE *DIWAN* WAS not the only safe haven in Kurdistan. Women fleeing from abuse and the wrath of their families had another as yet limited but growing option: women's shelters, which I at first simplistically viewed as a new and enlightened idea coming from the West. Only gradually did it dawn on me that the shelters had in fact arisen to fill the gap left by the shrinking number of *diwans.* The shelters were not so much an improvement on traditional Kurdish society as they were a replacement for a once-integral component of that society, now disappearing due largely to exposure to the West.

At the time of my visit, there were only two official public shelters, both in Suleimaniyah. Plans were in the works to open others in Dohuk and Erbil. Some organizations, including the women's branch of the Iraqi Workers' Communist Party, also took in women in need on a more informal basis.

The more easily accessible of the two official shelters was the Nowah Center, located in a quiet residential neighborhood on the outskirts of the city. A well-kept place enclosed by a high wall, it could accommodate a total of about twenty women. To the right of the entrance was an education and handicrafts area where the women took literacy and other classes, and in back was a communal kitchen.

The center's director, Bayan Mamoud, an energetic woman with sparkling eyes and lustrous black hair, told me that the shelter had been founded in 1999 by seven women's organizations. Most of its funding came from a German nongovernmental agency, and the shelter also received a small stipend from the PUK. The average shelter stay was three months, and rooms were usually half to fully occupied. Most of the clients heard about the center through outreach programs in their villages, on television, or on radio.

When a client arrived at the shelter, the staff quickly contacted her family. If her family were unaware of her whereabouts for any significant length of time, and especially overnight, her life would be placed in danger. Women whose lives were in danger did not stay at the Nowah Center, but were sent to a safe house run by PUK's Women's Union.

Bayan and her all-woman staff, which included lawyers, social workers, and her sister, next met with the woman's family, sometimes in the shelter, but more usually traveling to her village. "The process is very difficult," Bayan said. "In the beginning, the families do not hear us and are very angry. And sometimes we must meet with an *agha* or *shaikh*, and we are very afraid. We have difficulties with our car—it is very old—and in winter, the day is short. We sit with the *agha* or *shaikh* and many men, just two ladies—I often go alone with my sister—and we don't feel safe until we are back in Suleimaniyah. We don't bring the police, because if we did, the family would become even angrier."

I felt astonished at the women's courage: two young, unmarried, and well-educated outsiders meeting with large groups of angry and probably uneducated men.

"Often we must go back to a village many times, sometimes it takes ten visits," Bayan said. "But usually, we are successful. The families calm down, we find a solution, and they sign a contract, which we can use later in court if anything happens. We always follow up on the women after they leave here."

Most women came to the shelter because of marital problems, often due to arranged marriages, the taking of second wives, or the common Kurdish practice of *jin ba jin*, or "woman for woman." Prevalent among poor Kurds, the practice involves two families exchanging women as brides in a reciprocal marriage arrangement—usually, two daughters exchanged to marry two sons. In this way, the onerous bride-price, traditionally paid by the groom's family to the bride's, is avoided, and a double wedding can also be arranged. When no eligible daughter is available, a family might pledge a niece, cousin, or much younger child instead, to be wed upon reaching puberty. And, in a potentially heart-wrenching twist—luckily dying out—if one couple divorces, the second is expected to follow suit.

Bayan introduced me to some of the women at the shelter. Two were in their forties, but everyone else was disconcertingly young—most well under twenty. All were villagers, a fact that even I, after nearly three months in Kurdistan, could tell at a glance. The young women had a simple, direct, and capable way about them that spoke of hours spent toiling in the kitchen and fields, along with an air of puzzled watchfulness, as if working hard every moment to understand the urban world around them, so different from what they were accustomed to.

One of the girls, wearing an orange-and-white dress with a blue-and-white scarf and a fake diamond ring, told me that she was in the shelter because of *jin ba jin*. She didn't know exactly how old she was, but guessed fourteen or fifteen, she said as she nibbled on her fingernails, chipped with a deep red polish. She hadn't wanted to marry her husband, and when he took her home, he and his family "did nothing for me—no gold, no home, no furniture," she said, reminding me of how young she was. Instead they all lived together in a crowded house, and when she complained, her husband beat her and shouted, "Go to your own home if you don't like it here."

So she went back home, where her uncle and grandfather beat her even harder, saying, "If you were a good woman, why did they send you back? We don't want you here." Her uncle locked her in a closet, to drag her out later and beat her again. Three months pregnant, she lost her baby, and, after hearing an announcement on the radio, ran away to the shelter. Now she didn't know what to do. She didn't want to return to her husband or her father's home. But she had no other options.

I traveled on to the safe house, the Aram Center. Also founded in 1999, the Aram Center had admitted sixty-seven cases in the last three years, all but three of which had been resolved. However, life at the shelter, whose location was kept strictly confidential, was very difficult; most of the women and their children didn't dare go out on the streets.

One of the unresolved cases involved a rape victim. In her early twenties, she wore denim leggings, plastic sandals, and a black T-shirt printed with a rose and a letter written in English that read: "Darling . . . When are you coming back to me? I'm waiting." She couldn't stop crying as she told me her story.

Her brothers had been in prison when she was raped, but as soon as they came out, they began threatening her with talk about her "betrayal," she said. They found the man who assaulted her and forced them to marry, but still, it was a bad situation, and she was afraid she might be killed. Then her brothers did kill her father-in-law. She was pregnant by that time, but she managed to keep it hidden until she gave birth, when a kind judge helped her and her baby escape to the shelter. Now, her family said they wanted her home, but she didn't trust them, and she couldn't see any future for herself or her son, age two. "We can't even go outside. How will he go to school?" she sobbed.

Another unresolved case involved a woman in her late twenties, dressed in a polka-dot blouse and black pants. She and her husband had married against her parents' wishes, running away to Dohuk to wed, and then to Iran, where they lived for ten years. Money was exchanged between their families, and, assuming they were safe, they returned to their village. But ten days later, someone entered their house at night and shot them in their sleep. Her husband was killed, her son shot in the legs, and she was shot in the back, legs, and hands.

I listened in horror to the gut-wrenching stories. I'd been hearing occasional similar tales all over the country, but some had seemed like hearsay and others had just been statistics. It felt completely different to be hearing the painful details from the victims themselves. How could a part of Kurdish society, no matter how small, not only condone this kind of behavior, but glorify it under the name of "honor"?

One easy but highly unsatisfactory answer is that a cruel and seamy underside exists in cultures everywhere, differing in its particulars, but seemingly an inevitable part of human existence.

The number of honor killings in Iraqi Kurdistan is believed to have been holding steady or on the decline prior to the uprising. It spiked dramatically in the early to mid 1990s, and is believed to be on the decline again. Experts blame the spike on a variety of factors, including economic and social dislocation, the rivalry between the two parties, the Kurdish government's near-complete failure to address women's issues up until recently, the rise of Islamists, and the influence of the violent Baath regime. High unemployment rates, not enough schools, collective towns in which people are crowded together with nothing to do but gossip, and the mores of a deeply entrenched patriarchal order struggling to regain control over a chaotic new world undoubtedly contributed to the rise as well.

Activists estimate that since 1991, some four thousand women were victims of honor killings in Iraqi Kurdistan—a number that is impossible to verify, and one that may be grossly inaccurate, as some honor killings are disguised as accidents on the one hand, and different types of murders have been passed off as honor killings on the other, in the hopes of lighter sentencing. Whatever the numbers, most Kurds agree that the practice started increasing dramatically immediately after the establishment of the semiautonomous zone, when the political parties apparently killed women suspected of fraternizing with the Baathists and Arabs who'd previously worked in the region.

Only in 2001 did the PUK and in 2002 the KDP seriously address the issue of honor killings by finally repealing the Iraqi laws that allowed for the killings under mitigated circumstances and that sentenced its perpetrators to no more than three years in prison. By the time the Iraq war of 2003 began, honor killings in Iraqi Kurdistan were finally being treated like all other murders, putting the enclave in a far more humanist position than the rest of Iraq, where the repressive laws still stood. Increasingly powerful Kurdish women's groups, publications, and conferences abroad had also been instrumental in drawing attention to the practice, and some believed that such vigilance had already paid off impressively. The Suleimaniyah's Independent Women's Center, for one, estimated that the number of honor killings in the region decreased to 47 in 2001 from 171 in 1991.

If I wanted a negative example of how trauma affects a society, I thought, remembering the questions I'd had before arriving in Iraq, I would be hard put to find anything more dramatic than the 1990s spike in such murders. Publicly, the Kurds had accomplished a superhuman amount in their decade of semi-independence, making it appear as if they had passed through their recent horrific past more or less psychologically unscathed. But insidious disturbances were at work, created by wounds that will take many years, if not decades, to heal. For some at least, the Kurdistan "safe haven" had been safe in name only.

ONE MONTH AFTER I left Iraq, I was again vividly reminded of the precarious nature of life in the safe haven. Sitting snugly cocooned in my New York apartment one morning, I received a call from Zerrin Ibrahim, whom I had met in Dohuk. A lively, intelligent, and outspoken woman in her thirties, Zerrin worked for the United Nations, helping Turkish refugees who had fled to Iraq.

Zerrin had terrifying news. She had been imprisoned by the Baathists while on a routine U.N. visit to Mosul and now, back in Dohuk, had good reason to believe that she was on Saddam's hit list. The Iraqi regime had a history of sadistically murdering former prisoners after releasing them.

Zerrin was contacting me in the hopes that I could help influence the U.N. to transfer her to another post outside Iraq as quickly as possible. With thousands of miles between us, I felt both far removed from her sickening ordeal — how could it be real? — and fraught with helplessness. All I could think to do was make a few ineffectual phone calls. The situation was only resolved several weeks later when the Dohuk governor assigned Zerrin full-time bodyguards, who remained with her until the end of the war.

Zerrin had given me garbled details of her imprisonment over the phone and later sent me a detailed written report. She had gone to Baathist-controlled Mosul on June 1, 2002, to renew her passport, as did all U.N. local staff once a year. Parking outside the appropriate building, she proceeded to the second floor, where an officer said she needed to visit his boss's office regarding a few routine details. Two men would take her there.

Leaving the building, Zerrin felt a pistol in the small of her back. She was taken to the Mosul Intelligence Office. Three and a half hours later, a tall, bulky man with dark skin and an infected eye arrived. Accusing her of spying for the United States, Britain, Israel, and Turkey, he said that she had fifteen minutes in which to confess. If she cooperated, she could go back to Dohuk the next day. If she did not, she would be sent to Baghdad, where she would be executed. She asked what evidence they had against her, and he said that she was being uncooperative and would be sent to Baghdad.

Eight hours later, at 3 A.M., Zerrin heard a car arrive. Two men shoved her out of the detention room and into the car's backseat, covered with dried blood. They drove to a prison outside Baghdad, where she was forced into a cell on the building's fourth floor. Measuring about three by two yards, the room was painted dark red and was completely dark, except for a dim light above the door. Insects were everywhere.

A knock came, and a moment later—eyes blindfolded, wrists tied—Zerrin was taken to the first floor for her first interrogation of many. The guards never guided her on the way down and laughed whenever she fell.

Inside the interrogation office, six men waited. One accused Zerrin of being a spy for four enemy states, starting with Israel. His proof? Zerrin's department head, who worked in the Baghdad office, was a French Jew. Zerrin said that she had not known that he was Jewish and did not believe him to be a spy, but if they believed he was, they should be interrogating him, not her. The men slapped her so hard that her mouth filled with blood. Then, saying that that was enough for one day, they sent her back to her cell.

More interrogations followed, each targeting Zerrin's alleged connections to a different enemy country. Her contacts with an English aid worker and American researcher were brought up, as was her work with Turkish refugees. And whenever she did not provide the answers that her interrogators were looking for, they hit her.

Back in her cell, Zerrin was unable to eat. Her right side felt leaden, as if she'd had a stroke, and one horrific day was spent listening to the screams of another woman on her floor. The woman was in labor and kept crying out for a glass of water, but no one responded as she delivered her baby alone in her dark, dirty cell.

Finally one day, Zerrin was handed a letter calling for her execution and taken to a court within the prison. The "trial" lasted only fifteen minutes, during which time a judge read the accusations against her and said that she would be executed.

Two days later, Zerrin was told that she was being released. She fainted. Guards handed her back her clothes and drove her to the house of a Baghdad relative. One hour later, she left for Kurdistan. She arrived home at 7:30 P.M. on June 15, two weeks and a day after her arrest.

Just what had been the reason for Zerrin's arrest? Had the Baathists truly intended to execute her? Had they really believed her to be a spy? Or had her arrest been meant as a warning—both to her and to the United Nations?

CHAPTER FIFTEEN

Syrian Interlude

ₛ₍₍ₐ₍

ON MY WAY IN AND OUT OF IRAQI KURDISTAN, I TARRIED nearly two weeks in Syria, home to about 1.5 million Kurds, or 9 percent of Syria's total population of 17 million. After the heady freedom of Iraqi Kurdistan, Syria came as a shock. Gone was all celebration of things Kurdish. In its stead were the secrecy, uncertainty, and fear of a people living under a repressive, strong-armed regime.

For thirty years, between 1971 and 2000, Syria was ruled by President Hafez Assad, a shrewd, authoritarian, and at times brutal Middle Eastern leader known for his Arab nationalism and opposition to Israel. Assad allowed the Syrian people considerable cultural and religious freedoms — he himself was of the minority Alawite faith — but few political ones, and he was responsible for various human rights atrocities, most notoriously the 1982 massacre at Hama, during which ten thousand to twenty-five thousand people were slaughtered. When Assad died in 2000, many were hopeful that his successor, his soft-spoken son Bashar, would usher in a gentler, more open, and less corrupt era. Some improvements have occurred, but overall Syria has changed little since the elder Assad's death.

In general, the Kurds of Syria have not suffered from persecution as extreme as that inflicted on the Kurds of Iraq, Turkey, or Iran, and Syria today is more tolerant of its Kurdish population than are Turkey and Iran. Nonetheless, Kurdish has never been recognized as an official language — though it is allowed on the streets — and Syrian Kurds cannot legally publish, study, teach, or write in Kurdish, or hold Kurdish concerts. Books published in Kurdish must be sold surreptitiously, although their possession is allowed. Kurds suffer discrimination in the workplace, and while some Kurds have risen to high levels in government—including membership in parliament—their influence is limited. Kurdish political parties are technically speaking illegal, but some are informally recognized and allowed to operate in what is basically a one-party system run by the National Progressive Front (NPF), a body of allied parties dominated by Syria's Baath Party.

Worst of all, over two hundred thousand Syrian Kurds, or one-sixth of its Kurdish population, are denied full citizenship. The Syrian government claims that they are foreigners, or descendants of foreigners, who immigrated illegally into the country from Turkey starting in the 1920s. Never mind the fact that most of these "foreign" Kurds were born on Syrian soil and have no other nationality; they are denied such basic rights as the right to vote, run a business, work as a doctor or engineer, hold a position in the government, possess a passport, be admitted into a public hospital, or register marriages. Furthermore, "illegal" Kurds cannot own real estate or an automobile without the help of an intermediary who is a full citizen. "Foreign" men are not allowed to marry women who are full citizens.

The Syrian Kurds live in three separate geographic pockets in northern Syria: the northeastern part of the Jazira, a fertile plain, where most of the "foreigners" live; the northwestern part of the Jazira; and the Kurd Dagh, the only mountainous Kurdish region in Syria. Many Kurds also live in Damascus, which has had a large Kurdish population since the Middle Ages. Many Damascus Kurds have long been assimilated into Arab culture. And with few mountains to offer them protection and a community that is dispersed geographically, Syrian Kurds have never waged the sort of full-scale war against their government that has at times torn apart Iraq, Turkey, and Iran.

WHEN I ARRIVED in Qamishli, the Syrian border town, on my way back from Iraq, my host family was waiting for me. We had spoken only briefly on the phone, and I had never met our mutual contact, but in true Kurdish fashion, the family showered me with gracious hospitality. They had turned their cheery children's room into my guestroom, prepared an elaborate wel-

250 | A THOUSAND SIGHS, A THOUSAND REVOLTS

coming meal for me, and arranged to take time off from work to provide tours of the area. Before I left them five days later, they would also insist on taking me out to dinner several times, buy me a half-dozen CDs and a ring to remember them by, purchase my plane ticket from Qamishli to Damascus, and give me money for the taxi ride between the Damascus airport and my hotel. No amount of protestation on my part would deflect them from these purposes.

The family lived in a modern apartment on a street that was part Kurdish, part Arab. Qamishli was largely developed after the discovery of oil in the Jazira in the mid-1900s, and was inhabited by a mix of Kurds, Arabs, Turks, Assyrians, Armenians, and Syrian Orthodox. Portraits of President Assad, past and present, hung everywhere, sometimes four or five on one short block, along with dozens of statues of the father. The city had more than its share of slums and unpaved streets, but also housed luxury apartment buildings and upscale shops, including a United Colors of Benetton.

After lunch, my hosts took me on a drive due west of the city, through a land of wheat and barley fields and pastures teeming with sheep. At first, I took the many shepherds among them to be Arab, as all were dressed in long white *jalabiyya*, or caftans, and flowing head cloths. Then my hosts told me that, on the contrary, most were Kurdish. Kurdish dress is not allowed in Syria, they said, a statement that I later learned was not altogether correct. During periods of strong Arab nationalism, Kurdish men have been forbidden to wear traditional dress, but during periods of leniency, the male costume has been allowed and is still worn in the Kurd Dagh. Many Kurdish men also began switching voluntarily to Arab dress after World War I. Kurdish women have never been subject to any restrictions regarding dress.

My hosts were reluctant to let me talk to any of the people we passed or, later, to most of their neighbors. It wouldn't be safe, they said. They also advised me not to take notes, and to destroy all my Syrian Kurdish-related papers before leaving the country, as I could be searched at the airport. When the family arranged for me to meet a Kurdish politician, the event had to be carefully choreographed so as to appear to be a purely social occasion.

We passed by one village after another, all looking much alike: flat, poor nondescript places built of cement and clay brick, with drooping electricity lines. Yet my hosts could tell them apart. "Arab, Arab, Arab," they said as the apparently newer and better-laid-out villages flashed by.

We were now in the heart of al-Jazira, an Arab word meaning "the island," that refers to the northern part of the Mesopotamian plain between the Euphrates and Tigris Rivers. During Ottoman times, the Jazira—today divided between Syria and Turkey—was a giant grazing ground, used by Arab nomads pasturing their camels and sheep in summer, and by Kurdish seminomads herding their huge flocks down from the Anatolian highlands in winter. Uninhabited and remote from central government, the Jazira was notorious for its lawlessness, though relations between its Arab and Kurdish tribes were generally good. Then in the 1920s, an enormous influx of about twenty-five thousand Kurds and many tens of thousands of Armenians and other Christians escaping Turkish massacres poured into the region.

From the beginning, tensions between the newly arrived populations and the older ones flared. At the same time, as the settlers began cultivating the land, it became apparent that the region was highly fertile and could become the breadbasket of the then–newly created state of Syria, carved out of the old Ottoman Empire along with Iraq and modern Turkey. By 1945, the Syrian government was starting to speak ominously of the "infiltration" of Kurds into the increasingly important region, and in the late 1950s, in the wake of growing Arab nationalism, the government began its first crackdown on the Kurds. Those caught with Kurdish music or publications, previously allowed, were arrested, as were over five thousand political "suspects," many accused of belonging to the illegal Kurdistan Democratic Party of Syria. In 1962, the government conducted an unusual census that led to the stripping of some 120,000 Jazira Kurds, and their descendants, of their rights as Syrian citizens, proclaiming them illegal immigrants. Fears of Iraq's growing Kurdish nationalism and the discovery of oil in the Jazira undoubtedly had much to do with the government's actions.

The next year, an "Arabization" program similar to the one in Iraq was devised, with a Lieutenant Muhammad Talab Hilal drawing up a twelve-point plan. Among other things, Hilal proposed declaring all Kurdish land deeds null and void; denying Kurds education and employment; establishing a ten- to fifteen-kilometer-wide "Arab Cordon" along the Turkish border that would be completely devoid of all Kurds; replacing Kurdish religious leaders with Arab ones; and enticing more Arabs into the region with land and housing.

Due to the 1967 war with Israel, the "Arab Cordon" and other parts of Hilal's plan were never implemented. However, forty model Arab villages were built, about seven thousand Arab families imported into the region, some sixty thousand Jazira Kurds expelled or convinced to leave, and the remaining "non-Syrian" Kurds denied full citizenship. The harassment and arrest of the leaders of the Kurdistan Democratic Party of Syria also continued. One politician I met told me that he had lived six years on the lam in the 1960s, staying in a different house every night.

In the early 1970s, the state's persecution of its Kurdish minority eased, and in 1976, President Assad renounced the replacement of Kurds with Arabs in the Jazira. However, the denial of full citizenship continues to oppress more than two hundred thousand Kurds, while allowing the state to claim, on paper at least, that the Jazira is predominantly Arab. In addition, about seventy-five thousand of the two hundred thousand "non-Syrian" Kurds are descendants of "illegal" marriages between "foreign" fathers and Syrian mothers, meaning that they have no documentation or rights whatsoever.

"The policy is tragic and absurd," my hosts said. "The children of the illegal marriages were born here, but can't even go to primary school."

My hosts and I had reached Amuda, one of the largest towns in the Jazira. In the 1930s, the mystery writer Agatha Christie and her husband, noted archaeologist Max Mallowan, lived in Amuda, while Mallowan conducted digs in the area. Like Iraq's Shahrizur, the Jazira is covered with dozens of *tells*, or artificial hills, some dating back to Roman and Assyrian times, and others to prehistoric man. Christie had a deep appreciation of Syria but little good to say about her temporary hometown. "Amuda is mainly an Armenian town and not, may it be said, at all an attractive one," she writes. "The flies there are out of all proportion, and the small boys have the worst manners yet seen, everyone seems bored and yet truculent."

We drove by Christie's old home—a clay brick house with odd, heavy buttresses—a grim police station with indolent guards lolling around out front, and dozens more posters and statues of President Assad the elder. Then we turned onto a quiet side street lined with high walls, to enter a compound bursting with yellow and orange marigolds, a stately home, protective cypress trees, and a flagstone patio on which several aristocratic-looking women and a man were socializing. Joining them, we partook of tea and sesame-flour cookies, cherries and apricots, Turkish coffee and candy, and gentle conversation and laughter. The scene felt genteel, sophisticated, Old World, and far removed from anything I'd experienced in Iraq, where everything had felt so new and raw. So this is what cultured Kurdistan feels like when it hasn't been bombed into oblivion time and time again, I thought.

THE NEXT DAY, my hosts and I again traveled along a road heading west through the Jazira. But this time, the Turkish border, dotted with guard towers and strafed with barbed wire and mines, was often less than one hundred yards away. We passed through several villages that straddled the two countries, a wide military swatch in between. In the distance rose the mountains of Turkey, including Mardin, where some of my Iraqi Kurdish friends had lived in refugee camps. From the cassette deck came the voice of Zakaria, whose buoyant music I'd heard everywhere in the semiautonomous zone. I may have felt far from Iraq, but, in reality, we were only about forty miles away.

"Before the 1980s and the trouble with the PKK, the soldiers let the villagers go to the border and shout hello to their families at the end of Ramadan," my hosts said. "Sometimes they even let them shake hands and hug. But then the fighting started, and now if you get too close to the border, the Turkish soldiers will shoot you."

The PKK has as difficult a history in Syria as it has in Iraq. Shortly before the 1980 military coup in Turkey, PKK leader Abdullah Öcalan and other party members fled to Syria where they were welcomed by a regime hostile to Turkey. President Assad the elder offered the rebel group offices in various cities and a training ground in the Syrian-controlled Bekaa Valley in Lebanon—help that was "crucial to the initial success of the PKK," writes historian David McDowall.

At first, the Syrian Kurds wholeheartedly embraced the PKK. Here at last was a radical organization fighting for an independent Kurdistan. Young Syrian Kurdish men and women joined the rebels by the thousands, to take up arms and head to Turkey. About seven thousand never returned.

Syrian Kurdish anger toward the PKK grew. Not only were loved ones disappearing, but the PKK was heavy-handedly soliciting funds and services from the Kurdish community. Furthermore, the PKK declared that Syria had no indigenous Kurds of its own, that all Syrian Kurds were in reality displaced Kurds from Turkey who wanted to move back north—a claim that the Syrian regime welcomed, as it was perfectly aligned with their own. But most Syrian Kurds had no desire to leave their homes.

Not until 1998, after eighteen years in Syria, were Öcalan and the PKK suddenly forced out. Turkey had amassed a large force of troops on the border and was threatening to invade unless Syria expelled the PKK. Much weaker than Turkey militarily, Syria complied. Öcalan left, initially to seek asylum in Russia. It was the first step in an exile that would eventually lead to his capture in Kenya and life imprisonment.

My hosts, who had lost a boy and a girl cousin to the PKK, expressed nothing but bitterness toward the guerrilla group. "The PKK killed people who criticized Öcalan," they said. "Or they cut off noses and ears. And the police knew everything, but said and did nothing. They didn't care what happened to us."

Once again, it was all about politics and their ironic bedfellows, I thought. The Syrian government had supported the PKK while repressing their own Kurdish population in much the same way that the Turkish government had supported Iraqi Kurdistan while repressing their Kurdish population. And ordinary people, caught in the middle as usual, paid the price.

DUE WEST OF the Jazira and northwest of the historic city of Aleppo stretches the Kurd Dagh, the only mountainous Kurdish region in Syria. Dense with sleepy villages, rolling hills, olive and cypress trees, and terraced vineyards, the Kurd Dagh has been home to a relatively prosperous Kurdish community ever since Kurdish lords ruled over Arab vassals here in the medieval era. Reminiscent of Greece and other picturesque parts of the Mediterranean, the Kurd Dagh is the sort of place that attracts tour buses with its idyllic vistas, inviting roadside restaurants, pristine lakes and dams, and historic sites.

The Kurd Dagh has not suffered from the kind of abuse that has plagued the Jazira. However, as I toured the picture-perfect hills with a Kurdish politician and his woman associate—who preferred to remain nameless—I heard stories of Kurdish villages at times deliberately cut off from electricity and on-again, off-again road checks that necessitated the payment of bribes. Kurdish farmers were often denied the government subsidies that Arab farmers obtained easily, and Kurdish political meetings had to be held in secret, my companions said. As politicians, they also never knew when they might be arrested.

Their stories reminded me of Muhammad Hamo, a Syrian Kurd I'd met in Suleimaniyah. The former owner of a bookstore in Aleppo, Muhammad had been forced to flee to Iraqi Kurdistan in 2001, after the Syrian authorities had destroyed his shop and home library. Muhammad had been surreptitiously selling Kurdish books in his store for years, with long stretches of time passing during which he'd been allowed to operate in peace. But on three separate occasions prior to his final ouster, something had triggered the state's ill will and he'd been arrested. Once, he was locked in solitary confinement for six months simply for writing poems about freedom. "Before they locked me up," Muhammad said, "they asked me, 'Why do you write about freedom? You already have freedom.' "

Which was worse, I wondered as I remembered Muhammad's story and listened to my companions: constant predictable repression or periods of relative freedom abruptly interrupted by harsh crackdowns?

We spent the night in a small village, arriving at about eleven P.M. via a back road, after evading a Syrian police station in a nearby larger village. "We don't want anyone to know you are here," my guides explained as we slunk around the edge of the larger village, to fly through a moonlit landscape, fields on either side, no other signs of human life in sight. "They might make trouble for you and us, or throw you out." My guides had been making similar comments throughout the day. Each time they did, my heart started to thump and I had to resist the urge to slide down in the backseat.

The village was small, populated by no more than twenty families, some related to my guides. Driving into one of the compounds, we were warmly greeted by a bevy of older women, all dressed in colorful *dishdasha*. With no idea we were coming and despite the late hour, they did not seem at all surprised to see us and quickly began preparing a snack while we took seats on the carpeted floor.

"Our lives are good, we have no complaints," the women told me as they brought out dishes of yogurt, olives, various fresh cheeses, hummus, and baba ghanoush—the latter two dishes a Mediterranean influence, seldom served in Iraq. "Except the usual one. We work too hard! Our men do nothing but drink tea and talk!"

—

OVER THE CENTURIES, the fabled Syrian capital of Damascus, another of the world's oldest cities, has served as a place of exile for prominent Kurds. The last powerful Kurdish emir, Bedir Khan, whose family ruled the Botan emirate in what is now Cizre, Turkey, from the 1200s to the 1840s, lived out his last years here and is buried in the Kurdish Quarter, a web of steep streets etching the foothills of Mount Qasyun. The site of Kurdish troop cantonments during the Middle Ages, the Kurdish Quarter was also once home to Mawlana Khalid, the charismatic *shaikh* who almost single-handedly spread the Nasqhbandi Sufi faith in Kurdistan. Mawlana Khalid fled from Suleimaniyah to Damascus under mysterious circumstances in 1820 and is buried in a whitewashed tomb perched high above the city.

The best known of Damascus's former Kurdish residents, however, is Salah al-Din, better known in the West as Saladin. A preeminent hero of the Islamic world, Salah al-Din is most famous for having recaptured Jerusalem from Richard I—the "Lionheart of England"—in September 1187 after eighty-eight years of Christian rule. Generally regarded as a man of great integrity, intelligence, and chivalrous behavior in battle—in contrast to the barbarous Crusaders—Salah al-Din has almost as many Western as Eastern admirers. He has been lauded by writers ranging from Sir Walter Scott to Dante, who in Canto IV of the *Inferno* describes Salah al-Din as "sitting at a distance separately," in Limbo because although not Christian, he led a virtuous life.

Salah al-Din Ayyubi was born into a prominent Kurdish family in Tikrit in today's Iraq in 1138, but grew up mostly in Baalbek (Lebanon) and Damascus, as political circumstances forced his family into exile. At age fourteen, he joined his uncle in military service to Nur al-Din of the ruling Zangi dynasty, and so impressed the Syrian governor that he was appointed administrator of Damascus at age eighteen. In 1171, he became ruler of Egypt, and then succeeded in uniting the hitherto warring Muslim territories of Egypt, Syria, Palestine, and northern Mesopotamia. The founder of the Ayyubid dynasty, which governed Egypt and the Red Sea coast until 1250, Salah al-Din died of malaria in 1193, three months after signing a peace treaty with Richard the Lionhearted.

Salah al-Din is buried in the Old City of Damascus, in a modest mausoleum adjoining the Umayyad Mosque, one of the most magnificent buildings in the Islamic world. Several hours north of Damascus reigns the well-preserved Krak des Chevaliers, or Krak des Kurds, which Salah al-Din recaptured from Reginald of Chatillon just prior to his successful siege of Jerusalem.

And yet for all the accolades heaped upon Salah al-Din by both the East and the West, he is not especially appreciated by the Kurds, many of whom seem to believe he betrayed them by paying more attention to his Muslim rather than his Kurdish heritage. "If Salah al-Din had been a better Kurd, we would be ruling the Middle East today," was typical of the comments I heard. An unrealistic fantasy, I mused, given all that could have gone wrong between then and now.

WHILE IN DAMASCUS, I met a prominent modern-day Kurd living in exile: Karim Khan Baradost, *agha* of Iraq's powerful Baradosti tribe. Originally from Iran, the Baradosti are a fabled people, celebrated in one of the Kurds' most famous epics, the battle of Dem Dem castle.

Karim Khan was an imposing-looking man, dressed in a cream-colored, three-piece suit. We met in a four-star hotel over a welcome lunch organized by the PUK. The party's prime minister, Dr. Barham Salih, was in town to talk to Syrian politicians. Both the KPD and PUK had a good relationship with Syria and offices in the capital.

At the luncheon, I sat across from Karim Khan and next to his twenty-something son, Sidqi, who spoke good English and translated for his father. Educated in the United States, Sidqi helped to run an apparently highly successful family business that involved selling surge protectors throughout the Middle East. Another example of the Kurds' amazing ability to adjust to change, I thought as I listened to Sidqi's accounts of twenty-first-century capitalism with one ear and his father's accounts of the epic of Dem Dem with the other.

As the tale goes, Shah Abbas I, the Safavid king who ruled Persia from 1588 to 1629, once had a close alliance with a Baradosti prince, who supported the shah in many battles. During one, he lost his hand, which the shah replaced with a hand of gold, leading to the prince's nickname, Khan Lepzerin, or the "Prince with the Golden Hand."

The shah and the khan had a falling out. The shah invited the khan to his palace to discuss the matter, but the khan, fearing a trap, refused to go, and declared independence. The shah then laid siege to his headquarters in Dem Dem castle, situated atop a mountain south of Urumieh, Iran. The Baradostis put up a fierce resistance, fighting off their enemy for a year, but finally, the shah's army shut off the castle's water supply and the tribe knew that defeat was inevitable. Rather than wait for the end, the khan led his forces into battle, while the women of the royal family committed suicide, holding hands as they jumped off the castle's battlements. The khan and many warriors were killed, but one of his sons and the rest of the tribe escaped to Iraq, where they took up residence in Sidakan, near the Barzan Valley.

The Baradostis' modern history was also dramatic. In 1931, when Shaikh Ahmad, Mulla Mustafa's eccentric brother, apparently instructed his followers to eat pork and burn the Quran, it was the Baradosti religious leader Shaikh Rashid who led the attack against the Barzanis. This in turn led to a rout of Baradosti territory by Shaikh Ahmad, who forced Shaikh Rashid into Iran. Shortly thereafter, the Baradostis returned, and, a decade later, joined the Iraqis to force the Barzanis into Iran.

So it went throughout the rest of the twentieth century, as the Baradostis sided first with King Faisal, then with Brigadier General Abd al-Karim Qassem and, finally, with Saddam Hussein against their traditional enemy. King Faisal II was an especially close friend of the tribe, arriving on horseback with his retinue every year to spend a few days in Baradosti territory, known for its pristine lakes and mountains.

During the Iran-Iraq War, the Baradostis provided the Baathists with many troops, and Saddam Hussein awarded Karim Khan six medals in recognition of his tribe's efforts. But when the war ended, Saddam betrayed the tribe by demanding that they abandon their traditional lands, as they border Iran. "I gathered the tribe together and told them the matter," Karim Khan said, "and they said, we fought Iran for eight years, and now we are ready to fight the government. So from that time, our relationship with Saddam was cut."

Joining forces with the PUK, Karim Khan remained in Iraqi Kurdistan until 1996, when the Baath forces entered the region during the internal war. "That was the most dangerous time for me," he said. "I was in a very bad situation. I was in Erbil when the Iraqi army arrived, but fortunately I had seven hundred fighters with me and no one attacked. Saddam said,

'Stay, I will help you and give you weapons.' But I didn't trust him and I escaped, first to Iran and later to Damascus."

One year later, after the Iraq war of 2003 ended, I was in touch with Sidqi via e-mail. His family's exile was over; they were back in Iraq. "My father sends his best regards, he is very busy with the people of our tribe, and is very happy," wrote Sidqi, reminding me of an old Kurdish proverb: "Damascus is sweet, but home is sweeter."

CHAPTER SIXTEEN

Of Politics and Poetry

DEEP IN THE MOUNTAINS OF WESTERN IRAN RISES A SMOOTH-sided peak. In mid-May it is the green-blue color of flies' eyes, but by mid-September it has become gray and dark. The roads that skirt the peak to the east are narrow but paved, lined with clay homes sprouting ladders leading to roofs, and fields peppered with crackling mounds of harvested hay. Orchards spill small green apples out onto the street so that drivers must proceed with caution. The top of the mountain is bare, but to one side is a drop-off cliff, over which the women of the royal family are said to have jumped in the epic of Dem Dem. Up until the 1980s, when the Islamic regime cracked down on the Kurds, parts of the legendary castle still stood, and, in more recent years, the PKK used the mountain as a hideout. Now though, all is quiet atop the majestic peak, as it awaits the next chapter of its storybook history.

Less than an hour north of Dem Dem lies Urumieh, Iran's largest northwestern city, cut off from the rest of the country by a vast salt lake, its edges encrusted with lines of wavy white. Only the most primitive of fish can survive in its highly salty waters, but the lake attracts thousands of migrating waterfowl, including flamingoes, whose pink bodies bob upon its shiny surface like pieces of origami for a few weeks each year. Part Azeri Turkish, part Armenian and other Christians, and part Kurdish, Urumieh is said by some to be the birthplace of Zoroaster, the prophet who founded the Zoroastrian religion between 1000 and 700 B.C.

All around Urumieh stretches a fertile plain, once known as the "Paradise of Persia." Here, Ismail Simko, the Kurdish rebel who ambushed and drank the blood of the ninety-plus-year-old Armenian leader, staged his revolt against the Iranian government in the 1920s. The plain was also the battleground of what may have been the first revolt in the name of Kurdish nationalism. In 1880, Shaikh Ubayd Allah, a spiritual leader headquartered in Hakkari (Turkey) ordered his followers to invade Urumieh because the Persian authorities had harshly punished local *aghas* without first consulting the region's Kurdish governor. Sending a message to the British consul-general in Tabriz, Shaikh Ubayd Allah made an early call for Kurdish autonomy: "[The Kurds] are a nation apart. We want our affairs to be in our own hands."

The *shaikh*'s Hakkari troops were joined by numerous Persian Kurdish tribes. With eight thousand men, the *shaikh* laid siege to Urumieh, while one of his sons—leading fifteen thousand men—captured Mahabad farther south. Still others marched on Tabriz, but were badly defeated by the vastly superior Persian army, who went on to end the siege at Urumieh. Thousands of Kurdish troops and civilians fled to Hakkari, but many were massacred on the way. The Ottomans exiled the *shaikh* to Mecca, where he died a few years later.

During the siege of Urumieh, the Kurds had taken care to keep one population safe—the American Christians who had established the first Presbyterian mission in Persia in Urumieh in 1834. Though in general there was no love lost between Kurds and missionaries—hostilities at times erupting into massacres of the intruders—the *shaikh* owed the Urumieh mission a debt. Six months earlier, a Dr. Cochrane had saved him from a severe bout of pneumonia, remaining in the Hakkari mountains for ten days until the Kurdish leader was cured. Thus, Shaikh Ubayd Allah contacted the doctor before attacking, asking for the location of his residence and those of his people, so that no one connected with the mission was harmed. Honor takes many different forms among the Kurds.

I ARRIVED IN Urumieh one midmorning in September, traveling by plane from Tehran. What once must have been a beautiful town was now bursting from overpopulation, as is much of urban Iran.

At the Urumieh airport, I met Jaleh, a pleasingly plump, heavily made-up, Iranian-English Kurd, back in Iran after twenty-odd years of living in England, due to a second marriage. Her husband was away at the time of my visit, and, delighted to meet a fellow English speaker, she invited me to stay with her for a few days, to deluge me with stories about how much she missed England and hated Iran. Some of her complaints sounded legitimate: her neighbors ridiculed her for driving a car, and she'd had much trouble finding a live-in maid, as the Kurdish women couldn't stay away from home overnight. Others were more suspect: she'd heard of "many" Iranian stepmothers burning the babies of their husbands' earlier wives. Jaleh had had a difficult life, as she'd been forced to flee Iran at age sixteen, due to her brothers' political activities. In England, she had married a man who abused her for ten years. After finally breaking away, she'd become a dental hygienist and raised a son, now a college student. She was happy in her second marriage, but lonely; her husband was often away on business. The word *love*, encircled by hearts, was writ large in Magic Marker all over her bedroom walls.

Jaleh took me to the Kurdish village of Band, just outside Urumieh, where "people live like they did a hundred years ago," she said, clucking over the villagers' simple dress and homes. Like many who have left earlier worlds behind, Jaleh had something to prove.

Beyond Band stretched hundreds of round hills bristling with tan grasses cut evenly as a crew cut. Between them meandered a river framed with poplar trees and grazing cattle—a yawning vista that made me yearn to keep traveling along the empty highway before us, to roll on into oblivion, or at least Iraq.

That evening, Jaleh and I ate dinner in one of Band's outdoor restaurants, draped with multicolored lights and overlooking a small stream clogged with trash. Joining us was her cousin, a twenty-five-year-old civil engineer interested to hear that I'd been to Iraqi Kurdistan. He hoped to visit there himself one day, he said.

He had some bitterness toward the Iraqi Kurds. "The Iraqi Kurds have had many good chances, many more than the Iranian and Turkish Kurds," he said, "but the Barzanis and Talabanis have thrown them all away. They think only about their own pocketbooks. They are weak and corrupt."

Jaleh nodded in agreement, though I doubted she was paying much attention. She was much more interested in when her husband was coming home, and in whether she could convince him to move to England. "If

I can't, I might go without him, or else take along this cousin," she said, making eyes at the young man as she openly poured us all another round of beer.

I glanced around nervously. We were in the conservative Islamic Republic of Iran, after all, where the consumption of alcohol can lead to arrest. I'd already noticed the inhabitants of a nearby table looking at us askance, and had double-checked my head scarf and long black raincoat—they or something similar required wearing for all women in public in Iran—to make sure that no illicit body part, such as a knee, was showing. Jaleh pooh-poohed my worries. "They're drinking, too," she said. "And they're only giving us looks because they think we shouldn't be out alone with a young man."

"Jaleh says you're going to Mahabad," her cousin said. "You must be very careful. Three people were killed there last month for smuggling a carton of cigarettes, and four people were killed in a demonstration last week. They have an eleven-thirty curfew. It is a very dangerous city."

This was the first I'd heard of possible danger in Mahabad, and his words rattled me a little. However, when I arrived in Mahabad a few days later, the atmosphere was calm and quiet. Three people *had* been killed for smuggling a carton of cigarettes, but that was unusual; smugglers were usually fined or imprisoned. And during a demonstration protesting the killings, shots *had* been fired in the air, but no one injured or killed. Mahabad did have a curfew, but then so did Urumieh, and neither was enforced.

As I'd learned during my first visit to Iran in 1998, Iranians love conspiracy theories and related plots, often embroidering simple facts and rumors until they become complex tales filled with ulterior motives and nefarious misdeeds. Part of the tendency has to do with Iran's history—the Iranians have been betrayed many times, with some conspiracy theories turning out to be true—and part of it has to do with living under a regime that is repressive but also inefficient and unpredictable in its enforcement of that repression. In Iran, people never know exactly where they stand. "We have a red line that we cannot cross, but no one knows where it is," goes a popular saying.

MANY THINGS WERE different in Iranian Kurdistan as compared to Iraqi Kurdistan. The place felt more settled, less raw. In Iran, there were few signs of recent war and many signs of a long-functioning, sophisticated society at work—one into which many Kurds, numbering about 6.5 million out of a total population of 68 million, were comparatively better integrated. For all the problems that the Kurds have had with the Iranian government—almost as many as the Iraqi Kurds have had with their government—they have much in common with their compatriot Persians. Kurds and Persians share a similar language, a similar tolerance, a similar independence of spirit, and a similar outlook toward the Arabs, who conquered both their lands in the name of Islam in A.D. 637.

Iranian Kurdistan is not as isolated from the rest of Iran as the Iraqi safe haven was from the rest of Iraq, and many parts contain not just Kurds but large concentrations of other ethnic groups. Between a half million and a million Iranian Kurds also live in Tehran, where they go about their business much like any other Iranians, often unable to speak Kurdish, and often more concerned with issues that affect all Iranians—economics, for one—rather than just the Kurds.

Indeed, a major difference between Iran and Iraq, as well as between Iran and Turkey, is its considerably more heterogeneous population. Iran is only about half ethnic Persian, and holds many major minority groups—including Azeri Turks, Baluchis, Qashqais, Turcomans, Arabs, and Kurds. In contrast, in both Iraq and Turkey, the Kurds are the only sizable minority and make up a much larger proportion of their respective country's total population—about 23 percent in Iraq and 20 percent in Turkey, as compared to 10 percent in Iran. The Iranian government has therefore immediately cracked down on the separatist movements of all its minority groups, as the autonomy of any one group could lead to the breakup of the entire state. The sort of semiautonomy offered to the Iraqi Kurds in 1970 has not occurred in Iran. Conversely, the Iranian government has seldom felt quite as threatened by its Kurds as has its neighbors, and in recent decades has offered Kurds more cultural rights—though not political ones—than has Iraq or Turkey.

There are important historical differences as well. As early as the 1300s, much of Iranian Kurdistan was already a quasi-state, ruled by the Ardalan dynasty, whose territory reached far into today's Iraq. Later, with the rise of the Safavids, who ruled Iran while the Ottomans ruled Turkey and Iraq, the shahs used the Kurds to defend their territory, but never allowed most Kurdish princes the free rein that the Ottomans granted. After the Qajar shahs came to power in 1794, they replaced the region's Kurdish governors with their own administrators, a tradition that continues today with most of Kurdistan administered by non-Kurds—Azeri Turks in the north and Persians in the south.

When Reza Khan, founder of the Pahlavi dynasty, came to power in 1923, his first priority was uniting the many different Iranian peoples. This meant the enforced settlement of tens of thousands of nomads, including many Kurds. The shah's settlement policies were ruthless and disastrous, sometimes resulting in the near extermination of entire tribes. The Lurs, closely related to the Kurds, were decimated, while nearly ten thousand Jalalis, a Kurdish tribe, died following deportation to central Iran. Nonetheless, the government's policies toward the Kurds and others were never completely successful, as various unruly chieftains managed to retain their power, some through their cooperation with the regime.

Once the tribes were settled, they became easier to control and assimilate into society. Taxes became easier to collect; conscription into the army became easier to enforce; and trade across the frontiers became forbidden, forcing the Kurds to conduct more business with the central government, and erasing much of their previous self-sufficiency.

The power of the tribes revived somewhat in the 1940s and early 1950s, as the central government weakened during the turbulent World War II years. It declined again in the 1960s and 1970s as land reform broke the stranglehold in which the *aghas* had once held their constituents. A developing domestic capitalism and massive migration to the towns and cities also contributed to the breakdown of the tribe, leading the Iranian Kurdish leader Abd al-Rahman Qassemlou to say that by the 1970s, "Kurdish society in Iran can no longer be considered as a tribal society." Nonetheless, many tribes continued to exist and to exert considerable influence. Members of powerful tribal families still play leadership roles in Iranian Kurdistan today, and in some border areas, armed tribes are still used as government patrols.

I WENT TO talk with Ahmad Ghazi, editor of *Sirwe*, which means "word." The first and oldest continuously published Kurdish magazine in Iran, *Sirwe* was founded in 1985, and Mr. Ghazi became editor one year later. Prior to becoming editor, during the time of Mohammed Reza Shah Pahlavi, Mr. Ghazi was also imprisoned for four years for his political activities.

Sirwe's offices filled several airy upstairs rooms on a side street in down-town Urumieh. When I arrived, I found a small, round-faced man in his sixties waiting for me. Dressed in pants belted high on his waist and a button-down shirt, Mr. Ghazi spoke excellent, British-inflected English, perfected during his first career as a teacher.

The Iranian Kurds lived mostly in three provinces in northwestern Iran, Mr. Ghazi said, welcoming me with a glass of tea, which most Iranian Kurds drink Persian-style: through a sugar cube in the mouth. In the northernmost province, Western Azerbaijan, to which Urumieh belonged, Kurds spoke the Kermanji dialect and shared their territory with the Azeri Turks, a Turkic people with whom the Kurds often do not get along. The central province, Kurdistan, with its capital of Sanandaj, was almost 100 percent Kurdish, and its people spoke the Sorani dialect. And the southernmost province, Kermanshah, was again only part Kurdish and part other ethnic groups, most notably Lur and Persian. Most Kurds of Kermanshah also spoke Sorani, but at the edge of the province, bordering Iraq, lived the Hawraman, a "small and special colony" who spoke Gorani—a non-Kurdish Iranian dialect. They lived much closer to their traditional ways than did most other Iranian Kurds.

Another large group of Kurds lived separate from the rest in the Khorasan province of eastern Iran. They were the descendants of the tens of thousands of Kurds brutally deported from their homelands by the Safavids in the 1500s, to prevent them from siding with the Ottomans.

As in Iraq, most Iranian Kurds were Sunni Muslim, and of the Shafiite school, one of the four branches of Sunni Islam, which set them apart from the Arab and Turkish Sunnis in the region, most of whom were Hanafite. However, like the vast majority of Iranians, at least one-third of Iranian Kurds were Shiite, while others were Ahl-e Haqq. Both the Shiite and Ahl-e Haqq Kurds lived mostly in Kermanshah and neighboring Ilam.

"One-third of Iranian Kurds are Shiite?" I asked, surprised at the large number.

"At least, and one of the difficulties we have is that the Shiite Kurds don't join the Kurdish movements—cultural or political," Mr. Ghazi said. "This is beginning to change, but historically, the Shiite and Sunni Kurds have kept apart."

About two-thirds of Iranian Kurds now lived in large towns and cities. But even for those who remained in the villages, life had changed dramatically over the past twenty years. "Even the most rural areas now have schools, roads, electricity," he said. "There's a satellite television in almost every village. Illiteracy is going down, and we have universities in Mahabad, Sanandaj, Kermanshah, and other Kurdish cities."

Some tribal pockets did still exist, especially in the far northern and southern Kurdish lands, where the terrain was exceptionally mountain-ous—i.e., out of reach of the central authorities—and well suited for ani-mal husbandry. A few genuine nomads could even be found. "But fortunately, these pockets are few," Mr. Ghazi said.

" 'Fortunately'?" I was puzzled at his word choice.

"The breakdown of the tribes has been very good for the Kurdish peo-ple," he said. "The tribals were very traditional and fanatic. They were a great obstacle to our unity, governments played them easily off against each other. Fifty years ago, we weren't a nation, we were tribes, and the leaders of our nationalist movements were heads of big families, like Barzani and Qazi Mohammed [leader of the 1946 Kurdish Republic in Mahabad]. But now, everyone feels our nationalism. We are learning from each other, get-ting stronger. And the same is true for the Kurds in Iraq and Turkey."

I'd heard similar thoughts expressed in Iraqi Kurdistan, but only now did their full irony hit home to me. How strange that traditional Kurdish cul-ture, or at least an important aspect of traditional Kurdish culture, has to be destroyed in order for modern Kurdish culture to flourish.

"Do you think the Kurds will have their own country one day?" I asked.

Mr. Ghazi hesitated. "The time for fighting is finished," he said, echo-ing another statement often heard in Iraq. "We must now work for Kurdish rights through politics and other ways. But life is changing rapidly in the Middle East altogether. We have satellite TV and the Internet, we are in contact with others all over the world. . . . And I believe that a hundred years from now, borders will be regarded as a small thing."

I then asked Mr. Ghazi to compare the situation of the Iranian Kurds before and after the 1979 Islamic revolution. Before the revolution, Iran had been ruled by Reza Shah Pahlavi and his son Mohammed Reza Shah Pahlavi, both strong-armed authoritarian kings. After coming to power in 1923, Reza Shah had dragged the then-undeveloped nation into the twenti-eth century at a relentless clip, not only settling its nomadic peoples and establishing a strong central government, but also brooking no dissent and banning the wearing of the *hejab,* or Islamic covering for women—much to the horror of traditional believers. Mohammed Reza Shah, though a milder version of his father in some ways, had continued Reza Shah's policies of modernization, repression, and the denigration of Islam, while also forming a close alliance with the United States, establishing a powerful secret police known as SAVAK, and spending millions of petro-dollars—much needed elsewhere—on a sophisticated military arsenal.

By the late 1970s, many Iranians had had enough. Taking to the streets by the hundreds of thousands, they forced Mohammed Reza to flee Iran, to be replaced by the pious Shiite leader Ayatollah Khomeini, called back from exile in France. Representing all that the shahs were not, Ayatollah Khomeini and his supporters established the world's first Islamic Republic, to be governed in accordance with *sharia*. Women were forced to wear the *hejab*, an Islamic school curriculum was established, strict religious observance was expected, and all Western influences, including alcohol and music, were outlawed.

As a people who had been brutally repressed by the Shahs Pahlavi, the Kurds initially supported the revolution, seeing a chance to gain autonomy. During the 1970s, several dissident *mullahs* hid out in Kurdish territory and when in exile, Ayatollah Khomeini expressed sympathy for the Kurdish cause. But after the revolution, these quasi-promises were quietly forgotten. Khomeini cracked down on Kurdistan as early as August 1979.

"During the time of the shah, we could say we were Kurds, but we couldn't publish a book, or read a Kurdish poem in public," Mr. Ghazi said. "And many were in prison because of their political activities. I was in prison because I talked about autonomy, nothing more. It was a very bad time for the Kurds.

"With this Islamic regime, we have fought politically also, and after the revolution, conditions were very bad. There were many shot, many fled, it was unbearable. But now, especially culturally, things are much better. We have many publishing centers, we have about twenty representatives in parliament, we can vote freely. In the time of the shah, the Kurdish language and culture was being forgotten little by little, but now, it is blossoming."

"Did this happen before or after President Khatami?" I asked, referring to the moderate leader elected by a surprise landslide vote in 1997. Though much thwarted by the conservatives who largely control the Iranian government, Khatami has ushered in a period of some reform.

"The process began in the mid-1980s, but hastened in the time of

Khatami. Since his election we have many more cultural publications and can speak more openly. Our faction in parliament is pressuring the government for more Kurdish rights . . .

"Of course, we still suffer much discrimination. We are not allowed to speak of the destiny of Kurdistan or criticize too much. But I believe our situation is improving."

OTHER IRANIAN KURDISH intellectuals I met did not have as rosy an outlook as did Mr. Ghazi. After all, Kurdish political parties were still illegal in Iran and demonstrations were forbidden—although they took place. The Kurds had little administrative control over their own districts and, despite many parliamentarians, had no governors or ministers. Kurdistan was significantly poorer and less developed than was most of Iran, with few large factories or businesses, and extremely high rates of unemployment. The regime's Revolutionary Guards also kept a close eye on the Kurds, quick to throw into prison anyone suspected of political activity. Hundreds of Kurds were said to be languishing in Iranian jails, and three Kurdish activists were executed in the year before my visit.

Among the more pessimistic intellectuals I spoke with was Bahram Valadbaigy, director of Tehran's Kurdistan Cultural Institute. Only established in 2001, the institute was widely regarded as an important step forward for the Iranian Kurds—their first formal cultural institute.

The institute had four basic objectives, Mr. Valadbaigy told me through a translator on the afternoon we met. One was to develop a standardized written Kurdish. Another was to strengthen relationships with the Kurds of Iraq and Turkey through such things as student and cultural exchange programs. In addition, the institute advised and supported various Kurdish student publications, and published its own magazine.

Serious problems with the Islamic regime had already arisen over this last venture. The first issue of the magazine had run several political essays, and so the government had suspended its publication and was threatening to close the institute.

"There are many Kurdish publications in Iran now, but it makes no difference," Mr. Valadbaigy said with bitterness. "We still can't write about anything except folklore and culture. Tradition, only tradition . . . How does this help the Kurds? Our country has not improved. Khatami has done nothing. We were in the Islamic revolution and expected to gain our part. But all we have gained is war, fighting, poverty. . . ."

"But isn't the situation better now than during the time of the shah?" I asked, remembering Mr. Ghazi.

"Yes, but only because now they allow us to breathe!" Mr. Valadbaigy said. "But that is not enough! You cannot compare now to then. And why do we have a better situation? Because we fought for it! Many died for it. It was not a gift."

Nonetheless, Mr. Valadbaigy did agree with Mr. Ghazi on one important point. "Fighting has failed," he said. "And the world has changed. We must now use other ways to achieve our goals."

MAHABAD, ABOUT A ninety-minute drive south of Urumieh, was prettier than I expected. Perhaps because of its volatile political history, I'd imagined the place to be flat, harsh, and scraggly. Instead I found a clean, orderly town, population about two hundred thousand, surrounded by wide rolling hills, with fields and orchards in the foreground, smoky whipped peaks in the distance. Many streets were lined with trees, while here and there stood traffic circles and plazas, marked by statues and the occasional shrine. Mahabad had its share of Internet cafés as well, and an all-pedestrian street bustling with families and shrouded women in the late afternoon, boys and men after the sun went down.

Showing me around Mahabad my first afternoon there was Rojeen, a striking Kurdish woman in her mid-twenties, whom I met while traveling in a collective taxi from Urumieh. Rojeen didn't share my opinion regarding her good looks, however. She planned to get a nose job as soon as her life calmed down a bit. Try as I might, I couldn't see any way in which her looks could be improved—her nose, straight and of average size, seemed perfect to me. But I had read that nose jobs were all the rage in Tehran, and Rojeen was a fashion-conscious Tehrani.

Rojeen, who spoke some English but no Kurdish, was in Mahabad for only a few days, on one of her biweekly trips to take care of her family's estate. Her father, the son of a leading Mahabad family, had died of a heart attack three months before, and her mother was in no condition to look after anything. As the eldest of five daughters, it was up to Rojeen to make sure that the family's orchards were running smoothly.

As Rojeen and I talked more, I realized that she came from an unusual family. Two of her great-grandfathers had been powerful Kurdish *aghas*, one living in Mahabad, the other in nearby Bukan. When her grandmother married, they laid out a red carpet all the way between the two towns—well, at least some of the way, Rojeen amended. But her grandmother had moved to Tehran when Rojeen's father was seventeen or eighteen, and all the rest of her ten children had grown up there, learning only rudimentary Kurdish. Most had also married Persians, while their mother had become "very up-to-date," learning how to read and write, and becoming a film buff. "My grandmother is eighty years old, but always improving herself!" Rojeen said, laughing.

Rojeen's father had also been unusual. When his wife bore no sons, he was pressured to take a second wife, but he refused. He loved his wife and daughters deeply and felt no need for a son. "When I was born, my father took me in his arms," Rojeen said. "And some in my family said, 'Why are you doing that? You are an important man, and she is only a girl.' But my father was happy, he never cared I was a girl."

"Do people still care so much about having boys today?"

"Some people care," Rojeen said, "but not like before. And for the new generation, it's very different. We don't care at all. Some have only one child, no problem. Some have no children, no problem."

"What about honor killings?" I asked somewhat hesitantly, but wanting to take advantage of the turn in the conversation.

"What?" Rojeen had never heard of honor killings, and neither had any of the young urban Kurds I met later in Sanandaj and Kermanshah. Middle-aged Kurds knew what I was talking about, but except in the traditional Hawraman region, most told me that they hadn't heard of an occurrence in years.

"No one kills a woman for sex before marriage," Rojeen said after I had explained, "but women are expected to be virgins when they marry."

Rojeen herself had already been married and divorced. Her husband had been a handsome Kurdish doctor, but he hadn't liked the way she dressed—she'd shown too much leg. Also, he didn't enjoy going to parties, which Rojeen adored. She'd felt trapped and unhappy. Her parents had supported her in her decision to divorce, and now she was "very okay. I have a boyfriend, I am free." She did not intend to marry again for at least three or four years.

Hardly a typical Iranian woman, but then again, not altogether atypical either. On my earlier visit to Iran, I had met many strong and independent women pushing the envelope of traditional Islamic society, especially in Tehran.

Our tour of the downtown finished, we headed out of the city, to Rojeen's family orchards, passing hills so shiny they seemed plated with gold. From the tape deck came the music of Kamkar, a family of musicians from Sanandaj, whose songs are known around the world. Rojeen drove — women drivers were accepted in Mahabad, she said. It was a relatively liberal city, though nowhere near as open as Tehran, of course.

"Why are you wearing black?" Rojeen asked me, suddenly changing the topic. "I must, because of my father, but why are you?"

"What do you mean?" I looked down at my shapeless black *manteau* — the French word for "coat" usually used in Iran — that I'd purchased on my first trip to the Islamic Republic in 1998.

"No one wears black anymore," Rojeen said.

Strictly speaking, that was not true. Most of the women on the streets still wore black. But now I knew what she was talking about. My *manteau* was badly out of style. Arriving in Tehran about two weeks earlier, I'd been shocked to see the amorphous black *manteaus* of my earlier visit replaced by tight, tunic-length coats of maroons, greens, and tans. Despite all the discouraging news that had come out of Iran since 1998 — including crackdowns on the liberal press and arrests of liberal politicians — the atmosphere on the streets had lightened up. People were depressed over the failure of the moderate President Khatami to institute as much reform as they'd hoped, and yet, in some intangible way, they also seemed more buoyant — or perhaps the word was brazen — than they had before. Suddenly, it seemed, everyone had cell phones, everyone was on the Internet. The Tehran streets had been cleaned up, many of the once-ubiquitous murals of Iran-Iraq War martyrs removed, and more Westerners were in town.

Rojeen's family orchards grew apples and apricots as far as the eye could see. Her father had been a wealthy man who, like many prominent members of tribal families in Iran today, had operated as an absentee landlord. But Rojeen and her sisters had inherited only fifty of his hectares, in accordance with Islamic law, because the family had no sons. The other fifty had gone to male relatives. "It is still good because we have enough, but it is bad psychologically," said Rojeen.

Not far from the orchards was the FARHRIGAE STONE MASOLEUM, as a nearby sign read, though "Faqraqa" was a closer transliteration. It was one of Mahabad's must-see attractions, and yet when I went to visit it the following evening—with other companions, as Rojeen was working—at first there seemed to be nothing there. Parking our car on a silent dirt road, we walked at least a half-mile through an empty field bristling with sharp, pointy grasses. The crescent moon was rising, and I cursed under my breath as I stumbled in the semidarkness up an increasingly steep slope riddled with depressions and boulders. Then, the ancient tombs suddenly appeared, three black holes separated by columns yawning above—tantalizingly, mysteriously, just out of reach. The tombs probably dated back to the early period of the Medes, a people who lived in the region from about the 800s to the 500s B.C. Once, the Medes controlled an area that extended from the Caspian Sea in the north to the Zagros Mountains in the south to the ancient Assyrian capital of Niveneh in the west—in short, the land of the Kurds. Many Kurds believe the Medes to be their direct ancestors, perhaps making the Faqraqa tombs one of the oldest of Kurdish sightseeing attractions.

IN MAHABAD WAS a traffic circle still known among Kurds as Chowar Chira—Kurdish for the "four lamps" that once stood on its corners—though now officially renamed Shahradari, or "municipal." Nothing to look at, the circle marked a more modern—and much more legendary—Kurdish historic site. Here, on the sunny morning of January 22, 1946, fresh snow dusting the ground, a wiry man in a Russian army uniform and a shiny white turban climbed up on a wooden podium. Before him stretched a crowd of tribesmen and chiefs in traditional dress, and politicians and businessmen in dark suits, while from the surrounding rooftops watched the women. The man, Qazi Mohammed, began to speak: the Kurds were their own people, with their own country, a powerful new friend (the Soviet Union), and the same right of self-determination as all other nations, he said. He then formally declared the establishment of the autonomous Kurdish Republic, and off went a three hundred-rifle salute.

Fourteen months later, in the secret dead of night, Qazi Mohammed, his brother, and cousin were hanged in the Chowar Chira circle by Iranian authorities. No one living nearby heard or suspected a thing until the next

morning. The hangings so shocked the town that Mahabad remained politically quiescent for the next thirty years.

Shortly after leaving Mahabad, on my way back to Tehran from Iranian Kurdistan, I myself saw three hanged men, in an odd, coincidental
echo of 1946. Traveling overnight by bus, to enter the capital's Azadi
Square just after dawn, I unsuspectingly pushed aside a window curtain to
see an inert form hanging from the arm of a crane. I couldn't believe my
eyes at first—he looked just like a rag doll, in a loose, long-sleeved shirt
and mop of dark hair, but stiller and heavier than seemed possible. He
and his companions had been hanged—a rare punishment in the Islamic
Republic these days, though it once was common—for operating a prostitution ring, an especially serious offense under *sharia*. The early-morning
mists both muted and augmented the scene, turning the particulars into
the generic, to create a portrait of human cruelty that lay, and lies,
uneasily within me.

For the Kurdish people, the 1946 Kurdish Republic of Mahabad carries
enormous resonance. It marks the only real moment in modern times that
the Kurds have been in near-total control of their own government and
administration. Even the semiautonomous Iraqi Kurdistan of the 1990s—
dependent on Western air patrols and the United Nations' oil-for-food
program—does not compare, at least in the Kurdish imagination.

The Mahabad Republic came about during the tumultuous years of
World War II, when the Russians were occupying northern Iran and the
British were occupying the south. Due to his Nazi sympathies, Reza Shah
was forced to abdicate in favor of his son, Mohammed Reza. In the fall of
1942, a group of Mahabad Kurds secretly organized into a modern nationalist political party, Komala, with the help of the more politically mature
Iraqi Kurds of the Hewa Party. Three years later, the Russians supported the
Kurds in their bid for an autonomous state, and Komala, joined by members of Hewa and other groups, became the Kurdistan Democratic Party,
precursor of today's KDP in Iraq and the Kurdish Democratic Party of Iran
(KDPI).

Elected as president of the new republic was Qazi Mohammed, a judge
of Islamic law from Mahabad's leading family. The descendant of a long
line of judges, Qazi Mohammed had both a religious and informal secular
education. A decisive, charismatic, and sociable man who had married late
in life to a divorced woman—an unconventional move in those days—he

often offered his home as a safe haven to those fleeing the wrath of their families, tribal leaders, or the Iranian authorities.

Protecting the fledgling Kurdish Republic was a small army of about twelve hundred men from the immediate area and a larger group of twelve thousand tribesmen from farther afield, under the control of their traditional leaders. Most formidable among them was Mulla Mustafa Barzani, leading a contingent of twelve hundred *peshmerga*, their skills well honed after years spent fighting in Iraq. In a piece of fortuitous timing, Barzani and his forces, along with their families, had just been forced out of Iraq in the wake of their 1943 to 1945 revolt.

The Mahabad Republic aspired to control all of Iranian Kurdistan, but its reach did not include the important Kurdish city of Sanandaj and other regions to the south, which remained under Iranian control. And not everyone in Mahabad supported the idea of an autonomous Kurdish state. Among the less enthusiastic, and one of the first to surrender to the Iranians after the republic's fall, was my friend Rojeen's grandfather, patriarch of an influential Mahabad family.

During the Mahabad Republic, the Kurds published their own newspaper and magazines, established a radio station, set up a Kurdicized school curriculum, founded a Kurdish theater, and survived economically through agriculture, taxes, and smuggling. Citizens were free to carry arms, while the Soviet influence remained distant and muted.

But the hopeful days of the Kurdish Republic were short-lived. As 1946 wore on, the Russians began preparing for the breakup of their wartime alliance with Britain and the United States. They abandoned Mahabad, deciding to bolster pro-Soviet support within Iran instead. Withdrawing from the region, they left the Kurds to fend for themselves. On December 16, eleven months after proclaiming independence, Qazi Mohammed surrendered to the Iranians without a fight. The Mahabad area was disarmed, the teaching of Kurdish prohibited, and all Kurdish books burned. Three months later, Mulla Mustafa began his famous retreat to Russia and Qazi Mohammed, his brother, and cousin were hanged.

WHILE IN MAHABAD, I stayed with Ahmad Bahri, the editor of *Mahabad* magazine, and his family. They lived in a dark but spacious home near the edge of the city, making me think of the nineteenth-century traveler Isabella Bird (no relation), who had approached Mahabad through another of its lesser-known neighborhoods. Exploring the region on horseback in 1890, when she was sixty, Bird took a wrong turn, to find herself "on a slope above the town, not among the living but the dead. Such a City of Death I have never seen. A whole hour was occupied in riding through it without reaching its limits. Fifty thousand gravestones. . . . Weird, melancholy, and terribly malodorous."

One evening, Mr. Bahri arranged for me to meet with Mahabad's literary elite; the city was almost as well known for its writers as it was for its politicians. The Kurdish Republic of Mahabad had catapulted two modernist poets, Abd al-Rahman Hejar and M. Hemin, into Kurdish fame, and sparked a literary movement in the city that still continued.

Oversized pastel portraits of Hejar and Hemin dominated the Bahris' living room. And Mr. Bahri and two of his guests that evening—Mrs. Jaferi and Mr. Ashti—had been students of Hemin. Mrs. Jaferi, who had written a novel about the epic of Dem Dem from a woman narrator's point of view, was also Hemin's niece. Rounding out the party that evening was Mr. Khosrow, an Iraqi Kurd who had lived in Mahabad for years.

Each of the party was distinctive. Mr. Bahri, a small man in a three-piece green suit, was an expert in Kurdish folktales—especially rich in the Mahabad region, due to its historic isolation. Mahabad was home to the Mukrian people, a powerful tribal confederacy, and over the past twenty years, Mr. Bahri had recorded over two hundred cassettes of folktales told and sung by storytellers and troubadours.

This is the kind of scholarly research that is desperately needed in Iraq, I thought as Mr. Bahri described his work, especially when he told me that, no, unfortunately, he couldn't take me to meet any traditional storytellers and troubadours. They had all died out.

One of Mr. Bahri's favorite folktales was the story of Khadje and Siyabend, a tale popular among many Kurds. Beautiful Khadje is the daughter of a wealthy family; handsome Siyabend, the son of a poor one. Loving each other against their family's wishes, they run away to the mountains, where they spend three happy days and nights together. On the fourth day, Siyabend falls asleep with his head in Khadje's lap. A herd of deer passes by, and one, a big buck, seizes a pretty doe and runs away with her. Khadje weeps at the sight and one of her tears falls on Siyabend's cheek, awakening him.

Siyabend grabs his bow and chases the stag. As he takes aim, the buck attacks, flinging him into a deep ravine, where Khadje finds him mortally wounded. Weeping bitterly, she curses the beautiful forest around them for nurturing the evil buck and dies of heartbreak. A tree that is forever in bloom shoots up on the spot.

I could well understand why the tale was one of Mr. Bahri's favorites. It is so filled with contradiction.

We talked about Kurdish literature for a while. Modernism and post-modernism, and the dearth of both in Kurdish letters, seemed to be a favorite topic among my companions. They also lamented the limited number of Kurdish novels, as Kurdish literature has traditionally meant poetry—also the strongest literary form throughout Iran, where even illiterate villagers can recite long reams of poetry by heart.

Many of the writers' opinions were closer to those of the pessimist Mr. Valadbaigy's in Tehran than to the optimist Mr. Ghazi's in Urumieh. Publishing conditions were still a long, long ways from being satisfactory. "We all practice self-censorship in order to publish," Mr. Bahri said. The foursome also felt that the recent rise in the number of Kurdish magazines was misleading, as many were financed by the Islamic regime and so were perhaps being used to deflect the Kurds from more controversial goals.

"The life here is not good, not bad," Mrs. Jaferi said, summing up with a phrase that I heard often in Iranian Kurdistan, and one that contrasted in my mind with the Iraqi Kurdish expression, "This is the life," so often used after describing an atrocity. Both sentences implied endless suffering and stoic endurance, but one was muted in tone, the other an acute cry.

ONE AFTERNOON, MRS. JAFERI took me to a Kurdish wedding, only the third I'd attended in Kurdistan—a surprisingly low number considering how central weddings are to Kurdish culture. Since many weddings last two or three days, and involve hundreds of guests, I was constantly bumping into someone who knew someone who was giving a wedding and wanted to invite me along. But for one reason or another, most invitations hadn't worked out.

The first wedding I'd attended had been with my host family in Dohuk. Held in a vast modern hall built expressly for weddings, the party was mobbed, with a hired band playing amplified music so loud that it hurt the ears. "Awful," my companions said as we hurried away after a rushed "Congratulations" to the family.

The second wedding had been in Suleimaniyah. This had been an unusual mass celebration held in a sports arena, with a professional troupe of dancers and band. Fifty couples from poor families had married at the same time in order to defray the wedding costs—a brilliant idea, I thought, as the traditional Kurdish wedding has become prohibitively expensive. The brides wore billowing Western white; the men, dark suits with flowers in their lapels. They made a handsome sight as they wove in and out, dancing in the long gilded rays of the late-afternoon sun. The PUK subsidized the event, even providing each couple with a small monetary gift.

For the wedding in Mahabad, I was asked to dress in traditional Kurdish clothes—a request to which I had become accustomed. Everywhere I went in Kurdistan, people liked to dress me up and take my picture, often chuckling with great glee whenever I self-consciously emerged from an impromptu dressing room. Some costumes I modeled were everyday attire, but usually I was handed an elaborate affair of bright colors, shiny fabrics, brocades, and sequins. I never minded posing for my hosts—it was a small price to pay for their generous hospitality—but I was always happy to take the garments off. Wearing a stranger's clothes is too close to another's shape and smells, to another's life.

The costume of Mahabad differed from those I'd worn earlier. This was a long one-piece dress, worn with a cowl-like piece of cloth around the neck, and a thick sash around the hips. The sash looked stunning on younger women, as it elongated their slim waists, but thickened the silhouettes of the middle-aged.

The wedding was given by Qazi Mohammed's descendants, still one of Mahabad's leading families, and when Mrs. Jaferi—Nasrin—and I arrived at the compound at about two P.M., it was already packed with people. The main building was divided in two—men sitting on the floor to one side, women to the other—with constant traffic through wide, open doorways in between. Most of the women dressed traditionally, in brilliant gowns and much gold jewelry, but some of the younger women wore T-shirts and jeans. About half the men wore dark Western suits; the other half *shal u shapik*. Only a few older men wore turbans, different from the ones I'd seen in Iraq, with bits of string framing their faces and a tail-like piece of cloth descending in back.

We had arrived just in time for lunch, and, after kissing us three times on alternate cheeks, as is the Kurdish custom, young women took our hands to lead us into the middle of the women's side, where the others somehow made room for us on the crowded floor. Men balancing huge silver-colored trays laden with dishes wove through the crowd, serving everyone kebabs, rice, vegetables, and a thick Iranian stew known as *ash*. I expected one of the men to lose his footing at any moment and rain plates and food down upon us, but there were no mishaps.

Most of the women around us were under thirty, heavily made up, and clad in brightly colored dresses, no head scarves. They eyed me with curiosity.

"Who do you think is the prettiest among us?" asked one dark-haired beauty in a fire-engine-red dress with a gauzy black cowl and matching sash. Next to her, and seemingly waiting with bated breath for my answer, sat an older blond woman resplendent in creamy white and dangling gold earrings.

I couldn't answer. Even if I could have, I would not have dared.

After lunch, we retired out front, where dozens of red plastic chairs had been set up under the trees, for an afternoon of socializing, drinking tea, and dancing. In the center of things sat two beaming middle-aged women from Qazi Mohammad's family, who effusively welcomed me. A small band was tuning up to one side, while servants rushed to and fro with tea trays and three-foot-long blocks of ice, which they plopped into metal water coolers. The bride and groom were not in attendance, although the bride would arrive later, at around eight P.M., by which time Nasrin and I would be gone. It was the second day of a traditional Kurdish wedding, the time at which the bride says good-bye to her family and goes to the home of the groom.

The music started, and the dancing began. The line was short at first but grew steadily longer as people grabbed hands, including mine. We fell into a popular dance called *saypah*, or "three step." I had learned it in Iraq, and had grown to appreciate its slow, simple rhythm, which has a hypnotic and comforting quality as the notes twine in and out, the dance line goes round and round, and lazy minute after lazy minute passes, everyone moving closely together, all accepted, all protected, no one left out.

When I took a break, some men came up to me to talk about—what else?—politics. One day soon, the men predicted, the Iranian Kurds would have a semiautonomous state within a federated Iran. After Saddam Hussein was gone and Iraq set up such a system, it was only a matter of time before the same thing happened in Iran. And what about an independent Greater Kurdistan? The men shook their heads. The Iranian Kurds were too well integrated into Iran, for one thing; and the Kurds in general didn't have the economic or military might to support their own state, for another.

The youngest among the men, a medical student in *shal u shapik*, then said that he hoped the United States would soon bomb Iraq. All the other men disagreed, some vehemently. They wanted Saddam to go, but not if it meant the arrival of the United States. Like most Iranians, but unlike most Iraqi Kurds, most Iranian Kurds deeply distrust American foreign policy and intentions.

Writes the poet Hemin, in words that still resonate in Iranian Kurdistan today:

Young ones! *Peshmerga!* Brave ones! Fearlessness!
You pick up the sword and we sharpen the pen!
With God's help we will take out of the hands of foreigners
The clean Kurdish homeland—

CHAPTER SEVENTEEN

Land of Lions

THROUGH AN ODD SET OF CIRCUMSTANCES, I FOUND MYSELF
attending the region's first environmental conference, held in Sanandaj,
the capital of Iran's Kurdistan province. The two-day meeting had been
organized by a Kurdish ecological society to address the growing problem of
pollution in the Zagros Mountains. About a hundred men and women
were in attendance, and most were professionals. Many were also hikers, a
popular pastime in Iran.

The conference was held in a modern meeting center, complete with a
hotel. The friend of a friend who suggested I attend the event—it would be
a good way for me to meet Kurds from all over Iran, he said—deposited me
in the cafeteria, where breakfast was being served, and then disappeared.
Looking around, I wondered how exactly I was going to meet all these
Kurds. But then the conference's young organizers discovered me. Thrilled
to have a foreigner in their midst, they took me under their wings for what
would prove to be the rest of my stay in Sanandaj, showing me around,
inviting me to stay with their families, and introducing me to others. It was
the same kind of charming, magnanimous hospitality that I remembered
from my first trip to Iran, when people couldn't seem to do enough for me.

I could barely distinguish one organizer from another at first, as they
ebbed and flowed around me, asking questions, making conversation.
Later, though, two in particular took on a definite shape: Hiwa, a cameraman for a local television station, and Arash, a physics teacher.

I had no interest in attending the conference's actual lectures. After breakfast, I told my new friends that I would leave to explore the town for a while and return for the social part of the program. I had been in Sanandaj before—it had been my only stop in Iranian Kurdistan in 1998. But my new friends wouldn't dream of letting me go off by myself and insisted on helping me locate a contact name I'd been given—a middle-aged man who spoke good English and who was, in fact, expecting my call that morning.

About a half hour later, Mr. K arrived. Lean and balding, with a concave chest, he greeted me distantly, which I initially attributed to Iranian formality. But as the day wore on, I realized that his reserve went deeper than that. Although he treated me with great condescension at first, assuming that I knew nothing about Iran, he became increasingly nervous and suspicious when he realized that I was already well informed. By early afternoon, he was trying to convince me to leave Sanandaj on the next bus. "Sanandaj has little to interest you, you should go farther south," he said. He also followed many of his statements, innocuous though most were, with, "You can't write that."

Mr. K was not the only nervous middle-aged Kurd I met in Iran. The man who had deposited me at the conference had been vastly relieved to get rid of me, and others later made it plain they wanted nothing to do with me. It wasn't personal. These men had lived through the violent, desperate years following the Islamic revolution, and knew the cruelty of the Islamic regime all too well. They'd seen friends and family mowed down in cold blood, and some had been imprisoned and tortured themselves. They were always alert to danger and being seen with an American could cause problems.

Or not. The reactions of the Islamic regime are unpredictable, and Iran today is a more tolerant place than it was in the 1980s. Most young Iranians have no memory of extreme repression and so flout all kinds of Islamic laws, for which they usually receive nothing more than a reprimand or fine. And certainly most Iranians I met, young or old, Kurd or non-Kurd, did not hesitate to be seen with me, were indeed eager to be seen with me.

Why Mr. K agreed to show me around Sanandaj in the first place remains a mystery, but I suspect it had something to do with the Iranians' great politeness and sense of hospitality. It was better to take a small risk than to insult a guest.

At any rate, Mr. K and I left the conference center to wander downtown, past the nineteenth-century Friday mosque with its lovely Qajar tiles and the closed Sanandaj Museum, through the busy bazaar, and down a side street crowded with shops in which artisans were tooling exquisite inlaid backgammon sets. Woodworking, along with hand-woven kilims, is an art for which the Sanandaj Kurds are well known, although both industries are dying out. The younger generation has no desire to learn their parents' crafts, preferring to obtain university degrees.

Sanandaj was much as I remembered it—bustling and spacious, set high on a plateau, peaks soaring all around. The town had both an attractive devil-may-care air—young men defiantly strutting down the streets, as if they owned the world—and the feel of poverty. Sanandaj was neglected by the central Iranian government, which left its roads filled with potholes, its city services meager, while at the same time serving as a magnet for poverty-stricken villagers seeking work. Kurdistan was one of the poorest and least developed of Iran's provinces. Officially, its unemployment rate hovered around 20 percent, but unofficially it was at least twice and perhaps three times as high.

I did notice one significant change in Sanandaj since 1998, however: only a handful of Revolutionary Guards roamed the streets. Four years earlier, there had been many more. Though of course, a continuing steady presence of plainclothes intelligence agents could not be discounted. This was Iran.

Yet even Mr. K agreed with me—there were fewer guards on the streets. "We are going forward little by little," he said. "It's mostly related to changes in the world, not the government. We have the Internet now, we have satellite TV, we aren't so isolated."

Here and there in Sanandaj stood rectangular palaces made of a fine brown brick, built in the 1800s under the Qajar shahs. Constructed around overgrown courtyards, the romantic and largely abandoned buildings had a magnetic draw, seeming to hold within them dark secrets far removed from the modern world. Most were closed to the public, but one was being restored, and Mr. K and I ducked inside to wander through dust-filtered rooms, some adorned with intricate tiles and hand-carved wooden shutters. As we were leaving, a tall, bearded young worker addressed me in good English, startling me.

"Where did you learn your English?" I asked.

"In my town."

"Where is your town?"

"My town is Sanandaj and my country is Kurdistan," he said, proudly pulling back his shoulders and again startling me, this time with his Kurdish nationalism.

A handsome village couple walked by. The wife wore a long red dress with a heavy black headdress ringed with coins—once common among Kurdish women, but now increasingly rare—while her husband wore a *shal u shapik* and a black turban with a cloth tail in back. The couple was probably in town just for the day, to sell their wares in the market, and contrasted sharply with the *manteau*-clad women and men in Western clothes who dominated the streets.

Many of Sanandaj's brick palaces had once belonged to the Ardalan family, who governed the city during the Qajar period and all of Persian Kurdistan for centuries earlier. Still a powerful family, the Ardalan dynasty was founded in the early 1300s, and Sanandaj, then known as Senna, was their capital. Renowned for their love of culture and the arts, the Ardalans nurtured sophisticated courts filled with poets and musicians, and established Gorani as the Kurds' first literary language.

Prior to the rise of the Ottoman and Safavid Empires, the Ardalans controlled vast areas of land on both sides of the Zagros Mountains, in both Iran and Iraq. After the dueling empires came to power, the Kurdish dynasty was forced to choose sides. With their capital to the east, they cast their loyalties with Persia. The Ardalans were the only Kurdish princes allowed extensive semiautonomous rule under the Safavids.

In the early nineteenth century, the Ardalan ruler Aman Allah Khan came to power. A passionate builder, he greatly expanded Sanandaj, erecting a new mosque, public bathhouses, caravanserais, a bazaar, and other buildings, many of which still stand. But Aman Allah Khan was also a ruthless and pitiless man. Claudius Rich, an East India Company representative who traveled through Kurdistan in 1820, describes visiting him in the town of Baneh, where he found the khan "settling accounts"—i.e., pulling out the eyes of three men who'd displeased him and sending their wives and daughters to Sanandaj under guard.

One of Aman Allah Khan's projects was the palace of Khosrow Abad, built on a small hill. Rich describes coming upon it: "We were ushered up avenues of poplars of great height and beauty, to a magnificent garden-house of great elevation, with a fine square tank full of jets d'eau in front and at the back of it. . . . The pavilion was lofty, and elegantly painted and gilded in the Persian taste."

Khosrow Abad still stands. Although dilapidated, it is more magnificent in some ways now than ever. I went to visit it one evening, wandering through the empty, darkening streets of the quiet neighborhood that surrounds it, to arrive suddenly at its massive front door, studded with iron nails. With me were two companions, and we had to plead long and hard with the caretaker to let us in, as shadows gathered, obscuring an overgrown garden and leaf-clogged reflecting pool, its *jets d'eau* long gone. The caretaker finally relented, and we climbed up a dark steep staircase to view the haunted courtyard into which Aman Allah Khan and his retinue had once galloped on their steeds, splattering splendor and suffering in their wake.

WHILE IN SANANDAJ, I stayed with Arash, the physics teacher, and his family. His parents were both retired teachers, while his sister, Darya, and brother, Askhan, were university students. The family lived in a multistory apartment complex on the edge of the city, where the paved roads petered out into dirt and there were few taxis and no buses—meaning we often had long waits before catching transportation into town.

Like those I'd met in Mahabad, Arash, his family, and various friends had little good to say about President George W. Bush. "We call him Mullah Bush, because he is not smart enough to be an ayatollah," Arash said, chuckling. To become a *mullah* takes only a year of religious study, to become an ayatollah takes twenty years or more.

Also like most Iranian Kurds I met, Arash's family had lost loved ones in the Kurdish struggle of the 1970s and 1980s, and endured much bombing and suffering during the Iran-Iraq War—one of the bloodiest conflicts of modern times, with an estimated five hundred thousand dead on each side. Three on Arash's mother's side of the family had died due to politics, while one uncle had lost his mind following a five-year stint in prison during the time of the shah.

Arash took me to meet his uncle one morning. A middle-aged man wearing a tall skinny hat, he was sitting on the floor behind a small desk when we arrived, his atrophied feet folded beneath him as he dipped pens into various colored inks. He was hard at work on an English lesson, writing out sentences in a child's copybook, "*l*'s" and "*f*'s" looping above and below lines in a neat, confident hand.

"Why are you studying English?" I asked as I sat down beside him.

"It is amusing to me," he said in clipped English. "It is my hobby. I have written many books." He opened the cabinet beside him, to reveal several shelves weighted down with copybooks filled with his lessons.

"Tell me about when you were in prison," I said.

"I went to Iraq to fight, but Barzani put me in prison," he said. "I stayed five years. They beat me very bad, and now I can't walk."

"Were you in prison in Iraq or Iran?" I was confused by the reference to Barzani.

"Both. Prison is a business."

"Why were you arrested?"

"I can't tell you. You must read my secret dossier."

"When were you arrested?"

"I can't remember. I have a headache." He bent more closely over his copybook, willing me to desist, and I did, trying not to imagine what he had once been through.

Later, I learned that Arash's uncle had been the victim of another turbulent period in inter-Kurdish affairs. Though relations between the Iranian and Iraqi Kurds have usually been good, such was not the case in the late 1960s, when the Iranian government played them off against each other. The Shah of Iran was then sending aid to the Iraqi Kurds in the hopes of destabilizing the Baath government, and in return Barzani agreed to evict the Kurdish Democratic Party of Iran (KDPI) from Iraqi Kurdish territory, where some of its members were hiding. In 1968, he executed one Iranian Kurdish leader and handed his body over to the Iranian authorities, who paraded it triumphantly in Mahabad and elsewhere. Barzani then shipped others back across the border, to their death or imprisonment.

Two years later, alliances shifted again, as the Baath regime opened negotiations with Barzani, and the Iranian Kurds began operating out of Baghdad, with the support of the Iraqi government. But Barzani was still receiving aid from the shah, and despite everything, based on a long earlier history of cooperation, the Iranian Kurds did not feel they could attack the shah while he was still supporting Barzani. Thus, the Iranian Kurdish struggle was subjugated to the Iraqi Kurdish struggle until the Algiers Accord of 1975 when the shah withdrew his support of the Iraqi Kurds and the KDPI embarked on an armed revolt under its new leader, Abd al-Rahman Qassemlou, a socialist intellectual educated in France.

Once again, just business as usual in the wild and woolly world of Kurdish politics.

WHEN THE IRANIAN revolution swept the authoritarian, out-of-touch Mohammed Reza Shah Pahlavi off his throne in 1979, Iranian Kurds seized control of their region, believing themselves to be on the cusp of achieving both democracy for Iran and self-rule for Kurdistan. They hadn't bargained on the installation of an Islamic regime, and a Shiite one at that, or on a government so insecure that it immediately clamped down on all minorities. The regime's new constitution did not even acknowledge the Kurds' existence, leading them to boycott the referendum for its adoption. When the KDPI leader Qassemlou won over 80 percent of the Kurdish vote in the March 1980 parliamentary elections, but decided not to go to Tehran, Ayatollah Khomeini reportedly said, "It's too bad. We could have had him arrested and shot."

During the first years following the Islamic revolution, the Kurds found themselves in near constant battle with the newly formed Revolutionary Guards, who were aggressively imposing *sharia* on all of Iran. By as early as February 1981, an estimated ten thousand Kurds had died either at the hands of the Revolutionary Guards or in one of the many mass executions ordered by Ayatollah Sadiq Khalkhali, the "hanging judge." Attempts at negotiation were broached by both sides, but all failed.

When the Iran-Iraq War began, with Saddam Hussein invading Iran in September 1980, many Iranian Kurds initially viewed it as a way to distract the Iranians from the Kurdish struggle. But as the war escalated, with Kurdistan bearing the brunt of many battles, it proved disastrous. Thousands of civilians were caught between the Revolutionary Guards, the Iraqi army, the KDPI, Komala (a more left-wing Kurdish party), and the Iraqi Kurds, armed by Ayatollah Khomeini to keep the KDPI from escaping to Iraq. The year 1984 was especially devastating, as the Revolutionary Guards launched a huge offensive against the Iranian Kurds, capturing over seventy villages and towns. The KDPI fought back with aid from the Baathists, only to lose control of most of Iranian Kurdistan. By 1984, about 27,500 Iranian Kurds had died during the war. A mind-boggling 90 percent were civilians.

One Kurd I met, originally from Baneh near the Iran-Iraq border, told me that during the war, two thousand of his town's population of fifty thousand had been killed, with six hundred people, including seventy-six children, dying in a single Iraqi bombing attack. "Many border towns were attacked in this way," he said with a shrug. "Every morning, we went to the mountains for the day, when the Iraqis attacked, and came back at night. Except on cloudy days. It was safer on cloudy days."

After the war ended in 1988, over two hundred thousand Revolutionary Guards were stationed in Iranian Kurdistan, and Qassemlou, a passionate yet moderate leader who was always searching for peaceful solutions even while leading armed rebellions, decided to negotiate rather than continue fighting. In early July 1989, he flew to Vienna for a secret meeting with the Iranian authorities. On July 13, the Viennese police found his body crumpled in an armchair of a fifth-floor apartment, shot through the head. Two other prominent Kurds lay on the floor, also shot through the head. Many believe the killers were the very Iranians with whom Qassemlou was negotiating.

Qassemlou was regarded by many observers as the most capable of all modern Kurdish leaders, and his death decimated the Iranian Kurdish political movement. Three years later, his successor, Dr. Mohammed Saddeq Sharfkandi, was also assassinated, and under similar circumstances—while negotiating with members of opposition groups at a restaurant in Berlin. Today, the KDPI is largely based in Iraqi Kurdistan, where it is pushing for greater Iranian Kurdish rights through peaceful means, not separatism.

HIWA, THE CAMERAMAN I had met at the ecology conference, was a pale and serious young man with steady brown eyes. An artist and a dreamer, he aspired to become a filmmaker—his job as a TV cameraman was just a job. He had taken photographs for the conference's exhibit on pollution, and spent much of his time exploring the region's villages. Like other artists and scholars, he visited rural Iran as often as he could, to document the traditional life there before it faded away.

One afternoon, Hiwa took Arash, four other friends, and me into the countryside. We passed several dilapidated-looking villages and more of the dry, elephant-skin mountains and tall, elegant poplars I knew from Iraq. I also spotted ten-foot-high cones made of round, flattened pieces of cow dung, which the Iranian Kurdish villagers used for fuel during the winter. I hadn't seen any such cones, or as many cattle, in Iraq.

We headed east because there were no immediate checkpoints in that direction. I had to worry about those. My taxi had been stopped twice en route to Sanandaj, and although the Revolutionary Guards had been cordial enough, simply checking my passport, there was no telling when they might suddenly become suspicious about what I was doing in Iran, especially now that I was off the tourist path.

As we rolled over the wide brown hills, my companions talked about the September 11 attacks. With the exception of Arash, all believed that the attacks had been planned by the U.S. government, as a way to justify future American assaults against the Muslim world. Nothing I could say would convince them otherwise. Many other Iranian and Turkish Kurds I met shared the same viewpoint.

From the roadside, the village of Kelana looked much like the others we'd passed, but as Hiwa led us back into its winding maze of streets and alleyways, I realized that we had arrived in a small paradise, older and more settled than anything I'd seen in Iraq. Everywhere stood sturdy charming houses built of clay, stone, and brick, many with balconies brimming with flowers. The streets were spotless and the houses freshly plastered, some sporting nineteenth-century door knockers—round ones for female visitors, straight ones for male visitors; different tones alerted residents as to which gender was at the door. Women in brightly colored dresses gossiped on sod rooftops, amid sprouting grasses, and they called out an eager "Welcome to our village!" as we walked by.

"When my father was a boy in his village, they had a beautiful Newroz tradition," Hiwa said to me. "Groups of boys went up on the rooftops and lowered their belts"—i.e., the long cummerbunds—"through the holes for smoke, and the adults filled the belts with fruit and sugar. Then they tugged on the belts for the boys to pull up. And once, as a joke, they tied a big sheep to a belt. But my father's friend was very strong, and he pulled the sheep all the way to the ceiling!"

I loved hearing stories about the Kurdish past, which seemed so lush and magical.

"When my grandfather was a boy, and there was a wedding, the groom rode a beautiful horse into the bride's village," Hiwa went on. "He took a small boy with him, so they would have sons, and threw an apple or pomegranate hard, for good luck, which all the children tried to catch. And later they celebrated with horseracing and wrestling . . .

"Not all our lives are about suffering. Our pain is very deep, but our happiness is also very deep. We have suffered much, but we are rich."

I nodded. For all the horrific stories I'd been hearing in Kurdistan, there was a depth, an inner harmony, and a kind of buoyancy to the Kurdish world that made it seem fuller than many worlds I knew in the West—and not just because of its still-living traditions. Perhaps it came from living closer to the bone.

We had reached the edge of the village, bordered with fields as vibrant with color as the dresses of the rooftop women. Strawberries, apples, tomatoes, and sunflowers were all growing in abundance, along with poplar trees, walnut trees, and puffy purple-red bushes that when gathered and dried would be made into brooms. Irrigation ditches flowed between fields and a group of boys raced by, playing a Kurdish game resembling tag that involved a "stolen" hat. In the distance rose the purple-black Zagros peaks.

We stopped to talk to a farmer, who brought out his farm implements for show-and-tell—a scythe, a hoe, a primitive-looking plow. To create the small paradise around us involved endless, backbreaking work. And the villagers weren't as removed from the modern world as they at first seemed. The farmer had been to Sweden to visit a brother who'd been forced to flee Iran in the 1980s. Many of the villagers had relatives living in exile, he said.

Back in the village, we stopped to talk to a household of women. All wore deep-colored gowns with short black vests, and some flaunted near-iridescent orange hair, dyed from natural henna. One was working a drop spindle as we came up, while another told us stories about *her* trip to Sweden. The women invited us into their home, built around a courtyard with a grape arbor overhead, a clay oven to one side, and chickens to another. Traditional Kurdish homes often housed animals and humans in the same dwelling, with the animals usually on the ground floor or in front, humans up above or behind.

The women urged us to stay for tea, but some in our party were becoming restless. Village life was as foreign to them as it was to me—in fact, one of our companions had never been in a village before, she admitted as she checked her cell phone for messages.

Hiwa's mind was still in village life, reminding me of how unusual he was. "My grandmother is a very brave woman," he told me. "During the Iran-Iraq War, one of her sons and his wife escaped to Iraq because of politics. They had a baby in the mountains, but they were in a dangerous area, it wasn't safe, and the baby got sick. So my grandmother went by mule, took the baby, and brought him back to Iran. It took her three days to get back, and it was very cold. But they came back safe, through the snow and the mines, and she raised him until he was six. Now he's eighteen, and lives in London.

"I had a chance to go outside, too. Everything was ready for me to go to Sweden. But at the last minute I couldn't go. I couldn't leave Iran."

FROM SANANDAJ TO Kermanshah was a two-hour trip from the mountains to the plains, from an isolated all-Kurdish town to a crowded, traffic-jammed crossroads inhabited by a mixed population of Kurdish Sunnis, Shiites, and Ahl-e Haqqs, and Lurs and Persians. I had read that Kermanshah boasted a beautiful setting, backing up against a mountain range capped with snow year-round. But although the mountains were there, the snow wasn't, and the city shimmered with an ugly brown dust, heat, exhaust, and refinery fumes, making me long to return to cool, clear Sanandaj.

The nineteenth-century traveler Isabella Bird had a first impression similar to mine: "[T]he city impresses one as ruinous and decayed; yet it has a large trade, and is regarded as one of the most prosperous places in the Empire." I thought of those words as I wandered the city's streets, with its noticeable quotient of opium and heroin addicts—deposited here from all over Iran by the Islamic regime, some said.

Once an important stop on the trade route between Persia and Baghdad, Kermanshah dates back to about the fourth century A.D., when it was home to Sassanian kings, who established Zoroastrianism as the state religion. Later, the town's vulnerable location made it an easy prey for Arabs in the seventh century, Seljuk Turks in the eleventh century, Mongols in the thirteenth century, and Iraqis in the twentieth century. Kermanshah suffered some of the worst of the heavy bomb and missile attacks during the Iran-Iraq War.

During the nineteenth century, Kermanshah was considered to be the capital of Persian Kurdistan and boasted a robust Persian cavalry, made up mostly of Kurds trained by French officers. Then a walled city with a moat three miles in circumference, Kermanshah was also a stop for pilgrims en route to the holy Shiite sites of Najaf and Karbala, in what is now Iraq. By the late nineteenth century, at least 150,000 pilgrims and 8,000 of their dead relatives annually passed along the Kermanshah road, the latter headed for burial at the holy sites.

Many visitors still pass through Kermanshah, often stopping to see Taq-e Bostan, one of the most famous archaeological sites in Iran, dating back to the A.D. 600s. Built around a dark grotto, red walls carved with fine, giant bas-reliefs depict the Sassanian king Khosrow II on a royal hunt, with men riding horses and elephants, chasing stags and boar. Nearby stands Ardeshir II, receiving a wreath of friendship from the Zoroastrian god Ashura Mazda, while Ahriman, the god of darkness, lies defeated under his feet.

Behind Kermanshah looms Bisotun, a mountain upon which more famed bas-reliefs and inscriptions are carved. In 1838, the British soldier Henry Rawlinson, dangling from the end of a rope, copied down Bisotun's inscriptions and deciphered the Old Persian words.

The mountain is at least equally known for its connection with Farhad and Shirin, heroes of one of Iran's most beloved ancient tales, claimed by both Persians and Kurds. In one of the story's versions, Shirin, the beautiful wife of King Khosrow, falls in love with Farhad, a simple stonecutter. Desperate not to lose his queen, Khosrow consents to give her to Farhad if he can bring the waters of Bisotun to her castle, Qasr-e Shirin—the ruins of which still stood on the outskirts of a city of the same name until the Iran-Iraq War. Farhad's love gives him great strength, and he rapidly cuts a pathway through the mountains, constructing an aqueduct. He has almost succeeded at his impossible task when the frantic Khosrow sends him a message claiming that Shirin has died. An anguished Farhad jumps to his death, and Shirin dies of a broken heart.

Some Iranian Kurdish scholars attribute the doomed love affair to the tensions between the fierce Kurds of the mountains and the more docile Kurds of the plains, the latter often influenced by outsiders to betray their traditions and culture. In this interpretation, Farhad defaces the mountains, the Kurdish heartland, for his love of Shirin, who is in turn guilty of encouraging him in his task, at times with lies. Betrayal has been a Kurdish theme for centuries.

WHILE IN KERMANSHAH, I at first stayed with Kajal, the married sister of Arash, the physics teacher from Sanandaj. Their siblings, Darya and Askhan, had traveled with me to Kermanshah because they said they wanted to visit their sister. I suspected that the timing of their trip had much less to do with them than it had with me. In the gracious Iranian Kurdish tradition, my every need was subtly being taken care of.

Kajal spoke good English, as did a number of the family's friends, some of whom helped me find my way around the city. Together we visited the archaeological sites, the central bazaar, an upscale shopping district, a poor quarter, and a boarded-up Sunni mosque, the only major Sunni mosque in the Shiite-dominated city. Its outspoken and prominent cleric, Molla Mohammed Rabi'i, had been killed in December 1996 — "in disputed circumstances," according to Amnesty International — resulting in riots that had left at least several others dead and the mosque permanently closed.

Talking to Kermanshah's citizens, I learned more. Historically, the relationship between the city's Sunni and Shiite Kurds has ranged from poor to hostile. The Iranian government has used religion as a wedge between them; religion has proven to be more central to many Kurds' identity than ethnicity. Both groups have looked down upon one another, and the Sunni Kurds have resented the fact that only Shiites are appointed to positions of power — as is the case all over Iran. The country is officially 94 percent Shiite, with its 5 percent Sunni minority often treated as second-class citizens, so much so that some Sunnis convert to Shiism in order to move up socially and economically.

During and after the Islamic revolution, the Shiite Kurds wanted nothing to do with the struggle for Kurdish autonomy being waged farther north in Sanandaj and Mahabad. Many, in fact, agreed to fight against the Sunni Kurds, while among the most enthusiastic of the Revolutionary Guards during the Iran-Iraq War were Ahl-e Haqq.

All this lulled the Islamic regime into taking the loyalty of its Shiite and Ahl-e Haqq Kurds for granted. But in 1999, a curious thing happened. The arrest of Abdullah Öcalan, leader of Turkey's PKK, led to huge demonstrations on the Kermanshah streets, with some Kurds, as elsewhere in the world, burning themselves in protest. Even bigger rallies also took place in other Iranian Kurdish cities, with thousands gathering in Sanandaj, for one, but it was Kermanshah that caught the Iranian government completely by surprise. Apparently, Kurdish nationalism was no longer limited to its Sunni Kurds. Apparently, its Shiite Kurds were starting to feel at least as much Kurdish as Shiite. And perhaps the Islamic regime itself had encouraged this development, as Iran had aided and harbored the PKK during Turkey's civil war, hoping to clip its neighbor's growing influence in the region.

Just what, if anything, did those pro-Öcalan protests portend for the future of the Iranian Kurdish movement? Many Iranian Kurds I met seemed to feel that although their situation was not good, it was tolerable, at least compared to Turkey and Iraq under Saddam. On the other hand, thousands of Iranian Kurds, recently forced out of their villages by economic desperation, were now living rootless, alienated lives in crowded slums—ripe conditions for ferment.

AMONG THE KURDS I met in Kermanshah was the Najafi family, who invited me to stay with them. The Najafis were Hawraman, and had many relatives living in the isolated, mountainous Hawraman region, one of the most traditional Kurdish areas still left in Iran. They could help me travel to the Hawraman capital of Paveh, and even promised to take me to No Sud, the smugglers' town on the Iran-Iraq border.

The Najafi parents, Lotfallah and Maliha, were a middle-aged couple with three grown sons. Lotfallah, a gruff and hearty man of many opinions, dressed in Western clothes outside the home, but wore baggy Kurdish pants around the house, as did many Iranian Kurdish men. Maliha, who was often silent, wore traditional dresses both indoors and out. The couple's youngest son, Asoo, spoke moderately good English and often served as my translator. Tensile and intense, Asoo was studying for the nationwide university entrance exams, hoping to become a civil engineer.

One morning at daybreak, Lotfallah, Asoo, and I left Kermanshah for the Hawraman mountains. The plan was for Lotfallah to drop Asoo and me off in Paveh and then return to Kermanshah in time to go to work. In Paveh, Asoo and I would look up one of their relatives, who would drive us through the rest of the province.

We headed west down the still-dark streets and out past an oil refinery, Lotfallah already pontificating, while disconcertingly breaking off now and again to burst into song—a constant habit. Initially, I had thought it indicative of a poetic side to his blustery character, but as time went on, I realized that it had more to do with frustration, as he often started singing after a diatribe against his low salary or the government. And he wasn't singing just anything. His husky, mournful snatches of song, laden with mystery, were an exclusively Hawraman form of music called *siachamana*, meaning "black eyes," dating back to the Zoroastrians, though the significance of its name has been lost. Traditionally, the music was performed with the singer cupping his hands behind his ears, as if listening to the gods, and its heart-wrenching sound was unforgettable. I'd heard it only once before, in Halabja, where a man with a cancerous growth disfiguring his face had welcomed my companions and me into his rose-filled garden with a song as heavy with longing as an echoing call to prayer.

The land outside Kermanshah was rich agricultural territory, sprinkled with ancient combines and tractors, and the occasional village or dairy farm. Small rocky peaks poked up dead ahead, higher peaks behind, and, as we dove into them, Lotfallah broke off his talking and singing to ask me about the "red Americans"—a favorite topic among the Kurds, who see the Native Americans as a people much like themselves. In Turkey, especially, I met Kurds who knew an enormous amount about Native Americans, with large collections of their literature and music.

We plunged into an ocean of tan triangular mountains, bobbing around us as our battered car groaned its way along. Women and school-children waited for buses all along the roadside. Nearer Kermanshah, they had been dressed in dour *chadors*, but now bright traditional Kurdish clothes flashed by.

Villages built of clay homes with sleepy window lids climbed up steep mountainsides. Many had blue window frames and doors; some had balconies and ladders; and the roofs of one row often served as patios for the next, as the tiers receded, as evenly as a wedding cake.

Arriving in Paveh, we stopped at the home of a man I'd met at the Sanandaj conference, a well-educated professional who was an expert on the region. I didn't have his address, but Lotfallah knew where he lived. We knocked on his door at about seven-thirty A.M.—much too early to be calling upon a stranger, in my opinion, but considered the norm among some Iranians, who usually rise at dawn to say morning prayers.

As soon as the door opened, I realized that I had made a mistake. My erstwhile host had been cordial at the conference and on the phone when I called to confirm my visit, but I had sensed some hesitation in his manner. Seeing his sagging face, I now realized that, like Mr. K in Sanandaj, he really wanted nothing to do with me. He hadn't expected me to take him up on his invitation.

Nevertheless, he invited us in and bustled around for the next forty minutes or so as he got his children up and prepared breakfast, while his wife dressed for work. He talked mostly to Lotfallah and Asoo the whole time, barely acknowledging me, while I shifted uncomfortably, wondering how I should handle things when the activity quieted down.

To my surprise and relief, my host broached the subject of my presence himself immediately after his wife and Lotfallah left for work. "I am sorry, but I can't talk to you long, and I can only talk about the environment. This is a troubled area. The authorities will ask me later why you are here."

"But I'm not here to talk about politics," I said. "I'm mostly interested in the Hawraman culture."

"It doesn't matter. Last year, after a Japanese lady researcher was here, I was arrested."

My heart sank. How could I go bungling around so naively, putting others at risk?

And yet, how could I have known? He'd invited me to visit him—twice. The Iranian authorities knew what I was doing in Kurdistan. I'd stated the purpose of my visit on my visa application. Many Iranian Kurds had also strongly urged me to visit the Hawraman area, saying that as long as I stuck to people and culture, and avoided politics, everything would be fine. But since when do theory and reality coincide?

"But you are here now," our host said, "and the authorities didn't keep me long. Ask your questions."

In fits and starts, I began, starting with queries about the environment, as he had requested. But as we quickly exhausted that subject and branched out into others, he didn't object, and he began talking more and more freely, with little urging on my part.

Iran's Hawraman region encompassed about fifty villages and, together with the Hawraman region of Iraq, had been a "field of war" ever since the days of the Safavids and Ottomans, he said. Because of the region's isolation, extreme even for Kurdistan, the Hawraman people had maintained their independence for many decades after most Kurds. During the reign of Reza Shah (1923 to 1941), one Hawraman leader, Jafar Soltan, fiercely fought off the Iranian government for fourteen years. And during the 1970s and early 1980s, the area served as the clandestine headquarters for the Kurdish political parties. That changed by the middle of the Iran-Iraq War, when the Revolutionary Guards overran the district, but the region was still regarded with great suspicion by the regime.

Because of the Hawramans' isolation, they had always been exceedingly self-sufficient, growing and making everything they needed, including their own hand-woven clothes and shoes, known as *klash*, which they now sold throughout Kurdistan. And the Hawramans' self-sufficiency had also gone far beyond the physical, to encompass the creation of a rich repository of unique folktales, folk remedies, songs, games, and ceremonies. Some of the greatest of the latter celebrated the life of Pir-e Shahriyar, a holy Zoroastrian linked with Mythra, the ancient god of light and the sun. On the anniversary of the Pir's death, hundreds converged on his mountain slope grave, playing the *daf* and chanting. And though the Hawraman were Muslim, they still honored Mythra on the fortieth day of winter, with sacrificial blood spilled at the first light of dawn, and hundreds of men dancing ecstatically in circles to the beating of the *daf*.

When our host was growing up in the 1960s, many Hawraman traditions were still flourishing, but over the past few decades, their prevalence had steadily diminished. The villages were no longer self-sufficient; few told stories anymore, and even the festivals were not as well attended as before.

The Hawraman culture also had its dark side. Life for women was especially hard. They worked long hours and had few rights, with families often forbidding girls to go to school. Honor killings still took place, usually in secret, with many villagers believing that the victims deserved what they got.

The region had its share of more modern problems as well. Men sought work in the south, leaving their families alone for large chunks of the year. Others worked as smugglers, risking their lives to cross the mine-studded border mountains, patrolled by the Revolutionary Guards, who killed perhaps a half-dozen men every year. The quality of the natural environment was worsening, too, through water pollution, air pollution, and deforestation.

Our host would like nothing better, he said, with longing in his eyes, than to take us out into the remote Hawraman countryside. But he was under constant surveillance because of his political activities in the 1980s. It would also be extremely difficult for Asoo and me to travel into the villages alone. Villagers would be suspicious of us, for one thing, but, more to the point, the authorities would stop us. If we wanted to protect ourselves, and travel on to the town of No Sud, where Asoo's relatives lived, as we had planned, we needed to go directly to the authorities upon leaving him to obtain permission.

That would be a good idea, Asoo agreed, a bit vaguely. He had often traveled in the region, but never with a foreigner. I was suddenly struck by the fact that he was only seventeen years old and we were both neophytes here.

Taking leave of our host, we did as he advised, descending into the heart of Paveh to enter a dark, utilitarian building that housed the region's administrative government. Here, we were passed from one office to another by unsmiling, bearded men in loose, long-sleeved shirts and sandals. Some picked up the phone after studying my passport, to talk with their higher-ups, and I could understand much of their conversations: *No, no, she has no official documents, just a visa. She says she is a writer. She is alone. She is American.* It sounded suspicious even to me. It was strange that I was here at this time, with my country on the brink of war with Iraq, less than thirty miles away. With a sinking heart, I grew more certain that permission to go to No Sud would be denied, when one especially unpleasant-looking man suddenly washed his hands of us by sending us down the street to the local police department.

Here, we were greeted with equal unfriendliness and suspicion, especially after one officer discovered a slight irregularity with my visa. But then a higher-up arrived and, with a beaming face, ordered up more rounds of tea. "We are so happy you are here. Writers are always welcome in Iran." He handed us a letter granting us permission to proceed to No Sud and told us to call him should we run into trouble.

WITH THE LOGISTICS of the trip finally taken care of, we took a quick look around Paveh, a web of bumpy roads and brick-cement buildings spread up and down steep hills. Carpets hung from balconies, tractors cruised, and most of the men wore billowing pants with cummerbunds. Most of the women wore *chadors*. Behind the town rose Atashgah, a rugged peak that was once a sacred Zoroastrian site.

After a simple lunch of rice, yogurt, tomatoes, and flat bread, we headed west, to be sure to arrive in No Sud before sundown. The road leading there, threading around some of the highest mountains in Kurdistan, was too treacherous to travel after dark. It had no guardrails or lights, and along the forty-five-kilometer stretch were exactly 274 turns — many of them dangerous, said our driver, who traveled the route often.

We made stops along the way in a few roadside villages. In one, an old man with a bristly mustache and lopsided turban said that before the Iran-Iraq War, his village had housed 105 families, but now held only thirty-five. Most had left to look for work in the cities.

"Do you know the history of the Hawraman people?" he then asked.

"We are the descendants of Rostam"—the hero of Iran's national epic, the *Shahnameh*—"who once lived near Mount Damavand, near Tehran. But Darius the Mede expelled us, and we ran away here, to the safety of the mountains. We have lived here for thousands of years."

The old man's story made me think of the Avroman Parchments. Found in a cave in the Hawraman mountains, carefully preserved in a jar, the documents date back to the first century B.C., and record the sale of a vineyard in both Greek and Parthian. One way or another, this was an astonishingly ancient land.

And the mountains were as advertised: one steep surging peak after another, many wider and smoother than the mountains I'd seen in Iraq, but just as breathtaking and formidable. On a late afternoon in October, slopes were bristly and brown, with few trees, but with a golden sheen of plumpness and plenty. Far beneath their rounded humps, the Sirwan River meandered along, en route to the Darbandikhan Dam in Iraq, while a silver slip of road curled and uncurled up ahead, playing hide and seek among peaks and valleys.

No Sud itself emerged around a final bend just as the sun was setting, at the end of a curved road that cut a fine brown line along a red cliff. Sailing around the semicircle, we cruised into town, slowing to a crawl as we passed through a plaza crowded with men and boys in baggy pants, then squeezed our way down a painfully narrow street along the edge of a cliff. Directly ahead plunged a valley, followed by a wall of mountains—Iraq. Directly behind lived Asoo's relatives.

They enthusiastically ushered us inside. We were just taking seats on the floor when the police arrived. We had been in town less than five minutes. Who was I? What was I doing here? The family looked tense, and my heart pounded. However, upon hearing the purpose of my visit and where I was from, the police beamed. Welcome, they said, we are proud to have an American writer in our town. Come visit us tomorrow for a glass of tea.

We never did make that visit, and, on the way back to Paveh the next afternoon, we were stopped by a group of grim Revolutionary Guards. Iran's police and Revolutionary Guards are two distinctly separate groups, and though we'd passed through other Revolutionary Guard checkpoints without incident, this squad paid little attention to our letter of permission from the Paveh police. They also refused to give the friendly captain we'd met a call. They didn't like my presence in the region. A guard then climbed into our car to accompany us all the way back to Paveh, a two-hour drive—dashing my hopes of visiting more villages. He was surly and menacing when he first got in, making me wonder if my luck in Iran had run out at last. What would happen when we reached Paveh? But as the miles rolled by, the guard lightened up and, when we arrived, spoke briefly to his commander, who waved us on our way.

Asoo's uncle was a burly shopkeeper in his sixties, dressed in baggy pants and a turban, married to a much younger woman wearing a turquoise caf-

Our host in No Sud

tan—his second wife, whom he had married after his first had died on the dangerous Paveh–No Sud road we had just traveled. They lived in two rooms on the second floor of the spare house, while his son, daughter-in-law, and grandson lived in two matching rooms below.

Though a man of little formal education, Asoo's uncle was well versed in the region's history, and he told me many complicated tales involving the Hawraman leader Jafar Soltan, who had resisted Reza Shah's army. He also spoke about the years of the Iran-Iraq War, when Qassemlou and his KDPI forces were based in and near No Sud, and the town was subsequently flattened. Once, No Sud had been many times the size it was now.

I had noticed No Sud's emptiness, but hadn't guessed its cause. It disturbed me to think that newcomers such as myself could come to a place like this and see it only as it was, with no inkling of all that had gone before.

The son who lived downstairs had been a victim of the Islamic regime, Asoo whispered. He'd simply disappeared one day two years earlier, and no one in the family had known where he was until his release from prison six months later. After eight years of surveillance, the authorities had suddenly decided to arrest and torture him for his political activities ten years before.

As we talked, night fell. Dinner had come and gone, and we were relaxing over fruit and glasses of tea, when the clip-clop of hooves sounded outside. Minutes later, more hooves clopped by, and then more and more, until it sounded as if an entire cavalry was arriving. Indeed it was: The nighttime's smuggling activities were beginning.

When I'd heard about the smuggling between Iran and Iraq, I'd envisioned small groups working covertly together, trying not to draw attention to themselves. I was completely unprepared for the scene that greeted me when we stepped outside. Hundreds of men and mules had gathered in the central square and in a lot down the hill, bathed in a wan yellow light. Many men were saddling up with blankets and ropes, or checking their cell phones—used to warn one another of danger en route—while milling about were a few businessmen, who would later ship the illicit goods into Iran's interior. Smuggling in No Sud was no clandestine operation; it was a town affair. Everyone knew about it, even the authorities, who, for all their harassment of the smugglers, were blatantly looking the other way. I hardly needed proof of that but got it anyway, when I spotted an armed guard actually sitting on the edge of the plaza, watching the men, looking bored.

Hadn't I noticed the big banks in town? my hosts asked, after I voiced my astonishment at the sight of the guard. There were two of them, both multistory and built within the last two years. A town the size of No Sud, with no legitimate business to speak of, hardly needed one big bank, let alone two.

Although smuggling between Iran and Iraq had existed for decades, it became big business only about five years before, the smugglers told me.

Some of the goods entering Iran—which included cigarettes, tea, alcohol, and electronics—were originally from Turkey; others came directly from Iraq. The Kurds sometimes smuggled goods in the other direction as well, out of Iran and into Iraq, but that was more unusual.

To travel to and from Iraq took six hours each way, with the men leaving about nine P.M., to return the following morning. On average, a man earned 6,000 *tomans* ($5), for his night's work, hardly enough to warrant risking his life—not all of the authorities were looking the other way, and there were mines to watch out for. However, there were few other ways to make a living in No Sud.

Each of the Iranian border towns specialized in the smuggling of different goods. No Sud had the tea and banana market all locked up, while other towns concentrated on alcohol or electronic goods. Of course, to smuggle alcohol and electronic goods was much more lucrative than to smuggle tea and bananas, the men acknowledged when I asked, but it was a lot more dangerous. They wanted to come home to their wives.

"What about Ansar al-Islam?" I asked. "Are they a danger for you?" The terrorist organization's headquarters were just over the border, not more than ten miles away.

The men shrugged. Not really, it seemed.

"Are they operating here in Iran?"

One man laughed. "Iran is too smart to let them operate here," he said.

It was getting late, and the smugglers started to leave, to be instantly swallowed up by the darkness beyond. What lay ahead of them that evening, I wondered as I watched them slip away, some so very young, many very thin.

Asoo, his uncle's son, and I climbed up a steep set of stairs to an old fountain. Surrounded by a garden, it had been a favorite haunt of Jafar Soltan, the Hawraman leader. It was also one of the only places in No Sud that had not been destroyed during the Iran-Iraq War, Asoo said, as we bought bottles of orange soda from a woman in a purple velveteen dress. She had been weaving a pair of *klash*, the traditional Hawraman shoes, when we came up, and went back to her work as we took seats in the unlit garden. Empty now, it was crowded during the day with men playing cards and backgammon. The late day, that is. With almost everyone in No Sud involved in the nighttime smuggling trade, most people slept in until afternoon. This was no ordinary world.

CHAPTER EIGHTEEN

"Happy Is He Who Calls Himself a Turk"

THE ROOM WAS DARK AND A LITTLE MUSTY. THE DAY WAS fading, the sounds from the street growing dim. The half-dozen middle-aged women around me, all wearing white muslin head scarves edged with lace, leaned forward a bit in their chairs. Their kerchiefs gave them an angelic look, but their eyes were haunted.

They went around the room one by one, as if they were telling stories around a campfire. Nezahat started things off, but only after lighting a cigarette and, before her story was finished, lighting another.

She and her family had moved from their village to Diyarbakir, the unofficial Kurdish capital in southeast Turkey, years before the fighting between the Kurds and the Turks began. They found a place to live on the edge of town and were eking out a living as shopkeepers when their oldest daughter became involved with politics. At age twelve, the girl saw Turkish gendarmes mow down two next-door neighbors in cold blood, a sight she never forgot. At age nineteen, when the PKK leader Abdullah Öcalan was arrested, she burned herself in protest . . . at home. Her mother, the only other person in the house at the time, was unable to do a thing; her daughter was engulfed in flames. She rushed the girl to the hospital, but it was too late—"she was a martyr." Nezahat's face was impassive, but her hands shook as she lit her third cigarette.

Seniha was next. Her son had joined the PKK at age fifteen. He was martyred one year later, she said. He died in Lice, a town just outside Diyarbakir that was all but flattened by the Turkish forces in 1993, in a rampage following a PKK attack. He was killed with twelve other friends from school; they had all joined the PKK together and were probably buried together in a mass grave. She and the other mothers only learned of their sons' deaths seven months after the fact, by which time it was too late to know where the grave was or claim the boys' bodies, authorities told them.

Sakine had once had five sons. One died in a prison hunger strike protesting conditions there, one was killed while fighting with the PKK, and one died in a traffic accident. Another was arrested in 1979, tortured, and repeatedly "raped with sticks," she said. Freed in 1992, he fled to the mountains ten days later to fight again, saying he couldn't stand the quiet at home. She hadn't heard from him since. She had lost her husband because of him and the son who died in prison. Her husband forbade her to visit their sons in jail, saying that respectable women don't visit jails. When she disobeyed, he divorced her. Now, she had only one son left at home, and she was very afraid for him. How could she keep him safe?

The women called themselves the Peace Mothers, and they were trying to reach out to Turkish as well as other Kurdish mothers who had lost loved ones in the civil war. "All we want is peace," said one of the women in the now almost dark room. Sounds from outside had ceased, but someone near me was weeping.

TURKEY'S KURDISTAN WAS a land of ghosts. I felt it as soon as I arrived, and the feeling lingered long after I left. The Kurdish-Turkish civil war may be over, but its footsteps are still echoing down streets, sneaking up from behind, as remembered assassins' bullets crack out. Ghostly victims are still being dragged into anonymous cars or lined up in rows to be shot. Long-destroyed villages are still burning, invisible young men and women are still dying. And another kind of ghost is here as well—alive on the outside, but dead on the inside, living in vast city slums, their homes and villages destroyed, their loved ones disappeared.

The Kurdish-Turkish civil war that raged in southeast Turkey from 1984 to 1999 was one of the greatest underreported stories of the late twentieth century. During its long, vicious course, about thirty-seven thousand

Turkish soldiers, Kurdish guerrillas, and civilians were killed, between 1 million and 3 million Kurds rendered homeless, and over three thousand Kurdish villages destroyed—almost as many as were destroyed in northern Iraq. Yet throughout—and even today, as the war's aftermath and human rights abuses continue—most of the world scarcely noticed.

The seeds of the Kurdish-Turkish civil war were sown shortly after the founding of the modern Republic of Turkey. Following the collapse of the Ottoman Empire and World War I, the Turks had found themselves in a humiliated position, with the Allies planning the breakup of their territories, promising different lands to different peoples. Some of the best parts of Anatolia, the Turkish homeland, were to go to Christian peoples, while the Muslim Turks themselves were to be relegated to a small, semibarren region with no access to the sea. There was even talk of giving territory to the Kurds.

Just when it seemed as if things couldn't get much worse, they did. The Greeks, with the encouragement of the British, took over Smyrna (now Izmir), home to a large Hellenic population, and began invading farther east. For the Turks, this was the last straw. Galvanized by the idea of a former subjected people inhabiting prized Turkish territory, they organized under the Ottoman general Mustafa Kemal, who'd previously served with heroic distinction in the Dardanelles campaign, to wage the 1919 to 1922 Turkish War of Independence. By the time it was over, the Turks had successfully driven the British, French, and Greeks from their homeland.

Mustafa Kemal rose to become not just a national hero, but "Atatürk," or "Father of the Turks," a near godlike figure who would in effect rule Turkey unilaterally until his death in 1938. A westernized career officer, Kemal sat down with the Allies in 1923 to hammer out the Treaty of Lausanne, which established the Republic of Turkey. He then began propelling his bankrupt land into the twentieth century as rapidly as he could, outlawing the Islamic veil, replacing the Arabic alphabet with the Roman, and building what would become a robust modern economy. With a parliament and constitution, the new republic was based on democratic principles, but with the authoritarian legacy of the Ottoman Empire still lingering and Kemal hailed as a savior, most Turks were happy to see their new president take on all-encompassing powers.

Initially, the Kurds supported Kemal, fighting alongside his forces in the war of independence and taking heart in the Treaty of Lausanne, which declared all citizens of the new republic equal before the law "without distinction of birth, nationality, language, race or religion." But already in 1922, Kemal had abolished the old sultanate system, which had helped to sustain the *aghas'* authority. In 1924, he began a pitiless campaign to assimilate the Kurds.

His aim was to create an indestructible nation-state with a monolithic Turkish identity, one that could never again be almost torn asunder by foreigners. To do so, he needed to deny the existence of the country's largest minority, making up one-fifth of its population; the only minorities recognized by the new republic were its small non-Muslim ones. On March 3, 1924, all Kurdish schools, associations, publications, and religious organizations were banned, the use of the Kurdish language was forbidden in the courts and government offices, and the word *Kurdistan* was excised from official documents. Kurdish dress, music, and names became outlawed, and, most incredibly of all, Kurds were declared to be "mountain Turks who have forgotten their language." Kurds who did not call themselves Kurds could still rise high in Turkish government and society, but any Kurd who dared utter his or her true identity risked arrest, torture, and imprisonment. As late as 1979, when a former minister of Public Works declared, "In Turkey there are Kurds. I too am a Kurd," he was sentenced to two years and four months imprisonment with hard labor.

March 3, 1924, also saw the abolition of the Islamic Caliphate, turning Turkey into a fully secular state and severing the religious link between Kurds and Turks that had united them for centuries. Many Kurdish Muslims, as well as Turkish Muslims, were deeply offended; they had not waged war to live in a secular state.

The events of 1924 led to Turkey's first modern Kurdish revolt, under the leadership of Shaikh Said of Piran. The *shaikh* and his forces succeeded in capturing over one-third of the Southeast before Turkish troops rushed in to suppress the uprising. Shaikh Said and dozens of others were hanged, thousands of civilians killed, thousands more deported, and hundreds of villages burned, establishing a precedence of cruelty in Turkish-Kurdish relations.

Two more major Kurdish uprisings followed in 1930 and 1937 to 1938, one in the foothills of Mount Ararat, and another in Dersim, now known by the Turkish name of Tunceli—many Kurdish place names have been replaced with Turkish ones over the decades. Again, thousands of civilians were killed—perhaps forty thousand in Dersim alone—and large regions evacuated. As many as 1 million Kurds were displaced between 1925 and 1938. Southeast Turkey was placed under military rule, and the revolts ended as the Turks forced the Kurds into an uneasy submission for the next thirty years.

A Turkish newspaper correspondent who visited Dersim a decade after the uprising wrote: "The place was desolate. . . . There are no more artisans, no more culture, no more trade. . . . If you speak to [the people] of government, they translate it immediately as tax collectors and policemen. We give the people of Dersim nothing; we only take."

Atatürk marginalized the Kurds yet further by "proving" a mythical Turkish history that declared that all the world's civilizations had been founded by the Turks, and that all languages derived from the "Sun Language," whose closest modern descendant was, of course, Turkish. Kurdish was said to contain only eight hundred words, and so was not a real language, while the word *Kurd* was said to have come from the sound of crunching snow—*kart, kurt, kart, kurt*—that the early Turks made while walking over snow in the Southeast's mountains. Many Turks, still reeling from the humiliations of the early twentieth century, eagerly embraced such absurd nationalist theories, which were taught in the schools and continued to be propagated long after Atatürk's death. Chauvinist sayings such as "A Turk is worth the whole world" became woven into the very definition of what it meant to be a loyal citizen of Turkey.

Life in Kurdistan improved somewhat in the 1950s, following Turkey's first free general election. Exiled *aghas* and *shaikhs* were allowed back into the region and began to accrue their old power, with some entering politics, while also becoming estranged from their constituents as they took up residence in the cities. A limited amount of cultural expression was also allowed. Nonetheless, Kurdish political parties continued to be outlawed, and the Southeast remained mired in poverty; the government did little to develop the area, although a good system of roads was built—the better to police the Kurds.

In 1960, a military coup overthrew an authoritarian civilian government and, surprisingly, instituted a new liberal constitution that gave the Turks much more democracy than before. However, the new constitution also established the powerful National Security Council, composed of an equal number of military and civilian members, but usually headed by a four-star general, designed to oversee the civilian government. In 1971 and 1980, the Turkish military staged two more coups.

The 1960s was a turbulent decade in Turkey, as left-wing students and other radicals organized large, antigovernment demonstrations, leading to mass arrests. However, it was the 1980 coup that brought about the harshest modern clampdown on human rights. Staged to end the violence between left- and right-wing radicals that had begun two years earlier, resulting in over five thousand deaths, the coup led to the adoption of another new constitution. This one institutionalized the power of the military, sharply curtailed civil liberties, and outlawed all political parties. The military junta also cruelly enforced and augmented the ban on the Kurdish language, while sending troops into the Southeast to arrest and interrogate tens of thousands of "political suspects."

Unbeknownst to the Turkish authorities at that time, however, Kurdish history was about to enter a whole new phase. Abdullah Öcalan and his followers had formed the Kurdistan Workers' Party (PKK). A tragic civil war was in the offing.

MY TOUR OF Turkey's Kurdistan did not begin in the Southeast, the Kurds' traditional homeland, but in romantic, sophisticated Istanbul to the northwest—seemingly as far away from Kurdistan as it is possible to get and still be in Turkey. But Istanbul is also the world's largest Kurdish city, as it is home to about 2 million Kurds, out of a city population of 12 million. The Kurds started migrating to Istanbul and other western Turkish cities when the evacuations of their villages began in the 1920s. What started as a trickle grew to a stream in the 1960s and 1970s—due mostly to economics—and to a flood in the 1980s and 1990s—due to the civil war. At least a third of Turkey's estimated 14 million Kurds, out of a total country population of 70 million, now live in its western cities, including Ankara, Adana, Mersin, and Izmir, as well as Istanbul.

Most of Istanbul's more recent Kurdish migrants are uneducated, unable to speak Turkish, and desperately poor. To Turkey's credit, however, many of the migrants who arrived in the 1960s and 1970s have become solidly middle class, their educated children working professional jobs. Well assimilated into mainstream Turkey, these Kurds live lives much like urban dwellers in any other modern capital, with all the accoutrements that go with it—computers, cell phones, nightlife, music, casual sex, Western fashion.

While in Istanbul, I stayed with one such middle-class Kurdish family, who lived in a pleasant neighborhood on the city's outskirts. The parents, Elif and Yakup Sevinc, were originally from a village in the Bingöl region—a northern, hardscrabble Kurdish province. They had moved to the capital over thirty years before. Elif was unable to speak anything but Kurdish when she arrived, while Yakup knew only the basic Turkish he'd learned while in the army. Yet they'd done remarkably well, not only living in a comfortable, modern apartment, but also becoming the proud parents of three well-educated sons. Ali, an economist, lived nearby with a family of his own; Atilla, now also known as Alan, had emigrated to New Jersey, and Aydin was a university student.

Ali and his English-speaking cousin Sheri, an architect, picked me up soon after my arrival to whisk me to my temporary home, where Elif was waiting. Round and motherly, with a lovely face always wreathed in smiles, and always ready with a hug, she took attentive care not only of me during my visit, but, it seemed, of the whole world all the time, as she cooked up enormous traditional Kurdish/Turkish meals for everyone every evening. All followed, of course, with fragrant tea served in tulip-shaped glasses. Elif had been to New Jersey to visit her son Atilla the year before and had just started taking literary classes, painstakingly writing out her homework at the kitchen table in the late afternoons. Whenever I thought of all the twists and turns her life had taken, I felt in awe.

In yet more of the generous Kurdish hospitality that I encountered everywhere, the rest of the family was also waiting for me. Ali would serve as my occasional chauffeur and informal historian, Yakup would introduce me to various friends, and Sheri and her English-speaking friend Sedef—an Azeri Turk whose family was originally from Iran—would serve as my interpreters. Most of all, Aydin, the youngest son, a tall and lanky man with an irrepressible smile, essentially took more than a week out of his life to help me navigate Istanbul and its difficult transportation system. Aydin's bedroom was a testament to his many passions, filled with books by Mehmed Uzun, a foremost Kurdish writer from Turkey; various Kurdish folk instruments; recordings of both Kurdish music and American rock and roll; posters of Che Guevara and the NBA, and the anarchists' flag. "I am a Communist and an anarchist," he proudly told me.

But for all these trappings of success and well-being, the more time I spent with my adopted family and their friends, the more I learned that, as usual, more than one reality was operating here. Yes, the family and their friends had done well, and, yes, they did not have to worry about chemical attacks, harsh Islamic laws, or Turkish gendarmes burning their villages, as did their fellow Kurds in Iraq, Iran, or Turkey's Southeast. However, what they had achieved had come at a steep price. The usual one: hard work. And an unusual one: a decades-long denial of who they were.

Although my new friends were, in fact, closer to their heritage than many middle-class Kurds in western Turkey, none of the younger generation spoke Kurdish. It was outlawed while they were growing up, as was Kurdish music and all other forms of Kurdish cultural and political expression. Like most urban Kurds now in their twenties, thirties, and forties, they had gone through school pretending they were Turk. And although that pressure originally came from outside, it was also internalized. To be Kurdish back then was humiliating and worse, as everyone "knew" that the Kurds were stupid and dirty, they were ugly and dark, they were aggressive and primitive—animals, really.

"I hated being Kurdish growing up," one thirty-something said to me. "I tried not to think about it, and I never said I was Kurd—I didn't even want my mother to come to my school conferences, because she spoke only Kurdish and then my friends would know."

"There was a boy I liked very much, and finally one day I told him I was Kurd," said another. "But he didn't believe me. He said, 'Don't talk about yourself this way! It's like swearing! Kurds are ugly and stupid. You're too beautiful and smart to be Kurd.'"

"In high school, the teachers said many bad things about Kurds," said one young filmmaker. "You could protest, but if you did, you would get hurt. Or you could say nothing, but then you ended up with psychological problems—I know many who were affected in this way. So I tried to find a third way. I didn't volunteer I was Kurdish, but if someone asked, I admitted it."

A similar scenario played out in the business world, with men and women denying their origins in order to both survive and get ahead. "We never told anyone we were Kurdish," said an owner of a large factory. "We were ashamed, and we wouldn't have had any business partners or customers if we had."

Arriving in the cities in desperate economic straits, most of the earlier generation of Kurdish migrants gave little thought to asserting or savoring their ethnicity. They just wanted to get ahead and see their children do well. And if that meant that their children had to speak Turkish, and pass for Turk, so be it. Teaching their children the Kurdish ways and language made little sense, especially since it could get them all in trouble, and they themselves didn't know how to read or write Kurdish anyway. So the parents continued speaking together in Kurdish while their children spoke together in Turkish, each having only an imperfect knowledge of the other's language and world.

I couldn't even begin to imagine the effects of all this. I thought about the brutal mistreatment of African Americans and other minorities in the United States and its numerous, deep-rooted repercussions: psychological, sociological, economic. But here was a people not only subjected to a harsh prejudice and repression at every turn, but also forbidden to even admit *who they were*, indeed forced to pretend to be the "enemy"—though many Kurds have close Turkish friends, adding another complicating layer to the mix. Whole generations had been "passing" for what they were not, with all the psychological baggage that that entails.

Generations had also been irreparably distanced from one another, sometimes in more ways than one. With Europe then in dire need of manual labor, and travel between Turkey and Europe relatively easy, more than 1 million Kurds migrated to the continent between 1950 and 1980, some three hundred thousand heading to West Germany alone.

Among them had been the father of Sheri, the architect; he was also my hostess Elif's brother-in-law. He, his wife, and three oldest children had arrived in Istanbul in the late 1950s, to live in a three-room apartment with three other families. For nine years, he earned a meager wage serving tea in a bank; then he heard that the Ford Motor Company was hiring workers in Germany. He applied, was hired, and departed for the European country, where he'd bunked in dormitories together with masses of other Kurdish men for fifteen years, returning home to visit his family just one month a year.

As with Elif and Yakup, the strategy had worked, and worked well, though the emotional toll must have been tremendous. Now retired, Sheri's father had managed to provide his family with a comfortable house and educate all six of his children. In addition to Sheri, two of his daughters were teachers, another was studying to be a journalist, and one of his sons was a mechanical engineer. His second son's career was harder to categorize, as he'd just been released from jail after serving five years due to his involvement with an illegal socialist political party. Not that his case had gone to trial: in Turkey, political suspects are incarcerated before trial and, because the legal system is so slow, are often in jail for years before their cases are finally heard.

Sheri's journalist sister had also run into problems with the Turkish state. She worked for Freedom Radio, which had been shut down eight months earlier for broadcasting Kurdish songs that promoted separatism, or so the authorities said.

"Our parents ask us, Why are you doing this? Why don't you just get good jobs, keep quiet, and make money?" Sheri said. "But we cannot."

Like many Kurds in Turkey under forty, and many over forty as well, she and her siblings were through pretending to be something they were not. The civil war had changed all that.

FOR MANY NONPOLITICIZED Kurds living in western Turkey, the shift largely began in 1991, when President Turgut Özal convinced the parliament finally to lift the ban on the Kurdish language and folkloric music recordings. Almost alone among Turkish politicians, Özal recognized that unless the government softened some of its harsh Kurdish policies, the civil war then escalating in the Southeast—to reach its peak in 1992 to 1995— could literally tear Turkey apart. The language ban reversal caused an uproar among the parliamentarians—who passed it nonetheless—yet in reality it was a limited measure, as it permitted only private speech, already taking place in the street. The ban on Kurdish broadcasts, education, and modern song lyrics continued. But by repealing the ban, Turkey was at last admitting that it had a Kurdish population. This alone was cause for widespread celebration among Kurds.

However, at the same time, the parliament also instituted a harsh new antiterror law. The ruling allowed the authorities to imprison anyone suspected of "disseminating separatist propaganda" or otherwise threatening national security. It was used to sentence hundreds of writers, publishers, musicians, and other nonviolent "offenders" to long prison terms simply for disagreeing with the government's Kurdish policies. One of the most outrageous cases involved Ismail Beşikçi, a sociologist of Turkish ethnicity who had already spent years in prison prior to 1991 for merely defining the Kurds as a separate ethnic group. He was sentenced to one hundred-plus years under the new law for continuing to write about Kurds. Even Turkey's best-known novelist, Yaşar Kemal, who is part Kurdish, was prosecuted under the law and handed a twenty-month suspended sentence in 1996 for publishing a pro-Kurdish essay in a German magazine.

Nonetheless, as the 1990s progressed, other small positive changes in everyday Kurdish life in western Turkey occurred. The word *Kurd* started appearing in the newspapers—"I couldn't believe my eyes, I never thought I would see it," one young Istanbul Kurd said to me—and Kurdish music and other forms of cultural expression became more prevalent. Most of all, ordinary Kurds increasingly flaunted rather than hid their heritage—as indeed, more politicized Kurds had been doing since the 1980s, if not before; many Kurds had been working for more rights by peaceful political means long before the rise of the PKK.

By the time of my visit to Turkey in the fall of 2002, the political situation for the Kurds was continuing to ease. Turkey was working to improve its civil rights record, in the hopes of being admitted to the European Union. The previous August, the parliament had approved a reform package allowing the Kurds limited broadcast and education rights, while also outlawing the death penalty. The antiterror law was still in effect, but the accused were usually fined rather than imprisoned. However, the Turkish government still did not officially recognize the Kurds as a minority and continued to deny them many basic civil, cultural, and political rights. Brutal police tactics, inhumane prison conditions, heavy censorship, and the constant threat of arrest and torture continued.

THE MESOPOTAMIA CULTURAL CENTER, devoted to Kurdish culture, was housed in a humble building on the Istiklal, one of Istanbul's most famous streets. From early morning until well past midnight, the thoroughfare teemed with enthusiastic tourists, beefy businessmen, and boisterous young Turks.

One afternoon, Aydin and I climbed the worn stone steps that led to the center—my first visit of many, as it was the meeting place of choice for many Kurds. We entered a dark, smoky room crowded with small tables, around which dozens of serious, bright-eyed, mostly young men and women were gathered—drinking tea, smoking, and passionately discussing things Kurdish. To one side was a shop that sold Kurdish CDs and books, while in back and upstairs were theaters, a recording studio, workshops, and offices.

The Mesopotamia Cultural Center was established in 1991, just after the ban on the Kurdish language was lifted, and it had branches in about a half-dozen other cities. Yet the centers were constantly being closed down, accused of "disseminating separatist propaganda," with the main Istanbul branch itself in danger of being shuttered at the time of my visit, pending a court decision. In the meantime, however, business was proceeding as usual, as hundreds of Kurds congregated daily in one of the few large Kurdish centers allowed in Istanbul.

And this, I would discover, was one of the curious things about Turkey's Kurdistan. For all the country's harsh repression, there was a tremendous amount of activity going on. Though it might have taken the Kurds of Turkey longer to get there than the Kurds of Iraq and Iran, they had become a politically mobilized people. In Iran, the Kurds I met had seemed much more subdued, while the Iraqi Kurds were now in a different stage, with organization coming more from above than from below. In Turkey, grassroots workers were everywhere, toiling tirelessly for more Kurdish rights, often at great personal risk. Their passion reminded me of the middle-aged KDP and PUK officials I'd met in Iraqi Kurdistan, those who risked everything for the Kurdish struggle.

I was also in Turkey at an unusual time, having arrived just six weeks before the November 2002 parliamentary elections, which would bring to power the Justice and Development Party, a moderate Islamist party. The election would take the world by surprise, as it swept out the entrenched old guard and gave Turkey a one-party government for the first time in years.

That afternoon, Aydin and I met with the Mesopotamia's director, Zubeyir Perihan, and a half-dozen musicians, filmmakers, and actors. We gathered together in a creaky office beneath a poster of Sarya, an actress who died for the Kurdish cause.

The musicians described constant harassment—of being arrested following concerts, of being charged fifteen times the going rates at recording studios, and of having to choose the words to their songs with great care, lest they be accused of inciting separatism. Their hero was Şivan Perwer, the most famous of all Kurdish singers, who defied the Turkish state in the mid-1970s by singing Kurdish songs in a public stadium, causing the crowd to go wild. Thousands of police stormed the stadium, but Perwer's many fans helped him escape to Germany.

The actors spoke of being arrested after one 1997 performance and

imprisoned for forty days, though they had permission to stage the play, and
of a civil servant who lost his job for attending the performance. And a filmmaker, Sevaş Boyraz, told of making a short film with his colleagues called
The Land, about forced migration from the villages, and entering it in the
1999 Ankara film festival, where it was accepted. Until, that is, the president
of the festival saw the film and prevented its screening. Öcalan had just
been arrested; the atmosphere in Turkey was tense. The Ministry of
Culture then also banned the film, and it was still illegal in Turkey, though
it had been screened in thirty or forty international film festivals.

Sevaş' hero was Yilmaz Guney, the director of *Yol,* or *The Road,* a film
set in the Southeast that shared the Palme d'Or award at the 1982 Cannes
International Film Festival. Guney wrote the film's script while in prison
for a murder that he apparently did commit. He smuggled the screenplay
out and it was filmed under the direction of his collaborator, Serif Goran.
Yol was banned in Turkey until 1992 but, for various financial and technical
reasons, was not shown publically until 1999, when it was screened around
the country—an apparent sign of a loosening political climate.

One of the best-known artists challenging Turkey's censorship policies
at the time of my visit was musician and composer Sanar Yurdatapan. With
other artists, writers, and intellectuals, Yurdatapan—who is Turkish, not
Kurdish—had devised an unusual, and devious, campaign of producing a
constant stream of pamphlets (forty-two by late 2002) that deliberately
flouted Turkey's censorship laws. Each pamphlet was produced by dozens
of joint publishers, meaning that the Turkish judiciary had to initiate separate trial procedures against each and every publisher for each and every
booklet—a time-consuming process that resulted in much negative public-
ity for the Turkish authorities and, often, acquittal for the publishers,
though Yurdatapan had been imprisoned twice for brief periods. As
Yurdatapan later told me, chuckling, "Every year on January 23, our 'birthday,' we publish a pamphlet, cut a cake, and send pieces to the judges, to
the police. This will be the start of the end of military rule in Turkey."

ON A DESOLATE hill on the outskirts of Istanbul, in an area known as
Bagcilar, stretched a poor neighborhood cobbled together out of rough
cement apartment buildings, hovels built of clay and sticks, dirt-streaked
mosques, and litter-speckled empty lots in which boys played soccer. To

reach Bagcilar from the city center took two hours by multiple buses, a trip that some of its residents took daily, to work or to look for work.

Arriving in Bagcilar one morning, Aydin, our interpreter Sedef, and I met three women by prearrangement. We wound our way back through dirt streets, watched by skinny men in baggy pants and old women in dazzling dresses, white muslin covering their heads. The atmosphere was tense, the result, someone said later, of constant police surveillance and occasional raids. The neighborhood was home to many PKK families.

Climbing several flights of stairs, we entered an echoing, unlit apartment, where we were welcomed by more women, teenagers, and children, and ushered into a spartan living room. Around its edges sagged broken sofas, while on the walls hung black-and-white photographs of fathers and sons—thick hair brushed back, dark eyes shiny, frames draped with black. I could have been back in northern Iraq.

Our hosts were an extended family, originally from villages near Bitlis, in the heart of the Southeast, who had migrated to Istanbul in 1994, after their villages were burned. Most were middle-aged women, dressed in floral-patterned gowns and long vests similar to the ones I'd seen in Dohuk. The Kurds of Dohuk and those of southeastern Turkey share a similar dress, food, and traditions, as well as the Kermanji dialect. The women's lovely muslin head scarves edged with lace were an almost exclusively Turkish custom, however. Some of the head scarves covered only the head, while others wrapped around the head and the chin, turning faces into cameos.

We took seats, as teenage boys and girls bustled in with glasses of tea, and one boy sat down in the middle of the room with two teapots, at the ready for refills. Other children, women, and relatives crowded into the room. Faces blended into one another, as our hosts began to talk, their words translated first from Kurdish to Turkish by a young woman for Aydin and Sedef's benefit, and then from Turkish to English by Sedef for my benefit, an unwieldy process and constant reminder of the language divide between the Kurdish generations.

Fatma, a strong-featured woman dressed in blue and green, spoke first. "One night in 1994, the Turkish gendarmes knocked on our door, tied up my husband, took him to the river, and shot him," she said matter-of-factly. "He was the fifth and last man to be killed in our village that day. They took all the gold jewelry in the house and put a gun in my baby grandson's mouth. They said they would kill him, too—he would grow up to be PKK. But they let him live. They pushed everyone into the center of the village. Tanks surrounded us, and we thought we would be killed. Instead they burned our houses and fields, and took all our animals. We went to the next village, where people helped us, and later, we came to Istanbul. We came for work, but there is no work."

"Do you get any aid?" I asked.

Fatma laughed curtly. "No. The government does nothing, and we have no foreign aid organizations here."

I thought of the many Anfal victims I had met in Iraq. Fatma's story mirrored theirs. But the Iraqi Kurds had the whole world in their corner, while the Kurds of Turkey had no one.

Nazdar, an equally strong-featured woman, spoke next. "My husband was a *shaikh*, and one day, the Turkish police arrested him—they said he was helping the PKK," she said. "They tortured him, pounded nails into his feet. After four months, they let him go. They told him not to leave the house. But he went to the mosque—he thought he could go to the mosque—and the gendarmes came and killed him. . . . The next day, the police ordered me to sign a piece of paper. I can't read, but I was afraid and I signed. The paper said my husband's death was a suicide."

Nazdar's daughter then joined the PKK. Age seventeen, the girl left the house one afternoon to visit a neighbor and never returned. Nazdar hadn't heard from her in five years. "And now our village is burned. Where will she go if she comes home?"

Mesut, a slight young man, had been twelve years old when the family fled to Istanbul. As a child growing up in the village, he'd watched friends a few years older than he pressured into supporting the government, arrested after guns were planted in their homes, or kidnapped by the PKK to become guerrillas. In school, his teachers, who spoke only Turkish, constantly praised the legacy of Atatürk, and beat those children who didn't go along. "Happy is he who calls himself a Turk," the teachers made the students say, repeating the country's favorite maxim. The teachers also harassed students who wore Kurdish clothes, and encouraged children to spy on others and report those who spoke Kurdish.

Sedef and I exchanged glances. As an Azeri Turk, she was as far removed from and disturbed by the Kurdish stories as was I. Like most

Turks, she knew next to nothing about what had been happening in the Southeast over the past two decades. The war had not been covered by the Turkish press and, even now, was rarely written about in any depth.

"Do you want to go back to your villages?" I asked our hosts.

"Of course," they said. They hated city life, and they missed everything about their villages, from their orchards to their animals. But they could not go back unless they signed a piece of paper saying that their villages had been destroyed by the PKK, not the Turkish gendarmes, and this was something they would never do.

"How do you feel about Öcalan now?" I asked. I'd heard that the PKK leader's decision to declare a cease-fire following his arrest in 1999 was deeply resented by some of his followers, who felt they'd lost too much to settle. And other Kurds, or so I'd read, blamed the PKK as much as they did the Turkish state for all they had suffered—an impression that I would gradually learn was badly out-of-date.

There was an awkward pause and nervous glances toward the door. Not because of any ambivalence, but because Öcalan's name wasn't usually brought up so openly. It wasn't safe; people could always be listening. Even now, the police could drop by any time, to question what I was doing here.

"Apo is still very close to us," said one of our hosts.

"I would go to the mountains and fight with him myself, except my eyes are not so good," said a grandmother, and the room burst out with laughter.

ABDULLAH ÖCALAN, BETTER known to his followers as "Apo," or "uncle," was born in 1948 in the southern province of Urfa, a mixed Kurdish-Turkish area. The son of a peasant, raised in the Kurdish village of Ömerli, he grew up speaking Kurdish but forgot most of it as a teenager. "I think and plan completely in Turkish," he once said.

After attending a technical high school in Ankara on a state scholarship, Öcalan entered the prestigious Faculty of Political Sciences at Ankara University in 1971. Here, he mingled with other young, disaffected Kurds and Turks, with whom he organized a Maoist group whose goal was a socialist revolution in Turkey. Dropping out of college, he moved back south to Diyarbakir. In 1978, with eleven others, he held the first PKK congress. In stark contrast to the earlier tribal-based Kurdish movements of Turkey, Iraq, and Iran, this Kurdish party was a left-wing ideological group, based on Marxist-Leninist principles, whose targets included not just the state's forces but also the Kurdish *aghas* and landlords "representing the chauvinist class." The PKK declared that there could be only one solution to the Kurdish question—a completely independent Kurdish nation-state, to be obtained through whatever means necessary.

In September 1980, the Turkish military staged its third coup in twenty years. By then, Apo and his followers were gone, to Syria and the Bekaa Valley, where they set up boot camps for young volunteers. Focused as much on political indoctrination as on guerrilla warfare, the camps attracted Kurds of all socioeconomic classes and both sexes from all over the world, though the vast majority were poor and Turkish. The war tactics that recruits learned were brutal, while their own lives were held in light regard; Apo once told an American journalist that the PKK could "afford to lose" 70 percent of its recruits in battle within a year of completing their training. Öcalan himself took up residence in Damascus, driving to the camps in his Mercedes, surrounded by bodyguards.

The PKK launched its first successful cross-border operation in 1984, attacking two military outposts in Turkey's southeast. Other successful raids soon followed, often carried out by less than ten rebels at a time. They targeted the Turkish forces and its "accomplices"—i.e., Kurdish landlords, and, later, village guards, or civilian militias recruited from tribesmen loyal to their progovernment chieftains.

Meanwhile, the Turkish gendarmes harassed Kurdish villagers by the tens of thousands, subjecting many to torture and harsh prison terms. This often had the opposite of its intended effect, provoking many to join the rebels. The country had returned to civilian rule in 1983, but rather than address the Kurds' many legitimate grievances, a move that might have defused the escalating conflict early on, the new government met violence with violence, instituting a massive military buildup and counterinsurgency campaign in the Southeast. As early as 1986, forty-five thousand Turkish troops were stationed in Kurdistan, a figure that would grow to two hundred thousand by the early 1990s.

In 1988, the conflict entered a new, more tragic stage, as casualties began to mount. The PKK began burning Kurdish schools and assassinating Kurdish teachers and civil servants, accusing them of promulgating the government line. The guerrilla group was now also in the habit of arriving in villages and demanding food, shelter, and money. Villagers who did not cooperate were severely beaten and, in some cases, massacred. Some teenage boys and young men were kidnapped and forced to join the guerrillas.

The villagers found themselves in an untenable position. If they refused to cooperate with the PKK, they suffered brutal reprisals. But if they did cooperate, they suffered equally horrific consequences. Martial law was now in effect throughout the Southeast, and the Turkish military forces had sweeping powers. Without warning, gendarmes would suddenly descend upon Kurdish villages to beat, arrest, torture, and, in some incidences, slaughter innocent victims. Suspects could be retained for thirty days without trial; press reports regarding the state violence were banned; people could be deported out of the region at the governor-general's will.

The campaign to recruit village guards also escalated. Each community was expected to provide a platoon of men, who were armed and paid by the local gendarmes, to keep the PKK out of their village. Communities who refused to become village guards were viewed as PKK sympathizers and subject to yet more violence.

The Kurds became a deeply divided community, with some families supporting the PKK, others becoming village guards, and others still trying to remain neutral. But as the Turkish government did absolutely nothing to protect its ordinary Kurdish civilians — most nonliterate and living in numbing poverty, with a per capita income less than half the national average — and the military committed human rights abuse after human rights abuse, grassroots support for the PKK grew. Young women as well as men joined the movement, which eventually recruited over thirty thousand guerrillas between 1984 and 1999, and more Kurds began speaking out. The failure of the Turkish government to extend aid to the Iraqi Kurdish refugees crossing into Turkey post–Gulf War also inflamed many Kurds in Turkey, who ultimately extended that aid themselves. The PKK's image in the Southeast slowly began to change from that of a marginal outlaw group into one of a nationalist movement.

In 1991, the ban on the Kurdish language was lifted and the government made some gestures toward the Southeast, saying that it would "recognize the Kurdish reality." But at the same time, the infamous antiterror law was implemented and bloody attacks by both sides confounded any moves toward reconciliation. Popular demonstrations broke out. Villagers who refused to become village guards disappeared, assassinations took place on public streets in broad daylight, and the destruction of the villages dramatically escalated. Before 1992, about three hundred villages had been destroyed; between 1992 and 1995, that number grew to over three thousand, as hundreds of thousands of villagers saw their homes burned to the ground, their crops destroyed, and their animals confiscated before their eyes; some saw loved ones killed.

The brutal work of the PKK also continued. Between 1992 and 1995, the group is believed by Human Rights Watch to have committed at least 768 extra-judicial executions, including teachers, civil servants, and political opponents, along with some children and elderly men and women. Nonetheless, the Kurds' support for the PKK grew exponentially, as pride in Kurdish nationalism soared, even among the many millions who deplored the group's tactics and had no interest in Marxism or separatism. Whatever its faults, the PKK promised to deliver what had hitherto been only a dream: equal civil liberties and the right to call oneself "Kurd."

Inflaming the Kurds' escalating nationalism was the increasingly well-documented fact that the Kurdish countryside was being destroyed primarily by the Turkish military, not the PKK, as the government liked to claim. A 2002 Human Rights Watch report, typical of many similar reports released over the past decade, reads: "Most displaced [Kurds in Turkey] were driven from their homes by government gendarmes and by 'village guards'" in "an arbitrary and violent campaign marked by hundreds of 'disappearances' and summary executions."

The Turkish government tried to keep the Kurdish conflict under wraps as long as it could. Even to admit that there was a conflict, after all, meant that Turkey would have to acknowledge its Kurdish population. The first reports in the Western press started appearing in 1987, but coverage was limited. Most of the reports, often delivered through Turkish news agencies, simplistically dismissed the conflict as a "separatist" issue.

The West had little serious interest in scrutinizing what was going on inside Turkey. As one of the Middle East's few democracies, albeit an imperfect one, and the only Muslim member of NATO, Turkey was a major Western ally in a part of the world where allies were scarce. The country had recently played a vital role in the Gulf War, and was, ironically, providing the bases needed for Iraqi Kurdistan's air patrols.

In addition, the PKK had engendered little goodwill for Turkey's Kurds internationally. Not only had the guerrilla group slaughtered many hundreds of innocent civilians at home, but it had also committed terrorist acts in

Europe. Germany and France outlawed the PKK as a terrorist organization in 1993, and Germany had two international warrants out for Öcalan's arrest.

Turkey was also the third-largest recipient of U.S. military aid, though well behind Israel and Egypt. Between 1985 and 1996, the United States sold Turkey $8.7 billion worth of weapons, making commerce another powerful reason to turn a blind eye on its human rights abuses.

As journalist Kevin McKiernan describes in his award-winning documentary *Good Kurds, Bad Kurds*, it was as if the United States had divided the Kurds into two distinct groups. "Good Kurds" were Iraqi Kurds who opposed the common enemy Saddam Hussein and were the innocent victims of lethal chemical attacks, rendering them worthy of millions of dollars of international aid. "Bad Kurds" were the Kurds of Turkey who waged war against a stalwart American friend, the Turkish government, rendering them unworthy of any attention at all. No matter that a near-equal number of Kurdish villages had been destroyed by both the Turkish and the Iraqi militaries, or that Turkey's Kurds—who outnumber Iraqi Kurds three to one—had been suffering under extraordinary civil rights abuses for the past seventy years. And no matter that many of the U.S. weapons being supplied to Turkey were being used against its own civilian Kurdish population.

Also, little wonder that I found little support for the United States while traveling through Turkey's southeast. Many Kurds there had grown up in terror of the sound of U.S. Black Hawks, Hueys, and Cobras, the army helicopters used to land Turkish troops in their villages. And although the Turkish troops did not typically kill large numbers of civilians during the evacuations, the Turkish Air Force at times used F-16s and other fighter-bombers, supplied and equipped by the United States, to attack Kurdish villages.

For a brief moment in 1993, peace seemed within reach. Öcalan declared a cease-fire and was no longer advocating separatism, while President Turgut Özal made various overtures toward the Kurds. But Özal died suddenly of a heart attack before serious negotiations took place, and the fighting resumed, to endure almost without remittance until 1998, when Öcalan, still in Syria, offered the government a unilateral cease-fire. By then, the PKK was on the defensive. The villages in which its forces had once found food and shelter were destroyed and its guerrillas were increasingly inexperienced, dying before they learned how to fight.

Turkey responded to Öcalan's offer by amassing troops on Syria's border and demanding that he be expelled. Quietly, the PKK leader fled to Moscow, and then, in a dizzying tale of international intrigue, sought asylum in Italy, the Netherlands, and Greece, before landing in Nairobi, Kenya, on February 2, 1999, expecting to move permanently to another African nation a few days later. But on February 15, he was abducted on his way to the airport and handed over to waiting Turkish special forces, who flew him back to Turkey, blindfolded, handcuffed, and drugged. Who turned him in? The Kurds blamed the Greeks, under whose protection Öcalan had been traveling, while the Greeks blamed the Kenyans. The Kurds also blamed Israeli and U.S. intelligence, although both denied playing any "direct" role in the affair.

Word of Öcalan's arrest set off waves of protest across the Middle East and Europe, as tens of thousands of demonstrators flooded the streets, with some attacking Greek and Kenyan embassies, and others setting themselves on fire. Turkey incarcerated Öcalan on Imrali Island, holding him incommunicado for nine days and allowing him virtually no access to his lawyers. The state then rushed his case through the courts in a trial denounced as unfair by human rights groups at the time and by the European Court of Human Rights since. The PKK leader was found guilty of treason and sentenced to death. But in August 2002, Turkey, which has not executed anyone since 1984, outlawed the death penalty altogether, and Öcalan's sentence was commuted to life imprisonment without the possibility of parole.

The PKK officially disbanded in April 2002, to re-form as the Kurdish Freedom and Democracy Congress (KADEK). KADEK advocated the pursuit of Kurdish rights through democratic means until September 2003, when it called off its unilateral cease-fire, saying that the Turkish government had failed to respond with reciprocal goodwill. In November 2003, the Kurdish group renamed itself once again: it was now the People's Congress of Kurdistan (KONGRA-GEL).

WESTERN JOURNALISTS AND others who have met Öcalan invariably describe him as tyrannical, egomaniacal, ruthless, dogmatic, and not particularly bright. He has been compared to the Chilean dictator General Augusto Pinochet and the Cambodian butcher Pol Pot, and the PKK is often equated with Peru's vicious Shining Path. Independent human rights organizations have repeatedly denounced Öcalan, and his handiwork is abhorred by many Iraqi and Syrian Kurds, along with humanists everywhere.

Yet to most Kurds in Turkey, Öcalan is a hero. He gave them back their identity, pride, self-respect, and hope. For all the atrocities that the PKK committed, many Kurds reason, the Turkish state committed far more. Öcalan may have made mistakes, some Kurds admit, but he gave us a voice and he gave us power. In effect, Öcalan has become more a symbol than a flesh-and-blood man.

Some regard the Kurds' veneration of Öcalan as indicative of their inherently brutal and vicious nature. See how the old and cruel tribal ways have festered in the modern era, they say. Yet that veneration can be read in another way: as an indication of how desperate conditions in Turkey were prior to the civil war.

CHAPTER NINETEEN

Alone After Dark

〰〰〰

TO FLY FROM ISTANBUL TO DIYARBAKIR TAKES JUST OVER an hour, but to leave the storied Turkish port with its romantic mosques, rococo palaces, and cobalt blue waterways to enter the struggling, overpopulated Kurdish city with its hulking basalt walls and tight-lipped crowds is to replace tourist brochures with reality, commerce and glamour with the grim aftermath of war. On the surface, life in Diyarbakir has returned to normal, as traditional Kurds crowd bazaars and teahouses and modern Kurds congregate in cheery restaurants, offices, and the town's new bookstore. But just beneath the surface, wounds are gaping and raw.

Diyarbakir, capital of a province of the same name, sits near the western edge of Turkey's southeast, atop a plateau upon which Kurds herded giant flocks of sheep and cultivated small farms for centuries. During the time of the Ottomans, the province was home to the Gray People, a nomadic confederation of Kurdish and Turcoman tribes, numbering about seventy-five thousand, who wintered in Syria and summered farther north, while next door lived the Black People, an equally large nomadic group. The Diyarbakir province is one of twelve southeastern Turkish provinces that are generally designated as predominantly Kurdish, although the region, like northern Iraq, has long been home to Armenian, Assyrian, Chaldean, Yezidi, Arab, and Turkish communities as well.

Flanked by the Tigris River, which once froze solid enough in winter to support crossing herds of camels, Diyarbakir was founded around 1500 B.C.

The city's most recognizable landmark is its medieval wall, which once ringed the entire town and still stands in many parts. Probably first built by the Romans, the present walls date from the early Byzantines. At almost six kilometers long, the wall is said to be second in length only to the Great Wall of China.

Most of Diyarbakir today sprawls outside its historic walls, but within the old city still winds a maze of narrow, twisting streets and alleyways lined with ancient mosques, churches, and residences inhabited by some of the town's oldest and poorest families. Often gathered beneath one old city gate are dozens of grizzled men with pushcarts selling fruits and vegetables, while in the teahouses near the bazaar cluster hundreds more men in suits or baggy pants with knitted caps, sitting on low, four-legged stools as they sip, smoke, and talk.

Foremost among the city's many historical attractions are two mosques, the eleventh-century Ulu Camii, built around a lonesome rectangular plaza, and the sixteenth-century Nebi Camii, sporting the alternating black-and-white stone banding that is characteristic of old Diyarbakir. House museums with lovely courtyards are open to the public, while other historic sites are undergoing a brisk sprucing-up as the city eagerly, wistfully, awaits what it hopes will be the start of a more prosperous era, one filled with guidebook-toting tourists, rather than arms-bearing "special forces."

SHORTLY AFTER MY arrival in Diyarbakir, I called on Suzan Samanci, a Kurdish novelist. A blond woman with wide cheekbones, round cheeks, observant eyes, and a ready smile, Suzan was the author of four books and wrote a column for the pro-Kurdish newspaper, *Yeniden Özgür Gündem,* or "New Free Agenda." Divorced, she lived with her two school-age daughters in a spacious modern apartment in a new section of the city. Suzan spoke no English, but we instantly fell into a writers' conversation about books and publishing, communicating through the help of her fourteen-year-old daughter, an aspiring filmmaker.

The daughter of civil servants, Suzan finished her first novel in 1990 and, with no connections in the literary world, published the book herself, through a poor-quality publishing house. Despite this, the book—which dealt with the problems of women in the Southeast—had been widely discussed, and her subsequent novels were published by first-rate Turkish houses. Her books had been translated into German, Italian, Spanish, and Kurdish, and one of her short stories had appeared in an English collection of Turkey's writers published by PEN International. She had won Turkish literary awards and was regularly invited to writers' conferences in Europe.

Like my friends in Istanbul, however, Suzan's success had come at a high price. In her case, that price had been estrangement, both from her former husband and the general Kurdish community. "Many in our society disapprove of what I do," she said, as she served me *kadayif*, a delicious Diyarbakir pastry made with walnuts and pistachios. "They think I should just sit quietly at home, have children, entertain guests. My neighbors gossip about me, and I have few people I can talk to about books." She usually spent her mornings writing, her afternoons reading, and her evenings with her children.

Although Suzan had never been imprisoned because of her writings, she had been arrested and beaten in 1991 for taking part in an antigovernment demonstration. She had also been tried and fined in State Security Court for having the audacity to say in public that no one rebels without a reason.

SUZAN AND SEVERAL of her English-speaking friends, who dropped by during my subsequent visits, filled me in on Diyarbakir's recent history. As the unofficial capital of Turkey's Kurdistan, the city has long been known for its rebellious politics, and after the 1980 military coup, suffered a disproportionately harsh crackdown on civil rights. However, Diyarbakir's darkest modern period really began only with the murder of Vedat Aydin in July 1991. A popular high school teacher and politician, who'd been jailed for ten weeks in 1990 for giving a speech in Kurdish at a Human Rights Association meeting, Aydin was taken from his home one evening by three men professing to be plainclothes policemen. Three days later, his body was found by a roadside, the back of his head punctured, his legs broken, and bullets lodged in his chest.

Aydin was the fourth human rights activist attacked by unknown assailants in the Southeast within a three-week period. Unexpectedly, his funeral attracted an outpouring of over twenty thousand Kurds. The event turned into an enormous pro-Kurdish demonstration, with the coffin draped in the red-yellow-and-green Kurdish flag and many shouting pro-

PKK slogans. Young Kurds started throwing stones at the barricades set up by Turkish security. Masked special forces returned the overture by shooting indiscriminately into the crowd, killing six people and wounding about a hundred others.

"The masked teams shot many people," Suzan said. "And every day afterward, people were taken into custody. They never came back. Many journalists disappeared, and, in 1993, the chairman of the Human Rights Association, Metin Can, and a doctor, Hasan Kaya, were killed. Their bodies were found under a bridge.

"Many intellectuals, teachers, and journalists were assassinated. Assassins killed on the streets in daylight, or they raided at night at two A.M. Every day, maybe eight people were killed on the Diyarbakir streets—and more in Batman, maybe ten in Batman.

"There were special forces on every corner. The forces said, Give us information, and we will give you a good job. But we pretended we were blind and deaf. No one went out on the streets unless he had to. We went to work or school and back, no more. Parents asked their children to look out to see who was on the street before they went to work. Women waited at home, and if their husbands or children were even five minutes late, they became very afraid. This went on for years, until the end of 1995. And even today, when we hear a car brake suddenly or hear footsteps behind us, we become afraid.

"But now, because of the war, we are strong. War makes of many people, one people. The war woke us up, we learned lots of things. Now villagers want to be doctors and lawyers, we want our own language."

ON A QUIET, rubble-filled street not far from the old city walls stood the offices of the Human Rights Association (HRA). Headquartered in Ankara, HRA has been publicizing and fighting against human rights abuses in Turkey since 1986. Independent and member supported, the organization has weathered the assassinations of fourteen members, numerous office bombings, and constant threats, as it has challenged the state on many issues. HRA publishes monthly reports on human rights violations, and has about fourteen thousand members and thirty-four branch offices.

Arriving at the HRA offices early one morning, I met Selahattin Demirtaş, a soft-spoken lawyer and chairman of the association's Diyarbakir branch. HRA took down the clients' testimonies and tried to help them seek justice through the courts, Demirtaş explained. However, that was often a near-futile battle, as the Turkish state had immense power, especially in the Diyarbakir and Sirwan provinces, where Emergency Rule was then still in effect. Implemented in the Southeast in 1987, Emergency Rule gave the state the right to hold suspects incommunicado for thirty days and took away the right to appeal, along with other strictures. Emergency Rule had been lifted elsewhere in the Southeast and would be lifted in Diyarbakir and Sirwan the month after I left, but even so, its effects were still heavily lingering everywhere. "There is no difference between before and after Emergency Rule—nothing has changed," a group of human rights lawyers later told me in Batman, where the law had been lifted, though, tellingly, none of the lawyers could remember exactly when.

Many laws in Turkey worked against the individual. Lawyers could not speak with their imprisoned clients alone, for example—a guard had to be listening—or remain with their clients during prosecutors' examinations in the State Security Courts. But HRA could record what they heard and saw, release press reports, keep international human rights organizations informed, and take cases to the European Court of Human Rights.

The Diyarkabir branch of HRA had recorded fifty-three types of human rights violations over the past fourteen years. The worst types, including assassinations, disappearances, and the destruction of villages, had occurred primarily during the civil war, but the office still received occasional reports of burned homes or murders by unknown assailants. Torture by the police and gendarmes, though not as rampant as before, was still systemic, and, of course, there was no freedom of expression.

However, one of HRA's most urgent current problems had arisen only since the end of the war. With the cessation of hostilities, the hundreds of thousands of displaced villagers—officially only 380,000, but more realistically, at least 1 million—naturally wanted to go home. But to return to their homes, the villagers first had to receive permission from provincial governors, permission often denied for "security" reasons. When it was granted, it was usually done so only after the villagers signed a form relinquishing all rights to compensation. Many also required the villagers to tick a box for their reason for migration, with alternatives ranging from "employment" to "health" to PKK-instigated "terror"—no box for "gendarmes."

Complicating the problem were the village guards, who had taken over many of the evacuated villages and fields. There were now as many as ninety thousand village guards controlling much of the countryside and preventing villagers from returning. Over the past year, the HRA offices had been receiving frequent reports of returning villagers badly beaten and in some cases killed by the village guards. An October 2002 Human Rights Watch report stated: "Villagers are extremely wary of heading back into an unstable countryside where their former neighbors, sometimes from rival tribal groups, are paid and licensed by the government to bear arms."

"The government says that fifty-one thousand people have returned to their villages, but this is not true," Demirtaş said. "Only a very few have returned. But even if it was true, fifty-one thousand is a very small number" compared to the displaced hundreds of thousands.

Unable to return to their homes, villagers continued to live crowded together in abominable conditions, usually on the outskirts of large cities, as I had witnessed in Istanbul. Diyarbakir's population had swollen from about three hundred thousand to over 1 million in the past decade. Throughout Turkey, the refugees were receiving almost no relief from the government or foreign aid organizations, and went largely without adequate nutrition, housing, health care, or schooling for their children, most of whom were growing up nonliterate, like their parents. Unemployment was rampant, as was depression.

Also escalating in the last year was the problem regarding Kurdish names. Between January and September of 2002, HRA-Diyarbakir had recorded thirty-nine instances of families wanting to give Kurdish names to their children, only to have their requests turned down by the birth registrar's office. Parents were told that a new rule was in effect and such names were not in line with Turkey's culture and traditions.

I thought of Turkey's August 2002 decision to allow limited Kurdish broadcasting and education rights. Much had been made of that ruling in the press, but here in the hinterlands, a more basic right was being newly curtailed. It was as if the state was giving the Kurds a signal not to make too much of the new reforms.

Demirtaş walked me down the hall to meet one of his colleagues, Muharrem Erbey, a writer and culture buff as well as a lawyer. As a boy growing up in Diyarbakir province in the 1960s, Erbey had heard many itinerant troubadours, or *dengbej*, he told me. They had often stopped by his family's home. But now, tragically, most were gone. "During the war years, we couldn't pay attention to art," he said. "We had to fight to survive, and day by day, we lost our culture. Now people say it is a 'luxury' to be interested in culture. But what is the Kurdish identity without culture?"

Not that the *dengbej* tradition had completely died out. A few of the old masters still lived, and an arts-and-culture festival featuring *dengbej* had been held in Diyarbakir the previous year. Yet the only traditional Kurdish art form that had truly flourished in the last decade was dancing. The PKK guerrillas had danced in the mountains before and after raids, and when honoring fallen comrades.

A FEW DAYS LATER, I met a third Diyarbakir lawyer, Sezgin Tanrikulu, a cofounder of the Diyarbakir branch of HRA and the recipient of a Robert F. Kennedy Human Rights Award. He had received that award mostly for simply staying alive and staying put, he told me with a curt laugh. Six of his lawyer friends had been killed between 1990 and 1995, "for nothing else than defending human rights," he said. He himself had been indicted several times for his activities as a so-called "terrorist lawyer." During the height of the civil war, even communicating with an international human rights group had been considered evidence of terrorist support.

A strikingly handsome man with thick dark hair, a mustache, and a decisive manner, Tanrikulu was especially known for taking cases to the European Court of Human Rights. He had been one of the first Kurdish lawyers to do so and had written a book to help guide colleagues through the process—an arduous one, not least of all because the statute of limitations on many of the crimes was running out. Only since the end of the civil war had most Kurds been able to speak out about the atrocities committed against them years earlier. And even when the Kurds presented and won their petitions against the state security forces, as they had in over forty judgments against Turkey issued by the European Court between 1996 and 2002, it rarely made much difference. "Every time we win a case, Turkey apologizes and says it will change, people will be punished, but there is no change," Tanrikulu said. "No one is punished, and the laws remain the same."

A. CELIL KAYA was a buoyant law student with a dimpled smile. Usually dressed in blue jeans, sneakers, a T-shirt, and jean jacket, he spoke excellent English, Turkish, and Kurdish—the latter not a small point, as most educated young people in Diyarbakir, despite its virtually all-Kurdish population, did not speak Kurdish. As in Istanbul, it had been drilled out of them in the schools.

Celil (pronounced je-leel) lived with two sisters in a high-rise apartment on the edge of the city, while their parents lived in another apartment nearby—an unusual arrangement in Kurdistan, where parents usually liked to keep a closer eye on their children, especially unmarried daughters. Celil's father was a shopkeeper, while one of his sisters was a high school teacher, and another, a recent college graduate with a degree in folklore. Like Aydin in Istanbul, the siblings lived surrounded by Kurdish-language books and music, and represented the new generation, celebrating rather than hiding their ethnicity.

Before meeting Celil, I had been struggling to find my way around Diyarbakir. Few people in the city, including the HRA lawyers, spoke any English. Even fewer people would speak English when I traveled outside Diyarbakir, I was told. Many Kurds in Turkey were nonliterate; English was not taught regularly in the schools, as it was in Iraq, and, of course, my beginner's Persian did me no good here.

I therefore hired Celil as my translator and guide. It was the first time I had worked with a full-time translator/guide, and I was loath to give up the more serendipitous experience that traveling alone provides. Yet to penetrate the Southeast to any depth on my own would have been very difficult, especially since I had less than three more weeks to spend in the region.

On our first afternoon together, Celil took me up on the city's ancient walls, to view the surrounding Mesopotamian plain, a green-and-brown tabletop with the Tigris River running through it. Pointing to the far-off ruins of the Pira Deh, or Ten Door, Bridge, Celil sang a Kurdish folksong about two lovers, one a poor Muslim boy, the other the daughter of an Assyrian priest, who plan a secret rendezvous under the Pira Deh. "Under the bridge, where it is very black, Suzan come look for me," Celil sang, confirming to me that I had indeed hired the right guide.

While on the city walls, Celil gave me a brief history of Turkey's Kurds. Some of his words still stick in my mind. "Thirteen million Kurds cannot be terrorists," he plainly said. Also, like virtually every other Kurd I met in Turkey, Celil was adamantly opposed to a U.S. attack on Iraq.

From the city walls, we traveled on to what had already become my most frequent stop in Diyarbakir—a neighborhood DEHAP, or Democratic People's Party, campaign office. Turkey's parliamentary elections were heating up, and the pro-Kurdish DEHAP party, like all parties in Turkey, had opened up numerous temporary offices all over the country in order to further its campaign. Everywhere I traveled, I passed through streets overhung with thousands of flapping triangular flags, imprinted with party logos, while on sidewalks fronting party offices sat dozens or sometimes hundreds of people on four-legged stools with woven tops, passionately arguing politics and drinking tea.

For the Kurds, it was all a heady and novel experience. Up until recently, they had not been legally allowed to congregate in large numbers. Even more important, for the first time in decades, many Kurds felt that the elections had a shot to be fair.

DEHAP was a new party, formed by former members of an earlier pro-Kurdish party, HADEP, or People's Democracy Party, together with two small, non-Kurdish parties, because Kurds were worried that HADEP might be banned from the elections on charges of acting as the PKK's political wing. More than one Kurd had told me that DEHAP/HADEP was to the PKK what Sinn Féin was to the Irish Republican Army in Northern Ireland. But so far, the news had been good, and would remain good, as a later attempt by Turkey's chief prosecutor to disqualify DEHAP was turned down by the courts.

To earn seats in the Turkish parliament, a political party must win at least 10 percent of the vote. Most outside observers were not expecting DEHAP to receive more than 7 or 8 percent—in the end, it would receive only 6.2 percent—but any doubts of anything less than a resounding victory were seldom expressed in my presence.

"Welcome, welcome," the enthusiastic DEHAP campaigners said whenever I appeared in their doorway, sometimes with Celil, sometimes not, as someone rushed over with glasses of tea. The large, airy, temporary office was a popular meeting place, and always teeming with people. Traditional Kurdish music was usually playing over a loudspeaker, although once I was startled to hear the familiar voice of Joan Baez singing, "We shall overcome."

Despite my warm welcome at the DEHAP office, and others like it elsewhere in the Southeast, being there sometimes made me feel desperately ill at ease. As a stranger, I never had any idea to whom I was speaking, or, more to the point, what he or she had lived through. As we exchanged pleasantries and political opinions, I often felt pain creaking around me, pain that usually remained unrevealed yet delineated everything, making every word I uttered seem beside the point.

I had arrived in Turkey's Kurdistan at an excellent time, the DEHAP campaigners told me. Not just because of the elections themselves, but also because, with all the activity, I would be less likely to be harassed by the Turkish authorities. The elections had thrown everything out of kilter, with no one knowing who would be in power next, and so the police and gendarmes weren't paying quite as much attention as usual to life on the street. The authorities might also be mistaking me for a pre-election observer, as other real election observers would be arriving within a few weeks, though I saw no other foreigners while in Diyarbakir.

The campaigners' words eased some of my worries. I hadn't been sure how the authorities would react to my presence in the region. Up until about two years earlier, foreign journalists had been banned from the Southeast, and one English woman I heard of, a teacher previously living in Diyarbakir, was thrown out about nine months earlier simply for expressing too much interest in Kurdish affairs. Before leaving for Turkey, I was advised by Kurdish Americans to keep as low a profile as possible and to try to pass myself off as a tourist. I wasn't especially concerned about my safety—as an American, the worst that would probably happen to me was deportation. Even so, I didn't want to leave Turkey before I was good and ready.

Despite my good timing, however, there was still a significant chance that I was attracting unwanted attention, as Celil frequently warned. He often spoke of how I should be prepared to be taken "under custody" and advised me to e-mail my notes home whenever I could, just in case. Won't it be worse for you if we are stopped? I asked one day. He shrugged. As a Kurd, he was used to being harassed. Besides, he grinned, he would disavow any knowledge of my activities should I be hauled away; he was just an innocent translator doing his job.

AS IT TURNED OUT, Celil and I were under surveillance only once that I knew of, and then only in a desultory fashion, during a visit to a shantytown on the outskirts of Diyarbakir. We had arrived from the downtown by bus, and met our guides at another temporary DEHAP office, from which we plunged into a dispirited hillside neighborhood, built of cement shacks overshadowed with a web of electricity wires.

We visited several different families, including one from Nadera village, near the town of Kulp. Nadera had once been a large and prosperous place, with over twenty-five hundred inhabitants and thousands of acres of fertile farmland, the family said. But one day in 1993, the gendarmes surrounded the village, forced all the men to lie on the floor, and tied their hands behind their backs. Eleven men were taken away, never to be seen again, and the rest let go, but not before all their houses and fields were burned to the ground and their animals herded off.

The villagers had tried to stay together at first, moving en masse in three groups to Kulp, Diyarbakir, and Muş. Later, economic desperation forced them to disperse, so that they were now spread out over many different cities. "We barely even recognize our own cousins anymore," sighed the patriarch Mehmet, in a lament that struck me as characteristically Kurdish.

The Nadera family, numbering fourteen, now lived in a cement-block house with three small rooms, thin rugs, television, and dozens of boxes and bags piled up in the corners. Mehmet and his sons had only intermittent work, while the older children collected iron to help earn money and the women stayed home. Life in the city was especially hard on the women, everyone agreed, because there was no place for them to go. The men could at least leave the house to look for work or socialize in the teahouses.

"What was your village like?" I asked the family, and for the first time, I saw light in their eyes.

"It was a beautiful place, a mountain place, with lots of trees, nuts, fruits, and a river," they said, all speaking at once. "You can't even imagine the paradise! We had thirty *donums** and one hundred sheep, and some of our neighbors had had much, much more. We grew tobacco and wheat, and fruit and nuts. And we never knew cancer or diabetes, like we do now in the city. . . ."

On our way back to the DEHAP office, we passed a half-dozen beaming women who flashed us the "V" for victory sign, apropos of the upcoming

---

* One *donum* = 0.618 acre or 2,500 square feet.

election. The women wore their finest dresses, rich with vibrant color, as they were returning from a DEHAP celebration, and on their foreheads were small, blue tattoos, most of a geometric design. Tattoos were still prevalent in many parts of rural Kurdistan and were made with ash and a new mother's milk, Celil said.

Only when we neared the DEHAP office did we see the unmarked white car—characteristic of the plainclothes police—across the street, two burly men inside. I still would not have noticed them if the conversation around me hadn't abruptly stopped.

"Hide your notebook," Celil said. As I did so, the car backed up, so as to be partially hidden behind an obstruction.

Returning from a DEHAP celebration

"Are they here for us, or DEHAP?" I asked.

"Us, DEHAP, both," he said. "It's best not to pay attention."

We walked to a nearby bus stop, along with about a dozen gaunt men, who came out of the DEHAP office to say good-bye. The men had greeted us warmly when we'd first arrived and were now solemnly shaking my hand one by one, or placing their hands over their eyes, and saying *"Ser chaow,"* the Kurdish expression that means "on my eyes," or rather, "at your service."

It was in the grassy lot across from the bus stop that Musa Anter's body had been found one day in September 1992, the men told me. A foremost Kurdish journalist, author, and intellectual, and outspoken proponent of Kurdish rights, seventy-four-year-old Anter had been lured into the area by a young man who feigned interest in renting one of his fields. The Turkish authorities blamed the murder on Islamist extremists, but made virtually no attempt to solve the crime, with Prime Minister Suleyman Demirel remarking shortly thereafter, following other similar mysterious assassinations, "Those killed were not real journalists. They were militants . . . they kill each other."

By the time the minibus arrived, the white car was gone, and we didn't see it again, although I kept a close eye out. Just another day in Kurdistan, Celil said, shrugging.

IN THE CENTER of old Diyarbakir reigned three historic churches, one Chaldean, one Assyrian, and one Armenian. At the Chaldean sanctuary, a caretaker gave me a long and informative tour of the ornate building, just as if we were in the middle of peaceful, tourist-filled Paris or Rome. At the Assyrian church, a surly custodian reluctantly roused himself to show me an intimate, third-century chapel. And at the Armenian site, an arthritic old man with a curly white mustache shook himself out of a catnap to unlock a gate opening into an enormous ruined cathedral, filled with rows upon rows of gaunt black pillars and arches, reaching toward the open sky.

Of Diyarbakir's once-thriving Christian communities, only about thirty Chaldean families, fifteen Assyrian families, and ten or twelve Armenians in total were left. All three groups had been decimated by the Turks' campaigns against the Christians, often carried out with the help of the Kurds.

For centuries, Kurds and Christians, and especially Armenians, had shared the Anatolia plateau, often relatively peaceably so, despite tension and sporadic hostility between them. But by the late 1800s, the Kurdish tribes were exploiting and sometimes terrorizing the minority Christians, and in 1894 to 1896, the Ottomans ordered the Hamidiye, militias composed of Kurdish tribesmen, to repress an Armenian rebellion against taxation. The Hamidiye did so, and then extended their raids to other Armenian villages, to massacre at least a thousand civilians.

By far the worst massacres occurred during World War I, however, when the Ottomans suddenly ordered the evacuation of the Armenians from Anatolia, out of fear that they would side with the Russians or try to establish their own independent state. An estimated 1.5 million Armenians were then either massacred outright by the Turks, with the help of Kurdish tribesmen, or else died during brutal enforced marches east to the Caucasus. Many terrified civilians also fled south into what would become Iraq and Syria, as the massacres grew to include all Christian groups and some Kurds, who also lost tens of thousands in the campaign.

The Armenian massacres were a massive crime against humanity, the first major ethnic cleansing of the twentieth century. Yet the Republic of Turkey, though not responsible for the killings, continues to deny they ever happened, instead calling them part of a civil conflict instigated by rebel Armenians. The United States does its share to collude in the denial, as proposals in the U.S. Senate to observe an Armenian American day are repeatedly defeated by politicians and lobbyists reluctant to offend a critical major ally. In 2000, a resolution in the U.S. House of Representatives to officially label the massacres "genocide" was tabled.

IN THE CENTER of new Diyarbakir hummed the creaky, third-floor headquarters of the women's branch of DEHAP, thronging with so many people that Celil and I could barely get through the door when we arrived one afternoon. I had visited other women's centers in Istanbul, and would visit more elsewhere in the Southeast, yet every time, I was astonished anew by the enormous number of involved Kurdish women in Turkey—far more than in either Iraq or Iran. Most of the women were under twenty-five if not under twenty, and invariably dressed in pants or jeans, with no makeup and with simple hairstyles.

Much of the intense activity that I was witnessing was due to the upcoming parliamentary elections. Overall, too, the Turkish Republic was a more liberal society than its neighbors, with Istanbul women in particular living independent lifestyles much like women in the West. But the primary cause behind the Kurdish women's involvement—the license that had gotten them out of the house in the first place—was the PKK. Though most Kurdish women in Turkey still lived highly circumscribed lives, the rebel group had dramatically changed the image of women by welcoming them into its guerrilla army. Women guerrillas had their own camps and commanders—albeit few in the highest ranks—and Öcalan frequently spoke out in support of women's rights, often comparing the oppression of women in Kurdish society to the national oppression of the Kurds. "We want to put an end to the stereotype of the old-fashioned kind of Kurdish woman; it is vile," he once said.

Öcalan's feminist consciousness had been largely raised by his wife, Kesire Yildirim, whom he married in the late 1970s. Yildirim was an original member of the PKK's first Central Committee and a member of its Politiburo for a decade. She and Öcalan divorced in 1987, and she fled to Sweden, after apparently trying to replace him as Politburo chairman. Thereafter, Öcalan accused her of being a Turkish agent, but he did not backpedal on his championship of women's rights.

In the PKK army, guerrillas of both sexes were expected to put the Kurdish cause before all individual desires. Men and women were encouraged to postpone marriage and children until after the Kurdish revolution was won, and sexual activity and even fraternizing between the sexes was discouraged. These last strictures came out of the party's Marxist-Leninist philosophy, which denounced courtship and marriage as bourgeois concepts made hopelessly exploitative by capitalist societies, but also fell nicely in line with traditional Kurdish mores.

That afternoon, Celil and I made our way to the back of the women's headquarters. About two dozen young women crowded in a room, all making up flyers and posters. In its corner sat the only older woman among them, a small, toothless grandmother wearing a traditional blue dress with a knitted blue vest. Every time I looked at her, she broadly grinned and flashed me the victory sign. Later I learned that she had been arrested the year before and tortured for four days with electric shocks for taking part in a demonstration.

Seeing the roomful of young women reminded me of a mid-1990s description of a women's PKK camp that I'd read: "There are women everywhere; single files of them, in combat gear, carrying rifles. . . . The astonishing thing is how young they all are; most in their teens, the oldest in their late twenties, unsmiling, earnest, youthful faces, some with rimless glasses, their hair pushed up beneath berets and tied in ponytails."

Replace the combat gear and berets with pants and sweaters, the rifles with pens, and the description applied to the scene before me. Many Kurds in Turkey, like their Iraqi and Iranian counterparts, had been telling me that the time for fighting was over, the time for politicking begun, and here was one small proof of that happening—the estimated five thousand PKK fighters still in hiding in northern Iraq notwithstanding.

Emblematic of the changing status of women was Jiyan Giya, whom I met a few days later in Batman. Now a capable-looking, confident woman of about forty, with a few wisps of gray hair in her black ponytail, Jiyan had married her first cousin at age thirteen, as per her father's wishes, and had two children. As a young bride, she was filled with anger toward her father and fear of her husband, but she never questioned the arrangement. Then, sometime in her twenties, she discovered the PKK. A few of her younger friends joined as guerrillas, and she supported the movement from home until she was arrested in a raid in 1992. Her husband divorced her, and her children were raised by relatives. She remained imprisoned for ten years, during which time she was tortured, rarely saw her children, and went on four hunger strikes.

She was also sexually abused, she said—though she gave me no particulars. Sexual abuse is not uncommon in Turkish prisons; a 2003 Amnesty International report stated that women detainees were frequently stripped naked by male officers during questioning, often forced to undergo "virginity tests," and sometimes raped. Speaking out against such abuse was extremely difficult, as it seldom led to justice and often led to ostracism. As in Iraq, the concept of preserving one's "honor" prevailed.

Jiyan had been released only a few weeks before we met.

"How does it feel to be outside again?" I asked, marveling at her calm manner and stylish appearance.

"When I came out, I saw that everything has changed," she said. "I hardly know my children anymore, and every place has been destroyed. Of course, it's very good to be outside, but I also feel I have entered a bigger prison, especially when I see the conditions of women. I did not see the conditions of women so clearly before."

A FEW HOURS WEST of Diyarbakir were Batman and Hasankeyf, one a sanitized oil town reeking of death, the other a fairy-tale mountain retreat straight out of *Lord of the Rings*. Celil and I left Diyarbakir to visit both one morning, heading first to the magical town.

We drove across a dusty land, barren hills flanking either side. Animal carcasses lay by the road and the smell of petrol filled the air. Then we entered a shallow gorge and the wide, lazy Tigris River appeared, caves speckling the cliffs above. A wedding caravan flashed by, adorned with red, green, and yellow streamers. "Every wedding is like a small demonstration," Celil said with a grin.

Approaching Hasankeyf

The caves became more numerous and suddenly, there was Hasan-keyf—an entire town built into hundreds of caves honeycombed up a mountainside. On top soared a delicate, pointed minaret, while in the Tigris below hulked two flat-topped pillars that had once supported an enormous bridge.

One of the oldest settlements in Turkey, dating back at least five thousand years, Hasankeyf is overlaid with a mosaic of civilizations, including the Assyrians, Sumerians, and Romans. It was the Byzantines who first turned the natural fortress into a thriving town, augmenting its cave dwellings with stone castles and palaces. Later, Hasankeyf was ruled by a powerful Kurdish family, the last remnant of the Ayyubid dynasty, descended from Salah al-Din. The family's patriarchs minted their own coins and reigned over the surrounding countryside for centuries.

Celil and I had lunch at an inviting riverside restaurant at the base of Hasankeyf—each "table" a floating platform, covered with rugs and cushions. Around us flowed the mighty Tigris, which I had first crossed on my way into Iraqi Kurdistan many months before. Known as the Diçle in Kurdish, the Tigris is celebrated throughout northern Kurdistan. "Oh! Thou River. Let the river run, let the river run. . . . This is greatness," goes one folksong.

Celil and I ascended to the town via a staircase tunnel that burrowed up through the mountain to open into a cave on top. Walking out, we found ourselves surrounded by dozens more caves, most part of a giant outdoor museum, complete with teahouses and souvenir shops, though some caves were still occupied. At the crest of one hill were the ruins of the Grand Palace, said to once hold four hundred rooms, while at the crest of another were the ruins of the Great Mosque, originally built as a church. The place thronged with tourists, domestic and foreign.

Though it seems inconceivable, Hasankeyf is currently being threatened by the possible construction of the Ilisu Dam, a project that also promises to submerge about one hundred Kurdish villages and much farmland, displace thirty thousand villagers, and destroy dozens of archaeological sites. Plans for the dam were unveiled decades ago, but it is still in its planning stage, as it has elicited worldwide controversy. Some foreign governments that were once interested in funding the project have pulled out, thanks to the hard lobbying work of concerned activists.

The Ilisu Dam is part of Turkey's Southeast Anatolia Development Project, better known as GAP, itself highly controversial. An audacious, $30-billion plan to harness the Tigris and Euphrates Rivers for energy and irrigation purposes, GAP calls for the construction of twenty-two dams and nineteen hydroelectric plants, some of which have been built. Turkish politicians initially presented the project as one that would benefit the Kurds, by providing employment, but many experts believe that the opposite is the case, as most Kurds do not have the skills necessary for the jobs, and a total of over seventy thousand Kurds would be displaced by the project. In addition, GAP has elicited heated protest from Syria and Iraq, whose water supplies would be drastically cut by the dams. Water, some experts say, may become as valuable as oil in the Middle East in the decades to come and the cause of the region's next great wars.

CELIL AND I wandered the storybook town, stopping here for a glass of tea, there for pastry—much needed fortification, as it turned out, for Batman, where the horrors of recent life in Turkey's Kurdistan hit me especially hard.

In and of itself, the city wasn't especially bad to look at, though nondescript. Largely established over the past half century, after the discovery of oil in its nearby hills, Batman centered on a downtown built of wide thoroughfares lined with modern three- and four-story edifices. Banks and businessmen's hotels stood on many corners, along with restaurants and Internet cafés. The banality was deceiving.

Upon arriving in town, Celil and I headed straight to the branch offices of *Yeniden Özgür Gündem,* the pro-Kurdish newspaper, to look up Celil's friend, journalist Nihat Çelik. Gendarmes were lounging in a Jeep in front of the building, keeping a hostile eye on a DEHAP campaign office next door, outside of which an especially large number of men were assembled on the usual four-legged stools, sipping tea. Above them flapped the small, triangular campaign flags. No women were in sight.

Several of the men came up to welcome me. When they heard where I was from, they asked me what the American people—not the U.S. government—thought about the suffering of Turkey's Kurds.

Perhaps I was too honest.

"How can the American people not know about our suffering?" they cried. "We have been shouting for the last twenty years. Why hasn't America heard us?"

The hallway leading into the newspaper's office was lined with over a dozen black-and-white photographs. I had been in Kurdistan long enough to know what that meant.

The paper had started life in 1992, the year after the ban on the Kurdish language was lifted, though it was written in Turkish, in order to reach a wider audience. Initially known as simply *Özgür Gündem,* it was closed down in 1993, to be followed in succession by a long line of other publications, each bearing a different name, but all essentially the same paper.

From the beginning, the newspaper was dedicated to publicizing the human rights abuses committed by the Turkish security forces in the Southeast. Sometimes called the "PKK daily" by its critics, it had at times run a column penned under a false name by Öcalan—politics for which it paid a heavy price. The newspaper offices were bombed, its papers confiscated, and its employees arrested, tortured, and killed, as they were accused of supporting the PKK. By April 1994, seventeen of the paper's journalists and distributors had been assassinated or disappeared.

Five of the murdered journalists, including one woman, were from Batman, and their ghosts cast a pall over the newspaper's worn offices as Nihat, Celil, and I sipped tea and talked. Since the end of the civil war, the paper had broadened its coverage to include more stories on culture and social issues, but its dedication to covering human rights abuses continued unabated. Threats to the paper had dwindled and no journalists had been killed by unknown assailants since the mid-1990s. However, the *Özgür Gündem* staff still navigated the city's streets with great caution, never venturing out into empty areas or after dark alone.

They weren't the only ones. During the civil war, the Batman area had been the assassination capital of the Southeast, with over 180 civilians killed in 1992 to 1993 alone. The assassins had often been men in masks who killed in broad daylight, either riddling their victims with bullets or approaching from behind, to shoot once in the back of the head. Among the most famous of their victims had been Mehmet Sincar, a Kurdish politician gunned down with a fellow politico one Saturday afternoon in 1993 while walking through the Batman bazaar. The police escort that was with the men mysteriously disappeared just moments before the shootings, convincing the Kurds that the state was behind the killings, while the state blamed Hezbollah.

Unrelated to the far-better-known Shiite group of the same name based in Lebanon, Hezbollah was a small Islamist group headquartered in the Batman area in the early to mid 1990s. An Islamic revival was then taking place in the region, with local religious leaders arguing that the PKK and traditional politics had failed, and radical Islam was the answer. Yet curiously enough, of the approximately five hundred journalists, human rights activists, and professionals indeed believed to have been murdered by Hezbollah by late 1993, all were actively pro-Kurdish, and none of their killers have ever been found. Many Kurds and outside observers believe that Hezbollah and the Turkish state were working together, certainly at the local level and possibly nationally as well.

The killings abruptly stopped in 1995. "It was as if a rope had been cut," one Batman resident said. "For years, there were six, seven killings a day, and then, suddenly, there were none. If it had been a true ideological movement, the killings would have stopped more gradually."

EYE DOCTOR AND writer Shakir Kakaliçoölu was an unusual man. Of Turkish ethnicity, he had moved to Batman from the Black Sea region twelve years before, because he wanted to live "where there were troubles" and he could do some good. I knew that he had spent time in prison—due, I assumed, to his writings. I was wrong: Kakaliçoölu had been imprisoned because of his medical work. Accused of treating PKK guerrillas, he was first jailed in 1995 and held seven months, during which time he was "systematically tortured," he said. In the following three years, he was arrested twenty more times and sometimes imprisoned. Finally, things got so bad that he fled to Germany in 1998 for three years, returning after the war ended. He was still followed by the civilian police and his phone was tapped, but as he said: "Medicine doesn't care if one man is Kurd, another Turk, one guerrilla, another gendarme. It is a doctor's job to help all people."

Artist Fevzi Bilge was another unusual man. One of the founders of the Mesopotamia Cultural Center in Istanbul, he had lived most of his life in Turkey's western cities, only moving to Batman three years before. A teacher as well as an artist, he had come because he saw "great potential for art in Batman," and was now giving art classes. "The people here are hungry for art," he said, after showing me his rich, deeply colored paintings. "They have suffered much and have much buried inside. I want to help them express themselves. For many years, I lived in Istanbul and improved only myself. But now I am finished with that."

Abdul Rahman G. was extraordinary as well, though for considerably different reasons. Originally from Dikbayir village outside Batman, Abdul Rahman had been pressured to become a village guard. When he refused, he was forced to leave his village by his brothers who had become guards. Resettling in Batman, he became a member of the pro-Kurdish political party, then known as HEP, and was arrested seventeen times. In 1993 to

1995, the police also raided his home three times, and once he, his wife, and children were all arrested together, herded into one room, and ordered to take off all their clothes.

Then in 1997, Abdul Rahman was arrested again, imprisoned for three months, and tortured with electrical shocks. And ever since, he had been impotent. "They kept threatening to take away my sexuality, and then they did it," he said, squirming in his seat as he spoke and Celil, also squirming, translated. "I don't know how they did it, maybe they injected something?" He didn't know about these things—did I?

He had told his story to a human rights lawyer and now his case was before the European Court of Human Rights, he said—or hoped. Many of the villagers I spoke with told me that they had or were planning to take their cases to the European Court, with many, I suspected, having no real idea of what the process entails and no definite plans to apply. Yet the European Court represented a hope hung onto tightly, in much the same way that Iraqi Kurds held onto their idealized image of the United States.

"I never did anything wrong," Abdul Rahman concluded. "I was never a guerrilla and there are no guerrillas in my family. My only crime was refusing to be a village guard. And being Kurdish."

NIHAT, CELIL'S JOURNALIST friend, helped us find our way around Batman during our stay. Thirty years old, with a beard and glasses, dressed in jeans and a flak jacket, he was knowledgeable, compassionate, and deeply committed to both his profession and the Kurdish cause.

During our first evening in Batman, Nihat took Celil and me to a teahouse with a large garden, lit by sickly yellow lights, where we sat on four-legged stools, ordered multiple rounds of tea, and bought a bag of salted watermelon seeds from a passing vendor. I was the only woman in the place, as I was the only woman in almost all the teahouses and restaurants I entered in Batman. Most of the city's restaurants didn't even take women, and I saw virtually no women out after dark. Batman's ambience was far different from lively Diyarbakir, where I'd seen many women on the streets and some modern young couples eating out alone together, at least during the day near the university.

Batman's rigid sexual codes were due to the youth of the city and its huge influx of refugees in the wake of the war, Nihat said. At only fifty years old, Batman had developed no urban social structure to speak of, and so the arriving refugees had imprinted their traditional, patriarchal values on the city, rather than the other way around, as was usually the case with rural to urban migration. However, at the same time, Batman's lack of a social structure also meant that the arriving villagers had even less solid ground beneath them than did most war refugees. Which probably helped account for the city's extraordinarily high suicide rate, most committed by women.

Though no real data was available, suicide among women was up all over the Southeast, but especially in Batman. The reasons were many. Crowded into poverty-stricken shantytowns, many village women were profoundly alienated, unable to either enter into the new world in which they found themselves or leave their pasts behind. They couldn't relate to the television that some took so much pleasure in, or communicate with the Turkish-speaking officials in offices and citizens on the street. Their old neighbors—the ones they once shared ribald jokes with, swore in front of, traded gossip with—were gone, and their emotions and feelings went unexpressed. A rise in the suicide rate is also typical at the end of a conflict, one doctor told me, as the initial relief that one has survived subsides and repressed fears and depression come to the fore.

Kurdish women in Turkey usually committed suicide by hanging themselves or jumping from high structures; sometimes, they shot themselves. Though these last deaths were suspect. They could be honor killings, which were widespread in the Southeast, especially in the wake of dislocation and war. Some experts estimated that at least two hundred women and girls were killed by family members each year in Turkey, though those numbers, as in Iraq, were highly speculative. The murders were often committed by minors, forced to kill their sisters or cousins by their parents, as they would receive reduced prison sentences—a pattern that may now change, as Turkey, like Iraqi Kurdistan, passed reforms in June 2003 that did away with reduced prison terms for honor killings.

Turkey was a land split in two, and not just between its Turks and its Kurds, but between its modernity and its tradition, its democracy and its repression. Half of Turkey was firmly twenty-first century, the other half claustrophobically feudal. Turkey was a genuine democracy in some ways, a brutal military state in others. The civil war had brought out all the country's darker tendencies. Perhaps now, with peace, there was hope for change.

When Celil and I left Batman, Nihat walked us to the bus station, just a short stroll from the downtown. But instead of leaving us there and returning to the town on foot, he climbed onto the bus with us, to have the driver drop him off in front of his office. It was already ten P.M. To walk back alone after dark was too dangerous.

CHAPTER TWENTY

Not for Money

ꞏ ꞏ ꞏ ꞏ ꞏ

ACCORDING TO KURDISH LEGEND, ALEXANDER THE GREAT once had two horns growing out of his forehead. He could not get one hour's rest for the pain they caused him, and none of his physicians could cure him. One day, God appeared to him in a revelation and told him to travel into the Land of Darkness, to the Water of Life. Obeying, he passed the Sea of Dark and entered the province of Diyarbakir, where he drank from the Tigris. Its waters relieved his pain, though the horns remained. Continuing, he came upon the springs of today's Bitlis, located deep in the narrow Taurus Valley, and spent seven days drinking from their pure cold waters. On the seventh day, one of his horns fell off.

He summoned his treasurer, a man named Bedlis, and ordered him to erect an impregnable citadel on the cliff by the springs. The treasurer constructed a fortress with high walls upon which astrologers performed magical incantations. Returning from his conquests, Alexander approached the completed castle, but Bedlis forbade him entrance. Enraged, the Greek warrior laid siege. For forty days and forty nights, a fierce battle stormed, and on the forty-first day, a swarm of yellow bees the size of sparrows emerged from a cave at the base of the fortress and descended on Alexander's army. All fled in despair, including the commander. Whereupon, Bedlis put the keys of the castle in a jeweled pouch and with countless treasures and gifts went to Alexander, kneeling at his feet. He had done as his master had commanded, he said, and built an impregnable fortress that even the greatest of warriors could not conquer. Alexander forgave him and named the castle in his honor.

BITLIS WAS ORIGINALLY an Armenian town. But sometime in the twelfth century, Kurdish nomads took possession of the mountains surrounding it, and, in 1207, it fell to the Ayyubids. Four hundred years later, Bitlis rose to become a preeminent Ottoman principality, with the Turkish sultan relying heavily on the advice of a noble Bitlis statesman and scholar, Idris Bitlisi. It was Bitlisi who persuaded the sultan to offer the Kurdish princes semiautonomy in exchange for paying taxes and providing militias—a move that greatly aided the Ottomans in their battles against the Safavids. Later in the century, the town was home to another foremost Kurdish scholar, Sharaf Khan Bitlisi, who wrote the 1597 *Sharafnameh*, a history of the Kurdish tribes.

The famed Turkish traveler Evliya Çelebi spent months in the emirate in the mid-1600s. In his *Seyahatnameh*, he describes it as composed of several districts, including the fertile Muş plain, and controlled by an elite confederation of twenty-four tribes, united by a *mir*. Ruling over dozens of lesser tribes, who provided the principality with its fighting forces, the confederation's members were "not brave and warlike like the other Kurds, but sophisticates, men of learning and culture, with henna on their hands and beards and antimony on their eyes."

A center of commerce, craftsmanship, and learning, seventeenth-century Bitlis boasted 110 prayer niches and over twelve hundred shops, most dedicated to making weapons, weaving, and working leather. To one side rose the main citadel, which contained three hundred houses, while around it clustered seventeen city quarters, containing five thousand houses, seventy primary schools, twenty dervish lodges, nine caravanserais, seventy fountains, and at least seven palaces. Thousands more homes, summerhouses, orchards, and elaborate gardens—in which parties were held "day and night"—blanketed the surrounding hills.

As for the Bitlis people, they lived to be great ages, with men of "ruddy complexion and strong constitution" still hunting and riding horses when they were close to one hundred years old. Women were always well covered and kept strictly in the harem. "If they see a woman in the marketplace, they kill her," writes Çelebi.

CELIL AND I arrived in Bitlis, about 150 miles northeast of Diyarbakir, one cool, azure autumn day, climbing out of a sleek, air-conditioned bus and into a raggedy marketplace. Dilapidated fruit and vegetable stands lined dark cobblestone streets, while dirty snatches of streams emerged between litter-strewn alleyways and under footbridges. Hundreds of grizzled, unemployed men, many in knitted skullcaps, sat on four-legged stools crowded so closely together that knees, elbows, and shoulders bumped. Overhead, triangular campaign flags flapped. Bitlis's days of power and prosperity were long gone.

Shouldering our overnight bags, Celil and I wandered through a twelfth-century mosque and sixteenth-century caravanserai, both once celebrated by Çelebi, now dank and dour. We followed a footpath up to the ruins of the castle overlooking the city. From there, I could see that Bitlis had a beautiful setting, built into a narrow valley, with cliffs, mountains, and poplar groves all around. But its former romance had been lost.

Of the citadel, too, there was little left. Only the retaining walls and a few ramparts still stood, and I could not even begin to guess where once had stretched the castle's central square. There, Çelebi had once watched entertainers bewitch crowds with "magician's bowls, fire, bodily prowess, maces, bottles, cups, jugs, hoops, games of hazard, somersaults, shadow-figures, puppets, bowls, tightropes, monkeys, bears, asses, dogs, goats." Celil and I saw only two old men in baggy pants, no cummerbunds or turbans, sitting on their haunches, passing the time of day, and a younger, vaguely menacing loiterer.

Descending from the castle, we passed a rooftop upon which three middle-aged men sat, sipping tea. They called out to us. It was the first welcome we had received in Bitlis. Most of the town had barely seemed to notice us, and no one had made eye contact.

"We're leaving Bitlis," the men said, after we had shared a glass of tea. "There's no work here and too many villagers have moved in. When we were young, Bitlis had many fine families and was famous for its honey and tobacco. That was a tobacco factory." They pointed to a long white building on a hill across the valley. "But now, most of the old families have moved out. The factory has closed. And the villagers are too ignorant. They can't read or write. They vote for *shaikhs*. This is an insult for us! Bitlis was once famous for its learning!"

"*Shaikhs?*" I asked. I'd heard that the Bitlis area, along with Van to the east, Hakkari to the southeast, and Urfa to the southwest, was one of the most tribal regions in Turkey's Kurdistan, but this was the first I'd heard of *shaikhs*.

"Didn't you notice all these political parties?" the men said, pointing with disdain to the flapping campaign flags. "They're all controlled by *shaikhs*—all except DEHAP. The *shaikhs* are the cause of all our troubles, they are why we have not entered the industrial age."

Later, I learned that after the abolishment of the Kurdish emirates in the mid-1800s, Bitlis became a center for fanatic Naqshbandi Sufi *shaikhs*, where influence continued, albeit in a milder form. Before the late 1800s, Bitlis had been home to Kurds, Turks, Armenians, and other minorities, all living side by side. But as the old order fell apart, the *shaikhs'* fanatical preaching led to massacres of the region's minorities, while at the same time, giving rise to major Kurdish uprisings against their Ottoman overlords.

"What about the *aghas?*" I asked the three men. "Do they still have power?"

"Yes, of course—*aghas, shaikhs*, they're all the same," they said. "All they care about is politics and money."

Though I wasn't in the Southeast long enough to penetrate its tribal culture, I remembered the men's words often as I continued my travels. Because once outside Diyarbakir, especially in an election season, the close association between the Kurdish *aghas* and politicians was obvious—indeed, many Kurdish tribal leaders *were* politicians, with many living in Ankara, the center of Turkish government. Such an association also existed in Iraq, of course, and to a lesser extent in Iran, but it was more out in the open in Turkey, in part because it is a more democratic country, with its back-office machinations more visible, and in part because many parties—not just two, as in Iraq—were vying for the tribal vote. Which Kurdish *aghas* were bargaining with which political parties was speculated on in the Turkish press during my visit, as the tribes, many numbering in the tens of thousands, with many non-literate members, would vote largely as instructed by their leaders.

Historically, most Kurdish *aghas* have sided with the Turkish state during elections, voting for its rightist political parties, and against leftist Kurdish-Turkish parties—one of several complex reasons why DEHAP won only 6.2 percent in the 2002 parliamentary elections. Proponents of the status quo, the last thing most *aghas* want is any threat to their position, which has grown more powerful than ever since the mid-1980s, thanks to the village guard system. *Aghas* who provided the state with village guards were offered ample rewards, while also gaining armed control of the countryside—as in earlier, more unruly centuries, when the Kurds were known for their brigandry. Though nominally under the command of the Turkish military, village guards were in actuality controlled by no one, and free to act with impunity, attacking everyone from suspected guerrillas to rival tribal members.

Yet even without the village guards, the Kurdish tribes have been gaining rather than losing strength in Turkey since World War II, according to experts. In 1946, Turkey became a multiparty democracy based on a district system, meaning that the parties had to build grassroots support if they wanted to survive. In the Southeast, this meant winning over the Kurdish tribes. Politicians began offering *aghas* business contracts and other rewards in return for blocks of votes, and choosing tribal leaders as local candidates. Rival *aghas* joined, and continue to join, rival parties, often switching allegiances from election to election, depending on which party offered what. Traditional tribal interests and conflicts have become tightly entwined with modern politics.

FROM BITLIS, CELIL and I caught another spic-and-span bus, this one heading farther east, to Tatvan, on the shores of Lake Van. Built in the nineteenth century, Tatvan was the easternmost stop for trains arriving from Istanbul and Ankara, whose wares were loaded onto ferries to travel on to Van, a larger city farther east. During the civil war, the railroad also transported Turkish troops.

A long, skinny town, Tatvan wasn't much to look at, but Lake Van glittered like the world's largest sapphire, twisting and turning in the sun's lengthening rays as our bus pulled into town. One mile above sea level, Lake Van is the second-largest lake in the Middle East, covering 1,425 square miles. Snowcapped mountains flank its waters to the west, southeast, and north, while farther north soar the Greater and Lesser Mount Ararats.

Often bathed in an extraordinary silver-white light, the entire region was formed by volcanoes, with Lake Van created when huge lava flows blocked the area's western drainage. With no outlet, the lake's waters are brackish, home to only one fish, a kind of herring.

Celil and I checked into a cheap hotel, had a cappuccino in a modern café, and read our e-mails at an Internet center. Despite Tatvan's apparent isolation, it had all the modern conveniences. Then Cecil gave Nevzat Turgut a call on his cell phone. Nevzat was a well-known local business-man to whom we had an introduction.

Fifteen minutes later, a tall, balding man in a suit and tie arrived to take us to his home. He held his head at an awkward angle, due to a pain in his neck, caused by a misjudged dive he'd taken as a young man. He'd seen several doctors in Istanbul and tried physical therapy, but nothing helped; the pain always came back.

Nevzat had been arrested for periods in 1980, 1990, 1993, and 1995, he told us in good English soon after we arrived in his large but threadbare home, smelling of a kerosene heater and poverty. The reason for his arrests? Suspected separatist activities, of course. He'd been imprisoned in 1980 because of his involvement with a trade union, and in 1995, because of his work with a pro-Kurdish political party. But the 1990 and 1993 arrests had been the most unfair, coming about simply because he owned campsites from which German tourists were kidnapped by the PKK. "Because I was the owner, they said I also must be PKK," he said. "But why would I kidnap people from my own campsite?"

Nevzat was no longer in the campsite business, and he had leased out a small hotel he owned in order to serve as head of the Tatvan business asso-ciation. It was a tricky, often exasperating job that involved acting as liaison between local businessmen and the authorities. But despite Nevzat's many problems and difficult history, he hadn't given up his dreams and hopes for his people—not by a long shot. He planned to run for mayor, perhaps in the next election.

"If I were mayor," he said dreamily. "I would give animals to all the peo-ple and send them back to their villages. If I were mayor, I would build fac-tories for jobs and hotels on the lake and restaurants and ski resorts. I would put more fish in the lake so people could eat more protein, and bring in credit banks so people could start businesses. I would improve the schools and start a university. I would build an amusement park, if I were mayor . . ."

THE NEXT MORNING, Celil and I stopped by Tatvan's tourist office, equipped with an information officer and glossy brochures. Before the early 1990s, the Lake Van area had attracted its share of intrepid travelers, mostly backpackers and lovers of the outdoors. Some had even continued visiting during the height of the civil war and since its end, tourism was on the rise.

At the office, we met Mehmet, a large, sunburned man with a tan-and-white shirt stretched tight over a paunch, dirty maroon jacket, bad teeth, and a rusting minivan, seemingly held together with paper clips and rubber

Heating water atop Mount Nemrut

bands. Looks were deceiving; Mehmet was an experienced and honorable guide, with a great fondness for foreigners, and his van was capable of going anywhere. "The first time, everyone is only a passenger with me," he said in broken English, as Celil and I joined him on the front seat. "But the second time, they are my guests, they stay in my house—free."

Mehmet drove us along the lonely western shore of Lake Van, blue waters lapping against black sand, and on up Mount Nemrut, an inactive volcano whose lava flows had helped to create the lake. Up top, in an expansive crater, lazed yet more lakes—one large and deep blue; another smaller, darker blue; and a third, murky green. Hot springs bubbled in parts of the green lake, cooking a dead frog, while around us rustled the red, gold, and brown colors of autumn. Poplar trees with spinning yellow leaves, round as coins. Cattails with rusty stalks and gray plumes. Russet-colored grasses.

Otherwise, Mount Nemrut's slopes were covered with black volcanic residue and devoid of human life. Until, that is, we came across a cluster of young women in traditional dress washing clothes by a stream. One fed a fire built beneath a heavy cauldron of water, others laid out clothes on rocks to dry. They froze when they saw us, only slowly coming back to life as we said hello.

Behind the volcano was Mehmet's picturesque village, straight out of a storybook, scattered over a gradual slope with long views of Lake Van. Fat haystacks twice as tall as humans rose between enclosed compounds, homes made of clay and cement, and a small mosque with a pretty minaret. Several women squatted in the sun, baking bread or washing clothes, while a man on a tall handmade ladder repaired an electricity line. On the slope above the village grazed hundreds of sheep, some goats. Young women in bright colors moved among them, milking the goats.

Finally, I have arrived in a Kurdish village in Turkey, I thought. Visiting villages in the Southeast wasn't so easy. Aside from the fact that many settlements had been destroyed during the war, the highways were guarded by gendarmes and the byways by village guards. Our bus had pulled into two military checkpoints en route to Tatvan—all identification papers collected and examined—while along the smaller roads, travelers were usually asked whom they were planning to visit and why. As a foreigner, I could only cause trouble for people by arriving in their village.

"What exactly are the authorities so afraid of?" I had asked Nihat, Celil's journalist friend in Batman. The ban on visiting villages didn't make any sense. The story of the destroyed villages had been out for years, and I hardly needed to be physically in a village to talk to victimized villagers. "In fact, it is senseless," Nihat agreed. "It's just a way of controlling people."

Mehmet's home was cool and small, with a thin rug on the floor and bedding piled up along one wall. His wife and grown daughters brought refreshments—fresh cheeses and yogurts, flat bread and tea—while he brought out a notebook. Inside were pages crammed with comments from his many earlier visitors—most Israeli, some European and Australian, and a few Japanese and American. Many had stayed in his home for a night or two, and some had stayed for weeks. "Not for money," Mehmet beamed proudly. "Never, never. Everyone is free."

Mehmet was eager for us to stay with him, too, and was disappointed to learn that we had an earlier engagement. "Not for money, not for money," he kept saying anxiously, only somewhat mollified when we promised to try to return another day.

We were almost finished with our third round of tea before we learned that Mehmet's village was picturesque on the outside only. Although it had not been destroyed during the war, only half of its forty-odd houses were occupied, and of those, about half belonged to village guards. In earlier years, Mehmet himself had been pressured into becoming a guard, but had fled to safety in Istanbul for two years, successfully moving back in 1994. Now, he ignored his village guard neighbors, and, mostly, they ignored him.

But not always. Sometimes, they harassed him or had him arrested, asking him why he brought so many foreigners into the village, and why he charged them no money. "They do everything for money, so they think money is everything," he said bitterly.

THE ROAD BETWEEN Tatvan and Van ran flush along Lake Van, blinding cobalt waters to one side, dull tan hills to the other. En route, about sixty miles from Tatvan and a mile offshore, glittered rocky Akdamar Island, home to Akdamar Kilisesi, or Church of the Holy Cross. One of the region's most famed historic attractions, built by the Armenians in A.D. 921, the church was reachable only by motor boats that ran only when enough people had assembled. Disembarking from a bus in what seemed like the middle of nowhere, Celil and I despaired of reaching the island for many hours, when suddenly a dozen other waiting people—Kurds, Turks, and foreigners—materialized out of nowhere. *They* had been waiting for *us.*

"Tamara, what happened to your lover?" Celil sang as we puttered away from shore, and told me the island's legend. Tamara, the beautiful daughter of an Armenian priest, fell in love with a Muslim boy. Every night, she lit a lamp in an isolated spot and he swam out to the island to meet her. But one night, the lovers were spotted, and the next night, Tamara was locked in her room. Others then set out in a boat, with a lamp, to cruelly lead the Muslim boy farther and farther away from shore until he drowned.

Akdamar Kilisesi was notable for its vivid relief carvings, most in superb condition, depicting biblical stories: Adam and Eve, Jonah and the whale, Abraham and Isaac. And on the mainland across from the island, written in large white boulders on a hill, read the words: THE FATHERLAND CANNOT BE DIVIDED.

VAN WAS THE area's largest city, population five hundred thousand. Set back some distance from the lake, it boasted a modern, busy downtown in which fashionable young men and women in leather jackets bumped shoulders with poor villagers and a few older women draped in black—the first completely "covered" women I'd seen in Turkey. Celil, who had never been in Van before, had an instant negative reaction to the place. "It doesn't smell Kurdish," he said, while I remembered a warning from Mehmet. "Be careful in Van, there are many plainclothes police there."

Crowning a hill on the edge of the city loomed the ruins of an enormous, unwieldy Citadel, dating back to the ninth century B.C., when Van was the capital of the Kingdom of Urartu, an alliance of tribes especially known for their skilled metal work. Often at war with their neighbors the Assyrians, the Urartians fell from power in the sixth century B.C.

Celil and I visited the Citadel in the late afternoon, shortly after our arrival in Van. Steps carved in rock led to the fortress and halfway up were cuneiform inscriptions praising a Urartian king. On the summit stretched a long expanse of ruins that included several towers and funeral chambers.

But it was the ruins visible at the base of the Citadel's far side that interested me more. An eerie patchwork of foundations and pillars stretching deep into the darkling plain, these ruins marked the site of the old city of Van, destroyed during World War I. In 1914 and 1915, bands of Armenian guerrillas had been collaborating with the Russians in the hopes of establishing an Armenian republic, the catalyst that led nervous Ottomans, their power already on the wane, to order the deportation of the entire Armenian population. Massacres and evacuations began, with some Armenian villagers fleeing to Van to barricade themselves into its Armenian quarter along with the city's residents. The Ottomans, with the help of Kurdish tribesmen, laid siege, ultimately destroying Van and slaughtering untold thousands of civilians. After the founding of modern Turkey in 1923, a completely new Van was built, about three miles east of the old site.

Perhaps it was this tragic earlier history, and not the most recent Kurdish-Turkish struggle, that gave Van its slippery feel. This was an artificial city, built almost overnight and largely without the people that had once formed its heart and soul. The Armenians had lived in the Van area since the sixth century B.C. The land belonged as much to them as it did to the Kurds.

TUCKED INTO THE far southeastern corner of Turkey, just hours from both the Iraq and Iran borders, was the town of Hakkari. Surrounded by some of the country's highest peaks, it was said to be one of the most beautiful places in Kurdistan. It was also said to be difficult to visit. The 130-mile-long road between Van and Hakkari was studded with military checkpoints, while in the town itself, visitors were usually met by the police the moment they arrived and escorted around town until they departed.

Nonetheless, Celil and I left for Hakkari late one afternoon, just as the sun set, boarding another of the sleek buses that roamed the countryside. The road twisted and turned from almost the moment we left Van and a bus attendant came down the aisle, splashing out the perfumed hand wash that is a common amenity on Turkish buses. About an hour later, we passed beneath the eerie white ramparts of Hoşap castle, built by a Kurdish *agha* in 1643. Isolated atop a rocky outcropping, the Citadel was lit by floodlights, a seeming reminder of the still-lingering power of the tribes.

Though I was worried about the military checkpoints, the enforced stops—five in all—were uneventful, albeit time-consuming. At each, gendarmes boarded the bus and collected identity cards from my traveling companions and my passport. Sometimes they took everyone's ID, sometimes only a select few, sometimes they checked names against lists, sometimes they searched luggage bins, sometimes they paid extra-close attention to me, sometimes they ignored me. But every time they climbed on board, everyone in the bus became preternaturally still.

Watching the gendarmes, I noticed how young most were—late teens or early to mid twenties. Many were probably nervous if not terrified to be here, in unsettled enemy territory. The Turks as well as the Kurds had lost many thousands in the civil war, and the three-year-old peace was still tenuous.

"He looks horrible," Celil said of one gendarme, a stocky, muscular young man with blue cheeks and a grim, clenched jaw. But I couldn't agree, and pitied him his job, climbing aboard bus after bus filled with hostile passengers.

By the time we disembarked in Hakkari, it was after ten P.M., and no policemen were in sight. But they knew we were here, Celil assured me; the guards at the checkpoints would have called. The cold streets were poorly lit, dusty, and empty, with black mountains on all sides and a black sky flecked with mica overhead. Celil and I hurried into one of the town's only two hotels, a wan place with a lobby as empty as the town and a sleepy desk clerk, who did his best to welcome us.

The next morning, the same clerk was on duty, along with two policemen now stationed in front of the hotel and others across the street. They looked Celil and me over when we stepped outside, but made no attempt to follow as we wandered down the block.

Downtown Hakkari consisted of one short main street lined with rundown storefronts, many of which were abandoned. Rising up here and there were building projects in various stages of completion, while at the end of the town trotted a large statue of Atatürk on horseback, surrounded by Turkish flags and a banner trumpeting words that I had seen placarded all over the Southeast: HAPPY IS HE WHO CALLS HIMSELF A TURK. Hakkari's population had more than tripled in size during the 1990s—from about thirty-five thousand in 1991 to well over one hundred thousand in 2002—as displaced villagers flooded in, but at ten A.M., the streets were still largely empty. White-blue peaks, as perfectly triangular as in a child's drawing, ringed the cold, lonesome scene—inaccessible crags and precipices, high valleys deep with snow.

Partly for lack of anyplace else to go, Celil and I stopped into the local DEHAP campaign office, a large hall where a few men in baggy suits with long coat jackets milled about. Mehmet, a small man with a lopsided face and alcohol on his breath, welcomed us in English, a language he'd taught himself while imprisoned for seven years in the 1980s. He'd once been a successful businessman, with a bookshop and restaurant, but imprisonment, bad luck, and the war had changed all that.

He did still have a young and beautiful wife, however, whom he'd like us to meet. In fact, she and the rest of the family were getting ready to go to a wedding, or, more precisely, to pick up a bride in a nearby village for a wedding the next day. Would we like to come along?

So it was that an hour or so later, Mehmet, his wife, Medya, their ten-year-old son, another relative, Celil, and I were crammed into a taxi heading out of Hakkari. I was paying, to Mehmet's great embarrassment. I am very sorry, he said over and over again that morning, but you see how it is, we have no work, we have no money.

We spiraled down the mountain at a rapid clip, the slopes of other nearby mountains seemingly close enough to touch. Piney treetops were dusted with powder until we neared the bottom, where winter gave way to a still-green valley, centered on the Zab River. We came to a checkpoint. One of the lead cars stopped to offer a bribe, and the rest of us sailed by unharassed.

Medya was indeed young and beautiful—I'd had my doubts—and seemed beside herself with excitement as we cruised along, snapping her fingers, clapping her hands, singing snatches of a Kurdish song. We were going to pick up the bride! Tomorrow would be a wedding! Tall and slim, green-eyed and chestnut-haired, Medya was dressed in a two-piece gown of bright lilac beneath, velveteen black, purple, and green on top. She wore five or six gold necklaces, lipstick and mascara, while cinched around her waist was a silver belt. Every few minutes, she climbed up to sit halfway out the car window, shout and wave the "V" for victory sign.

She wasn't the only one. Women in cars in front and behind us did the same, twirling handkerchiefs in the air. We were part of a cavalcade of fourteen vehicles, with a Toyota truck in front equipped with a video camera pointing backward, and many of the cars draped in streamers of the familiar red, yellow, and green. "See what I mean? Every wedding is like a small demonstration," Celil said, as people by the roadside returned our victory signs. He nudged me. One of the people flashing back the "V" had been an armed village guard. Often pressed into service against their will, many village guards secretly supported the Kurdish nationalist movement.

We followed the Zab River for ten or fifteen miles before pulling off onto a muddy road crowded with vehicles. Parking, we joined a throng of people pouring from the cars and down surrounding slopes to converge on a simple house by a rushing stream. An electric band played and women were dancing. Like Medya, all were dressed in long, luscious, deep-colored gowns as they held hands, bent, swung, and swayed, while the men, drearily ordinary in Western dress, watched from the sidelines.

Medya and I joined in the dancing for a while—the same *saypah* step I knew from Iraq and Iran—and I took pictures. Then the music abruptly changed and some ran toward their cars. The bride was coming out! They wanted to be ready to follow in the cavalcade. Others waited as a woman draped in a sheet dyed yellow, red, and green was helped down the stairs and into a waiting wedding car. Her head, face, and body were all completely covered, and would remain so until she was in all-women's company in Hakkari. When she was finally uncovered, she would not smile, as Kurdish brides should not give the impression they are eager to marry.

We drove back the way we came, with much singing, laughing, clapping, flashing of victory signs, and climbing halfway out car windows. Medya seemed even more excited than before, and several times I was afraid she might fall out of the car altogether. But we made it back safely and retired to the groom's home for lunch. A sea of shoes had already collected outside the door by the time we arrived, and a boy was turning their toes around, so that all would be pointing forward when the guests left.

LATER THAT AFTERNOON, back in the DEHAP campaign office, now buzzing with activity, Celil and I were besieged by dozens of men and women, all eager to tell us their stories. We formed a large circle of chairs at one end of the room, and everyone began talking at once, some tripping over their words in their haste to get them out. They had so much to say, and so few had listened—Hakkari seldom received visitors. Gaunt faces, hollowed-out cheeks, and unblinking eyes surrounded me.

The villagers' stories were similar to others I'd heard. "Before, we were all okay," said a man from the village of Kavalkoy. "Even the poorest family in our village had a hundred sheep, enough to live on. We made our own yogurt and cheese, and bought only sugar and clothes from the city. But now, we are ninety percent unemployed and have nothing."

Even more than most I'd talked to, the hardest thing for many of the Hakkari-area villagers to endure was the loss of their livestock. The Kurds' economic mainstay for centuries, livestock was especially important in the region as it was not conducive to farming. But the gendarmes had either stolen the villagers' animals outright or forced the villagers to sell them at low prices. "We sold them in a hurry because we were worried about our lives," said a man from a village near Çukurca. "And sometimes the buyers came from the Western cities and paid by checks that were no good."

Later, I learned that in 1984, the province of Hakkari had contained 5 million livestock; by the late 1990s, it contained less than one-half million.

In 1970, livestock had accounted for 12.3 percent of Turkey's GNP; by 1997, it accounted for 2.2 percent.

Because of Hakkari's critical position near the Iran and Iraq borders, it was also subject to especially harsh surveillance and security measures. According to the villagers, the town was surrounded by barbed wire, mines, and watchtowers, from which the gendarmes kept track of all movement, using thermal cameras to determine when large groups of people got together. "Until the election process started six weeks ago, we couldn't gather in large groups like this," said a DEHAP representative. "Five or more people was considered illegal. And for wedding ceremonies, people had to ask permission."

The election process was proving to be fraught with difficulty as well. Gendarmes were preventing DEHAP representatives from traveling out into the countryside to campaign, and villagers were being intimidated into voting against the Kurdish party. A report from the London-based Kurdish Human Rights Project later estimated that as many as twenty-five thousand people had been prevented from voting in the Hakkari region in the 2002 elections.

But such practices were not government policy, a young Kurdish journalist from Hakkari told me a few days later in Istanbul. "Turkey wants the elections to be free and fair," he said. "Turkey wants to join the European Union. But Hakkari is far away from central government and election observers. In Hakkari, the gendarmes and village guards make the law."

CHAPTER TWENTY-ONE

Kurds Among Nations

⟩ ⟩ ⟨ ⟩ ⟨

WHEN I FIRST STARTED SERIOUSLY RESEARCHING THE KURDS in early 2002, many Americans barely knew who they were. Just over a year later, that dramatically changed. Anyone paying even the slightest attention to the war in Iraq knew that the Iraqi Kurds were the most stalwart of American friends, providing *peshmerga* militias to fight alongside the U.S. troops, welcoming the occupying soldiers with an unadulterated joy—in contrast to the Arabs' far more ambivalent stance—and, in the months of escalating violence after the war's official end, offering what was still Iraq's only real safe haven. Soldiers serving elsewhere in the country went to Iraqi Kurdistan for R&R.

Any American paying even slightly more attention to the war also knew that there were issues between Turkey and the Kurds. On March 1, 2003, the Turkish Parliament voted against providing troops to help invade Iraq— a bold and democratic act (over 90 percent of Turkish citizens were against the war) that infuriated the United States, which had taken that support for granted. Democracy was all fine and good, the United States seemed to be saying in its unfortunate message, as long as it supported U.S. policy, but a different story altogether when it did not. One of Turkey's major objections to the war was the fear that it might encourage Turkey's Kurds to fight for more autonomy, perhaps joining together with the Iraqi Kurds to try to form a separate, independent Kurdistan.

As much as I had adamantly believed in the necessity of ousting the Baath regime, I was against the war or, rather, against the arrogant manner in which the war was waged. I believed that with more adroit diplomacy and more time, the United States–Britain alliance would not have had to go it alone, and the removal of Saddam Hussein could have been undertaken by a larger coalition of allies, if not the United Nations. I saw then, and see now, the winning of a short-term victory for the United States at the cost of a long-term defeat for the entire world, a deepening of the already tragic East-West divide that will have repercussions for decades to come. Even in the best-case scenario—the quick establishment of a strong democracy in Iraq—I failed to see how exactly that would bring about a fundamental shift in the region, with other despotic regimes following suit, as the neoconservatives argued. I also questioned America's long-term commitment to the Iraqi people and was horrified by the obvious lack of postwar planning, made most manifest by the insufficient number of troops in the country, leading to much unnecessary death and destruction.

After the major hostilities were over, my reservations became beside the point. Saddam Hussein was gone! There could be no better immediate outcome than that. I was ecstatic for all Iraqis, and especially my Iraqi Kurdish friends. I had seen firsthand how they lived while he was in power.

During and after the war, everyone I knew in Iraqi Kurdistan was doing well. In Dohuk, my host family, Majed and Huda, had another child, a son, and Zobayda, the sister who helped me most during my stay, was studying in France—both events that would have happened with or without the war, but that nevertheless seemed a product of post-Baath optimism. Yousif, the cousin from San Diego, got a job translating for the U.S. Army, while his sister Fatma had married and her husband moved to the United States. Amin was back teaching at the art institute and my tightly covered translator Bayan got a job with a demining company. Dr. Shawkat, who had first helped orient me to Kurdistan, was now handling public relations for Mosul, a much larger city than Dohuk, and the site where Saddam Hussein's two sons died in a shootout in late July 2003.

Those I had met in the Erbil and Suleimaniyah governorates were also doing well. Dr. Adil Karem Fatah, the Halabja doctor who'd fled into exile in Damascus in fear for his life, was back in Iraq. He had no reason to seek asylum now and wanted to be in his own country, helping his people. Nizar

Ghafur Agha Said, the Kurdish American businessman who'd served as my translator in Suleimaniyah, was working as a regional adviser and interpreter for the U.S.'s Coalition Provisional Authority. The Rozhbayanis, one of my host families in Erbil—the mother a parliamentarian, the father an editor—had returned to Kirkuk, their hometown. Many outside observers had believed that Kirkuk would be the site of a bloodbath postwar, with Kurds and Arabs—as well as the Turkish army, if given the chance—violently fighting for control of the oil town. Kurds would ruthlessly attack those who had settled in their homes during the Baathist "Arabization" program, the experts said. But despite some ethnic tension and sporadic ugly incidents, by the fall of 2003, that scenario had yet to happen. Kurdish leaders had urged their followers to exercise restraint and settle questions of ownership by lawsuits, not guns, and most people listened.

Of all those I knew in Iraqi Kurdistan, the person whose life changed especially dramatically after the war was Nesreen Mustafa Siddeek Berweri, the woman minister of Reconstruction and Development, who had helped me so much throughout my stay. In early September 2003, the Iraqi Governing Council, assembled the previous July to help U.S. officials govern postwar Iraq, appointed Nesreen to serve as the country's minister of Municipalities and Public Works, overseeing forty-five thousand employees. The only woman minister in the new twenty-five member cabinet, Nesreen's responsibilities included urban planning, environmental sanitation, and, most important at first, drinking water. It was her job to get the drinking water of Iraq flowing again. Within days of her appointment, she was meeting with the Coalition Provisional Administrator L. Paul Bremer III and President Bush.

Nesreen was one of four Kurdish ministers in the Iraqi cabinet, while the twenty-five-member Iraqi Governing Council included five Kurds— numbers that boded well for the future of Kurds in Iraq. Other ministries headed by Kurds included the all-important department of foreign affairs and the group framing the new constitution. From the perspective of the fall of 2003 at least, it looked as if the Iraqi Kurds were finally getting their chance and would be an integral, and quite powerful, part of whatever happened next in their country. Of all Iraqis, they were in an especially good position postwar, thanks in no small part to their enthusiastic support for the United States. The Kurdish region was also in better economic and organizational shape than was most of the country, as it had been least subject to U.N. sanctions and recent Baathist rule.

Impressively, too, the KDP and PUK were managing to work together. Though behind-the-scenes tensions continued, each had reopened offices in the other's territory even before the war began, and Massoud Barzani and Jalal Talabani were presenting a united front to the world, issuing joint statements as they pressed for Kurdish interests.

Nonetheless, I couldn't help but mourn a little for the death of the semi-autonomous zone. In many ways, that zone had not been a good situation; the Kurds had been living in fear, and the United Nations had had too much power. Yet during their semi-independent years, the Kurds had flown their own flag, circulated their own money, run their own militias, and largely governed themselves and only themselves in what had been a unique, interesting, and overall quite successful experiment. Now, they were being ordered to fly the Iraqi as well as the Kurdish flag, their currency was being withdrawn, their *peshmerga* were to merge into a national army, and they were to share with others in the governing of a new multiethnic Iraq. The Kurds' relatively self-sufficient days of collecting tolls at checkpoints, smuggling oil between Baathist-controlled territory and Turkey, and receiving generous oil-for-food revenues were over. In the future, they would have to compete for national resources with other parts of Iraq and work within a budget administered out of Baghdad. Arab tourists were flooding the Kurdish region, and the Arabic language, shunned during my visit and unintelligible to many younger Kurds, was once again being heard on the streets. The magic kingdom was disappearing.

Such changes were inevitable, of course, if a new Iraq were to be created. Much more alarming for the Iraqis in general was the escalating postwar violence and growing presence of Islamist extremists in the country. Much more alarming for the Iraqi Kurds in particular was the flickering possibility that perhaps a strong federalist system would *not* be established, that Kurdish interests would be subsumed by Arab nationalists pushing for a strong central government. The troublesome issue of sending Turkish troops into Iraq also resurfaced. Once again, the Kurds were adamantly opposed to the proposal—as were the Arabs, who had their own distasteful memories of the Ottomans. Until the last minute, however, when Turkey finally abandoned the plan, saying it would not send troops unless invited by Iraq to do so, the Americans and Turks seemed to be settling the matter between themselves. This was big-time politics, no need to take the position of a minor ally like the Kurds into consideration, the Americans seemed to be saying. An indication of future U.S. policy in the region? Before and during the war, the United States had needed the Iraqi Kurds. But now, all bets were off.

In the end, the whole Iraq question would take years to be settled. Nation building is a long and arduous process, and many outside powers in addition to the United States—Iran, Turkey, Syria, Saudi Arabia, Russia, France—would seek to influence the fledgling nation, both politically and economically. Widespread ethnic hostilities might still erupt, extremist groups could take even more serious hold, occupying troops would probably be required far longer than initially thought. Yet despite my deep worries regarding the broader impact of the war, and the immediate future of Iraq, I was cautiously, albeit conditionally, optimistic about the Iraqi Kurds' future—if the violence could be eradicated, if the United States stayed the course, if a strong federated state were created. The Iraqi Kurds were now known around the world, and they weren't about to disappear inside a totalitarian state again. Positive as well as negative developments were occurring; it was early yet.

ALTHOUGH THE EYES of the world were largely focused on Iraq throughout 2003, dramatic changes were also taking place in Turkey—changes that could have as great an impact on the Kurds' future as the Iraq war of 2003. The surprise election of the Justice and Development Party (AKP), headed by Recep Tayyip Erdogan, now Turkey's prime minister, in November 2002, quickly led to a series of significant reforms. As a moderate Islamist party with a strong pro–European Union stance, the AKP's rise indicated both a turning away from Turkey's old-style politicians, with their often-unquestioning support of the United States, and an embracing of Western democratic values by Muslim traditionalists. Some worried that the AKP might have a hidden Islamist agenda, but they disavowed the accusation and throughout 2003, placed their emphasis on reform, not religion.

By that fall, the Turkish Parliament had passed four sets of laws and regulations aimed at improving Turkey's democracy and chances to join the European Union. The first two packages, introduced in January, made it more difficult to close down political parties, try party members, and get away with acts of torture or mistreatment. The packages also expanded the freedom of the press and made it possible to retry cases deemed unfair by the European Court of Human Rights. One of the first cases to be retried was that of Turkey's longest-serving political prisoners: Hatip Dicle, Orhan Dogan, Selim Sadak, and Leyla Zana—the latter the only woman and winner of the 1995 Sakharov prize. As Kurds and former members of parliament, the foursome had been imprisoned since 1994 for alleged links with the PKK. The evidence against them had been flimsy, and based primarily on their wearing the banned Kurdish colors during their swearing-in ceremony and using Kurdish words during or after taking the oath of office.

The Turkish Parliament passed two more reform packages in July. One lifted the infamous Article 8 of the antiterror law, the one used to sentence hundreds of writers and other nonviolent offenders to harsh prison terms simply for criticizing the government's Kurdish policies. And the second, and most significant of the reform packages, greatly curbed the power of the Turkish military by reducing the National Security Council to an advisory body. Equally composed of military leaders and senior politicians, but usually headed by a four-star general, the council had previously had the right to step into politics whenever it deemed the civilian authorities to be losing control. Now, the parliament decreed that the council no longer had such power, and that the hitherto secret military budget had to be subject to parliamentary review. Even a few years earlier, such reforms could have led to the military again seizing power, but broad support for more democracy in Turkey now made that scenario less likely.

The reform packages marked a major step forward for the republic, and one that earned it the right to start accession talks to the European Union in late 2004. Yet the larger question of implementation remained, and remains. "Pass all the laws you want," Sezgin Tanrikulu, the human rights lawyer I'd met in Diyarbakir, said in an interview after the reforms were passed. "The courts and law enforcement agencies will in the end apply them as they see fit."

And indeed, throughout 2003, Tanrikulu was right. The retrial of Leyla Zana and her three colleagues, begun in early spring, proceeded at a snail's pace, with the prisoners and observers complaining about new rounds of mistreatment. By that fall, the case still hadn't been resolved, even though far more dangerous criminals are routinely released from Turkish prisons after serving shorter terms. Kurdish language courses did not begin until over a year after they became legal, and then only in one city at first, as applicants had to jump through innumerable bureaucratic hoops before receiving permission to offer the classes; state objections ranged from too-narrow doorways to too-few pictures of Atatürk in the proposed classrooms. Giving children Kurdish names continued to be banned until September, when they were allowed as long as they didn't contain the letters "*q*," "*x*," and "*w*"—letters found in the Kurdish but not the Turkish alphabet. The limited amount of Kurdish broadcasting authorized by the parliament in July 2002 did not begin until nearly eighteen months later, and torture and other human rights abuses were said to be continuing.

Why can't the Turks just lighten up? I thought as I read about the stonewalling. During the height of the Kurdish-Turkish civil war, the Turks had perhaps had some justification for their harsh techniques, but PKK/KADEK had stopped calling for independence in the mid-1990s, when their focus shifted to equal civil rights, and all major hostilities ended in 1999. The local Turkish officials' refusal to institute even such simple reforms as Kurdish language classes seemed like paranoia to me—as had the general Turkish reaction to the Iraq war of 2003, when many Turks expressed a histrionic fear that the Kurds of Iraq and Turkey might join together to fight for an independent Kurdistan. Anyone who had spent much time in the region knew that such a scenario was unlikely. With the United States on their side, the Iraqi Kurds had far too much to lose, while Turkey's Kurds were too exhausted to begin another war. In addition, PKK/KADEK and the Iraqi Kurds were still at loggerheads.

Mainstream Turks' attitude toward the Kurds reminded me of mainstream white Americans' attitude toward black Americans before the civil rights era—and still all too often today—when fear of the "other" led to ascribing to the minority group all the worst attributes of human-kind. Racism was rampant in Turkey and, even if the reforms were miracu-lously instituted overnight, would probably take a generation to signifi-cantly lessen. It was unfortunate, too, that much of Turkey's impetus for change was coming from outside European Union pressure rather than from within.

Among the July reforms passed by the Turkish Parliament was an offer of amnesty to some rank-and-file PKK/KADEK guerrillas. The offer should have signaled a new beginning, but instead it led to heightened hostilities. The rebels felt that the amnesty was an insincere gesture, as it did not include PKK/KADEK leaders and granted reduced sentences only to those who informed on others still at large. KADEK subsequently called off its four-year unilateral cease-fire, saying that Ankara had failed to respond with reciprocal goodwill. The rebel group added, however, that the end of the truce did not mean war, and only a handful of skirmishes broke out over the next few months.

With the amnesty largely a failure, the question of what to do with the approximately five thousand PKK/KADEK rebels still hiding out in northern Iraq remained, and remains. Under the leadership of Osman Öcalan, Abdullah Öcalan's brother, the rebel group had kept a low and peaceful profile since 1999, but also said that it was not giving up the fight. Turkey wanted the United States to help flush out the guerrillas in exchange for providing peacekeeping troops, but even before the troops' proposal was abandoned, the chances of the United States pursuing the rebels were slim—things were unstable enough in Iraq as it was. Curiously, too, KADEK seemed to be supportive of the U.S.-British presence in the region. Osman Öcalan told journalists that he wanted to cooperate with the West to help establish a democratic Iraq and had no objections to Turkish troops passing through Iraqi Kurdistan on their way to peacekeeping missions farther south.

In the end, the verdict on the reforms in Turkey, like the verdict on the war in Iraq, was still unclear. Both countries were at a historic crossroads, with changes in the works that could have enormous implications for the Kurds. And while the situation in Turkey, like the situation in Iraq, could still go many different ways—the military could still step in, implementation could take too long, Turkey could backtrack—I was also cautiously optimistic about Turkey's Kurds' future. Unlike Iraq, Turkey already had a functioning democracy, repressive though it was in ways, and a serious desire to meet the reformist standards of the European Union. Corruption and abuses of power were deeply ingrained in the state, but both Turks and Kurds were demanding change.

Of course, there were still plenty of wild cards, several of which were dealt shortly before this book went to press: the United States' decision to hand over sovereignty to the Iraqis on June 30, 2004—far earlier than originally planned; the capture of Saddam Hussein; Grand Ayatollah Ali al-Sistani's call for a full-scale general election prior to the transition of power. And if, say, Iraq fell apart and the Iraqi Kurds split off from the Iraqi Arabs and Turkey panicked . . . Anything could still happen.

Immediately before, during, and after the Iraq war of 2003, I received worried e-mails from my friends in Turkey. Saddam Hussein might attack the Southeast, masked special forces were back on the streets, Emergency Rule might be reinstated. But as the war came, went, and receded, the e-mails became reassuringly mundane. In early October, my translator Celil wrote: "Nowadays people in Diyarbakir are curious about the health condition of Öcalan. . . . But yesterday there was a festival in Batman and Ciwan Haco the most famous Kurdish rock singer (now living in Sweden) came to Batman after 23 years and we all went to Batman. It was fantastic."

My Kurdish friends in Iran and Syria were also wrapped up in their everyday lives. I received no reports from either country of increased repression or any other fallout—bad or good—from the war. Events in Iraq and Turkey were undoubtedly already affecting Iranian and Syrian Kurdistan behind the scenes—Iranian politicians were nervous, I read—but on an everyday level, nothing had changed.

I THOUGHT BACK to the many questions I had had at the beginning of my journey. How had the Kurds kept going after all they had suffered? They kept going because they had no other choice. How were they juggling the old and the new? With two steps forward, one step back. Were they still their own worst enemy? At times. Had they reinvented themselves? Yes.

AS FOR THE question of an independent Kurdish state, that remains open. For the most part, Kurds in Iraq, Turkey, Iran, and Syria today are not talking about independence but, rather, about equal civil rights and the need to establish federated political states. Yet floating in the back of many Kurdish minds—how could it be otherwise?—are dreams of complete independence, with some regarding it as only a dream and others viewing the federated states as a stepping stone to the larger goal.

Many enormous impediments stand in the way of Kurdish independence. None of their nations would let them go without a fierce struggle— ironic, considering the way Kurds are mistreated and looked down upon by their respective compatriots. After eighty years of separation by international borders, the Kurds have also become considerably estranged from one another; each group has taken on some of the characteristics of their nation. And the divide between the Iranian Kurds and those in Iraq, Syria, and Turkey dates back far earlier—to the days of the Ottoman-Safavids and, before that, the Ardalans. A large number of Kurds, especially in Turkey, are well integrated into mainstream society and no longer live in predominantly Kurdish areas or speak Kurdish. The Kurds also lack a strong military, adequate financial and economic resources, organization, education, and, perhaps most important, a unified, Pan-Kurdish leadership. The Kurds remain a fractured people on many levels—torn between countries, regions, political parties, tribes, families, dialects, outlooks, the old and the new.

And yet, and yet . . . Modern technology, coupled with oppression, has changed everything. Through satellite communications and the Internet, the Kurds have their own television shows, radio broadcasts, publications, and websites, all of which are theoretically available to every Kurd anywhere in the world. Hundreds of thousands of Kurds, forced out of their homelands by politics, now live in Europe or the United States, where they are steadily gaining advanced degrees, power, and influence. The Kurds may not have their own physical nation, but they do have an international cyberspace state, along with a quickening sense of national identity that, decades from now, may yet give rise to Pan-Kurdish unification—perhaps in the form of a federated Kurdish nation-state. I do believe that the time of armed Kurdish conflict is over, at least for the foreseeable future—the Iraqi *peshmerga* are not what they once were, while the Kurds of Iran and Turkey are ineffably weary. The Kurds are also a smart, pragmatic, industrious, and increasingly modernized people. They know that there is more than one way to win a war.

I THOUGHT BACK to my last stop in Kurdistan—Dogubayazit, Turkey, situated at the northern edge of Kurdish territory. Celil and I had traveled there from Hakkari, backtracking through Van to continue farther north along the eastern shore of Lake Van, over a dry, brown plateau enclosed by a powder blue dome of sky. Along the way, we passed Çaldiran, the site of the 1514 battle that established the boundary between the Ottoman and Safavid empires and divided the Kurds. Built largely of cement block homes with corrugated iron roofs, Çaldiran looked neglected and flimsy. I wondered how many of its citizens even knew of the momentous battle that once took place there.

Nearing Dogubayazit, the landscape changed. Ridge after ridge of mountain hills, each a different brown, appeared, along with giant cow-dung patties of hardened black lava. On the reddish earth between the patties sprouted green grasses upon which sheep grazed. In the distance rose the smooth, cone-shaped peaks of the Greater and Lesser Mount Ararats, shrouded in mist from afar, but bathed in shafts of sunlight closer up, with stocking caps of snow.

With Iran less than twenty miles away, Dogubayazit was a frontier town, containing a handful of muddy streets lined with small storefronts, an Internet center or two, and many poorly kept businessmen's hotels. The gendarmes said to have dominated the place even a year before had been replaced by villagers with pushcarts and animals, and a surprising number of tourists. Israeli, European, and Japanese, they were in town to see Mount Ararat and the Ishak Pasha palace, spectacularly perched on a red outcropping, outlined against the sky like a dream.

An amalgam of Ottoman, Georgian, Persian, and Armenian styles, the palace was a hundred years in the making, begun in 1685 and completed in 1784 by the Kurdish chieftain for whom it is named. Dominating its silhouette was a pointy striped minaret and a round dome that reminded me of the caps that many Kurdish men in Turkey wore.

The drive to Ishak Pasha took us past a huge military outpost filled with rows of tanks and trucks, and up a steep red road that quickly burrowed into the hills. Arriving at the palace, we passed through a towering arched gate to enter a serene courtyard in which a young British artist sketched. We wandered through empty room after empty room, past window after window, each with heart-stopping views of the mist-filled plain below, the silver snows of Mount Ararat gleaming in the distance. From a loudspeaker overhead came a lonesome Kurdish melody, sung by a woman *dengbej*. "Mother, mother, today is Saturday, come and wash my hair and braid it," Celil translated. "Lawike Metini, my beloved, come and ask my father for my hand, and if he refuses, kidnap me."

Beyond the castle was a mosque, and the tomb of Ahmad-i Khani (circa 1650 to 1706), the most famous of all Kurdish poets. Probably originally from Hakkari, Khani is best known for his long literary poem *Mem u Zin*, which he versified from a famous Kurdish folktale. Revered by the Kurds as their national epic, *Mem u Zin* tells the story of handsome Mem of the Alan tribe and Zin of the Botan tribe, who fall in love. But Zin is already betrothed to another, and her father, the Botan emir, has a villainous minister named Beko, who tries to keep the two would-be lovers apart. Beko suggests that the emir and Mem play chess; if Mem wins, he may have Zin, and if he loses, he will be imprisoned. Mem agrees and is winning the match until Beko distracts him. He is thrown into jail. When he is released, he dies suddenly. Zin visits his grave and dies of heartbreak, to be buried beside him. Mem's good friend Qeretajdin, who has been out hunting, returns to the city and goes to the cemetery with the emir and Beko. The graves are opened, and Mem and Zin are found embracing. Beko sticks out his head to leer and Qeretajdin beheads him. A drop of blood falls between the lovers and a thornbush grows between them, separating Mem and Zin even in death. Whenever the bush is cut down, it grows back again.

But Khani's *Mem u Zin* is about much more than doomed love. Living at a time of great tribal conflict, with the Kurds divided between the Ottomans and Safavids, Khani was the first to give written voice to the Kurds' longing for self-determination—one century before the French Revolution conceived of the idea of a nation-state. Scholars posit Mem and Zin as the two parts of Kurdistan, divided between Ottomans and Safavids. Beko personifies the disunity between the Kurds that keeps them apart; for all the Kurds' powerful external enemies, their most dangerous enemy comes from within.

Nation building even before the term was invented, Khani begins his poem with a long introduction in which he praises God and discusses the place of the Kurds among nations. He writes of his people's subjugation, dispossession, divisiveness, independence, and courage. His words resonate as much today as they did three hundred years ago:

> Look! Our misfortune has reached its zenith,
> Has it started to come down do you think?
> Or will it remain so,
> Until comes upon us the end of time?
> Is it possible, I wonder, that for us too,
> A star will emerge out of the firmament?
> Let luck be on our side for once.

Notes

For background information, I am especially indebted to the works of two foremost scholars of Kurdish studies, David McDowall and Martin van Bruinessen. *After Such Knowledge, What Forgiveness?* by Jonathan Randal and "When Worlds Collide: The Kurdish Diaspora from the Inside Out," a Ph.D. dissertation by Diane E. King also inform much of the Iraq section, while *Atatürk's Children: Turkey and the Kurds* by Jonathan Rugman and Roger Hutchings, and *Turkey's Kurdish Question* by Henri J. Barkey and Graham E. Fuller inform much in the Turkey chapters. *The Kurds: State and Minority in Turkey, Iraq and Iran* by James Ciment, *The Kurds: A Concise Handbook* by Mehrdad E. Izady, Michael M. Gunter's works on Iraq and Turkey, Human Rights Watch publications, and the listserv articles of the Washington Kurdish Institute were also especially helpful.

CHAPTER ONE: *Through the Back Door*

8–10: population figures: based on estimates in David McDowall, *A Modern History of the Kurds*, pp. 3–4 and 466; Jonathan Randal, *After Such Knowledge, What Forgiveness?*, p. 16; and Diane E. King, "When Worlds Collide: The Kurdish Diaspora from the Inside Out," Ph.D. dissertation, p. 19.

10: growing national consciousness of Kurds: Henri J. Barkey and Graham E. Fuller, *Turkey's Kurdish Question*, pp. 1–4; McDowall, *A Modern History*, pp. 455–60; and Martin van Bruinessen in Susan Meiselas, *Kurdistan: In the Shadow of History*, p. 374.

10: Xenophon quote: cited in Randal, *After Such Knowledge*, p. 21, from *Anabasis*, IX, 1–3.

10: Kurds' first loyalty to tribal leaders: McDowall, *A Modern History*, p. 21.

10: "golden age": Mehrdad Izady, *The Kurds: A Concise Handbook*, p. 41.

11: tension between Muslim and Kurdish identities: King, "When Worlds Collide," pp. 253–55.

12: successful balance of power in Ottoman-Safavid era: McDowall, *A Modern History*, p. 25 and following.

13: "a thousand sighs": cited in Randal, *After Such Knowledge*, p. 12, from Rene Mauries, *Le Kurdistan ou la mort*, 1967, p. 1; and Thomas Bois, *The Kurds*, p. 136.

14: Prometheus in the Caucasus: Yo'av Karny, *Highlanders: A Journey to the Caucasus*, p. xv.

14: *bilad es-siba'*, "refreshed and in motion": Carleton S. Coon, *Caravan: The Story of the Middle East*, p. 295.

15: number of villages destroyed: the often-cited figure of four thousand refers to the total number destroyed while the Baath Party was in power. Carole A. O'Leary, "The Kurds of Iraq: Recent History, Future Prospects," p. 2.

CHAPTER TWO: *Arrival*

20: Mulla Mustafa's revolt continuing to present day: Michael M. Gunter, *The Kurds of Iraq: Tragedy and Hope*, p. 19.

21: "inability of the feudalist": cited in McDowall, *A Modern History*, p. 343, from a PUK publication, *Revolution in Kurdistan*.

22: elections deemed mostly free and fair: "Elections in Iraqi Kurdistan (May 19, 1992): An Experiment in Democracy," a report from international election observers, sponsored by the European Human Rights Foundation, London/Brussels.

25: comparison of KDP and PUK: James Ciment, *The Kurds: State and Minority in Turkey, Iraq and Iran*, pp. 19–20; and International Crisis Group, "War in Iraq: What's Next for the Kurds," p. 2.

25: populations: 2003 estimates from World Food Program, United Nations.

26: double-edged sword of Ottoman arrangements: McDowall, *A Modern History*, p. 31.

31: "fear and dread": Ely Bannister Soane, *To Mesopotamia and Kurdistan in Disguise*, p. 367.

CHAPTER THREE: *The Little Engine That Could*

40–41: Algiers Accord overview: Randal, *After Such Knowledge*, pp. 145–82, and Ismet Sheriff Vanly in Gerard Chaliand, *A People Without a Country: The Kurds and Kurdistan*, pp. 167–77. Pike Report quote as cited in Chaliand, p. 170. Kissinger quote as cited in Randal, p. 166.

41: "I trust America": cited in Randal, *After Such Knowledge*, p. 156, from Barzani interview by Jim Hoagland, *The Washington Post*, 1973.

53: Hussein as the perpetrator of all evil: King, "When Worlds Collide," p. 10.

CHAPTER FOUR: *After al-Anfal*

55–56: Anfal overview: Human Rights Watch/Middle East, *Iraq's Crime of Genocide: The Anfal Campaign*, pp. 1–22; Randal, *After Such Knowledge*, pp. 210–35; McDowall, *A Modern History*, pp. 257–63.

55: numbers killed in Anfal: Human Rights Watch estimates 100,000. The Kurds, using figures compiled by the PUK, estimate 182,000.

56: total number killed during Baath regime: O'Leary, "The Kurds of Iraq," p. 2.

56: " 'a final solution' ": Human Rights Watch and Physicians for Human Rights, *The Anfal Campaign in Iraqi Kurdistan: Destruction of Koreme*, p. 7.

57: "I will kill them all": from 1988 audiotape of meeting of Iraqi officials. Available from www.hrw.org/reports/1993/iraqanfal/APPENDIXA.htm.

CHAPTER SIX: *Balancing Acts*

88: "covered their heads with a veil": Claudius James Rich, *Narrative of a Residence in Koordistan*, pp. 153–55; King, "When Worlds Collide," pp. 40–41.

89: "the place was a desert": A. H. Layard, *Nineveh and Its Remains*, p. 142.

96: decline in Muslim-Christian relations and Layard's reaction: Martin van Bruinessen, *Agha, Shaikh and State*, pp. 230–31. "cause of much jealousy": Layard, *Nineveh*, p. 156.

98: losses during Kurdish-Turkish conflict: official government figures are 37,000 people killed, 3,165 villages destroyed, and 378,335 rendered homeless. Human rights groups estimate the number of homeless to be at least 1 million. Kurdish Human Rights Project estimates 3 million; Human Rights Watch, between 1 and 2.5 million.

99: PKK-Iraqi Kurd relations: Barkey and Fuller, *Turkey's Kurdish Question*, pp. 48–53, 160–61; Michael Gunter in Robert Olson, *The Kurdish National Movement in the 1990s: Its Impact on Turkey and the Middle East*, pp. 50–62; and McDowall, *A Modern History*, pp. 383–91.

99: "combat the PKK": cited by Gunter in Olson, *Kurdish National Movement*, p. 52, from *Foreign Broadcast Information Service—Western Europe*, Dec. 18, 1991, p. 55.

99: "Öcalan is the enemy": Ibid., p. 58, from *FBIS-WEU*, Sept. 5, 1995, p. 30.

100: "Kurdistani" identity: O'Leary, "The Kurds of Iraq," p. 7.

CHAPTER SEVEN: *Questions of Honor*

109–10: honor as central to Kurdish society: King, "When Worlds Collide," pp. 224–31; Nazaneen Rashid, paper presented at Department for International Development conference on "Violence Against Women in Iraqi Kurdistan," Oct. 18, 2002. Available from www.kurdmedia.com/reports.asp?id=1103; David Morgan, "Honor Killings in Iraqi Kurdistan: Seminar Report," Aug. 9, 2000. Available from www.kurdishmedia.com/reports.asp?id=9; and Sheri Laizer, *Martyrs, Traitors and Patriots: Kurdistan After the Gulf War*, pp. 161–69.

111: In "Matriarchy in Kurdistan? Women Rulers in Kurdish History," *International Journal of Kurdish Studies*, Vol. 6, 1993, Martin van Bruinessen argues that Kurdish women acquire leadership roles in Kurdish society only through high birth or marriage.

114: Iraqi-Turkish oil trade: *New York Times*, Nov. 29, 2002; and interview with Nesreen Mustafa Siddeek Berwari, minister of Reconstruction and Development, April 2002.

115: "Fearing death I roam the steppe": as translated in Richard F. Nyrop, *Iraq: A Country Study*, p. 12.

116–17: Zembil Firosh tale: as related by van Bruinessen in "Matriarchy in Kurdistan?" p. 35, from A. Gernas, "Zerbilfiros," *Roja Nu* 33, 1992, pp. 10–14.

117: "basic paradox of folklore": William R. Bascom, "Four Functions of Folklore," *Journal of American Folklore*, 67 (1954), p. 349; as cited by Michael Lewisohn Chyet,

" 'And a Thornbush Sprang Up Between Them': Studies on Mem u Zin, A Kurdish Romance," Ph.D. dissertation, p. 363.

CHAPTER EIGHT: *The Cult of the Angels*

121: "cult of the angels": Izady, *The Kurds*, p. 137 and following.

123: political meaning of "original Kurds": Ibid., p. 136; and Christine Allison in Philip G. Kreyenbroek and Christine Allison, *Kurdish Culture*, p. 36.

140: "the enemy within": McDowall, *A Modern History*, p. 411, citing Turkish sources.

140–41: Sivas massacre: Hugh and Nicole Pope, *Turkey Unveiled: A History of Modern Turkey*, pp. 324–25.

CHAPTER NINE: *From Kings to Parliamentarians*

144: Turkish students arrested: Kurdish Human Rights Project, *The Trial of Students*, p. 5.

149–50: Turcoman population and boycott of elections: "War in Iraq: What's Next for the Kurds?" p. 6.

156–57: oil-for-food program statistics: Kurdistan Regional Government. Available from www.krg.org/986; United Nations' Office of the Iraq Program. Available from www.un.org/depts/oip. Official U.N. sum for unspent funds: *New York Times*, July 14, 2003, U.N. Letter to the Editor.

CHAPTER TEN: *Invitations*

164–65: Balisan attack: Human Rights Watch/Middle East, *Iraq's Crime of Genocide*, pp. 38–47.

165: death of Muhammad Jamil Rozhbayani: April 16, 2001, letter from Coalition for Justice in Iraq to Mary Robinson, U.N. High Commissioner for Human Rights. Available from www.krg.org/newsletters/20010419184439.html#11.

166: oil production in Kirkuk: "War in Iraq: What's Next for the Kurds?" pp. 1, 19.

166: "Arabization" statistics: Human Rights Watch, "Iraq: Forcible Expulsion of Ethnic Minorities," pp. 3, 11. Available from www.hrw.org/reports.

174: Erbil folksong: as quoted in Ralph S. Solecki, *Shanidar: The First Flower People*, p. 154.

CHAPTER ELEVEN: *Along the Hamilton Road, with Side Trips*

177: "roads essential for law and order": A. M. Hamilton, *Road Through Kurdistan*, p. 73.

178: spring in Gali Ali Beg: Ibid., p. 58–59.

182–83: Simko's violent history: Randal, *After Such Knowledge*, p. 328.

183–84: land mine statistics: interview with Mines Advisory Group, May 2002; *Iraqi Kurdistan Dispatch*, July 2002.

186–87: "marched for fifty-two days": cited in Gunter, *The Kurds and the Future*, p. 10, from Dana Schmidt, *Journey Among Brave Men*, pp. 109–10.

188: "betrayed the country": cited in Human Rights Watch/Middle East, *Iraq's Crime of Genocide*, p. 27, from *Al-Iraq*, Sept. 13, 1983.

189: Qushtapa as encouragement to use same techniques again: Ibid., p. 4.

190: "finding of flowers": Solecki, *Shanidar*, p. 250.

CHAPTER TWELVE: *In the Land of the Babans*

202: 80 percent of books in Sorani: Randal, *After Such Knowledge*, p. 24.

202: "The Baban Land": C. J. Edmonds, *Kurds, Turks, and Arabs: Politics, Travel and Research in Northern-Eastern Iraq*, pp. 57–58.

206: assault on Central Security Headquarters: Randal, *After Such Knowledge*, p. 40.

208: *sherim*: King, "When Worlds Collide," pp. 203–04.

209: ambush of Ali Askari: McDowall, *A Modern History*, pp. 344–45.

211: Goptaka attack: *Iraq's Crime of Genocide*, p. 117–20.

CHAPTER THIRTEEN: *Judgment Day*

217: "on the threshing floor . . .": *Encyclopedia of Islam*, Vol. 9, p. 218.

219: Adela Khanoum, "of pure Kurdish origin": Soane, *To Mesopotamia*, p. 226; van Bruinessen, "Matriarchy in Kurdistan?" p. 27.

222–23: for more details on the chemical bombing and Halabja Post-Graduate Medical Institute, see Washington Kurdish Institute website, homepage at www.kurd.org.

227: names of chemical companies released: *New York Times*, Dec. 21, 2002.

CHAPTER FOURTEEN: *Safe Havens*

229: "horsemen came galloping": Soane, *To Mesopotamia*, p. 173.

231: Piramerd poem: Edmonds, *Kurds, Turks, and Arabs*, p. 45.

244–45: reasons and estimated number of honor killings: Morgan, "Honor Killings in Iraqi Kurdistan"; Rashid, paper, Department for International Development. See note for p. 109.

CHAPTER FIFTEEN: *Syrian Interlude*

252: not an attractive town: Agatha Christie Mallowan, *Come, Tell Me How You Live*, p. 57.

253: Syrian help crucial to PKK: McDowall, *A Modern History*, p. 479.

253: growing Syrian Kurdish anger toward PKK: Ibid., p. 479.

256: "sitting at a distance separately": cited by Vera Beaudin Saeedpour in "The Legacy of Saladin," *The International Journal of Kurdish Studies*, Vol. 13, No. 1, 1999, p. 55.

CHAPTER SIXTEEN: *Of Politics and Poetry*

261: "a nation apart": McDowall, *A Modern History*, p. 53, from *Parliamentary Papers*, Turkey No. 5 (1881).

265: "no longer . . . a tribal society": A. R. Ghassemlou, in Chaliand, *People Without a Country*, p. 97.

266: urban-rural breakdown: no census figure exists. One 1993 report estimated that the five western provinces of Iran, including the Kurdish provinces, were only 47 percent urban (Kooli-Kameli, Farideh, *The Political Development of the Kurds in Iran*, p. 138), but many Kurds I met used the two-thirds figure.

269: no Kurdish governors or ministers: President Khatami appointed a Kurd, Abd Allah Ramazanzadeh, as governor general of Kurdistan province after his election in 1997, but Ramazanzadeh was later removed from office.

276: "City of Death": Isabella Bird, *Journeys in Persia and Kurdistan*, Vol. 2, p. 206.

276–77: Khadje and Siyabend tale: as related by Bois, *The Kurds*, pp. 65–66.

280: Hemin poem: as translated on the Kurdistan Democratic Party-Ankara website. Available from www.kdp-ankara.org.tr/literature.html.

CHAPTER SEVENTEEN: *Land of Lions*

284: "settling accounts": Rich, *Narrative of a Residence*, pp. 211–12, 245.

284–85: "avenues of poplars": Ibid., pp. 199–200.

287: "arrested and shot": Ciment, *The Kurds*, p. 70

287: ten thousand dead by 1981: McDowall, *A Modern History*, p. 262, citing *Daily Telegraph*, Feb. 11, 1981.

287: 27,500 dead by 1984: David McDowall, *The Kurds: A Nation Denied*, p. 77.

291: "city impresses": Bird, Vol. 1, pp. 101–2.

292: interpretation of Farhad and Shirin tale: Izady, *The Kurds*, p. 189.

293: Iran 94 percent Shiite: Human Rights Watch estimates Iran to be about 80 percent Shiite, 20 percent Sunni.

294: slum conditions possibly leading to ferment: McDowall, *A Modern History*, p. 279.

CHAPTER EIGHTEEN: *Happy Is He Who Calls Himself a Turk*

305: losses during Kurdish-Turkish conflict: see note for p. 98, Chapter Six.

306: creation of monolithic state: Rugman and Hutchings, *Atatürk's Children*, p. 26.

306: minister of Public Works sentenced to hard labor: Ibid., p. 26; McDowall, *A Modern History*, pp. 413, 417.

307: "the place was desolate": cited by Kemal in Chaliand, *People Without a Country*, p. 63, from *Son Posta*, April 1948.

318: "think completely in Turkish": as cited in Rugman and Hutchings, *Atatürk's Children*, p. 30.

319: "chauvinist class": Ibid., p. 29.

319: "afford to lose" 70 percent: Randal, *After Such Knowledge*, p. 238.

320: Thirty thousand PKK recruits: Human Rights Watch, "Displaced and Disregarded: Turkey's Failing Village Return Program," October 2002, p. 12. Available from www.hrw.org/reports/2002/Turkey.

321: number of villages destroyed: McDowall, *A Modern History*, p. 440.

321: PKK 768 extra-judicial killings: Human Rights Watch letter sent to Italian Prime Minister Massimo D'Alema, Nov. 21, 1998. Available from www.hrw.org/press98/nov/italy-ltr.htm.

321: "driven from homes by government gendarmes": Human Rights Watch, "Displaced and Disregarded," p. 3. A 1999–2001 study by the Migrants' Association for Social Cooperation and Culture (Goç-Der), a Turkish nongovernmental agency found that 83.7 percent of Kurdish refugees cited the actions of the Turkish security forces and emergency rule as primary reasons why they left their homes, while only 1.1 percent cited fear of the PKK.

322: $8.7 billion in U.S. military aid to Turkey, Turkey third-largest recipient of U.S. military aid: Human Rights Watch, *Weapons Transfers and Violations of the Laws of War in Turkey*, addition of figures on pp. 28, 30.

322: use of U.S. fighter-bombers: Ibid., p. 61.

323: "Öcalan's arrest: *Time*, March 1, 1999. Available from www.time.com/time/daily/special/ocalan/bitterend.

CHAPTER NINETEEN: *Alone After Dark*

329–30: village resettlement: Human Rights Watch, "Displaced and Disregarded," Oct. 2002; forced to sign form relinquishing rights to compensation: p. 35; number of village guards, p. 42; "villagers are extremely wary," p. 42.

331: forty judgments against Turkish security forces: Kurdish Human Rights Project, press release, London, July 11, 2002.

337: "those killed were not real journalists": cited in McDowall, *A Modern History*, p. 433, from *Middle East International*, no. 433, Sept. 11, 1992.

338: 2000 resolution on Armenian genocide tabled: *New York Times Book Review*, Oct. 19, 2003.

339: "we want to put an end": cited in Michael M. Gunter, *The Kurds and the Future of Turkey*, p. 144, from *Kurdistan Report*, Nov./Dec. 1996, p. 56.

339: "there are women everywhere": Michael Ignatieff, *Blood and Belonging*, pp. 153–55.

340: sexual abuse in prison: Amnesty International, "Turkey: End Sexual Violence Against Women in Custody!" Feb. 23, 2003. Available from www.amnesty.org. Index # EUR 44/006/2003.

342: "let the river run": "Chave Mini, You Are My Eyes: Songs from Turkish Kurdistan." Recorded in the field by Gregory Scarborough and Jordan Bell. Translated by staff of Medya TV, Cultural Cornerstones, 2002.

344: seventeen journalists and distributors killed: Rugman and Hutchings, *Atatürk's Children*, p. 55.

344: 180 killed in Batman: Ibid., p. 55.

344: five hundred murdered by Hezbollah: McDowall, *A Modern History*, p. 432.

344–45: connection between Hezbollah and Turkish state: Ibid., p. 433.

347: two hundred honor killings annually: *Washington Post*, Aug. 8, 2001.

CHAPTER TWENTY: *Not for Money*

349–50: Alexander the Great and Bitlis legend: Robert Dankoff, *Evilya Çelebi in Bitlis: The Relevant Section of the Seyahatname*, pp. 49–57.

350: "not brave and warlike like other Kurds": Ibid., p. 63.

350–51: "ruddy complexion," "If they see a woman": Ibid., p. 79.

351: "magician's bowls, fire": Ibid., p. 93.

353: Kurdish tribes gain strength since World War II: Martin van Bruinessen, "Kurds, States, and Tribes." Paper presented at the conference "Tribes and Power in the Middle East," London, Jan. 23–24, 1999. Available from www.let.uu.nl/~martin.vanbruinessen/personal/publications/Kurds.

360: Hakkari population growth: Kurdish Human Rights Project, press release, London, Nov. 28, 2002.

362–63: livestock figures: McDowall, *A Modern History*, p. 448.

363: report on 2002 elections: Kurdish Human Rights Project, press release, London, Nov. 28, 2002.

CHAPTER TWENTY-ONE: *Kurds Among Nations*

368–69: Turkey's 2003 reform packages: "Europeanisation of Turkey's Democracy?" Centre for European Policy Studies Sept. 23, 2003. Available from www.euractiv.com; *New York Times*, Aug. 4, 2003.

369: "pass all the laws you want": *Radikal*, Aug. 25, 2003.

371: Osman Öcalan wants to cooperate with West: *Guardian*, Oct. 8, 2003.

375: *Mem u Zin* story: as related by Michael L. Chyet, "And a Thornbush Sprang Up," pp. 6–9.

375: Khani's message of self-determination: Ibid., pp. 61–62, quoting earlier scholars Amir Hassanpour-Aghdam, Roger Lescot, and Ferhad Shakely; Kreyenbroek and Allison, *Kurdish Culture*, p. 11.

375: "Our misfortune has reached its zenith": Khani poem, as translated by Shahin Baker and Bawermend. Available from Kurdish Poetry, www.welat.50megs.com.

Bibliography

Amnesty International. *Iraq: Human Rights Abuses in Iraqi Kurdistan Since 1991.* New York: Amnesty International, February 1995.

Barkey, Henri J., and Graham E. Fuller. *Turkey's Kurdish Question.* Lanham, Md.: Rowman and Littlefield Publishers, 1998.

Bird, Isabella. *Journeys in Persia and Kurdistan.* Vols. 1 and 2. London: John Murray, 1891. Reissued, London: Virago Press, 1988.

Bois, Thomas. *The Kurds.* Trans. M. W. M. Welland. Beirut, Lebanon: Khayat Book and Publishing Company, 1965.

Brosnahan, Tom, Pat Yale, and Richard Plunkett. *Turkey.* Oakland, Calif.: Lonely Planet Publications, 2001.

Bulloch, John, and Harvey Morris. *No Friends but the Mountains: The Tragic History of the Kurds.* New York: Oxford University Press, 1992.

Chaliand, Gerard, ed. *A People Without a Country: The Kurds and Kurdistan.* New York: Olive Branch Press, 1993.

Christie Mallowan, Agatha. *Come, Tell Me How You Live.* New York: Dodd, Mead and Company, 1946.

Chyet, Michael Lewisohn. " 'And a Thornbush Sprang Up Between Them': Studies on Men u Zin, A Kurdish Romance." Ph.D. dissertation, University of California at Berkeley, 1991.

Ciment, James. *The Kurds: State and Minority in Turkey, Iraq and Iran.* New York: Facts on File, 1996.

Coon, Carleton S. *Caravan: The Story of the Middle East.* New York: Holt, Rinehart and Winston, 1961.

Dankoff, Robert, ed. *Evliya Çelebi in Bitlis: The Relevant Section of the Seyahatname.* New York: E. J. Brill, 1990.

Drower, E. S. *Peacock Angel.* London: John Murray, 1941.

Eagleton, William, Jr. *The Kurdish Republic of 1946.* New York: Oxford University Press, 1963.

Edmonds, C. J. *A Pilgrimage to Lalish.* London: Luzac, 1967.

———. *Kurds, Turks, and Arabs: Politics, Travel and Research in Northern-Eastern Iraq, 1919–1925.* New York: Oxford University Press, 1957.

Encyclopedia of Islam. Vols. 1–11. Leiden, Holland: Brill, 1960 to present.

Findy, Rasheed, et al. *A Guide to Duhok Governorate.* Trans. Sardar Mohammed Ali and Hizrat Tayeb. Duhok, Iraq: University of Dohuk/Islamic Law Press, 1995.

Fromkin, David. *A Peace to End All Peace: The Fall of the Ottoman Empire and the Creation of the Modern Middle East.* New York: Henry Holt and Company, 1989.

Goldberg, Jeffrey. "The Great Terror." *The New Yorker,* March 25, 2002, pp. 52–75.

Guest, John S. *Survival Among the Kurds: A History of the Yezidis.* New York: Kegan Paul International, 1993.

Gunter, Michael M. *The Kurds and the Future of Turkey.* New York: St. Martin's Press, 1997.

———. *The Kurds of Iraq: Tragedy and Hope.* New York: St. Martin's Press, 1992.

Hamilton, A. M. *Road Through Kurdistan.* London: Faber and Faber Limited, 1937.

Hansen, Henny Harald. *Daughters of Allah: Among Kurdish Women in Kurdistan.* Trans. Reginald Spink. London: Allen and Unwin, 1960.

Hay, W. R. *Two Years in Kurdistan: Experiences of a Political Officer 1918–1920.* London: Sidgwick and Jackson, 1921.

Human Rights Watch. *Syria: The Silenced Kurds.* New York: Human Rights Watch, 1996.

———. *Weapons Transfers and Violations of the Laws of War in Turkey.* New York: Human Rights Watch, 1995.

Human Rights Watch/Middle East. *Iraq's Crime of Genocide: The Anfal Campaign Against the Kurds.* New Haven, Conn.: Yale University Press, 1995.

Human Rights Watch and Physicians for Human Rights. *The Anfal Campaign in Iraqi Kurdistan: Destruction of Koreme.* New York: Human Rights Watch, 1993.

Ignatieff, Michael. *Blood and Belonging.* New York: Farrar, Straus and Giroux, 1993.

International Journal of Kurdish Studies. Vols. 6–16. Brooklyn, N.Y.: Kurdish Library, 1993–2002.

International Crisis Group. "War in Iraq: What's Next for the Kurds." ICI Middle East Report No. 10, March 19, 2003. Available from www.crisisweb.org.

Izady, Mehrdad R. *The Kurds: A Concise Handbook.* Washington, D.C.: Taylor and Francis, 1992.

Kahn, Margaret. *Children of the Jinn: In Search of the Kurds and Their Century.* New York: Seaview Books, 1980.

Karny, Yo'av. *Highlanders: A Journey to the Caucasus in Quest of Memory.* New York: Farrar, Straus and Giroux, 2000.

King, Diane E. "When Worlds Collide: The Kurdish Diaspora from the Inside Out." Ph.D. dissertation, Washington State University, 2000.

Kooli-Kamali, Ferideh. *The Political Development of the Kurds in Iran: Pastoral Nomadism.* London: Palgrave MacMillan, 2002.

Kreyenbroek, Philip G., and Christine Allison, eds. *Kurdish Culture and Identity.* Atlantic Highlands, N.J.: Zed Books, 1996.

Kurdish Times. Vols. 1–5. New York: Cultural Survival, 1986–1991.

Kurdish Human Rights Project, Bar Human Rights Committee and Human Rights Association. "The Trial of Students." London: Kurdish Human Rights Project, 2002.

Laizer, Sheri. *Martyrs, Traitors and Patriots: Kurdistan After the Gulf War.* Atlantic Highlands, N.J.: Zed Books, 1996.

Layard, Austen Henry. *Nineveh and Its Remains.* Vols. 1 and 2. New York: George P. Putnam, 1849.

——. *Discoveries Among the Ruins of Nineveh and Babylon.* New York: G. P. Putnam and Company, 1853.

Lennox, Gina, ed. *Fire, Snow and Honey: Voices from Kurdistan.* New South Wales, Australia: Halstead Press, 2001.

Longrigg, Stephen Hemsley. *Four Centuries of Modern Iraq.* Beirut: Librarie du Liban, 1968.

Lovat, Francois-Xavier. *Kurdistan Democratic Party.* London: G.I.D. Editions, 1999.

MacDonald, Charles and Carole A. O'Leary, eds. *The Kurdish Identity in an Unsettled World.* Forthcoming in 2004.

MacKenzie, D. N. *Kurdish Dialect Studies.* Vol. 2. New York: Oxford University Press, 1961.

Makiya, Kanan. *The Republic of Fear: The Politics of Modern Iraq.* Berkeley, Calif.: University of California Press, 1998.

Makiya, Kanan. *Cruelty and Silence: War, Tyranny, Uprising and the Moslem World.* New York: W. W. Norton, 1993.

McKiernan, Kevin. "Turkey's War on the Kurds." *The Bulletin of Atomic Scientists* 55, no. 2 (March/April 1999): 26–27.

The Meaning of the Glorious Koran. Translated by Mohammed Marmaduke Pickthall. New York: Penguin Books USA, n.d.

Meiselas, Susan. *Kurdistan: In the Shadow of History.* New York: Random House, 1997.

Milns, R. D. *Alexander the Great.* New York: Pegasus, 1969.

McDowall, David. *The Kurds: A Nation Denied.* London: Minority Rights Publications, 1992.

——. *The Kurds of Syria.* London: Kurdish Human Rights Project, 1998.

——. *A Modern History of the Kurds.* New York: I. B. Tauris and Company, 1997.

Mojab, Shahrzad, ed. *Women of a Non-State Nation: The Kurds.* Costa Mesa, Calif.: Mazda Publishers, 2001.

O'Leary, Carole A. "The Kurds of Iraq: Recent History, Future Prospects." *Middle Eastern Review of International Affairs* (MERIA) *Journal,* Vol. 6, No. 4, December 2002.

Olson, Robert, ed. *The Kurdish Nationalist Movement in the 1990s: Its Impact on Turkey and the Middle East.* Lexington, Ky.: University Press of Kentucky, 1996.

Pope, Hugh, and Nicole. *Turkey Unveiled: A History of Modern Turkey.* Woodstock, N.Y.: Overlook Press, 1998.

Power, Samantha. *"A Problem from Hell": America and the Age of Genocide.* New York: Basic Books, 2002.

Randal, Jonathan C. *After Such Knowledge, What Forgiveness?: My Encounters with Kurdistan.* Boulder, Colo.: Westview Press, 1999.

Rich, Claudius James. *Narrative of a Residence in Koordistan.* London: James Duncan, 1836. Reprint, London: Gregg International Publishers, 1972.

Rugman, Jonathan, and Roger Hutchings. *Atatürk's Children: Turkey and the Kurds.* London: Castle Wellington House, 1996.

Roux, George. *Ancient Iraq.* New York: Pelican Books, 1980.

Sadie, Stanley, ed. *The New Grove Dictionary of Music.* Vol. 14. New York: Grove Dictionaries, 2001.

Schmidt, Dana Adams. *Journey Among Brave Men.* Boston: Little, Brown and Company, 1964.

Soane, Ely Bannister. *To Mesopotamia and Kurdistan in Disguise.* London: John Murray, 1926.

Solecki, Ralph S. *Shanidar: The First Flower People.* New York: Alfred A. Knopf, 1971.

Tapper, Richard, ed. *The Conflict of Tribe and State in Iran and Afghanistan.* New York: St. Martin's Press, 1983.

Tripp, Charles. *A History of Iraq.* New York: Cambridge University Press, 2000.

U.S. Government, Secretary of the Army. *Syria: A Country Study.* Washington, D.C.: U.S. Government Printing Office, 1988.

van Bruinessen, Martin. *Agha, Shaikh and State: The Social and Political Structures of Kurdistan.* Atlantic Highlands, N.J.: Zed Books, 1992.

van Bruinessen, Martin, and Hendrik Boeschoten. *Evliya Çelebi in Diyarbekir.* New York: E. J. Brill, 1988.

Waheed, Sheikh Major A. *The Kurds and Their Country.* Lahore: University Book Agency, 1958.

Wigram, Rev. W. A., and Edgar T. A. Wigram. *The Cradle of Mankind: Life in Eastern Kurdistan.* London: Adam and Charles Black, 1914.

Wilcken, Ulrich. *Alexander the Great.* Trans. G. C. Richards. New York: W. W. Norton and Company, 1967.

Yalcin-Heckmann, Lale. *Tribe and Kinship Among the Kurds.* New York: Peter Lang, 1991.

INDEX

Page numbers in italics refer to illustrations.